BEYOND SEX ROLES

BEYOND SEX ROLES

Alice G. Sargent

WEST PUBLISHING COMPANY

ST. PAUL · NEW YORK · LOS ANGELES · SAN FRANCISCO

CREDITS   Photography on the following pages by Ellen Ebert: Page 6 (bottom photo and upper left); page 18 (bottom photo and upper right); page 140 (bottom photo and upper left); page 144 (upper left); page 274 (upper left); and page 352 (upper left).

Photography on the following pages by Carla Green: Page 6 (upper right); page 7; page 18 (upper left); page 19; page 144 (bottom photo); All preceding photos courtesy of Pacific Oaks Children's School; and the photo on page 274 (upper right).

Photography on the following pages by David Ostroff: Page 141 and page 352 (upper right).

Photography on the following pages by Linda Wolf: Page 140 (upper right); page 144 (upper right); page 274 (bottom photo); and page 352 (bottom photo).

Other credits are as follows: Page 86 cartoon. Copyright 1975. Reprinted by permission of *Saturday Review* and Bill Hoest. Pages 148–49 cartoon by Evert Opie. Reprinted from *The New Yorker* by permission of *The New Yorker*. Page 179 cartoon by James Stevenson. Reprinted from *The New Yorker* by permission from *The New Yorker*. Page 233 cartoon. Copyright Jules Feiffer. Reprinted with permission from Jules Feiffer.

Library of Congress Cataloging in Publication Data

Sargent, Alice G   1939–
    Beyond sex roles.
    Bibliography: p.
    Includes index.
     1. Androgyny (Psychology)   2. Sex role.
I. Title.
BF692.2.S27   155.3'3   76–23392
ISBN 0-8299-0104-3

1st Reprint—1978

To all our changing sex roles

a personal preface

What has growing up female or male meant to you? What dreams have you suppressed because you were a prisoner of your sex role? What feelings have you not expressed because they were unmasculine or unfeminine? How would you change your life if you were not confined to your sex role?

Beyond Sex Roles invites you to see yourself among your masks, roles, obligations, expectations, rules, and stereotypes, and to free yourself from inhibiting behaviors. The first step toward change is to engage in self-exploration, reflection, and introspection in order to discover which of your attitudes and behaviors are role-related—more specifically sex-role related. You are invited to take this opportunity to discover yourself further—to see where the *woman, man, child, parent, lover, worker, amateur, professional,* and *poet* are within you. You can then see which sex-role expectations inhibit you. Perhaps you will be able to experience once more a curiosity about your life and let go of a few of your role inhibitions. This is how it happened for me.

As a teacher, practitioner, and as a person, I have focused on the field of sex roles and on understanding my own androgynous identity for only the past four years. For more than ten years, however, I have been involved in group dynamics and have worked with people who want to increase their self-awareness and skills in interpersonal communication in order to become effective agents for social change. Four years ago, I began to look more and more at how sex-roles imposed limitations upon my own personal growth. It had been clear to me throughout school, as well as in the professional world, that expectations of me as a woman greatly limited my options and created a conflict within me regarding my goals for myself. I had worked in a world of men, used them as my role models, and felt inadequate when I could not be as single-minded as they.

I realized that the time had come for me to pause and reflect upon what it meant for me to be a woman. What, if anything, did I have in common with other women? What were the positive and negative characteristics of being a woman? What did I want to give up, and what did I want to retain? It was not an easy process of evaluation. Much of my professional life had been encouraged by some very helpful and competent men in this field, together with a couple of extremely effective women. But these few women were my only female professional role models.

As I begin to explore who I was, I wanted to know what being a woman had uniquely contributed to my identity and what I had in common with other women. So, I began to ask myself the question which is embodied in the sentence completion exercise, "Since I am a woman I must. . . if I were a man I could. . . ." And this was my first step toward exploring what the masculine and feminine sides of my personality were—what I allowed myself, what I forbade myself, and what I required of myself because I was a woman. For a long time, when I did the sentence completion column on "If I were a man," it abounded with options. I could be more single-minded, more focused; I did not have to cook dinner every night; I could put myself first more often. On the other hand, my column on "Since I am a woman" was filled with role-related responsibilities which were quite constraining.

It became clear that I could not go very far alone. With myself and with colleagues, I began to explore what it meant to be a man and what it meant to be a woman. I felt a great desire and energy to reach out to women, and yet I also felt hesitant as so many of us do. Whenever I was with a group of women, I would ask myself, "What do I have in common with them?" I thought I should know the answer, and I was quite uncertain about asking it aloud. When I did articulate my question, I was surprised to discover that the other women not only did not pull back in horror at my ignorance, but they too were in pursuit of the same answers. What we had in common often turned out to be of negative import: We found that we enjoyed fewer interesting relationships with other women because women valued men more highly than other women. We found that for the most part we did not share our competence with other women, but rather that we saved our brilliant conversation and our efforts at collaboration for the men with whom we worked and lived and loved.

We had not had great secret sharing or pal relationships with our mothers, but rather we identified deeply with our mothers' frustrations and disappointments. This created a negative self-identity about being a woman. I am not describing women like the Queen Bees who left the hive to enter successfully into the work world and rise to the top, nor am I describing women who were quite fulfilled as wives and mothers. I am rather describing women like myself who had multiple-role identities, who were ambivalent, autonomous and dependent, who wanted meaningful relationships with others as well as a strong sense of their own identity. We tried to be "super women." We felt that we had to fulfill all the roles of worker, wife, and mother, and we ended up with partial fulfillment, few satisfactions, little room for self, and a lot of pain.

As I continued my questions, new doors began to open in relationships. It was interesting and fun to be with women and there were many opportunities for sharing our feelings and our lives. Simultaneously, changes began to take place in relationships with men as we talked about what it meant to be a man and a woman. I became less helpful to men than I had been, and my relationships became uneven. I grew more selective about the men with whom I worked, ruling out those who were particularly oppressive, unexpressive, or unaware. I found an increasing number of men who regretted the emotional sparseness in their relationships with other men, and who preferred to be more collaborative in their relationships with women. More and more men said how tired they were of looking exclusively to women to meet their needs for warmth and tenderness. They were tired of spending endless hours involved in task relationships with other men which were highly unidimensional and unfulfilling. These men expressed not only sadness from feeling cut off from their children, but also their failure to devote themselves to developing these relationships. They wanted to share more of their emotional life with other men but said they did not know how to begin. They wanted to develop increased sharing in their relationships with women but were fearful of being exploited.

As my own consciousness grew, I found myself spending more and more time dealing with *sexism*, that is, dealing with the kind of behavior that was expected because the person was a male or a female. Now, four years later, both professionally and personally, I find most of my energy focused on the destructiveness of sexism in organizations, work relationships, and couple and family relationships. My underlying concerns remain the same: a desire for direct and authentic communication between people; intentional, proactive behavior rather than reactive behavior; and adult relationships rather than one-up, one-down communication. I am concerned about shared resources among people rather than a hierarchical view of resources.

I have become an advocate. More and more I try to deal directly with how sexism inhibits these values. I confront the oppression women feel from men, men feel from women, and the competition women experience from other women for the approval of men. I am deeply concerned that organizations include more women and minorities in the work force. Yet the culture of these organizations needs to change, so that they do not merely absorb minorities and women, but instead alter their values to include those of the new work force.

My first concern in this book is for the role liberation of women and men so that each of us has the potential to develop a role-free human identity which encompasses both male and female characteristics—androgyny. Simultaneously, it is necessary to help men and women develop the skills necessary for androgyny—autonomy, intimacy, and interdependence. Then, individuals can join together to restructure the institutions in our culture which maintain the status quo, that is, the family, the schools, business, social services, religious institutions, and government organizations.

I am constantly engaged in my own struggle to achieve greater self-actualization, rather than submitting or succumbing to living for and through others. Many times I have been tempted to abandon my total self to a lesser sense of self, thereby letting the noise of life drown me. After all, I am just a woman with work, teaching and groups, husband, a child, friends, and parents. Many times I wish I had someone to prepare dinner, play with our child, plan my social life, and soothe my confused ego. Many times I give in and find myself *living to work and problem-solve* as many people do, rather than *working and problem-solving to live*. Many times, I lose my focus and start living for others to the exclusion of myself; then I scan those around me for their expectations rather than charting my own course. I start fulfilling my sex-role proscriptions of being deferential; smiling a lot; not being too assertive with men or confronting with women; looking for confirmation of my work competency and femininity from men, and affirmation of my competence as a mother and homemaker from women. After that, for a brief space, I become refocused and feel a solid balance between my concern for others, my interest in work, my sense of my own competence, my direction, and my sense of fun and joy in my life. I feel like a sailboat that is righted after having been inundated by a strong wind, and I let go for a while until the next gust.

For all of us, beyond the women's movement and the men's movement, is the cause of human liberation—the raising of consciousness in both men and women so that life styles can emerge which transcend traditional, automatic role relationships, and instead, are self-managed and human. Some of the questions before each of us in our search are:

What if I could look at issues such as self-actualization, developing boundaries, building relationships, and becoming secure, without regard to being a woman or a man?

Could I then find meaning, experience loneliness, be authentic, be tough, be tender, be creative, be productive without regard to my sex roles?

What if I could be primarily concerned with the fulfillment of my human potential rather than with the fulfillment of my gender identity?

What would it be like not to behave out of guilt or a sense of imposed role-related responsibility to others, but rather out of a sense of self-fulfillment?

What if each time I acted I asked the question: what am I getting out of this, as well as what am I giving? Am I fulfilling my own expectations of myself or am I trying to please someone else?

Keep these questions in mind, as you use this book to explore new ways of being and changing. I would like to hear about your experiences with this book if you would care to share them with me. We are embarking upon one of the most important journeys of our lives. We may experience moments of incredulity and of pain which cannot, and should not, be avoided. At the least, our curiosity will be engaged. At most, we may realize that it is *"only our life"*—*"our only life"* that is at stake!

Alice G. Sargent

acknowledgments

I am most indebted to the contributors to this book, many of whom are friends and colleagues. They demonstrated a high commitment to this project and worked with a diligence and involvement that far surpassed any customary sense of responsibility. In the process, this became much more than a book to all of us. Many colleagueships were developed among the forty of us which link us together for future efforts.

I am grateful to the students who participated in the sex-roles courses at the University of Massachusetts and in a number of programs in Continuing Education at the University of California at San Diego where these exercises were developed. I would also like to express my appreciation to the employees at Charmin Paper Products, a division of Procter & Gamble, especially to Ken Richardson and Cecile Follansbee who confirmed the relevance of this work in an industrial setting. These people came together to look openly at some of the toughest issues of identity and values before us today. Their increased awareness about sex-role stereotypes, changes in their behavior, and their continuous growth was the greatest incentive and reassurance that what was going on was meaningful.

The antecedents of this book began a long time ago with my family, who encouraged women to be super-persons—adequate as both women and men. That includes my competent and caring parents, Adele and Harold; my brother, Bob; my devoted and gentle/tyrannical grandfather, Harry; my two super-aunts, Ruth and Gertrude; and my warm friend, Gertrude Streety. These same expectations continued in my former marriage with Dann. Our lives together and independently for those thirteen years seemed frequently to be an exciting and painful microcosm of the complex social issues facing many families today. I valued Dann's commitment to knowledge and independent thinking.

I would like to dedicate this book to my daughter, Elizabeth, who gives me joy beyond any I might have imagined, with the heartfelt but futile wish that as she grows up she might enjoy the richness of being a woman-person without knowing the pain. Her love and curiosity have contributed immeasurably to my work and life.

I am most appreciative of my own support and consciousness-raising network which has developed over the years in San Diego, Amherst, and in Washington, D.C., and has served as a frequent reminder of the genuine interdependence between women and men. I would especially like to thank the following people: Melinda Sprague and Dee Appley, whose friendship and colleagueship have constantly attested to the strengths, warmth, and pain that women can share with each other; Jim Thickstun, whose encouragement of "just me" over the past two years has often lightened my own sense of life's issues and kept my autonomy before me; Joe Litterer, who has contributed his compassion, encouragement, and professional and personal vision over the past five years; Herb Shepard, who for several years participated in a lot of my personal and professional growth and who is now a special colleague; Len Goodstein, Orian Worden, Al Ivey, and Edie Seashore who have been significant for their enthusiasm, caring, perspective, and sense of direction; and a number of people connected with the National Training Laboratories Institute and the Institute for Educational Leadership in Washington D.C. who have also contributed significantly to my learning.

The rest of my extensive support system includes three spectacular women: Joan Corwin, who not only typed and retyped this manuscript a number of times, but encouraged and managed, cajoled and ordered many steps along the way; Linda Schrade, who has taken care of, loved, learned with, and taught both Elizabeth and me so much about being an extended family over the past three years; and Elizabeth Kamansky, who managed our home in an unbelievably orderly manner.

I am most appreciative of Len Goodstein's critical reading and extensive comments on this manuscript. My gratitude goes to Jane Pemberton for her constructive editorial assistance and to the staff of West Publishing for their confidence throughout the many different stages of this book.

Without this vast network, a great deal less would have been possible and what did happen would not have been the learning, caring, fun, rich, and human experience that it was.

contents

Life Planning Exercises   67

PART II
Awareness of Sex-Role Stereotypes   141

Awareness   145

Personal Change   275

BEYOND SEX ROLES

a guide to the
use of this book

As you read *Beyond Sex Roles* you are invited to relate differently to these exercises and readings from the way you would customarily use a book. The process of this book emphasizes individuality and growth: You, the reader, are encouraged to be spontaneous and analytical; to express yourself at the moment; and to reflect upon the implications of events for the future. Hopefully, you will be stirred to consider your own development as a man or a woman and examine the impact that your sex-role stereotypes have had on your professional development, and on your relationships with other men and women. You may want to recall that pain and resistance along with joy and curiosity are essential ingredients in any important developmental experience.

This book is both didactic and experiential. Experiential education emphasizes how much you can learn from your own experience when you are able to abstract and generalize from its common and unique facets, and affirms that the learning process involves both reason and emotion, the rational and the irrational. The book embodies both an inductive approach to learning whereby you collect data on your attitudes and behavior, as well as the traditional deductive teaching method by which you learn from reading about current concepts and research in the sex-roles field. Feelings are emphasized not only to involve you, but because emotions reflect significant data which all too frequently are denied or ignored. You are encouraged to unite the world inside you with what is going on in the world outside you.

You are embarking upon a difficult undertaking, trying to become aware of behavior which has been reinforced for many years. In order to make changes in your attitudes and behavior, you may need support groups, diaries, encouragement from close relationships, time to reflect, and a constant awareness to put yourself first more than you have in the past. From time to time, you may find that you are covering familiar ground and that you are using the exercises and your support group simply as an opportunity to see if your own feelings have changed and to hear what others think about a familiar issue. You may go over some attitudes repeatedly, such as: the difficulty of being autonomous and intimate at the same time; your lack of assertiveness in certain situations; the value of being able to swing flexibly from intense involvement to a participant-observer posture; how to take a win-win approach in situations which have previously been win-lose; how your feelings about some part of your body affect your identity; how your fears about conflict impair your effectiveness; or how to value your own spontaneity and authenticity rather than your own control. Your work with the group is like viewing yourself through a kaleidoscope. The pieces keep falling into place a little differently. But it is a very special kaleidoscope because from time to time you may insert a new piece, since as you grow and behave in new ways, you are incorporating a new part into your identity.

You may want to read through the book quickly to get an overview before you begin to do any of the exercises. *Beyond Sex Roles* is divided into four sections: Exercises, Awareness, Personal Change, and Social Change. The format throughout invites you to look at your own experiences and to reflect upon them before talking to others in your group or reading what the contributors have to say. You may use this workbook as an experience in self-confrontation or you may wish to share your perceptions with others, either in "stranger-groups" (people you do not know well), or in "family groups" (people with whom you work closely). Neither group is mutually exclusive. In fact, each group can undoubtedly be relevant at one time or another.

The exercises lend themselves to use as modules in a training program at work, in a weekly on-going group, or in a class as topics arise. The intent of this book is to mix personal data with cultural data. After you have compared your own experiences, there are essays on the personal, interpersonal, and social issues. Each of these essays was written expressly for *Beyond Sex Roles* and frequently reflects the author's attempt to condense a rather complex subject area into a brief presentation. Some of the contributors are psychologists, sociologists, and linguists who are specialists in the area of sex roles. Others are applied behavioral scientists who have a rich background in experiential education, organizational change, and social action.

use of the book in the group

If you do elect to use the book in a group, it is important that your first agenda is to become acquainted. To develop cohesiveness, trust, and a concern for the members of your group is necessary in order to feel comfortable sharing your life with them and learning from them. It is very helpful to begin your group with an extended session, perhaps for four hours including dinner, or with a one-day workshop during which time you begin to overcome some of the stiffness and unfamiliarity.

Your goals for the extended workshop might include:

becoming acquainted and comfortable with each other;

beginning to encounter similarities and differences in each other;

increasing your awareness of your own sex-role stereotypes and how these affect you;

testing out what changes you are able to make in attitudes as you become aware of stereotypes; and

feeling freer to select from a large set of options rather than merely fulfilling of a sex-role script.

After this extended workshop, your group will have begun to develop and to feel freer to deal with the content of sex-role stereotypes. Nonetheless, there will be plateaus in individual development, breakdowns in effective communication, and lapses in the group's movement. Like any effort at change, the path to sex-role liberation has ups and downs, pauses and sprints, immobilization and a sense that there is light at the end of the tunnel.

guide to the experience

There are a variety of ways to structure your group[1] experience. Probably the majority of you will be meeting weekly for an hour and a half or so. In a "stranger-group", such as a class, a group of people gathered from business for the first time, or a newly formed consciousness raising group, you have the double agenda of becoming a group as well as moving into the topic. If you invest some effort initially in the development of good communication and cohesiveness within your group, you will be able to move more quickly and deal richly with the subject of your own sex-role stereotypes.

design for a class

After the opening extended session of the class, you might utilize one of the following structures:

1). Divide the subsequent twelve classes into six personal sessions followed by six more cognitively-oriented sessions in which the students give presentations of topics, generated from the readings. This division enables the group to get deeply involved in reliving their own sex-role socialization because they feel totally responsible for developing the content of the course from their own experiences. It may be difficult to pull people back from their own data-collection to the content of the readings.

or 2). For the first hour of the twelve sessions discuss a topic selected from the readings and then move to personal sharing of attitudes and behavior related to that topic. This design helps provide a balance between personal and cognitive sharing throughout, but it does run the risk of the group not going deeply enough into personal socialization.

[1]Also see the chapter, "Consciousness-raising groups: A resocialization process for personal and social change" later in this volume.

The experiences take on much greater vitality if responsibility for leading them is rotated through the group.

The topics that could be covered over the twelve weeks are:

1.   What psychology and biology tell us about socialization

2.   Female-female relationships

3.   Male-male relationships

4.   Male-female relationships

5.   Issues of minority men and women

6.   My own socialization

7.   Stages of adult development

8.   Life planning

9.   Assertion training

10.   Organizational barriers to women's success

11.   **Organizational expectations of men**

12.   Racism and sexism—the economic implications

13.   How to create change

**design for a
two hour
session**

For a brief, several-hour session, particularly with a larger group, the following design has been effective:

Self-confrontation

20 minutes	Exercise—Who Am I. Exercise—Since I am a woman/man, I must. If I were a woman/man, I could.
20 minutes	Let the group enumerate on the newsprint stereotypes they generated on men and women.
20 minutes	Theory sessions—Socialization research as in the "Stereotypes, Socialization, and Sexism" by Carol Tavris.
40 minutes	Exercise—Share in groups of three a good and bad experience with someone of the other sex. How does it fit with your stereotypes?

design for an extended workshop

The optimum environment for an extended workshop is away from home in a live-in situation where there are a minimum of distractions. Frequently there are summer camps for rental for such experiences. Dividing the work of making the arrangements, getting food, and cooking frequently builds a sense of community within the group, and generates as much data as the exercises do about sex-role expectations and the dynamics of group interaction. Particularly in a co-ed situation, how these tasks are handled interjects "real life" data about the participants into the history of the group.

It is helpful if the participants read in advance "Consciousness-Raising Groups: A Resocialization Process for Personal and Social Change" in advance of the weekend workshop.

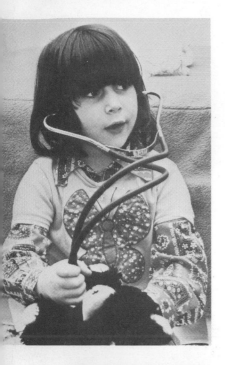

1 toward androgyny: the new woman and the new man

Consciousness about sexism—women's and men's liberation is fomenting a revolution in a variety of social institutions including marriage, the family, the schools and organizations, as well as in individual personal development. At the heart of this revolution and of this book is a growing dissatisfaction with the sexist values of our culture, the processes of socialization with regard to sex-typing, the current allocation of sex-linked behavior, and the manner in which our institutions have helped to build and maintain the status quo which is prejudiced in favor of men and against women. To date, women and men have learned to fill very different roles without regard for the attributes, visions, likes, and dislikes of the unique individuals of each sex who have had to play these unchosen parts in their life's script. We are only now beginning to recognize the cost of squashing both women and men into these highly limited sex roles. One of the rallying cries of the movement for sex-role liberation is, "Women are not sex objects; men are not success objects."

The law has provided great assistance to the sex-role revolution, particularly with respect to women's rights. The extent to which women are an oppressed group is reflected in the passage of new legislation and the creation of special commissions: the 1963 Equal Pay Act; the 1963 President's Report on the Status of Women; Title VII of the 1964 Civil Rights Act; the Equal Employment Opportunity Commission and its guidelines over the past seven years; Title IX as overseen by the

Office of Education; and the Equal Rights Amendment, possibly less than one year from passage. The need for such legislation can be seen in the following 1973 employment figures for women: 2 percent of the engineers are women; 5 percent of the lawyers are women and 9 percent of the physicians are women. (These figures may be compared with the fact that 32 percent of the engineers, 37 percent of the lawyers, and 79 percent of the physicians are women in the Soviet Union. There is, of course, the other issue that while women work in the USSR, they are also, traditionally, homemakers at the same time.)

Consider that in the United States four out of five working women are in seven fields: teaching, nursing, music, social work, accounting, auditing, and library work. Ninety-seven percent of all registered nurses are women, as are 92 percent of all dieticians, 85 percent of elementary school teachers, and 70 percent of all health technicians. Consider the 1970 median incomes of full-time workers: white men—$9,447; minority men—$4,160; white women—$5,536; and minority women—$2,043. The hierarchy of earnings for the following nine groups in America is as follows: white men, black men, other ethnic men, white women, Japanese-American women, Philippine women, black women, Chicanas, and American-Indian women.

Sex-role expectations are at the core of child-rearing practices and the modeling behavior of parents and teachers, as well as at the root of the behavior which the world of work rewards and punishes. They have come to us through such august sources as St. Augustine, the Bible, Freud, Erikson, D. H. Lawrence, Dr. Spock, Madison Avenue, and Sesame Street. We have learned that men's work is to provide a living for the family; women's work, in addition to whatever else they do, is to make babies and to care for the home.

If a daughter has, for eighteen years, seen her mother care for the home, the children, and her father while subjugating her own emotional and intellectual needs, she will not easily shed the feeling that she too should someday also fulfill these helpful, deferential roles. If a young man has for years seen his father arrive home from work, read his newspaper, and ask his wife when dinner will be ready, he is unlikely to change this behavior in his own home. This is particularly true if his wife does not work outside the home as one contribution to their lives. Underneath both these sets of role behaviors are unique individuals whose emotions and abilities undoubtedly cross sex lines. They may, however, spend their entire lives without ever fully understanding that many of their frustrations result from being constantly pinched by sex-role expectations.

socialization   As we have read many times and experienced for ourselves, women have been socialized to be expressive, reactive, dependent, and to meet the needs of others by caring for their physical as well as emotional needs. Not only have women had few role models or female mentors to support their professional development, but they have not become competent in the skills of the marketplace, such as being analytical problem solvers, independent, and developing the ability to generalize and abstract. In contrast, men have been expected to be task-oriented, egocentric, strong, silent, responsible, effective problem solvers, and competitive. Men's self-esteem has tended to come from their evaluation of themselves with respect to other men. Women's self-esteem has come primarily from men's evaluation as well.

To a large extent, male behavior is linked with what is effective in the marketplace and within the bureaucracy. Many of the skills men learned so well that help them to be successful at work are less useful in intimate relations or in organizational settings where there is a concern for relationships. Close friendships, spouse, parental, and other relationships require more expressive behavior in addition to the rational, instrumental, problem-solving style of the marketplace. Intimacy demands of us spontaneity, impulsivity, risk taking, a willingness to make oneself vulnerable, a commitment to go the extra distance when necessary in order to make human contact. It is paradoxical that intimacy involves a desire not to be destructive of another person, but rather to be supportive even at costs to oneself; while at the same time we must work furiously to see that our own needs are also met. The value system required for intimacy is a commitment to growth and learning rather than a survival orientation.

parenting

To date, men have not been encouraged to express themselves deeply as fathers. As conveyed by the media and literature, the stereotyped role of the father has been construed as the provider and the disciplinarian, as well as someone to be protected from family pressures at home because of the work pressures he faces. Father deals with weighty issues all day, and in the remaining time after he has finished his work, he is the rule giver, judge, punisher, and the member of the family who is in charge of fun for everyone for an afternoon, probably over the weekend. Mothers, in contrast, are expected to be caring, involved, efficient, and self-abnegating. The motherhood mystique almost sounds as if women possess a biologically-based maternal instinct. As women have begun to speak out about their lack of total fulfillment in caring for the family—saying that meeting the needs of children and a husband does not necessarily lead to complete self-fulfillment—there has been a growing recognition that some women want to be deeply involved in mothering and others do not. And some fathers might be more involved in fathering if given the chance.

Rossi (1968) describes the parental role as including "spontaneity and flexibility, the ability to be tender and loving and to respond to tenderness and love from a child, as well as to have boundaries and a sense of self." Many men are inadequately prepared to be fathers in the sense Rossi describes, not because they lack the time to be significantly involved in their children's lives, but because they do not have the interpersonal skills for intimacy, namely spontaneity and a sense of their own emotional life. On the other hand, many women may have the necessary nurturing behaviors for parental and couple relationships, but lack the ability to be assertive and express anger directly, which are also significant skills in intimate relationships. Many women tend to feel a loss of autonomy and privacy and become bored and anxious if they are responsible only for nurturing and meeting the needs of the next generation, particularly if they do not have ample opportunity to develop their own personal identity.

Until recently, highly successful professional women have tended to come from very different backgrounds from most other women. As Hennig's (1973) case studies of the family constellations of one hundred top women executives point out, these women are likely to be oldest or only children, raised by both parents to be like both women *and* men, not simply to be like women *or* men. Both parents valued their daughter highly for her femaleness and her achievement, her activity and competitive success. Both parents also valued themselves and their partner as separate persons and supported each other's role choices, behavioral styles, and other relationships. This background is in sharp contrast to the more highly differentiated socialization with respect to sex roles that most men and women experience.

sexuality

Another revolution is taking place in attitudes toward sexuality. Many women have been socialized to see sex and intimacy as inextricably linked; many men have grown up with the opposite viewpoint—that sex is not related to intimacy. Both sexes seem to be approaching a more encompassing view of sex as being both fun and intimate, sensual and sexual. Masters (1974) says:

In the past the prevailing attitude was that sex was something a man did to a woman. The woman usually accepted this fact and engaged in sex as a duty. Changing attitudes gave women the proper idea that they too should enjoy sex but the mistaken notion that sex is something the man has to do for her. We've changed from the man doing it *to* a woman to doing it *for* her. This idea places tremendous pressure on the man knowing he has to please the woman (p. 1).

This sexual revolution, with women assuming equality with men in taking responsibility for sexual acts, with women enjoying sexuality for itself rather than as a conjugal duty, will substantially change the relationships between the sexes both within and outside of marriage. It is difficult to know what these changes will be but they are clearly potential by-products of changes in traditional sex roles.

the need for change

Until recently, many women and men who chafed under the constraints of their roles felt maladjusted, personally inadequate and insecure, rather than feeling that societal expectations were unreasonable. For some women it is a real awakening to discover other women for whom motherhood is not a totally satisfying experience; for some men it is an enormous relief to discover that having responsibility is not only threatening but unfulfilling to other men. This demystification comes about as individuals get in touch with what the cultural expectations are, how dissatisfied many others are with them, and what the long-run costs are to the culture of maintaining individuals in roles which underutilize women and overutilize men. These costs manifest themselves in terms of poorer physical and mental health for both men and women, crime, apathy, and alienation. The effect of a consciousness-raising experience is to point out the numerous manifestations of sexism in the culture and the costs to the individual.

Basic to the problem of sexism is the perceived lack of political strength by men and women to eliminate sexism. The Redstockings' Manifesto of July 7, 1969, says:

Because we have lived so intimately with our oppressors, in isolation from each other, we have been kept from seeing our personal suffering as a political condition. This creates the illusion that a woman's relationship with her man is a matter of interplay between two unique personalities, and can be worked out individually. In reality, every such relationship is a class relationship and the conflicts between individual men and women are political conflicts that can only be solved collectively (Hole & Levin, p. 137).

This manifesto could be applied equally to women's relations with men at home and at work, to relations among men, and to relations between men and women.

The problem of sexism also exists because of the lack of awareness of its dimensions and the lack of knowledge of how to deal with this social problem. Only recently have there been widespread social efforts through consciousness-raising groups; national organizations such as Women's Political Caucus, NOW, Federal Women's Program, Feminist Counseling Collectives, and the Affirmative Action program to effect widespread change. Women now are a political group, a "class," and can exercise poitical power if they form a coalition. The very process of consciousness raising works to overcome the psychological isolation of women and men.

strategies to combat sexism

There are a variety of change strategies, based on different value systems, which could stimulate alternatives to presently defined masculine and feminine behavior. The range includes political, legal, community organizing, and educational approaches. Political change through the election of women and the placement of women in power positions in various sectors of the society would be very effective. Mass education, if it could work, would be a much more efficient process. Yet, this book focuses primarily on a change process that encourages developing individual awareness through consciousness raising about

the strengths and weaknesses of our current socialization and allocation of sex-role behavior. The process of personal liberation through
consciousness raising seems to be an arduous and time-consuming
course to follow, particularly if the ultimate goal is to create massive
cultural change.

Yet the core issue is that the consequences of our socialization run
so deep in our culture that a long-term effort at increasing awareness
is necessary. It seems necessary—just as it was with black people—for
a critical mass of women and men to be aware of what the impact of
the sexist culture has been on them. Until women and men are aware of
sexism and begin to work on their own personal, unique liberation,
they cannot mobilize for widespread social and political changes.
Furthermore, from a value standpoint, if the movement for sex-role
liberation is truly committed to individual self-actualization rather
than exhorting persons to fulfill still another role and follow another
ideology, then the means for change need to be highly individualized.
When a critical mass of women and men have participated in the consciousness-raising process, then perhaps their effect in individual
households and organizations around the country may become noticeable.

The second strategy is to teach relevant behavior for change to
women and men. If women and men learn to express their wants and
needs more effectively and then negotiate ways in which to meet each
other's needs, there is the opportunity for collaborative relationships.
This could then lead to the building of support systems to facilitate self-
confrontation, changes in personal life styles, and collaborative uses of
power. As new behavior is tried, the support network is there, ready to
offer encouragement and to be a sounding board if there are setbacks.

The third strategy is to teach men and women about institutional
power realities so that they will be able to develop social change
strategies to eliminate sexism. This will require support systems and
change teams within the organization where the change is being
attempted. The uniqueness of the women's movement and now the
men's movement has been the grass roots organization and the focus on
personal change. To date, the movement has not created oppressive institutions of its own. Unfortunately, certain social issues are so entrenched in the hands of the power elite and so resistant to change that
they require organization and political action. This includes training
persons in change-agent skills in order to initiate the necessary organizational and political changes. In addition, men and women need
to learn how to develop support groups to facilitate such organizational
changes, how to form coalitions and organize for political activities,
how to influence decision-making processes in both the public and private sectors, and how to have an impact on the power structure of the
system. Some of these skills are covered in the second part of this book.

The fourth strategy involves a concerted program of social action to challenge the institutional sexism which is so pervasive in our society. In order to alter the existing power structure, each person needs to become intentional about the impact of his/her behavior on others, particularly on those who feel powerless. If a woman has been successful on her own and is not concerned for other women's search for identity and for a meaningful place in society, she is, in fact, part of the problem. If white women are oblivious to issues facing their sisters of color, then they are supporting the oppressive system they are trying to change. Sisterhood, brotherhood, and coalitions between groups are necessary to alter the patterns of sexism in the family, work, the schools, and governmental institutions. Furthermore, an understanding of how to deal with power realities is necessary at this stage. Collaboration may not produce adequate change and confrontation may be necessary.

This book encourages self-awareness, increased effectiveness in male/male, female/female and male/female relationships, but recognizes that in addition, organization for social change must take place. There are cultural differences, value differences, and drastic inequities in the current allocation of power in our society. Jones (1972) says: "The culture creates and determines the nature of its institutions. The institutions socialize the individuals, and the individuals perpetuate the cultural character" (p. 5). The culture, through its institutions, has distributed privileges unequally to men and women and has limited the life options of both women and men through role expectations. New members of the culture will continue to be socialized along these lines until there is massive change.

The movement for sex-role liberation has been predominantly white and middle-class—almost as if those of us who have certain needs met at the survival level are then free to look at areas of psychological pain. Unless, sex-role changes have meaning for all oppressed peoples, we are deluding ourselves that what is occurring is a significant revolution. Regrettably, there are those in whose best interest it remains to keep racism and sexism separate. Then advocates of each will compete among themselves for a minimal portion of power rather than coalescing to obtain a large share of the action. It is essential to be mindful that as long as there are the oppressed, there are oppressors. We therefore live in a win-lose culture that uses power and influence competitively rather than a win-win culture that uses power in a collaborative and synergic manner.

the future

What will society look like eventually? We have yet to know. We see the beginnings of the new women and the new men and they overlap. Behavior that was thought to be in the exclusive province of one or the other is now an option for both. The ultimate goal of this revolution is self-actualization and the fullest expression of the masculine and feminine sides of our personality in whatever proportion we wish, for we all have that range buried somewhere within us.

With the increasing democratization of the family and work environments, there is a slow shift from paternalistic structures to more collaborative ones. Blue collar blues and white collar boredom has precipitated a crisis in business which requires organizations to value more highly the resources and needs each individual brings to the market place (Slater, 1970). The role expectations for doctor, policeman, lawyer, teacher, are expanding to include, expression, feelings, and empathy as important to the work. The definition of the manager in an organization is now someone who develops the internal human resources of subordinates as well as assuming responsibility for the technological and task area. The emphasis on stricter analytical, rational decision-making styles are yielding to encompass greater humanity supportiveness and nurturance.

The new man is not punished for showing his tender, needy side, or expressing his fears and concerns for relationships. It is not surprising for a man to say to a woman, "I am tired of being responsible for what goes on between us; I would like you to be more in charge and for us to share more." And, in return, the new woman may respond, "I need some time for myself because I have some other things that are important to me right now, but I would like to get reconnected soon."

The new woman is allowed, without punishment, to be assertive, to be more direct, to live less vicariously, to be less nurturant, and to be less helpful. She is more autonomous, more competent in dealing with a larger world, less deferential and more self-centered.

The process of change is arduous, grinding, depressing, debilitating and, sometimes, exhilarating. The institutions of our culture move ponderously and haltingly. Many individuals seem to move forward one moment and back the next. The social revolution around sex roles will not be completed in our lifetimes, but there is no mistake that it has begun. Hopefully, through reading this book, many of you will become change agents and find ways in your family and work environments to expand sex-linked options. The revolution is within us! It begins with the myriad of decisions we make every day, and entails a commitment to not settling for being less than yourself. To join this revolution is to embark upon a course of pain and joy. But not to risk is to banish a part of ourselves and leave it to die. Those of us who grew up on Cinderella must wean ourselves from such art to prepare ourselves for life.

references   Hennig, M. P. 114 in I. E. Low, Family attitudes and relations. In R. Knudsin (Ed.), *Women and success.* New York: William Morrow & Co., 1973.
Jones, J. M. *Prejudice and racism.* Reading, Mass.: Addison Wesley, 1972.

Restocking manifesto 1971. In J. Hole & E. Levine, *Rebirth of feminism*. New York: Quadrangle Books, 1971.

Rossi, A. Sex Equality: The beginning of ideology. In C. Safilios-Rothschild (Ed.), *Toward a sociology of women*. Lexington, Mass.: Xerox Publishing Company, 1972.

Slater, P. *In the pursuit of loneliness*. Boston: Beacon Press, 1970.

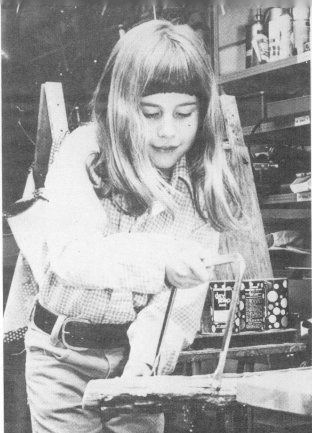

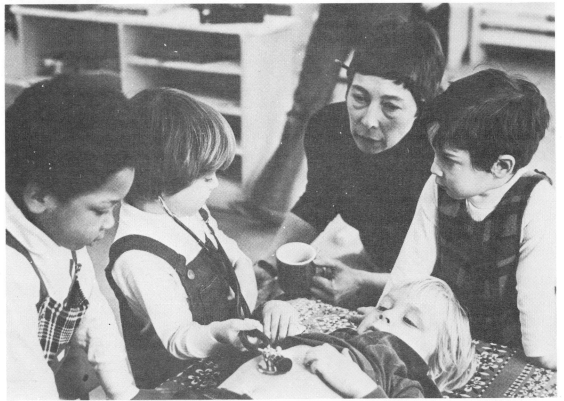

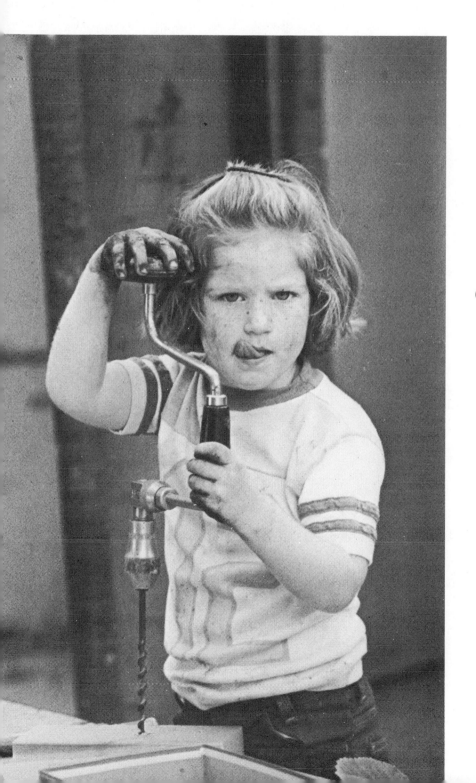

exercises

critical
incident form

personal goal

Since our recollections about group experiences often blur and the specifics of a new learning are forgotten if not recorded, a diary or a log is strongly suggested. Perhaps this critical incident form will suggest a helpful format.

directions

Try to complete this form after each session of the group. Be as *specific* and *objective* as possible in your descriptions. There may be "clicks"—moments when you become aware of a fact of social sex-role discrimination through an everyday incident.

Name _____ Date_____

**critical incident related
to the small-group
consciousness raising
experience**

Think of your experience in your small group today and describe the incident (a situation) in which you were involved that had the *most* impact on you (either positive or negative.)

1. Describe the situation (include date and time); background or activities that led up to or influenced your behavior, namely, what was going on before and at that time.
2. Describe exactly what you did, said, or thought.
3. Outcome—analysis of how your behavior, intervention, or lack of overt behavior, influenced the group and how you felt about it.
4. How would you in retrospect have liked to respond? What do you think you will do the next time a similar situation arises?

Contributed by Professor Dee G. Appley, Department of Psychology, and Professor Don Carew, School of Education, Univ. of Mass., Amherst, Mass.

experience in
data collection*

personal goals

To begin to become comfortable sharing information about yourself with your group; to get in touch with your experiences with respect to birth order, sex differences, and leadership and to articulate them; to explore myths about these categories; and to confirm or discard some of these myths through listening to other people's experiences.

directions

Since it will be quite relevant for discussion of sex roles and stereotypes to be aware of how to collect data, you may want to begin by testing a less emotionally loaded topic such as your family experience as a result of "*birth order.*"

birth order

1. Divide into four groups: the oldest children in one corner of the room, middle children in another, youngest children in the third, and only children in the fourth.
2. In the next 15 to 20 minutes find out what you have in common because of your birth order.
3. In a total community session the leader for this exercise collects data from each of the four groups about the experiences they shared in common.

**additional
areas for data
collection**

men and women
1. If the group seems ready, divide into two groups, one of men and one of women, and answer the question: "What do women or men have in common with each other?"
2. At the end of this discussion, the groups reassemble and report

21

what the men said and what the women said. Were any myths exploded? What experiences were there in common?

goals for attending this workshop

1. Go to the corner of the room that best describes your goal for attending this workshop (the person managing this exercise designates each of the corners of the room as representative of one of these goals).
   These goals include:
   a. work on personal issues,
   b. educational goals,
   c. career choice, or
   d. mixed.
2. Discuss what your choice says about you. How are you similar to and how are you different from the others in your group?

attitudes towards leadership

1. Go to one of the four corners of the room on the basis of your attitude towards leadership: (again the leader assigns an attitude to each corner in advance).
   a. to follow it,
   b. to fight it,
   c. sometimes to go along with it, sometimes not,
   d. to try to be a leader.
2. Discuss your attitudes and look for similarities and differences.

orientation to a new experience

1. Go to one of the four corners of the room based on your attitude towards a new experience such as this workshop:
   a. trustful,
   b. cautious,
   c. confronting,
   d. withdrawn.
2. Discuss your set and look for similarities and differences.

*The following exercises were written and designed by Alice Sargent unless otherwise indicated.

introductions

exercise 3 _____

personal goal   To learn more about other people in the group and allow them to know you on a more personal basis.

directions   1. Select a group of three people to meet with. Go around the circle answering each of these questions:

a. When I get in a new group I, _____
_____

b. When I am in a group with women, I _____
_____

c. When I am in a group with men, I_____
_____

d. Towards the end of a group, I _____
_____

e. Over the past year a critical issue in my life around being a woman or man has been ____
_____

2. Put an "M" after those activities you prefer to do with a man. Put a "W" after those activities you prefer to do with a woman. Put "M or W" after each activity you would like to do with either sex. At a later date you may also want to put the name(s) of the person(s) in this group with whom you would like to do these activities.

a. Whom would you prefer to:
go to the movies with?_____
go on a vacation with?   _____
go to New York with? _____

23

get angry at? _____

go to a desert island with? _____

cry with? _____

go shopping with? _____

go to a doctor for a physical? _____

watch a football game on TV with? _____

have as your boss? _____

talk about your sex life with? _____

3. Discuss your responses with each other and your feelings about the introductions process.

4. Select one person in your group of four to introduce to the larger group. Note some of the person's responses that intrigue you and with his or her permission share these in the larger group.

explanation   This experience can be very important in setting the norms of the group. How the information is received about each person, whether people are interested or can express caring to each other set the tone for how quickly cohesiveness will develop.

heroes and heroines

_____

personal goal   To be in touch with and share your dreams and visions of your ideal self.

directions   Introduce yourself to the group through a favorite childhood fairytale character, a sports hero/heroine, cowboy, a politician. Describe what qualities this character had that are significant to you.

explanation   As we have read many times and experienced for ourselves, women have been socialized to be expressive, reactive, dependent, and to meet the needs of others by caring for their physical as well as emotional needs. Women's role models, particularly within the middle class, have included nurses (Cherry Ames), detectives (Nancy Drew), social workers (Jane Addams), lovers (Lady Chatterly and now Erica Jong), sex objects (Ursula Andress), politicians' wives (Lady Bird Johnson, Jacqueline Kennedy, and Betty Ford), writers (Jane Austen, George Eliot, Joyce Carol Oates, Denise Levertov, Doris Lessing, and Anne Sexton), and now finally politicians (Shirley Chisolm, Barbara Jordan, Elizabeth Holzman, Sissy Farenhold, Bella Abzug, Ella Grasso, and Yvonne B. Burke). In contrast, men have been expected to be task-oriented, egocentric, strong, silent, responsible, effective problem solvers, and competitive. Their role models include cowboys (John Wayne), playboys (Hugh Hefner), movie-star motorcycle riders (Steve McQueen), detectives (Richard Roundtree and Perry Mason), sports heroes (Willie Mays, Mickey Mantle, and Evel Knevil), astronauts, explorers (Tom Swift), intellectuals, doctors, teachers, lawyers (William Kunstler and Eliot Richardson), and political heroes (from Martin Luther King, Robert or John Kennedy, Howard Baker, Sam Ervin, Lowell Weicker, to Jerry Rubin).

pictorial history
of my sex roles

personal goal To recall some of the experiences which remind you that you have learned a sex-role identity.

directions Each person in the group selects a crayon. The color may be important to you or you may want to swap as you get involved in your picture.

Begin to draw vignettes from your life, depicting how you developed your sex-role identity. Start with the earliest incident you can remember. Each scene should convey how you told yourself, or how someone else told you, the appropriate behavior for a boy or girl, or a man or woman. In my picture, for example, the boy next door might be telling me that his mother said we could no longer wrestle because I was a girl.

explanation This exercise can be a "fun way" for people to become acquainted and to begin to get in touch with what they have in common. How many women and men were told many of the same "myths" about what they should do and should not do? The experience of drawing rather than writing often serves surprisingly well to cue people in to many childhood memories. It is helpful if each person can pick something from each stage of his/her life: elementary school, junior high, and so on. This is not an art test, although participants may be surprised that they have not allowed themselves to advance beyond third-grade stick figures.

materials Large poster paper
crayons
masking tape

Allow approximately half an hour for drawing.

26

who am I?
what are my sex-
role stereotypes?

personal goal

To articulate your self-concept and your sex-role stereotypes as well as to see what sex-role stereotypes members of the group share in common.

directions

This experience is designed so that you can "data collect" about yourself. Its value is lost if you do not attempt to confront yourself honestly. Do not let the possibility of sharing later interfere now with self-disclosure during the exercise. It would be better to be honest with yourself and not share with the group at a later time.

Divide your paper into three columns. Head the first column *Who am I?* and answer the question at least ten times. People think of themselves in a variety of ways—in terms of roles they play; likes and dislikes; things that would be phoney for them to do; important values and beliefs; the way they would like to be—their ego-ideal; other people who give their life meaning; personality traits; kinds of relationships that they build.

After you have finished enumerating them, you may want to rank your responses. Number one should be the quality, adjective, or role, without which you would feel most unlike yourself. In effect, it is your "emblem," or the word you would most likely include when telling about yourself. Put a plus next to the other ones that are precious to you and a minus next to the ones that you want to give up.

After this part of the exercise is completed, start the next two columns. At the top of one column write *Men are*, and at the top of the next column write *Women are*. Fill in each column with adjectives that describe men and women *as you see them*. Perhaps it would help to picture a situation in your mind. For example, You are going to a party where you do not know many of the people. You walk into the room. On one side is a group of five men you don't know talking to each other, and on the other side are five women. Toward which group do you gravitate? What are you saying to yourself about the difference, if any, between the climate in each of the two groups? What makes you choose one group over the other? Rank your responses so that No. 1 seems to be the essence of that sex.

You may want to pause to compare your responses to *Who am I?* with your *Women are* or *Men are* to see how many overlap.

In order to "data collect" on the total group, use either a blackboard or post two sheets of poster paper titled "Men are" and the other "Women are." People in the group may simply call out their adjectives while someone writes them on the papers. Is there consensus? Do people like their sex?

Next to each quality put a + (plus) if you want to keep it or a - (minus) if you want to give it up. Also number the qualities in order of importance to your identity.

explanation — spirit of the exercise

The "Who Am I" exercise is usually a very important one for participants and can also move the group to a more meaningful level of sharing. It can be quite painful to share this exercise if a large part of the group does not react to the data. In the event that this happens, it is important to stop and to take a look at the group process in order to determine what is going on. Possible issues are that the task seems irrelevant or threatening, or that many group members came to get for themselves and not to give to others. If these issues prove relevant, then the group needs to talk about norms before proceeding with the experience if the Who Am I's are to be meaningful. This exercise usually takes two and a half to three hours in a group of ten to twelve persons.

Who am I?	*Men are*	*Women are*

sentence completions

personal goal To increase your self awareness by helping you get in touch with some of your "shoulds".

directions Perhaps from your "Who am I?" you can identify salient words which you would like to explore further through sentence completions. For example:

Nice girls are (complete each sentence 10 times or as many as you can) _____
_____

Nice guys are _____
_____

Angry people are_____
_____

Bitches are _____
_____

Bastards are_____
_____

Responsible men are _____
_____

Aggressive people are _____
_____

The little boy in me is _____
_____

The little girl in me is _____
_____

The man in me is _____
_____

The woman in me is _____
_____

The worst thing a woman can call a man is (insert word) _____
_____

The worst thing a man can call a woman is (insert word) _____
_____

The worst thing a man can call a man is (insert word) _____
_____

The worst thing a woman can call a woman is (insert word) _____
_____

The human in me is (answer 10 times) _____
_____

Men are superior to women because (answer 10 times) _____
_____   _____

Women are superior to men because (answer 10 times) _____
_____

It is more advantageous to be a man because (personally) _____
_____

(professionally) _____
_____

It is more advantageous to be a woman because (personally) _____
_____

(professionally) _____
_____

Free associate words with each of the following categories:

Housewives _____
_____

Single women _____
_____

Successful women _____
_____

Married women _____
_____

Men in education_____
_____

Women in business _____
_____

Divorced women _____
_____

Househusbands _____
_____

Women managers _____
_____

Single men_____
_____

Women in education _____
_____

Men in business _____
_____

Married men_____
_____

Men managers _____
_____

Divorced men _____
_____

explanation   Frequently people organize their behavior around "shoulds" or "expectations" for themselves. These policies filter behavior along certain lines and require them to fit into a mold; for example, "Good mothers always love their children," "Good children always love their mothers," "Mature men are responsible," "Women shouldn't be too assertive."

role models

personal goal To increase awareness about the influence of your sex-role identity in your life.

directions Describe five "role models" whom you have used in elaborating your identity, such as mother, father, a teacher, and so on. The concept of role is used here to mean a set of expectations that has an objective reality. Enumerate ten characteristics of each model and put a rank order on each characteristic to indicate how important you feel it is. Contrast these characteristics with your answers to "Who am I?".

role models

Name	1	2	3	4	5

a. Who are some role models you might choose in the future?

explanation Role models or mentors play a significant part in shaping the expectations and prohibitions we hold for ourselves. It is so important to recognize their sex, when their influence was most significant, and what it is like to live without role models as many women and men do who are changing from heavily sex-linked identities.

32

our mothers' and fathers' sex-role commandments

exercise 9 _____

personal goal   To help understand how you learned your sex roles as part of growing up.

directions   List ten commandments you think your mother gave you about how to be a girl/boy.

1. _____
2. _____
3. _____
4. _____
5. _____
6. _____
7. _____
8. _____
9. _____
10. _____

List ten commandments you think your father gave you about how to be a girl/boy.

1. _____
2. _____
3. _____
4. _____
5. _____

6. _____

7. _____

8. _____

9. _____

10. _____

explanation   Parents typically offer children a variety of commandments which in turn influence behavior either positively because the commands are accepted, or negatively because they are resisted. Sharing these with others can increase understanding about their origin and their similarity to cultural norms.

sex-role expectations

exercise 10 _____

personal goal   To further understand your own sex-role expectations and limitations.

directions   List as many items as you can for each category:

	I am *required to*	*I am* *allowed to*	*I am* *forbidden to*

1. Since I am a woman (man).

	I could	*I would*	*I would not*

2. If I were a woman (man)

3. The "human" in me wants to _____
_____
_____

4. The most important thing in life for a man is _____
_____
_____

5. The most important thing in life for a woman is _____
_____
_____

explanation   This exercise is a further attempt to help you explore some of the dimensions of your own sex role and to understand what other options might be available.

35

my role expectations

personal goal   To increase awareness of your role relationships and how you might change them to be more satisfying.

directions   Enumerate role expectations you see in each of the following roles. For instance, think of how much power, intimacy, achievement, competence, and influence are related to that role. List about a dozen words you associate with that particular role.

Spouse _____
_____
Child _____
_____
Parent _____
_____
Friend _____
_____
Lover _____
_____

Cite one way in which you could *change* each of these relationships to be more personal and less role-related and thereby express more of yourself. What behaviors increase intimacy in each of these relationships? What behaviors make you more powerful in each of these relationships?

List the changes you wish to make:

Spouse _____
_____

Child _____

_____

Parent _____

_____

Friend _____

_____

Lover _____

_____

Would you like to consult with the group or with any helpful person in the group about how to change any of these roles?

explanation   Often we are trapped in either/or modes of behaving. This experience offers an opportunity to collect a range of options by soliciting the opinions of the other members of the group.

alter-ego

personal goal   To get in touch with more of your feelings.

directions   Select someone in the group with whom you are particularly in tune, and let that person know how you feel.

Divide into pairs in which at least one person feels in touch with the other.

The group continues with its work but the member of the pair who feels in touch with the other person serves as the alter-ego. The alter-ego may sit a little behind the person with whom he/she is working, although it is necessary to see facial expressions and body posture.

As the group member expresses himself/herself, the alter-ego may speak up to express what the person is *feeling* but is not saying openly to the group. The alter-ego may add to something the person has said, or may contribute something completely on his/her own, perhaps from nonverbal cues such as facial expression or posture.

The person then agrees or disagrees with his/her alter-ego.

To what extent are the alter-egos and their partners mixed along sex lines? Are there some feelings in common about whether it is easier or more difficult to be an alter-ego for a person of the same sex or a different sex, or does it depend more on the person?

explanation   This exercise is an attempt to make available more data about the feelings of the group.

fishbowl: — group building experience

exercise 13

explanation

At certain points in the development of the group, attention needs to be paid to the process of the group in order for it to continue effectively with the task of increasing awareness about sex-role stereotypes. The foregoing group-building experiences are included as possible ways to unblock the group and to increase communication. They should be used when relevant.

personal goal

To improve observation skills of group processes.

directions

Divide into two groups either male and female, or simply two equal groups. The women, or half the group, interact in the center of the group for half an hour while the men, or the other half of the group, observe. Each person selects another person to observe. Observe both verbal and nonverbal participation.

The observers share their observations and then change places.

Group A seated in a circle on the outside;
Group B seated inside.

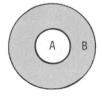

Observe for:

1. Listening—does the person attend to what is being said or is he/she concerned with something else, perhaps what he/she is going to say next?
2. Empathy—does he/she hear feelings as well as content?
3. Open versus closed questions—does the person invite others to share more, or is he/she quite specific? Open: How were you feeling when you said that? Closed: I hate people who do that, don't

you?

4. Does he/she listen more to feeling or to content?
5. Communication—how clear are the messages the person sends?
6. Power—who has the power or influence in the group?
7. Who talks to whom?
8. Does the person expect others to take him seriously, or does he/she just let her comments trail off without bothering to look for a reaction?
9. Does the person refer to himself/herself as "I," or as "you" or "one" (as in "one does thus and so")?
10. What does the person's posture indicate? Is he/she bent like a pretzel or relaxed? What other nonverbal messages are being sent?

how to give feedback on observations

1. The best way for feedback to happen is "naturally." People simply ask how they are coming across and others share their reactions with them.
2. When you offer feedback to someone it is important to check whether or not the person wants to receive it.
3. If the feedback is wanted, then it is helpful to be as specific as possible in your response. "When you said this to me, I felt. . ."
4. It is also very important to check out whether other members of the group experienced the person this same way.
5. If it is a personal "vision" rather than a collective experience, then you need to explore your own perception and feelings further to see what is going on inside you.

explanation

In the early stages of the group, as people are getting to know each other, it is less likely that feedback is actually taking place. Instead, people are becoming acquainted and clearing up distortions through the exchange of information. In order to promote active participation as well as effective communication, it is necessary for group members to check out their perceptions with each other. As the group develops members may indeed give each other feedback about such behaviors as sending mixed messages; that is, communication in which the affective or nonverbal message is different from the verbal statement.

This observation list was generated by Professor Allen Ivey, School of Education, University of Mass., Amherst, Mass.

taking the pulse of the group—group building experience

personal goal   To get a clear reading of what is happening in the group.

directions   If the group seems to be fragmented or if there are a number of sub-groups, or if the group seems to be depressed, it is sometimes helpful to go around the circle and have each person try to express in one word what she/he is feeling at that moment (*not* what he/she is *thinking*).

Keep going around in the circle until everyone has finished sharing all feelings. Often people "catch" each other's feelings and those who were depressed become more optimistic. Having shared their depression, they are less alienated. Hopefully, they have not simply spread their depression around. Participants in the group become aware that they are not alone in how they feel and possibly the cheerfulness and warmth of someone close to them in the group makes them feel better.

The expression of feelings might run as follows: down, turned off, angry, sad, rejected, bored, frustrated, curious, confused, involved, eager, hopeful, turned on, and so on.

explanation   This experience is intended to encourage members to be open about their feelings within the group rather than dumping disgruntled or positive feelings after the group is over, when they cannot be part of the collective awareness.

consciousness-raising groups

personal goal   To encourage you to construct your own model for discussing sex-role issues.

directions
1. Separate into a male group and a female group.
2. Each member of the group imagines a same sex group with whom you want to participate in a consciousness-raising experience. Enumerate on a sheet of paper twelve topics that would increase awareness about sex roles. When that is completed, expand on each topic by writing two questions about that topic.
3. The male group and female group return to the total group and share your lists.
4. Divide into pairs of one man and one woman. Each person selects one topic about which you would like to interview the other person. Ask each other three questions about sex roles.
5. Sometime within the next week interview someone else outside the group about your topic.

force-field analysis

personal goal   To help give you a better understanding of what the climate of a group or an organization is so that you can participate more effectively.

group goal   To get a reading of the group climate.

directions   One of the ways to assess what is happening in a group is a Force-Field Analysis. The Force Field concept reflects the forces at work at a particular time, and can be drawn individually by each member or as a composite for the entire group. It helps to assess strengths in the group and to select forces to remove in order to create change. The theory of change, suggested by Kurt Lewin who developed the force field analysis, is that while driving forces may be more easily affected, shifting them could increase opposition and add restraining forces. Therefore it may be a more effective change process to remove restraining forces. A force field for your group might look as follows:

done by the women

Driving forces *that help this group meet my needs*	Restraining forces *that keep this group from meeting my needs*
I like the people in this group	I came to talk about political ideas not to talk about myself. This personal sharing isn't meeting my needs, and it's making me anxious.
I'm beginning to feel something in common with the other women in this group.	When I came into this group I was satisfied with my marriage. Now I'm afraid I'm beginning to wonder. It's making me feel uncomfortable.
I'm starting to like the women in here better than I ever liked women.	So and so seems to be much more aware than I am. I'd better not open my mouth.
I'm starting to feel it's all right for me to express anger in here.	No one in here seems to care when I say anything. They just move on to another person.
I'm beginning to enjoy touching and being touched by other people.	It takes me time to get to know people. I just can't start talking about myself this quickly.
All this time I thought I was the only person who had these feelings. I can't believe other people feel the same way.	My boyfriend is putting pressure on me to stop coming. I certainly can't tell the group that, so I had better keep quiet.
If I stop coming, people will think I'm afraid.	I really don't have anything to contribute.
Ineffective group	*Effective group*

done by the men

Driving forces that help this group meet my needs	Restraining forces that keep this group from meeting my needs
I'm beginning to feel much more in common with other men than I ever thought I would. ⟶	This movement is the women's thing. Probably I shouldn't participate. ⟵
I'm beginning to feel attracted to some of the other men in the group. ⟶	I'm really angry at women who sit around and bitch. What are they doing with their lives? And yet I can't say that. It's boring in here. ⟵
I'm finding that it's all right to express all kinds of feelings that I've kept locked away. Sometimes I hurt a lot or I'm afraid, but I don't let anyone know. ⟶	I'm beginning to feel attractive to some of the other men in the group. I look forward more to informal time before and after the group. I feel like I'm on show in here. ⟵
It feels good to acknowledge that I'm not as sure of myself or as cool as I pretend. ⟶	I'm beginning to feel attracted to some of the women in here. But I can't say that or else they'll say I'm turning them into sex objects. I'd better keep quiet. ⟵
It feels good to share how lonely I am—that what I really want are some friends—both women and men. ⟶	I'm feeling anxious that my wife may start to make some demands on me to help more at home. I like things the way they are. ⟵
I hope my wife does start to change. She's not nearly as interesting as she used to be when we were first married. I don't mind if she is home less, just so she's happier and more involved. ⟶	I don't know what I'm going to get out of this. I wish I were a woman. I think they have it so good.
Ineffective group	Effective group

For further information on Force Field Analysis, see Kurt Lewin, *Resolving Social Conflicts* (New York: Harper & Row, 1948).

explanation   It is to be hoped that the use of the force-field analysis will demonstrate to the group the range of forces pressing on the group at a particular moment. This form of analysis can increase the group's optimism that it is possible to strategize and plan for change.

affirmative action

directions: Write a force-field organizational analysis on the environment in your organization for women.

Driving forces	Restraining forces
————————————————→ ←————————————————	

A hard place for women to work.   A good place for women to work.

the problem-solving process

Select one or two restraining forces which you might have power to change. For example, a restraining force might be lack of cohesiveness among the women, or lack of awareness of the organizational constraints, or the lack of empathy among most of the men. Do not be trapped by selecting areas of need which have little hope of being changed.

You may need to try out another force-field analysis of the particular restraining force.

Select one restraining force you want to change. Brainstorm (without evaluating) possible actions you could take to remove the restraining force. For example, if you select the lack of support among the women in the organization, you might want to consider calling a meeting of the women in your division to discuss this.

Assess the payoffs and lack of the particular alternatives for the force you are considering. If, for example, you want to invite the women to meet together, what reaction might that produce in the men? How could you deal with their responses? Ignore them? Not hold the meeting? Meet with the men informally or formally to explain what your goals are?

Decide on a next step and inform the relevant people of your decision.

my body

personal goals

To increase your awareness about your body and how these feelings effect your image of yourself.

directions

Draw an outline sketch of yourself—your whole body. (A roll of butcher paper or newsprint is easiest to use.) Try to imagine your whole physical self and express all the feelings you have, cosmetic, sexual, good, and bad, in the drawing. Try to discover if all these facets are integrated or not. If not, how would you like them to be relative to each other? Remember to set your own values; integration may not be what you want. There is no right or wrong, better or worse. Let your drawing show how you feel you are and how you would like to be. Draw your sensory organs big or small to indicate the ones you rely on more or less, such as your eyes, nose, mouth, feet (for balance), ears, hands and genitals. Please don't worry about your artistic ability; this is not an art test. Just concentrate on the things that you are trying to communicate.

Now draw another picture of *yourself as a member of the other sex.* How do you differ?

Divide the group into pairs and share the feelings with which you are in touch.

Return to the total group and talk about your body and senses. How do the women feel about their bodies? How do the men feel about their bodies? Are the men's feelings different from the women's?

Were the senses the women used different from the men's?

explanation

Very few women and men are satisfied with their bodies. "The most minute blemish on a total person—a pimple, excess weight, a 'funny nose,' larger than average breasts—can ruin a day, or years of agonies of constant awareness of it."[1]

Women have grown up appraising their bodies on the basis of how

47

sexually attractive they are, how they compare to certain ads in magazines or television. Many men learn to evaluate their bodies competitively—how well does a body work in athletics; how well coordinated and how fast is it; how much can it endure; and how responsive and sexually active is it?

Women's expectations of their bodies tend to rely upon a Madison Avenue image rather than an appreciation of individual differences. To a lesser extent, so do men's expectations. In reality, there are a wider variety of images of men and women, for example, in the art of Modigliani, Renoir, Braque, or Giacometti.

[1]Hole, J., & Levine, E. *Rebirth of Feminism.* (New York: Quadrangle Books, 1971).

relaxation

exercise 18 _____

Wendy Wyman Kritchevsky

personal goals   To relax in order to participate more fully in some of the other exercises. To continue to learn more about your body and how it does and doesn't work for you.

explanation   There are several ways to approach relaxation. These include tension release, imagery, breathing exercises, and activities which leave the body in a relaxed state. While these exercises may appear less obviously sex linked, they are critical to developing a self concept of a whole person. Our feeling's about ourselves are so intrigal to how we feel about our mind, our relationships and our body.

One of the leading scholars on tension/release relaxation is Dr. Edmund Jacobson who speaks of residual tension which builds up when the individual uses more energy then is needed on a particular task or event.[1] Specific exercises allow participants to locate and release these areas of tension in the body. The focus is on learning to let go from the inside. With practice one is able to locate and release tensions at various places in the body (e.g., stomach, eyes, back of neck) simply by focusing on letting go from the inside.

**tension
release
relaxation**

directions: I call this exercise "giving your body a hug" (i.e., "give your hand a hug and let it go" instead of "find the tension and let it go.")

These exercises can be done sitting or lying down:

1. Begin by lying down on your back on the floor, arms at your sides. Close your eyes.
2. Become aware of your breathing. Try not to change it, but rather just allow yourself to listen to it. If you like, locate the place on your torso where you feel the rising and falling of each breath.
3. Begin by tightening your hands into fists, then let them go. Repeat 2-3 times, allowing yourself plenty of time to experience the release.
4. Tighten your arms and let them go. Do not make your hands into fists, but allow them to remain flat on the floor. You may want to bring your hands up to your shoulders and let them go for variation, especially if you are sitting rather than lying down. Repeat 2-3 times, again allowing yourself enough time to experience the release.
5. Curl your toes and let them go. Repeat 2-3 times.
6. Tighten your legs and let them go. Again, if you are sitting, you might want to bring your knees toward your chest and then let them go. Repeat 2-3 times.
7. Tighten the stomach and pelvic area and let it go. Repeat 2-3 times.
8. Tighten the face as a whole or part by part, and let it go. Repeat 2-3 times.
9. Tighten your whole body and let it go. "Give your whole body a hug."
10. Check your breath (step two) and see if it is any lower or deeper than when you started the exercise.

[1]Edmund Jacobson, *Modern Treatment of Tense Patients.* (Springfield, Illinois: C. C. Thomas, 1970).

imagery relaxation

The success of imagery exercises depends largely on the participants' willingness to be involved in the particular fantasy and the appropriateness of the image chosen by the leader. In imagery relaxation sessions, it is important to encourage individual interpretations of the experience. For example, we don't all "fly away on clouds." Instead, each individual is asked to imagine a way to move through the air. Responses have included flying, floating (alone, or on something such as a leaf or a cloud), sliding on a rainbow, and being blown by the wind. All are valid and accepted. Basically, the individual is allowing his/her mind to create an image which is then responded to at an intense kinesthetic level. The person does not get up and act out the fantasy, but rather lies passively on the floor and imagines his/her body going through the experience. From the image, the participants can weave a story.

Here is a simple one. Speak quietly and allow plenty of time for individuals to experience each image.

1. Imagine that you must transport yourself by air to another place. How will you get there? Experience the voyage through as many senses as possible.
2. Find a way to land.
3. Explore the environment. What temperature is it? Can you feel it? What do you see? Move through it. What do you touch? (Note: the environment might change for some people at this point as they allow more possibilities to come to consciousness.)
4. It's time to leave. Take a last look around. You might want to bring something back with you or just say good-bye to it.
5. When you're ready, find a way to transport yourself back home. Experience the journey.
6. When you are back in this room, allow yourself to feel the floor supporting your weight, and the texture of the rug or wood beneath you. Become aware of your breathing. Check to see if it is any lower or deeper. Slowly open your eyes. This is a good time for sharing, if individuals so choose.

melting

Melting is an imagery activity which many people find enjoyable.

1. Begin by standing in a comfortable position, feet parallel, eyes closed.
2. Imagine that your little finger is melting, now your entire hand. Carry the melting feeling up your arm.
3. Repeat step 2 on the other arm.
4. Allow the melting feeling to travel across your shoulders and into your neck and back. Let your head go with it.
5. As the melting feeling moves down into your legs, your knees bend.
6. Keep melting until all of you is lying on the floor in a "puddle." Experience yourself melting across the floor.
7. Now gather yourself together until you feel your body boundaries again. (Note: The leader may want to trace participants' bodies with his/her hand to re-establish body boundaries.) Open your eyes!

breathing exercises

1. One person sits quietly and breathes normally. The other person simply listens for his/her partner's breath and tries to breathe in the same rhythm. Reverse. How was your breathing different from your partner's? What did you learn about the way you breathe? Variations: exaggerate your breath or your partner's by moving a body part in rhythm to the breathing. An example would be to lift and lower your shoulder. Gradually take the rhythm into the entire body. Try moving through space maintaining this rhythm.
2. One person sits quietly and breathes normally. The other person tries to locate the breathing by placing a hand on various parts of

his/her partner's body (e.g., the chest, stomach, back). Reverse. Could you feel how deep or shallow each breath was? What did you learn about the way you breathe? Variation: try this exercise on yourself.

Here is an exercise to try alone.

3. Find a quiet place to lie down. Center your breathing. Try breathing in and out through various parts of your body. Examples: up your toes and into your legs; down your legs and out your toes; up your fingertips and into your arms; down your arms and out your fingertips. Breathe in and out of your upper back. Give yourself plenty of time to experience the process. Become aware of any sensations such as color or temperature so that you may experience the area that is "breathing." Note: center your breathing after working on each area.

rocking

1. Experiment with different ways to rock yourself; front to front, side to side, in various positions. Try it to music. Allow yourself plenty of time to give in to the rocking.
2. With a partner explore different ways to rock together. Some ideas: sit cross-legged facing each other and hold hands. Try to maintain eye contact as you rock back and forth. Sit back to back and rock with your eyes closed. Become sensitive to the rhythm that you are creating together.
3. In a group (3 or more people) explore rocking together. Begin by making contact only with your hands. Gradually involve more of your body. Soon a group rhythm will develop. Stay with it. Sense your individual rhythm and your relationship with the group.

floppy doll   If you have one to demonstrate with, so much the better!

1. Begin by lying on the floor on your back, arms at your sides, ankles uncrossed.
2. Try to make your body as loose and floppy as possible.
3. The leader or partner gently grasps the wrist of the person lying down and flops the hand back and forth. If the hand is very tense and you can feel the individual anticipating the movements, try moving individual fingers. Then return to the whole hand.
4. Now grasp the wrist gently, lift the arm, and let it flop to the floor. If it is relaxed, it will fall gently. If it is tense, it will come down with a crash. To avoid the latter, use your free arm to break the fall and catch the arm. As the person learns to relax, this step can be eliminated. Repeat steps 3 and 4 with the other arm.
5. Holding both wrists, lift the arms and let them flop to the ground. Try to make and maintain eye contact with the person on the floor.

6. Grasp behind the ankle and knee of the person lying down and gradually flop the leg up and down and side to side. Repeat with the other leg.
7. Now lift the leg gently from behind the ankle and allow it to flop to the floor. Again, use your freehand to catch the falling limb until the individual is relaxed enough to let it go without increasing tension in the area.
8. If the participant is very relaxed, stand behind him/her, grasp both wrists and lift the arms high enough so that the head comes off the ground and falls back. Encourage the participant to close his/her eyes and enjoy the sensation. Slowly return the head to the rug and lower the arms.

swinging

This is a quick way to find out how tense or relaxed an individual is.

1. Begin by having one person lie down on the floor on his/her back.
2. One person stands behind the head and firmly grasps both wrists.
3. Another person stands in front of the feet and firmly grasps both ankles.
4. At a given signal, both people lift the person from the ground and gently swing him/her back and forth. Depending on the degree of relaxation, the head will drop back and the individual will allow him/herself to give into the swing.

discussion:

In groups of four, composed of two women and two men, discuss your feelings about these exercises noting differences that might be sex linked. Both women and men have received fairly constricting commandments about how freely to let their bodies flow. Many men have been encouraged to use their bodies competitively while women have limited their range by not being athletic enough. These exercises are a simple beginning to feeling greater power and gentleness in our physical being.

play

personal goal To express another dimension of ourselves.

directions We all have different childhood memories about playing with other girls or boys. For some of us it wasn't a particularly successful time. For the men in the group play was probably highly competitive, a time to prove toughness, but fortunately also an opportunity to express some boyish curiosity and enjoy oneself with abandon. Some of the women in the group may have tried to be "one of the boys" at times and on other occasions tasted the magic of dolls and stuffed animals and tea parties.

1. Try to recreate some of that play by recalling a favorite scene of yourself playing with another child.
2. Select a person of the same sex in the group and share that scene.
3. Select a partner of the other sex and compare notes with that person.
4. Now bring the play into the meeting. Select a person in the group. Kneel facing the person and place the palms of your hands together. Some people prefer to close their eyes.
5. Begin to explore each other's hands in an effort to make contact and get to know each other in another way. Feel whether the other person's touch is gentle, pushy or tough.
6. Now let your hands dance together without talking.
7. Pretend you have a fight at the dance.
8. Make up after the fight.
9. Your hands share a secret with each other.
10. It is time for your hands to say good-bye to your partner's hands.
11. You can move on and select another partner if you like.

explanation Some members of the group may feel freed by this exercise which gives permission to be less serious, less of a learner. Others may experience some tension as they are being asked to perform, one more time, in yet another manner.

54

sexuality

personal goal   To explore our fears of homosexuality, fears which often tend to interfere with establishing closeness with persons of the same sex.

directions   On a sheet of paper, each group member should answer the following
question anonymously: I am not homosexual because _____(10 times).
   Place the responses on the floor in the center of the group and invite
each group member to select a paper which is *not* his/her own.
   Read your paper to the group and suggest what the feelings might
have been of the person who wrote the paper.
   After the reading, the group may then want to engage in a discussion
of bisexuality and homosexuality. No effort should be made to get members of the group to disclose their responses.

explanation   One of the areas that holds back male/male, female/female relationships so much is the fear of homosexuality. These strong cultural taboos have only very recently come into question. This exercise is suggested in order to demystify homosexuality; so that fear of it does not
hold back very basic steps toward emotional contact among men and
among women that might take place in these groups.

sex-role
reversal

personal goal   To expand your options for initiating and responding sexually.

directions   During a sexual encounter, you might try role-playing the other sex to see if that offers any increased options in getting or giving sexual pleasure. Does it make any difference in the movements you allow yourself, in your position, your breathing, the noise you make, the length of time you are involved, whether you think of yourself as a woman or a man during sex? How do you feel about the difference? If there is no difference, you might try trading off your rituals whatever they are, with your partner.

explanation   Many people do not own their own sexuality within them, but rather experience it as a response dependent on someone else. This experience is an attempt to explore some constraints that might hold back sexual self-expression.

my feelings: love — joy — fear — anger — pain

exercise 22

personal goal   To be in touch with your range of emotional experiences.

directions   Below are five emotions. In the past week have you experienced all of them?

	Not at all	Hardly	Sometimes	Often	Almost all the time
Love					
Joy					
Fear					
Anger					
Pain or sadness					

Last time you experienced these emotions, what were the conditions? Fill the lefthand column below with your answers. How would you change that scene if you could replay it? The righthand column is for your answers.

Love	
Joy	
Fear	
Anger	
Pain	

Compare how men in your group differ from women in their responses. How are they the same?

explanation   Frequently there are important sex-linked differences in our range of emotional expression (see Carol Tavris' article), although for many of us the contexts in which we work seem not to give permission for much emotionality at all. This experience is intended to increase options within the group at least.

my emotions
collection

personal goal To be in touch with those emotions which may not be as readily available to you.

directions
1. Reflect on how related you feel to each of the members of the group. Take about ten minutes of silence and look from member to member assessing where you are with each person.
2. Did you recognize that you have been collecting "trading stamps" with respect to a particular person or emotion?
3. Are there any members of the group with whom you would like to alter your relationship either to make it better or worse?
4. Could you talk directly to that person and share with him/her what you have collected?
5. Could you check out whether they see themselves as sending these messages?

explanation Eric Berne[1] talks of "trading stamps" which people collect "as the by-product of legitimate interactions" and save for use later. Some people collect "trading stamps" to confirm a depression, to justify alienation, or to reassure themselves that other people are not really trustworthy, hence they need not relate to them in order to confirm their right to become angry or to confirm other guilts or fears. In fact, "People like to show their collections of feelings to others and talk about who had more," or better "angers, hurts, guilts, or fears, etc." Fortunately, some people collect positive emotions and share their joys and good feelings.

[1]Eric Berne, *What Do You Say After You Say Hello?* (New York: Grove Press, 1971).

anger

personal goals   To help confront and release tension in the group. This experience might be useful if there seems to be too much tense silence within the group; if the group seems to have reached a plateau and is having trouble going further; or if the group is having difficulty expressing negative feelings such as anger or fear.

directions   For about ten minutes, silently fantasize how each person in the group might express anger. What sorts of behavior would various people exhibit if they became angry?

   If anyone is willing to share his/her fantasies, begin the sharing of ideas with that person. It is more helpful to wait to discuss the fantasies until after a number of people have shared them.

   Check with the person whom the fantasy is about as to how accurate it actually is. Of course, the fantasies may say more about the person who is sharing them than they do about the person who is the subject of the fantasy.

   Are the fantasies of how the women express anger different from those for the men?

explanation   The group members' fantasies and projections of how others might respond with anger undoubtedly inhibit a free exchange. Therefore, it seems critical to get these to the surface where they can be examined and confirmed or discounted.

support systems

personal goal   To become more in touch with how much you are willing to give to and get from others.

directions   There are different kinds of support that we need in our lives every day to get our work done, to make a home, to stay in touch with what our strengths and limitations are, to feel good about ourselves, and to make transitions to new ways of life. People, geography, objects, and activities give us comfort, are relaxing, familiar, and help us regain our equanimity. Particularly during a time of stress and change, such as moving to a new location or breaking up an intimate relationship, it may be very important to assess your support systems and to plan a variety of ways to comfort oneself.

In fact, support groups are being organized for some of these life transitions such as Life Planning Groups, Widow to Widow, Parents Without Partners, Parents Without Children, The Gray Panthers, and Seminars for the Separated. Children have such delightful props; we take pleasure in giving a fuzzy animal, a delightful doll, a snuggly blanket with satin binding to a child we care about. Yet, we are less likely to treat ourselves in the same fashion. What kinds of things do you give yourself for comforts? How healthy are they? (You are requested not to smoke while you make out this list.) It may be a walk in a special place, a phone call, listening to a record, a bottle of champagne, a bubble bath, sitting in front of the fire-place. When did you last comfort yourself this way?

Draw a pictorial representation of your present support network. Begin with yourself at the center and then, radiating outward, place the other members of your support system. You might include organizations as a part of your support system. If you can, try to distinguish between psychological—socio-emotional support and task support—coworkers—a mentor, babysitting, and household assistance people.

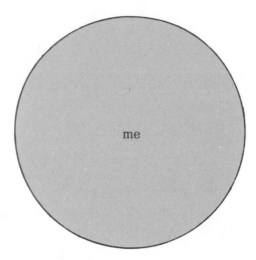

Or you may want to locate the other people in the group in terms of how intimately related you *feel* towards them.

Do you have many at different distances? Do you have a number of people you are holding equidistant?

Are people of different sexes scattered equally or do you tend to place people of the same sex closer or further away from you?

Do you want to change your picture at all? Is there someone you would like to bring further in or someone you would like to put further out?

Would you like to share with the group?

explanation   This exercise attempts to hold out a model for relationships which goes beyond role relationships to interdependence and mutuality.

conclusion to a session:
I learned

personal goal

To data-collect out loud rather than taking for granted or speculating about what each person learned from the session.

directions

At the end of each group session try going around the circle and asking each person to make several "I learned" statements regarding today's session. Take five to ten minutes to think about this first, or else it will be superficial and a foregone conclusion.

examples

I learned that I have difficulty talking in a group.
I learned that I am more liberated than I thought.
I learned that a lot of things I thought were "only *my* feelings" are actually shared by other people in the group.

explanation

Active participation is important here as always. Silence cannot be interpreted as agreement. Time and again you will be surprised when you actually hear from someone what is going on inside him/her. Making assumptions that we know where people "are coming from" without checking with them is the "role-related" way of putting people into stereotyped boxes and keeping them there. It may be necessary to listen particularly sharply to hear what each person is actually saying, rather than what you expect to hear them say. You may also need to remember to take yourself seriously enough so that you believe that the members of the group want to hear what you have learned.

individual assessment of
the group experience

exercise 27

group goal   To data collect anonymously about the climate in the group.

directions   At the end of the session, fill out the table and answer the questions that follow. Have someone tabulate the results. Present the results at the beginning of the next session.

1.   How involved were you in what went on in the session?

Very
involved   Not at all
                                                                            involved

2.   How involved were most other people?

Very
involved   Not at all
                                                                            involved

3.   How much do you feel you gave of yourself to the group?

A great deal
                                                                            Very little

4.   How much do you feel you received from others?

A great deal
                                                                            Very little

5. How free did you feel to say or do as you wanted in the group?

Completely   *Not at all*
free   *free*

6. How important do you feel your contributions were for the group?

Very   *Not at all*
important   *important*

7. How useful was the session for you as a woman/man?

Very   *Not at all*
useful   *useful*

8. The group increased my awareness about the kinds of problems women/men face:

A great deal   *Moderately*   *Not at all*

9. The group increased my trust in people:

A great deal   *Moderately*   *Not at all*

10. The most important contribution I made to the group was _____

11. The least important contribution I made to the group was _____

12. The behavior by someone else in the group that frustrated me most was _____

13. The behavior by someone else in the group that I liked best was_____

life planning (exercises 28-47)

The notion of life planning, and the development of Life Planning workshops and some of the particular exercises included here were done by Dr. Herbert Shepard, Stamford, Connecticut. The Life Planning exercises invite you to set aside a time to look at your total life space and answer the questions: where have you been, where are you now, and where are you going? There are many relevant populations who might want to participate specifically in the Life Planning Series:

people contemplating their first job
people considering a change in jobs
college freshmen who are planning their course of study
high school and college junior and seniors who are planning the next step in their career
housewives who want to explore other options
management development programs
career development workshops
couples who are concerned with growing as individuals or as a couple

These experiences offer the opportunity to consider the planning process of a person's entire life space: work time, leisure time, fun time, family time, friendship time, and alone time.

More important than emerging from the life planning experience with a definite goal, is that a person feels more in charge, has more options open, feels more capable of making decisions about his/her life. Many women, in particular, begin this experience feeling little control over their destinies.

life line

personal goal To look at your past to see what patterns emerge, what the high points and low points have been, and what you think is ahead of you.

directions Draw a life-line to depict your life up to the present. Think in terms of jobs and career, relationships with other women and men, education, peaks and valleys in your growth. Your representation may be graphic. Show what you have built along the way, including relationships, dreams and other monuments. You may want to draw two lines, one for your professional life and the other for your personal life. When you have finished, share these in your group.

Your line may look like this: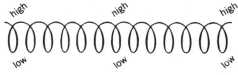

personal life

professional life

self-assessment

exercise 29

personal goal   To get a clearer sense of your own needs and wants.

directions   Complete the following sentences and share with someone else in the group.

I feel angry when _____

_____

I feel attractive when _____

_____

I feel nurtured when _____

_____

I feel feminine when _____

_____

I feel masculine when _____

_____

I feel afraid when _____

_____

I feel strongest when _____

_____

I feel alone when _____

_____

I feel controlled when _____

_____

I feel rejected when _____

_____

I feel competent when _____

_____

life planning career

personal goal   To look at the influences on your career

directions   We have been using words a great deal; let's try to find some other medium. Why not try drawing a picture which tells how you got to the present point in your career? Include about ten vignettes which show who influenced you along the way and what dreams you have held onto or discarded as you went along. Make an art gallery posting the pictures on the wall if you feel comfortable sharing your chef d'oeuvre with the group.

fantasy

exercise 31

personal goal   To increase your awareness about the conflict within you between both sex roles.

directions   Take a few moments to conjure up fantasy people who will tell you what they want you to be and do. Try to really hear them and write down what they are saying.

Fantasize a man and a woman in your head or on a television screen who each tell you what you should be like.

The woman is saying,   "Be _____

_____

"Don't be _____

_____

The man is saying,   "Be _____

_____

"Don't be _____

_____

Now the woman is arguing with the man over which you should/shouldn't be. What are they arguing about? _____

_____

Now they are in agreement about _____

_____

autonomy

personal goal   To try to get on top of your life, albeit momentarily, to see how you might feel more in charge.

directions   Draw a picture or make a collage of the areas of your life in which you feel you are in charge—where you are your own manager—including relationships, work, recreational activities, sex, personal growth, the condition of your body, vacations, and leisure time.

   Draw a picture of those facets of your life over which you feel you do not have as much control as you would like. In those cases where you know, draw a picture of the person(s) or the ghost(s) or the destiny that is in charge of those decisions or events.

explanation   As we have said, both men and women live under sex-role constraints which limit their ability to be autonomous. Being autonomous reflects a desire to know versus a desire to feel competent. Autonomy goes beyond independence. It is used here to describe the sense that there is a personal life-force within you to which you are responsive. In contrast to living to preserve your image, it is rather a sense of taking council with your inner self in order to decide how to behave and how to define your own uniqueness.

self inventory

exercise 33 _____

personal goal   To get in touch with the strengths you have demonstrated in your life to date.

directions   List six success experiences in your life. Enumerate resources that accomplishment required you to have.

	Success	*Resources*
1.		
2.		
3.		
4.		
5.		
6.		

Draw a line down the middle of a piece of newsprint making two columns.

In one column list your strengths and in the other your blocks to being more effective in a particular area of your life. Select from either the personal, work, or educational spheres. Your concern may be as a father/mother, a student, a change-agent, or manager.

Strengths	Blocks

Enumerate both your strengths and blocks to being effective. Hold these papers up in front of you and mill around the room encountering others in the group. See who has strengths that you would like to have and whose blocks are similar. To what extent are your behaviors sex-linked? Have you encouraged or prohibited yourself from learning some behaviors because they weren't quite "appropriate" for your sex?

Link up with one other person in the group and talk about a possible change you could make in one of your blocks.

best and worst day

personal goal   To look at what we like about our present life and what are some of the constraints.

directions   Draw a composite picture of your best and worst day in the past month or so. Include about ten episodes in each picture. Share these with the group.

Best

What kinds of experiences make a "good" day?

Worst

What are the common ingredients of a "bad" day?

life inventory

personal goal   To be in touch with how much we are permitting and encouraging ourselves to be expansive in our present life style.

directions   Select a partner with whom you feel quite comfortable. Interview each
other for half an hour, each writing in the other person's responses on
his/her inventory. The interviewer may ask open-ended questions in
order to stimulate the other person's responses.

	Work life	Personal life
Peak experiences I have had		
What I do well		
What I do not do well		
What risks I take		

	Work life	Personal life
What I would like to learn		
What I would like to have		
What I would like to stop doing		

The one thing I most want to accomplish is? _____

what I do for fun

personal goal To get in touch with how much or how little fun we have in our present life space.

directions List 20 activities that make you happy.

	Code			
List	a—alone p—people	r—risks f—familiar	i—intimacy	Put $ if costs more than $5.00
1.				
2.				
3.				
4.				
5.				
6.				
7.				
8.				
9.				
10.				
11.				
12.				

Code

List	a—alone p—people	r—risks f—familiar	i—intimacy	Put $ if costs more than $5.00
13.				
14.				
15.				
16.				
17.				
18.				
19.				
20.				

discarded dreams

personal goal   To expand our horizons for what we permit ourselves in our current lives.

directions   Write down some of the dreams, behaviors, values, attitudes that have been encouraged by the people who are important to you.

What are some of the dreams, behaviors, values, attitudes that have been discouraged?

Select one or two dreams that you would like to playout now. What encouragement would you need to follow through on them? How could you go about getting that support?

Share one of your dreams with the group.

proactive versus reactive approaches

exercise 38

personal goal   To assess to what extent we are in charge of our lives at the present.

directions   List about ten things and people for whom you are waiting before you move forward.

List about ten areas over which you have direct influence without checking with others at work or at home.

discussion   Frequently we adopt a mode of waiting for others to rescue us. If they don't, we grumble about "the world" or "those thoughtless people" rather than taking the risks to try and learn to get what we want for ourselves. To stereotype momentarily, it seems that men may expect to be rescued in their personal lives while women may want to be rescued from establishing professional and successful goals.

Is the women's list much longer than the men's list in terms of what they are "waiting for"?

Next to each of the items you are waiting for, note one step you could take to get movement in that area.

freedom and responsibility

exercise 39

personal goal

To look at the values you use to make decisions about your life.

directions

Select a decision you need to make about your career.

Choose two people in the room whom you know to feel differently about the degree of freedom and the degree of responsibility individuals should exercise with respect to their lives.

Sit between these two people; freedom on one side—responsibility on the other. Have the discussion about your decision with each of them arguing with you and each other about the direction you should take.

The rest of the group may either observe and eventually join in, or everyone in the group may want to break up into groups of three to go through this exercise at the same time.

Ultimately the members of the group may want to vote by positioning themselves in terms of their own preference as to the importance of freedom or responsibility.

decisions

personal goal To look at the person you carry around inside you and consult when you make a decision.

directions Write a letter to yourself about your life, about taking care of yourself, or about a choice you are facing in the near future. Who else might have written this letter to you? Does it include criticism or permission in it?

Fantasize a discussion with yourself about a decision you need to make. Begin to discuss the decision with yourself. For example, try to decide whether to go back to school, to go to graduate school, a new job opportunity, or whether to have a baby. Imagine you have a Board of Directors that is helping to make this decision. Who are the members of the Board? Who is taking your position on the Board? Who is the treasurer of the Board? Who has the most votes on the Board?

types of
decision-strategies

exercise 41 _____

personal goal   To increase your awareness about other options for making decisions.

direction   Select a decision-making strategy which describes your behavior in some situations. Test out this style with respect to a decision you currently need to make in your life. What does your style say about you? How is it related to your sex-role identity? What style would like to have?

Impulsive	*Fatalistic*	*Complaint*
Little thought or examination, taking the first alternative, "don't look before you leap."	Letting the environment decide, leaving it up to fate, "it's all in the cards."	Let someone else decide, following someone else's plans, "anything you say, Sir."

Delaying	*Agonizing*	*Planning*
Taking a moratorium, postponing thought and action, "cross that bridge later."	Getting lost in all the data, getting overwhelmed with analyzing alternatives, "I don't know what to do."	Using a procedure so that the end result is satisfying, a rational approach with a balance between cognitive and emotional, "weighing the facts."

Intuitive	*Paralysis*
A mystical, preconscious choice, based on "inner harmony," "it feels right."	The decider accepts responsibility but is unable to approach it, "can't face up to it."

Reprinted with permission from *Deciding* by H. B. Gelatt, Barbara Varenhoist, Richard Carey, p. 44, © 1972 by College Entrance Examination Board, New York.

couples life planning

personal goal   For couples to define both their individual and collective goals.

directions   Make a list of things you want out of life as a couple. Compare lists with your partner.

Make a list of things you want out of life for yourself.

Begin to negotiate with your partner about being a support system for getting your individual needs met.

"I'll tell you what I want. I want self-actualization as a woman in a societal modality in which a viable life-style is divorced from pre-conceived ideas of sexual role-conditioning, and I want it now!"

couples inventory

_____

personal goal   To look at how sex-role behavior influences decision making, autonomy, and intimacy in your relationship with your partner.

directions   Both partners fill out separate inventories and then compare statements.

1.   I am important to our couple because _____

_____

2.   What I contribute to your success is _____

_____

3.   I feel central to our relationship when _____

_____

4.   I feel peripheral to our relationship when _____

_____

5.   The ways I show concern for you are _____

_____

6.   The ways I encourage your growth are_____

_____

7.   The ways I deal with conflict are _____

_____

8.   The ways I have fun with you are _____

_____

9.   I get angry when you _____

_____

10.   I am elated when you _____

_____

11.   The way I get space for myself in our relationship is_____

_____

12.   The ways I am intimate with you are _____
      _____

13.   The ways I am jealous of you are _____
      _____

14.   I have difficulty being assertive when you _____
      _____

15.   You have difficulty being assertive when I _____
      _____

16.   The strengths of our relationship are _____
      _____

17.   The weaknesses of our relationship are _____
      _____

18.   Our relationship would be more effective if you _____
      _____

19.   I feel most masculine in our relationship when I _____
      _____

20.   I feel most feminine in our relationship when I _____
      _____

21.   I trust you to do/be _____
      _____

22.   I do not trust you to do/be _____
      _____

23.   I deal with stress by _____
      _____

24.   You deal with stress by _____
      _____

25.   The division of labor in household tasks is decided by _____
      _____

26.   Our finances are controlled by _____
      _____

27.   The amount of time we spend with our relatives is determined by ___
      _____

28.   Our vacation plans are made by _____
      _____

29.   Our social life is planned by _____
      _____

30.   Taking stock of our relationship is done by _____
      _____

31.   I am lonely when _____
      _____

32.   I need you to _____
      _____

transitions fantasy

exercise 44 _____

personal goal   To increase awareness about how supportive and how critical you are of your own dreams.

directions   Select a comfortable location in the room. Sit down. Try to relax. Begin to contemplate a change you want to make in your life within the next year. You may be considering a mid-career change, taking a trip alone, going back to school, having a baby, interviewing for a different job, changing your relationship to your parents, or changing your relationship with the person with whom you are living, making some new friends, or adding more fun to your life. Be very specific about what effects your new change might produce. Discuss for a few moments with yourself how you feel about this change.

Conjure up a tiny figure of a person in your support network. It might be yourself or someone else who cares a lot about your growth and development. Drop that support figure into a place in your body where you feel you get your support. Let the support figure begin to enumerate reasons why you can make this change: how competent you are; how important the change is to you; how you can do anything you set your mind to.

Conjure up a tiny figure of a resistor and drop that figure into your body where your resistance is. Let the resistor begin to tell you how foolish you were to even consider making this change: Who do you think you are?—You can't do this; there's no way. Look at the reasons—it's not possible. Let's be practical, logical, rational . . .

Now, let the supporter and resistor argue with each other and listen as they discuss your change. The moment of choice has come.

You must either yank the supporter or the resistor from your body. Whom will it be? That decides whether you make the change or not. Yank one of them out. Look at it in the face. Who is it? Look the other figure you left in your body in the face. Who is that?

If you feel comfortable doing so, share this experience with someone sitting near you.

This exercise was contributed by Dr. Charles Seashore, Washington. D.C.

a fantasy future

personal goal   To dream a little about some options you might want in your future.

directions   Fantasize a day in your life for tomorrow. Unless you make some changes, it will be the same as today. Be aware of how much you feel you manage your own life. Be aware of what your real preferences are—what is meaningful to you. What do you treasure? If you stop yourself from dreaming by censuring yourself, be aware of that. Are you frightened? Why? Try to be happy rather than just brave.

Relax and let's begin the fantasy. Think about it quietly to yourself for about ten minutes. Do not be concerned about sharing it with the group; that is not the most important part of this experience. This experience emphasizes being in touch with your own dreams.

Let's set the stage. You wake up in the morning. What time is it? Who, if anyone is next to you in bed? Where are you living, what town, what kind of building? You go to the closet to get dressed. What kind of clothes are hanging there? Are you going to work? What kind of work do you do? What does the person(s) living with you do? How do you spend your evening? What kind of friends do you have? How do you feel about your day?

If you feel like sharing with the group, then please do. We might all lie down on the floor with our heads together like teenagers around a campfire sharing great dreams for the future. If your fantasy seems too unreal, try one that is more realistic.

On the other hand, if you feel you confined yourself too much, try to dream some more.

Now go through the day again, being a person of the other sex. Make certain you do at least one or two things differently just because you are of the other sex.

a two-year plan*

exercise 46 _____

personal goal   To test a hypothetical plan that you are considering for your life in the
near future.

directions   Answer the following questions:

1.   What, specifically, do you want to accomplish in the next two years? (Not just what
you *should* do). _____
_____

2.   What specific steps do you plan to take to achieve this goal a)_____ b) _____
c) _____
_____

3.   What blocks in yourself will you have to overcome to achieve this goal? _____
_____

4.   What blocks in the world will you have to overcome to achieve this goal? _____
_____

5.   How do you feel about the possibility of achieving this goal? _____
_____

6.   How do you feel about the possibility of failing to achieve it? _____
_____

7.   Where will you go specifically for help in accomplishing your goals? _____
_____

8.   How strongly do you want to achieve this goal?

Hardly at all   *A great deal*

9.   How honest do you feel you have been in answering these questions?

Hardly at all   *Extremely*

10.   In a conversation with someone else with whom you feel very comfortable, discuss your responses.

the future

personal goal

To forecast the events in your life that will be important to you and the kinds of rewards you give yourself for the various activities in your life.

**an article
in your local
newspaper**

directions

Write a newspaper article to your college alumni magazine or local newspaper ten years after you have graduated.

Consider a variety of areas in your life such as your career, where you have been, where you want to go.

Consider how you obtain status and respect. Whom do you want to respect you? Who does?

Consider your personal relationships. How do you feel about your friends? How inclusive or exclusive are you?

Consider your leisure and pleasure activities.

How are you continuing to educate yourself?

Where do you get your energy? How do you renew yourself spiritually?

Consider whether your life style has been growth-oriented or survival-oriented. If it is growth-oriented, how are you trying to grow?

**your retirement
dinner**

directions

Fantasize that it is the night of your retirement dinner. What is the year? Where is it being held? Whom do you invite?

There are several speeches to be made about your life. Whom would you select to give them? Write out what they are to say. In a small group, try playing out this event, giving the speeches to people whom you would like to read them. What did you have colleagues do at the dinner? What did you have your family do at the dinner? What did you learn from the experience?

behavior change contract

_____

personal goal

To make change goals as overt and specific as possible in order to increase the likelihood that they happen.

directions

Make a contract to express emotions this week that were excluded on your list in Exercise 28.

behavioral change characteristics

The behavior must:

1. represent overt behavior
2. be individualized
3. be extremely specific

contract

Name _____

Specific, individualized, behavior-change goal _____

_____

Characteristics of failure_____   Characteristics of success _____

_____

Date _____   Signatures_____

_____

explanation

This contract encourages you to adopt a problem-solving mode and to have a support system in order to facilitate changing a pattern that you have identified as not helpful in your style.

assertiveness

personal goal

To try to increase your options for expressing your wants and needs.

Assertiveness is expressing your wants and needs without being destructive to another. It is characterized by an "I" (assertive), "I want to go to the movies tonight, will you come with me?" rather than a "you" (aggressive) statement, "You never take me to the movies." A passive attitude is: "What do you think we should do tonight?" (waiting or hinting to the other person but counting on them to intuit your feelings).

directions

Describe a situation in which you feel good about your assertiveness.

Describe a situation in which you feel you are not sufficiently assertive.

1. Write an assertive response to this situation.
2. State what the other person's behavior was that bothered you. Indicate one feeling that behavior evoked in you, such as closeness, fear, or anger.
3. Specify one change you would like to see the other person make.
4. Indicate what will happen if the other person does not hear you or respond to you (try to find a range of options which are not no-win).

explanation

Learning to be assertive offers something to people who are bullying and intimidating in order to get their needs met or to those who are self-denying martyrs. Assertive behavior emphasizes self-expression, self-management, and autonomy; but not blaming, rescuing, manipulative, deferential, or uninvolved responses.

man/woman dynamics: some typical communication patterns

exercise 50

Carol Pierce
Janice Sanfacon[1]

Many women and some men are beginning to examine their patterns of communication. A few have jointly been exploring how our non-androgynous conditioning has affected our interactions, or how "one-upness and one-downness" gets expressed in communication patterns and influences other behavior. We will outline eight models of communication that we have observed as a result of working with male/female groups for the past few years. We offer these models here for your discussion and hope they may eventually provide the basis for some research.

The basic dynamic we observed the most consistently in male/female interactions was a process of "psyching out." As in other human relationships characterized by a one-up, one-down dynamic, it is a survival mechanism resulting from feelings of a lack of power, but in addition this posture seems to predetermine and underlie other patterns of behavior.

the "psyching-out" process

A constant and subconscious process in the thought and behavior of women is the "psyching-out" of men. This behavior is so pervasive it can be considered a feminine life style affecting a wide range of interactions. We hypothesize that this phenomenon developed because:

Little girls are not urged to experience as active a childhood as little boys or to control their world by physical actions.

[1]We wish to thank our colleagues, Judith Palmer and Karen Stone Terninko, Marcy Murninghan and John Haskell, for their thoughtful and supportive contributions to this paper. We also thank the many women and men who were willing to deal with these touchy and elusive issues in groups.

Women are encouraged from childhood to feel it is better to have a
   man's approval than a woman's approval.
Women are set in competition with other women for male approval.
Women experience lines of power as going from women to men.
Women are taught to be reactive rather than proactive.
Women learn to live for and through others and to define themselves in
   terms of others.
Women are expected to be selfless helpers and not to have needs for a
   lot of space, both territorial and psychological.

On the other hand, men are taught: to be self-sufficient, intact, a closed
system; they are not expected to acknowledge their dependence needs.
The costs are high for men as well as women. Eventually men begin to
deny to themselves that they even have such needs. They lose touch
with their feelings, become task-oriented, compartmentalized, mechanical, totally rational and therefore totally dependent on women to fill
their needs for nurturing and caring of their own personal relationships and interaction with others (women playing the role of facilitator
between father and child, adult son and father, man and friends). Men
are now ripe for women's "psyching-out."
   For women this necessitates the development of mental processes
and styles characterized by continual forethought as to how to "use"
another person. Hence, women learn to be schemers. Women often
learn to gear their thoughts to what will make a man feel comfortable;
the best way to make a man appear pleasing and smart to others; what
problems a man needs to talk about; and how to make a man feel fas-
cinating and powerful. The cost to women in this process is that they
learn to deny their own wants and needs and, hence, do not gain a
sense of self-esteem, integrity as a individual, and autonomy. They
have little feeling of being powerful enough to shape their environment.
Women frequently "psych-out" to get male approval, to compete with
other women, to manipulate, because these are the modes familiar to
them. Whereas, in those interactions characterized by the sharing of
straight, factual knowledge, giving orders or advice, and the initiating
of sexual encounters, one sees the preponderant type of communication behavior of men in a male-dominated world. Many men are now
experiencing a revolution to learn those behaviors and expressions
necessary to grow emotionally and to relate in a more personal way.
   "Psyching-out" then is a mode of behavior where a person constantly takes on the responsibility of figuring out what is most helpful
and pleasing to another person, hoping the result will be that in return
he/she will be liked, appreciated and will receive attention. The problem is that because of role-stereotyping, the same kind of attention is
seldom initiated or returned to women, and the giver is frequently
neither noticed nor appreciated.

Lack of openness and honesty about one's real feelings characterizes the "psyching-out" phenomenon. When this mode of relating is carried into task-oriented groups such as offices, community organizations, education institutions, or human service agencies, it may become a block to decision making, orderly planning, procedure, learning groups, and personal helping relationships. *The following stereotypical communication models show graphically the phenomenon of "psyching-out," its behavioral styles, and results.*

model 1—
"the check-out"

"The check-out" shows a man and a woman. In our society, the respon-

sibility typically falls on women to initiate personal communication of a friendly, nonsexual nature. She has learned, mostly unconsciously, that she needs to initiate the "hello-how-are-you's" and pleasantries. Yet the woman may be fearful of seeming aggressive, seductive, or motherly unless she is the hostess where her role is quite clear. The man may have "blinders"—he may be reluctant to initiate contact with women as friends or as great kinds of persons with whom to be, because he has learned to wait for the woman's initiative in this situation. Many possible friendships are lost in a few seconds at the level of the "the check-out," because the woman, having carried all responsibility for initiating contact, has decided after a quick assessment not to continue the relationship.

model 2—
"the set-up"

However, many times a woman does decide she will initiate an explora-

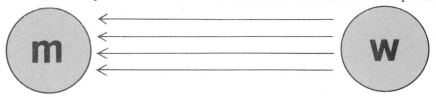

tory contact. She perhaps starts a conversation by asking the man about himself, complimenting him on a job well done, or asking how he feels about a certain issue. He responds by answering her questions and a lively discussion may very likely ensue around his interests and concerns. For the woman, the *topic* is the man's attitudes and feelings through the *vehicle* of the subject matter.

What is missing from this conversation is his asking her what her opinions are, what she is doing these days, commenting on how well she seems to be getting along. What often accompanies this transaction is the woman feeling that her thoughts and needs, if she can even get in touch with them, are unimportant or invalid, and the man without expectation that there would be anything the woman could or would want to say about herself or her ideas.

model 3— "the stand-off"

When a man plays host to a woman, the roles may change. This could

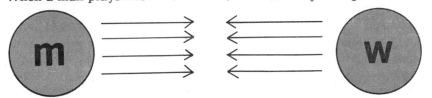

happen where a woman is a speaker at a meeting and the man is responsible for inviting her, so that casual conversation is necessary. The content of the conversation typically becomes factual. He asks such questions as: "Are you married? Do you have children? Do you ski? Have you ever enjoyed a certain vacation area?" Each one of these questions can be answered and a similar one asked back. A very lively and engaging conversation is carried on as long as factual material can be found. The basic quality of the transaction is information-sharing and neither of the sets of lines goes past the middle to touch the other person. Factual conversation can be delightful and relaxing with the two persons not making contact at an intimate level. Often such conversations are initiated as "openers," with speakers hoping to get to a deeper level by this route. But sooner or later, if the goal of the communication is to do something other than to confirm "what is," someone must risk contact by asking or sharing feelings.

model 4— "the run-around"

A possible variation on "the stand-off" might be the man making fac-

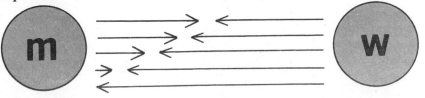

tual statements of the "stand-off" variety and the woman "psyching-out." If the conversation does start out this way, the balance of statements and questions from the man soon change to just statements about himself and his ideas. As the intense feeling of interest in the man becomes the backdrop of the conversation, the man may see the woman less and less as a person like him with interests, feelings, likes, and dislikes. In fact, the "Stand-off" most frequently develops shortly into the "the run-around" due to the woman's feelings of being responsible for the relationship. That is, his silence signifies a lack of interest in her so she colludes and fills the vacuum with another question about him.

Another version of this communication is where the woman states a feeling like: "I'm really feeling low today." And the man responds with either advice "Why don't you go out for lunch with a friend?" or with an evaluation: "I don't see why you should be feeling like that." Because he may feel pressured so by his own role expectations to be the protector or provider, he responds to the facts rather than to her feeling. Many men in groups reported that whenever they are asked a question, and especially when it comes from a woman, they feel they are obliged to provide a solution rather than investigate the cause.

model 5— "the dialogue"

"The dialogue" depicts an equal relationship where both partners

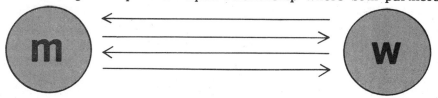

have comparable time for the concerns and interests of the other. This relationship is interdependent. It is characterized by mutuality in which persons share the "psyching-out" function, help each other to expand ideas, support each other's endeavors, share feelings, and try to understand each other. Many relationships of "the set-up" variety appear to have "the dialogue" status because the partners claim such happiness and contentment with the status quo.

It is important to remember that "psyching-out" on the part of women is in itself not always bad. The problem is that women learn to do it so well, men often feel no reason to learn such behavior to complement it. It needs to be part of a communication pattern where it flows back and forth, and is done for positive reasons, not negative reasons.

In the pattern of men and women stereotypically interacting there are times when the "psyching-out" process goes from men to women. Models 6, 7, and 8 are examples.

**model 6
"the conquest"**

Where the motivation is to establish a sexual relationship, until re-

cently the culture has assigned the initiative to men. This expectation is so deep in our culture that it is one of the great barriers to other man/woman friendships. Men often feel they have done their duty within a relationship when they have taken the initiative sexually.

When a woman is "psyched-out" by a man it is difficult to differentiate between a sexual interest and interest in her as a person or as a business colleague. Many women are ambivalent and fear concern from a male peer because it might be a camouflaged sexual approach. Yet they secretly hope that it is, because such interest confirms them as women. Many men have learned that when they do show great interest in a woman's thoughts and endeavors, it is the clearest route to a sexual relationship. This behavioral interaction puts an extra load on business and professional relationships for both women and men.

**model 7—
"the turn-off"**

An occasion when a man may be forced into "psyching-out" position

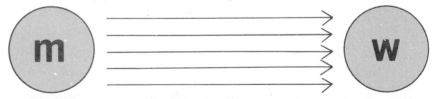

comes when a woman's behavior towards him changes, because she is suddenly spending more time on her own personal growth and less time focusing on his needs. This happens frequently when a woman joins a consciousness-raising group. Her own growth and change now dominate her thoughts and she also may be in touch with anger at men for their part in stereotypical role playing.

A man who may be confused by such sudden changes and who still cares about a relationship with the woman is now put into a position, out of feelings of self-preservation, of trying to "psych-out" the woman as to where she is and what she wants in relation to him. As shown by the "turn-off," a strong come-on by the man may result, but an equally possible behavior would be to retreat inside oneself.

model 8— "the revolt"

Another situation occurs when a woman stops doing the emotional

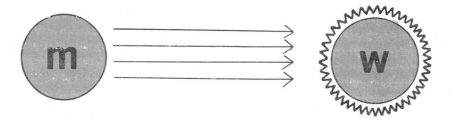

maintenance for the relationship. Since it has been solely her responsibility to maintain the man/woman relationship, always carefully nurturing it and attending to its tensions and crises, the time often comes when she throws her hands up and says, "I've had it. You never listen to me. You're never concerned about me. You do nothing for our relationship, I'm tired. I want out." At this point, if the man doesn't assume some share of the maintenance, conflict comes and the relationship may end, either physically, psychically, or both. If the man does want the relationship to continue he may try to listen, ask the right questions, show interest. Whether his efforts to mend the relationship are successful depends on how quickly he can change, how weary the woman is of carrying the burden of making the relationship successful, whether she can find other ways to self-actualize rather than simply demand change from him, and whether they can establish their own and other support systems to assist during the crisis.

At times "going into crisis" by a woman in order to be heard and to get some attention can become a life style and a way of relating, because it is the only time she is listened to with real concern.

directions

Write a sample of communication from your work or personal relationships, or one that you have observed in others interactions for each of the models described.

1. *"The Check-out"*
Personal

Work

2.   *"The Set-Up"*
Personal

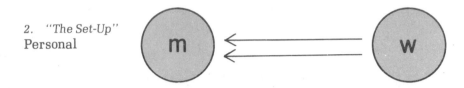

Work

3.   *"The Stand-Off"*
Personal

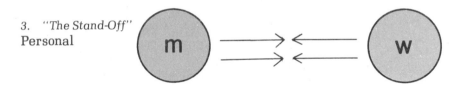

Work

4.   *"The Run-Around"*
Personal

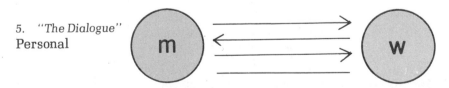

Work

5.   *"The Dialogue"*
Personal

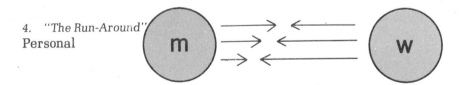

Work

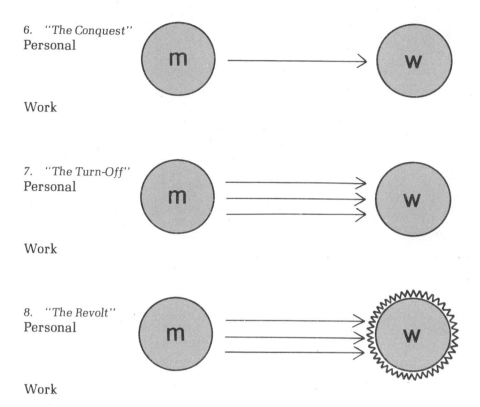

6. *"The Conquest"*
Personal

Work

7. *"The Turn-Off"*
Personal

Work

8. *"The Revolt"*
Personal

Work

follow-up   Identify one model that seems to be a frequent part of your communication patterns. Find someone you trust with whom you can discuss the communication pattern and who will give you feedback from an observer's position.

role reversal
in male-female
communication styles

personal goal   For each sex to experience the other's stereotypical rules for communication.

directions   Select a topic for discussion. During the discussion, the men will follow the women's rules for communication and vice versa.

The men are to follow traditional guidelines for women's communication style. The men will:

1. Be deferential—don't interrupt.
2. After making a point in the conversation, laugh or let your voices trail off in some discounting manner.
3. Smile a lot.
4. Look at the other group members a lot, particularly (in this case) the women, for approval.

The women will:

1. Be assertive.
2. Interrupt others if they don't complete their thought quickly enough for you.
3. Talk in paragraphs.
4. Ignore nonverbal cues.
5. Don't look at anyone in particular when you talk.

Discuss how you felt during the experience. Was it easier for the men to decrease their responses than it was for the women to increase theirs?

explanation   While these directions are exaggerated, they may help you experience some contrasting ways of responding and being responded to.

self assessment
in male-female
relationships

exercise 52

personal goal   To facilitate peer relationships between men and women.

directions   List your strengths and blocks in both work and personal relationships with the other sex. You might differentiate between work relationships and personal relationships by selecting one or the other or by noting next to the characteristics if it is exclusively a problem in a work relationship or a personal relationship. Women may be troubled by how to be more assertive with men, how not to be intimidated by men, how to deal with sexual attraction. Men may want to deal with what it feels like not to be in control with women any longer, when they have been brought up to be in control.

With men

Strengths   *Blocks*

List your strengths and blocks in both work and personal relationships with women.

With women

Strengths   Blocks
_____

Hold your paper up and walk around the room sharing with others to discover similarities and differences. Select three other people to link up with, one of the same sex, two of the other sex. In groups of four, for the next hour, share strengths and blocks.

Begin to formulate one change you might make to move out of being blocked.

Block   Action steps
_____

1.

explanation   It is hoped that through this experience you can formulate blocks as problems to be solved and, therefore, move to a different space in your relationships with some men and women.

scenarios for role playing male-female issues

Barbara Benedict Bunker

personal goal   To increase your options for responding in situations which raise issues about sex-role stereotypes.

directions   Divide into small groups to practice these role plays and then one person may act as a consultant to the role-playing group. It is important to take the roles and to speak from the role before getting involved in a discussion of the issues. It might be helpful to demonstrate one of the role plays in front of the entire group. Assign specific parts to the role players. Each person take a few minutes to think about the role. Take the roles seriously but do respond flexibly ("in role") as your feelings move you. Select a setting for the role play that is compatible with your work experience, that is, school, business or social agency.

scenario 1.   reactions of men and women to the newly assertive woman

It is the monthly meeting of the administrative staff of a government organization. This group meets weekly to do its business. Once a month there is a meeting to review the work relationships of the group. Jim, the principal, encourages staff members to discuss anything which is interfering with their working as an effective team. During the last month, one of the women in a group, Joyce, who had always been rather soft and supportive of others has changed. She has become quite forceful about her feelings and ideas, about the lack of support she has felt in the group, and about the competitive games she believes are going on. She backs up many of her statements with good data, and several men are beginning to look quite uncomfortable. Bob, who has been very active in the jab-and-parry type of participation, decides in this meeting to take her on and vents his rising feelings of irritation and anger. He tells her that he doesn't like the change in her. She was much more like a member of the group when she was soft and supportive; he liked her better then. Now, well, she is so aggressive it makes him feel uncomfortable. Several other men sit in by looking baffled and dismayed, but silent.

scenario 2.   male competition
for the attention of
an attractive young
staff person

The scene is the biweekly meeting of the residence hall staff at a small private college. The dean of residence halls is a woman in her early fifties who has held that position successfully for ten years. Nine other staff members are present, each head of a housing unit of some type. Cynthia is a young and attractive woman in her late twenties. There are three other women in the group. Two are pushing forty, and one is in her early fifties. None is so alive or attractive as Cynthia. Of the five men in the group, three are in their early thirties, and in quite obvious competition for Cynthia's affection and attention. Two are older—one, a former chaplain, is obviously on the sidelines of the competition, the other, clearly would like to be part of it but is hesitant to become too active, so is mostly very supportive of Cynthia. In the byplay around the competition for Cynthia, the other women are essentially ignored. Cynthia, who has shown signs early in the year of being a strong initiating leader in the group, has become passive and silent and very responsive to the three men. Although the group talks about other issues, the discussion has a hollow quality; the issue which is alive in the group, though unexpressed, is the competition for Cynthia.

scenario 3.   interaction patterns:
difficulty men have in
listening to women peers

This is the third meeting of a student committee appointed by the president of a large state university to make recommendations to him about counseling and advisory services at the university. It is composed of four women and six men. Jim Tompkins is the elected chairperson. The men have been quite active in getting the group moving; the women have been able to express feelings openly and respond to what has been happening. One of the women is very involved on the outside with women's issues, but seldom brings that up in the group. In the group, the women are more often interrupted by other women and men than men are. The women's comments have lower influence over the group than male comments. There have been several mildly hostile incidents between women in the group. There is a noticeable tendency to try to pair with the women on the part of several of the men.

scenario 4. the effects on women of attraction to male authority figures

This is the first graduate seminar in Psychology that Jack Tilotson has taught. He has been teaching for about five years at a major university. The seminar is about social behavior and ten men and two women are enrolled. One of the women is bright, attractive, and in her early twenties. The other woman in the group is an articulate and very forceful woman in her early forties who is alive, vigorous and has had a career in a voluntary agency as the executive director for the last ten years. Joan, the younger woman, is personally very attractive to Jack. He is aware that she gives him a lot of attention during the class. Early in the week she asked him if she could talk to him about the use of exercises in classroom teaching. This is an area in which he is personally very interested. They met and talked for an hour and had a great time. He found her very competent and the exchange of ideas was satisfying to both. They agreed to meet again the next week, but one of his children had an accident and he had to make a trip to the doctor. Now, in the seminar following that cancelled appointment, as he watches Joan, he thinks she looks sad and a little out-of-sorts. As he thinks more about her participation over the semester, he realizes she has moved from being quite outspoken, fun and involved, to being more of an on-looker and responder.

scenario 5. the less-conscious woman

Blaise is one of four women in a discussion group for single (divorced) parents with seven men. The women, with the exception of Blaise, are conscious of women's issues. They are supporting each other in efforts to have influence in the group; they are clearly kicking up their heels and having a great time. Blaise looks depressed. She often makes side remarks like "what all the shouting is about" and refers to not being a "libber." She looks annoyed and out of it when the women's group begins to push ideas or discuss topics of interest to them. Several of the men are rather paternal and protective of Blaise.

scenario 6.   the less-conscious woman under pressure

Mary is the mother of three children who are now in high school. She has never worked, has always accepted the female sex-role as her own model for relationship at home and has been active in volunteer activities. At the moment, Mary is in some turmoil. At a neighbor's house, she has begun to express to her friends her uncertainties about the future. Her friends, spurred by new attitudes toward women are going back to school, going to work, going on separate vacations away from their husbands. She finds it very confusing. She feels pressure to "do something about herself," has been praised by the other women as she takes greater initiative and is more expressive. They treat her as if she is on the threshold of a great breakthrough. Finally, she breaks into tears in the group and begins to express her conflict and stress.

scenario 7.   youth, attractiveness, and competence

Joy is just out of college. This is her first job on a team of hospital administrators and she spoke up a great deal at the first staff meeting. Other women in the group are older than she, and more established in their careers. Joy has an outstanding college record, a tour of duty in the Peace Corps, and a very responsible first job. On the whole, she was discounted during the first meeting. The men, and at least one of the women, treated her like a child. There were remarks like: "You're young enough to be my daughter."

explanation

Each of the descriptions raises issues around the current renegotiation of sex roles. These scenarios provide an opportunity to experiment with a variety of responses without repercussions.

sex-role negotiation

exercise 54 _____

Barbara Benedict Bunker

personal goal

To show how roles are groups of tasks or functions which need to be accomplished if the social system in which they are embedded is to be maintained. The identification and grouping of certain functions as "the woman's role" or "the man's role" is arbitrary and was the product of a different culture. Many couples and living groups today are assigning these functions rather than accept traditional sex-linked definitions.

A second goal was to help people distinguish two kinds of processes which makes role negotiation difficult. One is the external cultural labeling process in which others expect men, for example, to do certain tasks and women to do others. People who don't wish to organize their lives this way may be under pressure from others to conform. A second is the internalized acceptance and valuing of the sex-linked role functions: two woman, for example, who can't permit anyone else in her family to cook because she feels her womanliness would be less if she did; or the man who feels interfered with if a female member of the family takes some responsibility for a car repair.

directions and explanation

Any size group can do this exercise. Flexible seating is helpful but not essential. Step 3 is done in pairs, usually opposite-sex pairs if you have roughly the same number of men and women. If not, same-sex pairs provide a different but equally interesting experience. Unpaired persons can act as observers when same sex pairings are not desirable. If you decide to have both same sex and opposite sex pairings, participants may want to choose their partners.

The exercise is easily completed within eighty minutes. The duration is largely dependent on how much discussion you have with the total group.

introduction and overview

This exercise will proceed in three steps: the first is to be done alone, the second with others of the same sex, the third with a person of the opposite sex. We will examine how the two-person living unit works within the social system. Most of us have been taught as children what functions are appropriate for the female member of the household to fill and what functions the male should fill. This traditional division assumed that the woman's role was to run and maintain the home and raise the children. As more and more women work full time they find that they have acquired two full-time roles, their working role and their home role. Therefore, in many relationships where both parties are working, extensive renegotiation is going on about how the tasks necessary to maintain the living unit will be accomplished.[1]

materials

One copy of "Role Functions in Living Units" for each participant.

step 1

Read "Role Functions in Living Units." This sheet lists the tasks or functions which need regular attention in an ongoing living unit of two persons, one dog, one car, and no children. The tasks in each category are divided into the regular ones which require time each week and the occasional ones. Look over the tasks one by one and decide whether, in your personal view, they should be done by women, men, or either. Then label each task "M" if you think men should do it, "F" if you think women should do it, and "O" if either could do it. About the use of O: use only for those tasks you would be willing to do yourself or would be willing to learn if you cannot do them now. For example, cook meals. If you are a man, do you think women should cook? If yes, mark it "F." If you believe men should do almost all of the cooking, mark it "M." If you believe that either sex could do it and you are personally willing to cook or learn to cook, mark it "O."

(It takes approximately ten minutes to complete this form.)

step 2

When everyone has finished, form into 3 or 4 person groups *of the same sex.* During the next fifteen minutes compare your lists and try to generalize about which functions still are seen as associated primarily with men or women and which are more open to negotiation. What did the male groups find? Were their conclusions different from those of female groups?

step 3

Each person finds a partner of the other sex. It does not matter whether you know each other or not. It is equally interesting to do this exercise with a lifetime partner or with a stranger.

[1]See R. Rapoport & R. A. Rapoport, *Dual-Career Families.* (Middlesex, England: Penguin, 1971).

instructions

In the next 15 to 20 minutes you are to assume that you are going to be setting up a living unit with the person with whom you are now paired. Both of you will be working full time and about the same number of hours each week. Your job in the next 20 minutes is to negotiate a contract with your partner about what each of you will do so that all of the functions are allocated and there is an approximately equal division of labor. Use your own Role Functions inventory as a guide to establishing a contract that will be workable for you. In this exercise we will assume that your joint income is enough for two "regular" role functions (from the entire list) being done by someone hired by you. Therefore, you will need to agree which two functions you will pay to have done. You can begin your negotiations when you are ready.

discuss

This may take place either in groups of two or three pairs or in the total group. How did it go? What items did people have problems with? How did you resolve the difficulty? Do you have a contract that you think could work in real life? What did you learn about yourself? About the way you respond to the demands of others? About your views of sex-role linked functions?

**role functions
in living units**

Food

Regular

_____ cook meals
_____ plan week's meals
_____ shop for food, supplies
_____ wash dishes
_____ clean up kitchen

Occasional

_____ invite people for meals

Maintenance and cleaning

Regular

_____ light cleaning, dust, vacuum
_____ scrub floors, toilets, wax floors
_____ maintain, plants, garden, cut grass
_____ shovel snow
_____ make beds, pick up messes
_____ iron clothes and linens
_____ weekly laundry
_____ water houseplants
_____ walk dog, take dog to vet
_____ take out garbage

Occasional

____ wash windows

____ decide to send rug, drapes, furniture out to be cleaned

____ trips to cleaners

____ build fires

____ sewing and mending

Special maintenance

Occasional

____ electrical repair (lamp, sockets, plugs)

____ plumbing repair (washers, etc.)

____ repainting, wall papering

____ light carpentry (hang brackets, bookshelves)

____ redecorate room

Administrative

Regular

____ receive and pay bills

____ keep accounts against budget

____ plan recreation

order and pick up tickets

make reservations

____ supervise employed assistants

Occasional

____ make budget

____ errors in credit cards

____ read gas meter, call oil, paper delivery

____ plan vacations

arrange flights, hotel

____ decide to make major purchases or repairs

____ purchase gifts

Auto

Regular

____ take in for repair and maintenance

____ keep track of oil, battery, tire pressure

Occasional

____ minor repairs

____ change tires, snow tires

racism and sexism

personal goal   To attempt to demystify your notions about racism and sexism.

directions   At the tip of each spoke write a word which the concept evokes in you.

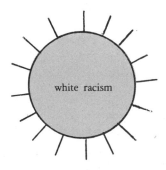
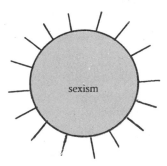

Question: in what ways do you see racism and sexism as similar? How are they dissimilar?

explanation   Often we say this is a sexist or racist culture without being specific about the personal, interpersonal, economic, political, and cultural implications of what we are saying. This exercise is a simple first step to enumerate some of the issues.

the ethnic me

personal goal   To get in touch with part of your own cultural identity.

directions   Think of yourself as having learned part of yourself from various cultures. Complete the following sentences:

The woman in me is _____

The man in me is _____

The black in me is _____

The white in me is _____

The Chicano (a) in me is _____

The Italian in me is _____

The Indian in me is _____

The minority in me is _____

Discuss your responses in groups of three people. Which were the most difficult to answer?

explanation   Depending upon the range of your life experience, you have encountered and contrasted yourself with people who have grown up in other cultures. This exercise is an invitation to explore which other cultures are familiar to you and in what way they influenced your identity.

boss/secretary
team-building inventory[1]

exercise 57 _____

personal goal   To maximize an easy flow of communication, a mutual sharing of resources, and a concern for the professional development of both the boss and the secretary.

directions   The secretary and the boss each fill out the inventory separately. They meet as a team to discuss their responses. They may want to consult with another boss/secretary pair as they talk to each other.

centrality

1. I am important to our team because _____
   _____

2. Our work relationship is important to me because _____
   _____

3. What I contribute to your success is _____
   _____

4. I feel central to our work relationship when _____
   _____

5. I feel peripheral to our work relationship when _____
   _____

6. The way we deal with my professional development is _____
   _____

7. The way we show concern for each other's personal life is _____
   _____

[1] I am grateful to David Nicoll, Organization Consultant, Del Mar, California, who interested me in the notion of dealing with the team building and sex-role issues so inherent in the Boss/Secretary relationship, and who developed this inventory along with me. (Alice Sargent.)

119

8. The way we deal with conflict is _____

_____

9. The way we have fun together at work is _____

_____

10. The way we make work satisfying/productive for one another is _____

_____

trust/
predictability

1. You are predictable because _____

_____

2. You are unpredictable because _____

_____

3. I trust you to do/be _____

_____

4. I do not trust you to do/be _____

_____

5. I deal with stress by _____

_____

6. You deal with stress by _____

_____

power/control

1. My work load is controlled by _____

_____

2. The tasks I undertake are determined by _____

_____

3. The planning for our team is done by _____

_____

4. Taking stock of our relationship is done by _____

_____

5. Decisions about how much time we spend working together are made by _____

_____

roles/
sex roles

1. I have difficulty being assertive when you _____

_____

2. You have difficulty being assertive when I _____

3. If I were boss/secretary, I would do the following differently at work _____

4. The strengths of our relationship are _____

5. The weaknesses of our relationship are _____

6. Our relationship would be more effective if you _____

7. Our relationship is masculine because _____

8. Our relationship is feminine because _____

9. I feel masculine in our work relationship when _____

10. I feel feminine in our work relationship when _____

11. Significant women in my life would characterize our work relationship as _____

12. Significant men in my life would characterize our work relationship as _____

13. A metaphor or epithet that characterizes our relationship is _____

explanation The boss/secretary team is a significant work-processing group. Their morale not only affects their work but it probably contributes significantly to the climate in the office. In the past, the job of secretary has been construed as almost analagous to "office wife" or as the technician subordinate to the boss. Currently there is a growing recognition that the two are a collaborative team who need to plan and divide work based on their competencies not on the hierarchical relationship. This inventory is designed as a way to assess the present relationship.

a workshop design for men in self-awareness and self-management

exercise 58

Richard L. Vittitow

The reader might find this workshop helpful as a sample design for a weekend.

If men continue to change, our way of life as we presently know it will be radically transformed. The American culture—its enterprise, its organization, its systems—is predicated on the willingness of men to follow a prescribed sex role. An increasing number of men are moving away from the constraints of this sex role toward a personal identity based on their own personal uniqueness. This movement is having a profound impact on them and on their relationships with women, with other men, and with organizations.

As important and as profound as these changes are for men and for our culture, little is being done to understand their implications or to build supports for the men involved. We can continue as a culture and as men to react to these changes and be directed by them, or we can begin to design ways of understanding them and move toward influencing and guiding them.

At the Center for Designed Change in Mill Valley, California, we have begun moving with the flow of these changes by designing a variety of workshop experiences for changing men. In this paper, I would like to share with you the design for a workshop entitled, "Self-Awareness and Self-Management for Men."[1]

workshop goals

Men are changing and need to understand the implications of those changes for themselves and for their relationships with others. In this

---

[1] I want to thank and acknowledge the contribution of Dr. James Bixler, San Francisco State University, who designed this workshop with me.

workshop we will examine the changes men are experiencing and examine some of the possible implications of those changes.

Since there is a strong taboo in the American culture against men being intimate with other men, it is important to create an environment where men can experience themselves as giving to and receiving support from each other. This workshop will allow opportunities for practice of these skills in a noncompetitive, open atmosphere.

Since men are struggling with their own emerging identity regarding what it means to be a man, it is important that they focus as specifically as possible on that struggle. This requires a special sensitivity to not taking over women's issues and struggles. We will attempt to verbalize current struggles for men, increase our awareness of their depth and breadth, and explore alternatives for managing our increased awareness.

Men, as the focal points of power in our culture, are under tremendous pressure to change. It is important in this workshop that we not increase that pressure, but that we allow the space to understand the pressures men are experiencing and prepare for determining what responsibilities they want to assume for change.

In their relationships, men tend to rely heavily on their rational, intellectual selves to the exclusion of their emotional, spiritual selves. In this workshop we have designed experiences which will allow men to experience many different levels of relating. For example, we will experience both the emotional and the intellectual, the body and the mind, the here-and-now, the past, and the future. We will work with myths and symbols, dreams and fantasies.

Men tend to base their identities on their work. In this workshop we will not concern ourselves directly with men's occupations or professional interests. Our focus will be to explore other aspects of their sex roles and their personal identity.

workshop schedule

Friday evening.   6:30-11:00 p.m.

6:30-7:30	Dinner (nice way to begin informally and allows time for people to arrive from work).
7:30-8:45	Getting acquainted. Experience 1
8:45-9:30	Setting contract and ground rules. Experience 2
9:30-11:00	Sensory awareness experience. Getting in Touch with your body. Experience 3

Saturday

7:00-8:00	Participant-led experience (Yoga exercises).
8:00-9:00	Breakfast.
9:00-10:00	Sharing night experiences. Experience 4
10:00-12:30	Masculinity mural. Experience 5
12:30-1:30	Lunch.
1:30-3:30	Private time.
3:30-5:30	Power, influence, and trust—a simulation. Experience 6
6:00-7:00	Dinner.
7:30-11:00	"What you always wanted to know about other men and were afraid to ask." Experience 7.

Sunday

7:00-8:00	Participant-led experience (Yoga exercises).
8:00-9:00	Breakfast.
9:00-10:00	Sharing night experiences. Experience 8
10:00-12:30	Body awareness experience. Meeting a person of significance. Experience 9.
1:30-3:30	Endings/beginnings. Exploration of what is ending for men and beginning for men. Experience 10.
3:30-4:00	Evaluation and closure.

getting acquainted

experience 1

personal goal   To allow individuals to introduce personal interests and aspects of themselves without having to rely on identifying who they are in terms of their work.

group goal   To create a climate that promotes sharing and intimacy and focuses on "here-and-now" concerns.

directions   The participants are asked to go through magazines and newspapers and select the representations, messages, pictures, and symbols that reflect concerns, issues, and aspects of themselves they can use in telling others about who they are. Some participants tend to choose three or four very different representations to indicate the variety of their present concerns while others prefer to elaborate on one or two basic themes.

Paper, paste, string, and poster paper are available for those men who would prefer to build an assemblage, rather than have separate representations.

In turn, each man introduces himself by giving his name and sharing the meaning of the representations he has selected regarding ideas, people, and things with which he is presently concerned.

Participants are encouraged to ask questions about the representations as they see and hear about them.

explanation   The use of pictures, messages, and representation allows men to review a wide variety of things that are happening for them, especially on the feeling level. Men tend to share the conflict and struggles they are experiencing and relationships that are important to them. This is particularly important in beginning a climate of sharing, risk-taking, focus on the here-and-now, and the use of creative means to express and talk about oneself.

facilitators'   Since the "Masculinity Mural" is designed for the next morning and it,
note   like this experience, relies heavily on symbols and representations, you may want to limit the participants to choosing no more than three representations to introduce themselves or to take no more than 20 minutes in choosing their representations. My experience has been that too rich an experience in the evening tends to take away from the depth and richness of the symbols in the morning.

materials   Ask the participants to bring from home four or five old magazines, poster paper, string, paste, magic markers, crayons, and any items that can be used in building a collage.

time   1 ¼ to 1 ½ hours.

setting the group
contract and ground rules

personal goals

To allow each individual the opportunity to check out his expectations for the workshop and to influence its design in whatever way may be desirable.

group goals

To discuss openly the ways we want to work together and agree on what activities will or will not take place.

directions

Share the schedule of events and time requirements. Allow the participants to ask questions and clarify what they will be doing. Check to see if everyone feels that the schedule is on target with what they want to do.

Go over the ground rules for working together. Some suggestions:

1. We can always change or add to our ground rules.
2. Throughout this 24-hour workshop, we will be working on increasing our awareness and management skills. This is one of the reasons we will ask those who can to keep a record of their night experiences and share them with us each morning.
3. The focus is on the personal, the here-and-now. We will talk about what is happening for us, not other men.
4. Let's create and build on a nonthreatening atmosphere by not pushing people to go beyond where they want to go and at the same time allowing individuals the space to take risks and experiment with new behavior.

explanation

Since this is probably the first experience for the participants in an all-male workshop, it is especially important to go over the design to relieve any anxieties about what will be expected of them. Many of the men will also be anxious about whether they will be using their time as "effectively" as they can. Giving them a chance to influence the schedule and design gives them a direct say in determining the use of their time. It is also important to use this experience to find out what resources and skills are in the group and to see if there are different ways of using them in the workshop. For instance, we had one participant volunteer to lead us in Yoga exercises each morning before breakfast.

time   45 to 60 minutes.

sensory awareness — getting in touch with your body

experience 3 _____

personal goal   To assist men in getting in touch with their bodies and bring a relaxing close to the day.

directions   Tension does not come from outside. I produce it. Excessive tension is a nonverbal message from my body asking me to become more attentive, receptive, permissive, to let go and allow relaxation.

Lie down on the floor, feet apart, and hands by your sides. Close your eyes. Experience your body in relation to the floor. When you can, allow your thoughts to move away; let words go and attend to how you feel—your bodily sensations and bodily processes as you experience them—not how you think you feel or how you would like to feel, but your sensations. Attend to those parts touching the floor.

When you are ready, shift attention to your feet and become conscious of what they are resting on. Take 15 to 20 seconds to experience (rather than think or imagine) these areas of the body:

feet (heels on floor)	back	cheeks
each toe	shoulders	nose
top of feet	arms	eyes
ankles	elbows	face
calves	forearms	forehead
knees	wrists	top of head
thighs	hands	back of head
buttocks	each finger	entire body
stomach	neck	sounds
chest	lips	how you feel on the floor now

Become aware of breathing. Make no effort to change. Just watch and allow. When you are ready, place both hands on upper chest, above breasts, with palms flat and fingers of one hand *not* overlapping or touching the other hand.

Experience hands on chest and how that feels.

Experience touch and space between hands and floor.

Place both hands slowly at your side. How does the chest feel now? Might the hands still be there?

Place both hands on your solar plexus, the area above the naval and attend to any movement there.

Put hands slowly down at sides and be with your feelings.

Place hands on lower belly, just inside your front hip bones and just above the pubis.

Experience touch and space between hands and floor.

In this position can you become aware of your nostrils and experience the air as it moves in and out.

Bring your hands to your sides and again experience your totality.

In your own time, open your eyes and come to sit in a large circle and let us share any experiences we might have found important for us.

explanation   There is no right or wrong in these experiences. They have the goal of feeling, allowing, being aware of your body. Any correct response is that which your body expresses. Don't judge, just be aware.

time   1 hour.

This experience was prepared and written by Dr. James Bixler, San Francisco State University. He is indebted to Richard Kramer who runs sensory awareness workshops in the San Francisco Bay Area and Bernard Gunther and his book *Sense Relaxation: Below Your Mind.* (New York: Collier Books, 1968).

night experience

experience 4 _____

personal goal   To furnish a continuity for the individual's night and day experience and allow persons to share what happened in the privacy of their dream life.

group goal   The sharing of night experiences contributes additional information that may furnish some keys or guides as to important issues and concerns for the group that would not be available to our consciousness.

directions   Those who want, have an opportunity to share any night experiences—dreams, feelings, sounds, and so on—that they feel important to share with the group.

Group members are encouraged to question and understand the night experience as it occurred for the individual but not to get into problem analysis of the person.

materials   Crayons and paper may be helpful for anyone who would like to make a visual description of a segment of his dream.

time   1 hour.

masculinity mural

experience 5

personal goal   To assist individuals in identifying the themes and issues of their masculine identity.

group goal   To let men know some other men's common issues and concerns about masculinity.

directions   On a 18 to 20 inch piece of butcher paper, participants are invited to draw a representation of what masculinity means to them.

After all the participants have finished drawing, each person takes a turn in describing his drawing to others. Questions and explorations of different perspectives are encouraged.

explanation   This is one of the most powerful experiences of the weekend. The participants will uncover a lot of material about themselves as men, some of which probably goes back to early childhood and adolescence. Often the content of the mural has messages and representations not immediately available to the person drawing it. Looked at from different angles, the messages may be altogether different. Allow the participants the time to move at their own pace. Note: you may want to examine how they handle territoriality and allocation of space among themselves around the mural.

facilitator's note	In one instance, this experience took five hours to process. The facilitator may want to contract with the group for a specific amount of time and then allow each participant so much time to relate and process his drawings.
materials	Butcher paper, 13 to 20 inches in length; crayons.
time	2 to 3 hours.

private time

There may be a tendency not to stress the importance of private time. Men seldom take the time to really explore what is happening to themselves in their own privacy. Private time has been experienced and used by previous participants as one of the most important parts of the workshop. Several participants have urged that more private time be allowed. None of them have recommended doing away with it.

time	2 hours.

pit (power, influence, and trust) simulation

experience 6 _____

personal goal	To create a situation where individuals get in touch with their feelings and attitudes toward issues of power, influence, and trust.
group goal	To create an experience where groups have an opportunity to develop positions of power, negotiation, and cooperation and examine the difficulties encountered for groups in such situations.
directions	In relationships between departments, between labor and management, and between governments, there are basic similarities which arise when these groups work toward accomplishing a task. Groups

often find themselves negotiating, using power and influence and developing varying degrees of trust or distrust in attempting to work with others to achieve their goals.

In the experience which follows, you will be working with a group under specific ground rules with the goal of maximizing your own position (that is, getting as many points as possible). I will review the rules. Make your own assumptions about anything I do not cover.

The simulation is built around the idea that in working with other groups you will often be making decisions that affect your group and the other groups involved.

1. The simulation is played with two teams. (Designate teams or as many pairs of teams as desired:
    a. The Brown team (6 to 10 members)
    b. The Gray team (6 to 10 members)
2. There are eight to ten plays, each play involving one decision.
    a. The Brown team has three alternatives; it must choose one for each play or turn. It may play White, Brown, or Black.
    b. The Gray Team has three alternatives, White, Gray, or Black.
3. Each team's choice is affected by the choice of the other team.
4. Refer to the following grid:

Brown Team choices
vertical): Points appear in square

			A	B	C
			White	Brown	Black
Grey Team choices (horizontal): points appear in circle	x	White	2 2	0 -2	6 −3
	y	Gray	−2 0	0 0	-2 0
Draw on newsprint	z	Black	−3 6	0 2	-6 −6

5. Brown team makes its choices from the vertical column designated A (white), B (brown), C (black). Thus, if Brown plays White its score will appear somewhere in column A. The Brown team's play places the vertical column within which their score will appear.
6. Gray team makes its choice from the horizontal columns designated X (White), Y (Gray), Z (Black). Its choice places the horizontal

column within which their score will appear. Thus, if Gray team plays White (column X) while Brown is playing White (column A) both teams will find their scores in the upper left-hand box of the grid. The Brown team would receive 2 points (score appears in square ⬜ and Gray team receives 2 points (score appears in circle O).

Other examples: If Brown plays Brown (column B) and Gray plays white (column X), then the score for each team will be found in the upper middle square of the grid. Brown would get 0 points and Gray would lose 2 points.

If both teams play Black, they will both lose 6 points.

If Brown plays Black (column C) while Gray is playing White (column X), then the Brown team would gain 6 points while Gray would lose 3 points.

Note: These instructions are best given verbally with examples—however, the trainer should avoid pointing out the advantages or disadvantages of any play; he should merely describe the scoring.

method of play

1. There are 8 (or more) plays in all. Each team meets separately and they have no contact during the play except for formal negotiation periods (see below).

8. First play: Each team decides which column it will play and delivers its choice to the trainer. Six minutes are allowed for the first decision. After the play, the trainer reports the results to both teams. (The teams have no direct contact.)

9. Second play: The same procedure as the first play—scores are accumulated. At any given time, a team may have a plus score, minus or zero.

10. Third play: The same as first and second.

11. Negotiation period. After the third play, the teams each appoint one negotiator. Ground rules: the two negotiators meet separately from their groups face-to-face. Their objective is to discuss ways in which each of their teams might play on succeeding turns to maximize the score for their own team. The negotiators cannot bind their team to any agreement they reach but must meet with their own teams to discuss the team's course of action. The negotiators meet face to face for five minutes and return to their teams—each team has six minutes to reach agreement on its choice for the fourth play.

12. Note: All players should be advised at the outset that the point values for the fourth play are doubled (for the fourth play only).

13. Fourth play: The same procedure as before except double value.

14. Fifth, sixth, and seventh plays: The same as initial plays (point values are as originally indicated.)

15. Negotiations: Same as previous negotiation. Teams informed at outset that scores for the eighth play are tripled. (Option: hold negotiation until after ninth play in a ten-play game.)
16. Eighth play—tripled.
17. Processing: This simulation is generally experienced very deeply with a lot of mixed feelings which need time for processing. It is especially important to discuss feelings about the other group and how individuals dealt with their own feelings around power and trust.

Areas for exploration: (a) Examine how trust develops or is destroyed. (b) Discuss the difficulties of negotiation when one cannot commit his group. (Note the intragroup conflict between a negotiator who wants to keep his word and the team that wants to "double-cross" its opponent.) (c) Be aware of the dangers of assuming that trust exists when it actually does not. (d) Examine the difficulties of achieving understanding and compromise in negotiation. (e) Note all kinds of communication misfires—"You promised you'd play White." "No we didn't, we promised we'd try to cooperate." And so on. (f) Significant communications issues appear during negotiation periods.

materials

Flip chart paper to keep score and use different colored magic markers.

explanation

This simulation demonstrates how power and influence are used in inter-group relations. It also shows how trust between groups grows (usually slowly) but can deteriorate rapidly. Things to watch for and comment on when the game is concluded (do not mention until game is over):

1. White is the cooperative or trust play—if both teams play white throughout an eight-play game, they can each score 22 points.
2. Black is the power play—it can gain the most for one team while maximizing the damage to the other. It is also the highest risk play—it can hurt the playing team the most.
3. Brown and Gray are basically defensive plays. They are risk for the player (the team can't be hurt, but the yield is low—zero in two out of three—only 2 points at most). But these plays have the potential of doing some damage to the opposition.
4. Based on the above: If a pattern of trust develops, both teams will play white (rarely). If win/lose attitudes prevail, Black plays will begin to appear "help us/hurt them." Often teams will forget about improving their own points and try to "hurt" the other. Black against Black plays will then result where both score 6 or Brown against Gray where a zero stalemate occurs.

Thus, when one team uses power (Black, Gray, or Brown plays), the other team must return in kind and both suffer or stalemate. This will be particularly interesting when more than one pair of teams are playing. One pair may be "destroying" each other while another pair cooperates and achieves better results than either of the "power" players. There are dozens of similar phenomena of group and inter-group interaction demonstrated throughout the play.

facilitator's note

My experience with this simulation is that men tend to pull some strong feelings from it. If, because of time demands, it looks like there will not be at least half an hour available for processing feelings at the end, then it is better not to do this simulation.

I found this simulation in my travels. Obviously someone made it up, but there is no name to attribute it to.

"what you always wanted to know about other men but were afraid to ask"

experience 7

personal goals

To give men an opportunity to ask other men questions about their experiences being men, especially relating to feelings and to gain information that is usually not available or comfortable to seek out.

group goals

To provide an experience for men where they can explore questions about themselves in nonthreatening ways and experience levels of support usually not available to men from other men.

directions

Ask the men to write out on a piece of paper questions they might like to ask other men, but generally feel some hesitancy or fear in asking.

In a "cream-off-the-top" method, take one question at a time and let anyone in the group respond to it until the group has dealt with all questions.

explanation

This is generally not an easy experience for men. Most of the questions will probably deal with male sexuality. Some participants will be risk takers, others will prefer to listen. It is important to acknowledge the uncomfortableness and to stay with the experience and allow it time to develop.

time   2 to 4 hours.

body awareness
experience: meeting a
person of significance

experience 8

personal goal   To assist individuals in identifying ways the body and mind work together in relating to the world and how the body expands or contracts in the use of energy when confronting persons of significance.

directions   All organisms from amoeba to humans have an energy, or life force which is physical in nature. This energy builds by the intake of food, fluid, and air, and is absorbed directly through the skin.

Energy streams rhythmically and continuously through the body from head to toe. It gives a pleasurable, glowing sensation of health and well-being. It is discharged by activity, excretion, emotional expression, thinking, conversion to body heat, and growth. The excess is stored for emergency situations like battle or exhausting work. When there is no emergency, it is felt in healthy individuals as sexual excitation. It is discharged as orgasm only if the individual is capable of full, healthy, loving, sexual fulfillment. If not, the discharge is not complete and energy is felt as tension and restlessness.

Man alone has prevented his own natural functioning by preventing the flow, build-up and release of his ergon energy by armoring—a process whereby we use certain muscles of the body to control emotions. Man and body are the same. Psychic and physical structure are functionally identical.

Come to a standing position and select a spot with minimum eye contact with others. When ready, close your eyes and in your own way imagine yourself to be five to eleven years of age.

If possible, imagine yourself then, standing before a significant person in your life whom you saw as an authority, perhaps a teacher or someone else.

Recall your feelings and stand in the way you would stand in front of this person.

Can you sense what the effect is on your body by standing this way? Do you notice muscles contracting and tensing? Can you feel the tight, stressful, braced, restricted parts of your body?

Is it possible to identify one or more spaces or areas in your body this way? Select one and exaggerate the stress and tension.

Relax and breathe, then exaggerate again several times.

Imagine what you'd like to say to the significant person. Then, in order to let the person know how you feel, try and verbalize what your body is saying. Say it to yourself, mumble it, then say it outloud.

Relax and breathe, then exaggerate.

Say No, No, No! I won't!!

Talk to the person and tell him/her—how you want that person to see you.

Exaggerate tension and repeat conversation.

Exaggerate the tense spot and answer the question, "How does this stance effect the way I experience time?"

Experience your feelings.

Come to standing in a comfortable way. When ready close your eyes, bring attention to your abdomen, and allow breath to flow there. Your belly expands and sinks. Allow your own rhythm. You may notice no pause on inhalation and a wait at end of exhalation. Can you attend to the quality of the pause?

Lie down on your side on the floor. Can you allow deep breathing and relaxation. How are the places where you touch the floor? Can you adjust the spots/places to release tension? Where are you now? Are you aware of areas that are ending for you? Can you identify old patterns of reaction? Who allows these to persist? Are there new-nesses emerging? Can you speculate about what paths are available to allow these newnesses to emerge?

In your own time, can we come to sitting in a large circle and share whatever we found important for us.

time   2 hours.

Adapted by Dr. James E. Bixler, San Francisco State University, from an experience in a workshop conducted by Dr. George Downing, Esalen Institute.

endings and beginnings

experience 9 _____

personal goal   To allow individuals to explore transitions occurring for them by examining those things that are coming to an end and those things that are beginning for them.

group goal   To explore as a group the transitions occurring for men and gain some insight as to the kinds of changes occurring for men in general.

directions   In change or transition, there are three basic occurrences: something comes to an end for us; something new begins for us; and from these endings and beginnings come a transformation—a different way of relating to the world.[1]

1. Explore what is coming to an end for you, particularly in your relationship to: yourselves (as individuals), other men, women, and organizations.
2. Explore what is beginning for you, especially in relation to your own selves, other men, women, and organizations.
3. From these endings and beginnings can we gain any indication of the future for us as men?

time   1 ½ hours.

[1]Stanley Keleman uses this concept around change and transition, and I borrowed the paradigm from him.

evaluation of the workshop

experience 10 _____

group goal   To discuss openly reactions to the learning and support that took place in the workshop.

directions   What in this workshop have we found most helpful to our learning and most supportive to us as men?

What in this workshop have we found least helpful in our learning and least supportive to us as men?

time ½ hour.

issues and learning evolving
from the workshop

issues

1. Although there are signs that men are becoming more open to participation in all-male workshops, there is still considerable resistance. Those working on first efforts may want to start by inviting friends and acquaintances rather than relying exclusively on mailing lists.
2. Women, by and large, are enthusiastic supporters of workshops for men and have been very helpful in advertising and promoting them. However, a few women did express resentment toward their partners for taking time away from them and from the family for a weekend, residential workshop.
3. Men value participating in a workshop with other men who are different from themselves in age, interests, and experience. In searching for participants we have looked for: men who are open to, excited about, and comfortable in exploring their maleness; men with as wide a variety of life experience, work involvement, age, and ethnic backgrounds as possible; men who are strangers to each other. A stranger group enhances the chances of an open atmosphere where participants can risk new and different behavior.

learning

1. Men are willing to take responsibility for a workshop when the facilitators act more as guides than gurus. Facilitators can fully involve themselves in workshop content and be experienced by men as helpful and supportive.
2. Male groups, like all groups, differ. This workshop design does not involve a specific experience of men touching each other. Some participants have felt that an experience in touching could be very important.
3. Men are involved in similar concerns and struggles, but tend not to know it because their present work involvements and personal relationships with other men do not support or allow for personal sharing.

4. The emerging identity of changing men is generally very different from the persons they thought they were or had to be as adolescents or early adults.

5. Stereotypic behavior usually attributed to men does not hold up. For the most part, men cry, share feelings, admit impotence and weakness, ask for help, take risks, and are not afraid of physical contact.

6. One of the biggest issues for men is dependency on women—both real and fantasied desires to be taken care of by women. Even though they can often recognize their dependency, it is not clear to them how to build towards interdependence.

7. Men experience themselves as less powerful or privileged as the women's movement would have us believe.

8. Changing men do share specific, unique struggles: defining who they are, searching for alternatives in a world built and maintained by the masculine image, not feeling culturally rewarded or valued for taking the risks of being different, and moving beyond the sex-roles prescribed for them.

9. Men can be important support resources for each other. They can quickly identify each other's games, share similar experiences and struggles, and offer different ways of responding to similar situations.

2 awareness of sex-role stereotypes

With men there is no break between public and private life, the more he confirms his grasp on the world in action and in work, the more virile he seems to be; human and vital values are combined in him. Whereas woman's independent successes are in contradiction with her femininity. The "true woman" is required to make herself object—to be the other.

—Simone de Beauvoir

For everything that was difficult in her position she blamed him . . . If he had loved her, he would have seen all the bitterness of her position and would have rescued her from it.

—Anna Karenina

In an important sense there is only one complete unblushing male in America: a young, married, white, urban, northern, heterosexual, Protestant father, of college education, fully employed, of good complexion, weight, and height, and a recent record in sports. Any male who fails to qualify in any one of these ways is likely to view himself—at least during moments—as unworthy, incomplete, and inferior. At times he is likely to pass and at times he is likely to find himself being apologetic or aggressive concerning known-about aspects of himself he knows are probably seen as undesirable.

—Erving Goffman

awareness

Until recently, psychological and sociological research has done little to help people understand the reasons for the differences in the behavior, values, and attitudes of men and women. Instead of studying how men and women could become more alike, psychologists have usually regarded gender-related traits as a given and have focused their attention on describing and contrasting male and female behaviors. This has often been the case, even in the research on individual differences. The work of psychologists in demonstrating clear-cut substantial differences between men and women has caused many scientists to overlook the question of the underlying basis for sex-linked behaviors. Similarly, these psychologists have taken race and social class as givens and attempted to study the myriad differences associated with race and class, giving little attention either to the problems in defining these categories or to their limitations. This has been true even of Leona Tyler and, to a lesser extent, Anne Anastasi—who have long been regarded as the intellectual leaders of the differential psychology movement.

The question that has not been explored is *why* men and women behave differently. For both the layperson and the psychologist, the answer to this question has been that behavioral differences between the sexes are an inescapable and a natural consequence of the biological differences between men and women.

145

In other words, the traditional view held by the behavioral scientists has been that, for sex-linked behavior, biology is destiny. For example, Rheingold (1964), a psychiatrist at Harvard Medical School, notes: ". . . anatomy decrees the life of a woman . . . when women grow up without dread of their biological functions and without subversion by feminist doctrine, and therefore enter upon motherhood with a sense of fulfillment and altruistic sentiment, we shall attain the goal of a good life and a secure world in which to live it." The sociologist Talcott Parsons (1955) classified the male role as instrumental and the female role as expressive, a compartmentalization based apparently on what he considered were innate or biological characteristics.

For a number of years there was no significant further exploration of the differences between the sexes. For example, in Terman and Tyler's (1946) review of sex differences, they state that "girls have a lower rate of delinquency, fewer school and home problems leading to clinical referral, and are rated higher by peers and teachers for various moral traits." They do not, however, go on to speculate about what child-rearing practices shape girls' behavior this way, or what such behavior costs girls.

If all human beings are both dependent and autonomous, how do girls handle their strivings to be independent? Tyler (1947) reports that "males tend to be higher in tests involving mathematical, spatial, and mechanical materials. Females average higher in verbal, perceptual, and memory tests, and in dexterity tests involving light, swift hand movements." Nowhere in her writing is there any speculation as to why these differences come about. She presents the data as a factor which is unconnected to the impact which the culture has had on the individual. It has been left to current research carried on by Lisa Serbin and Dan O'Leary at SUNY, Stony Brook to describe the differential responses of parents and teachers to boys and girls. They report that parents and teachers are more likely to give thorough directions to boys and not to offer assistance with tasks, thereby fostering independence and teaching them problem-solving skills; whereas girls are likely to receive the opposite treatment.

About twenty years ago, both psychologists and biologists began to question the assumption that only biological factors were relevant in determining differences between men and women. Studies were initiated to determine not only the dimensions of these biological factors but also how the biological influences are mitigated or enhanced by experience. There is now a substantial body of literature that reports on the ways, other than the obvious ones, in which men and women differ biologically. These studies began to demonstrate how the biological differences arouse differential psychological responses—that is, how biology and experience interact.

Ann Anastasi (1958), the other major student of individual differences, was more aware of sex differences as an underlying reason for sex-linked behaviors. Anastasi notes that "the amount of such sex differences in dominance varies widely from culture to culture as does the manner in which it is expressed." Sex differentiation in adult occupation differs greatly according to culture, as does play activity for children.

The clearest statement of the impact of culture on sex typing, made by Margaret Mead in 1935, has been overlooked by most researchers until the present. Regarding sex-linked behavior in play activities in other cultures, Mead notes that when dolls were presented for the first time to children on the island of Manus in New Guinea, it was the boys, not the girls, who were eager to play with them. In crooning lullabies, they behaved like their fathers, since it is the fathers who are principally responsible for child care on the island.

These contradictory traits of temperament, which different societies have regarded as sex-linked, are merely human potenialities isolated as the behavior of one sex. Mead writes:

We are forced to conclude that human nature is almost unbelievably malleable, responding accurately and contrastingly to different cultural conditions. The differences between individuals who are members of different cultures, like the differences between individuals within a culture, are almost entirely to be laid to differences in conditioning, especially during early childhood, and the form of this conditioning is culturally determined. Standardized personality differences between the sexes are of this order: cultural creations to which each generation, male and female, is trained to conform (p. 280).

In general, the traditional approach of differential psychology has provided little insight into the complexities of the development of sex-linked behavior, whereas the work of Margaret Mead, and now of psychologists Eleanor Maccoby and Caroline Jacklin, Walter Gove, Jeanette Tudor, the Brovermans, Michael Lewis, Lisa Serbin, as well as John Money and Anke Ehrhardt on biological differences points the way to a much more in-depth understanding of the development of sex-linked behavior.

references

Anastasi, A. *Differential psychology.* New York: Macmillan, 1967.

Mead, M. *Sex and temperament in three primitive societies.* New York: William Morrow & Co., 1935.

Money, J., & Ehrhardt, A. *Man & woman, boy & girl: The differentiation and dimorphism of gender identity from conception to maturity.* Baltimore: Johns Hopkins University Press, 1972.

Parsons, T. Family structure and the socialization of the child. In T. Parsons & R. F. Bales (Eds.), *Family, socialization and interaction process.* Glencoe, Ill.: Free Press, 1951.

Serbin, L. A.; O'Leary, K. D.; Kent, R. N.; & Tonick, I. J. A comparison of teacher response to the preacademic and problem behavior of boys and girls. *Child Development,* 1973, *44,* 796-804.

consciousness-raising groups: a resocialization process for personal and social change

Diane F. Kravetz
Alice G. Sargent

Consciousness-raising groups have evolved over the past seven years as a way for women, and more recently for men, to achieve personal and social change. These groups are often described as the cornerstone of the new feminism, as the heart of the Women's Liberation Movement:

The purpose of these groups is not therapy; it is to develop both an analysis of the society and an appropriate politics based on the experience of being female—the personal becomes political. As members of the group share experiences and attitudes, they become aware that the problems they thought were theirs alone are less a function of their own personal hang-ups than of the social structure and culture in which they live. Through sharing experiences,

women find that personal problems related to being a woman cannot be solved without an understanding of the society and often without attempting to implement changes within it as well (Polk, 1972, pp. 323-324).[1]

This sentiment is echoed in statements concerning men's consciousness-raising groups. "A basic change in the social upbringing of both sexes is needed for either sex to be free. For if women's liberation continues to press forward, then men's liberation will become a structural necessity. Ultimately, you cannot have a society of liberated females and chauvinist males. The condition of freedom for one is freedom for all" (Rueger, 1973, p. 77).

Consciousness-raising groups are generally same-sex groups of seven to fifteen persons that provide opportunities for women and men to share experience with others from a similar female or male culture. Acknowledging the economic and social differences within each of these cultures, the group focuses members' common attitudes, values, and experiences. An emphasis on commonalities for each sex allows group members to develop a meaningful understanding of the personal and social forces that have influenced them as individuals and as men and women. As common patterns are identified, the constraints and contradictions of sex-role stereotypes become evident and the effects of social discrimination due to sex become clear.

Many consciousness-raising groups emerge naturally both from informal friendship networks in the community and within formal organi-

[1]Women's Liberation: Movement for Equality, by Barbara B. Polk, in *Toward A Sociology of Women*, C. Safilios-Rothchild (Ed.). Copyright © 1972 by John Wiley & Sons, Inc. Reprinted by permission of John Wiley & Sons, Inc.

Drawing by Opie; © 1973 The New Yorker Magazine, Inc.

zations. Others are organized by women's political organizations, such as the National Organization for Women (NOW), and through women's and men's centers. The primary basis for membership in most groups is the desire to explore the psychological and social similarities and difficulties related to female and male roles. Some groups focus on problems encountered by women or men in specific roles. Some consciousness-raising groups commonly consist of working mothers, single career women, welfare mothers, older women whose children have "left the nest," women in work organizations, male professionals, or male college students. Although common roles and statuses provide the central theme for this type of group, individual issues and differences may receive equal attention as the group progresses.

Shepard characterized both the personal growth group and the consciousness-raising group as a "resocializing institution that provides conditions that disconfirm some mechanistic assumptions." In other words, it provides an atmosphere in which sex stereotypes are examined and changes considered. Such a group affirms the possibility of what a "different world could be like and provides a practical model of what it would be like. The alienating forces the participants bring with them largely disappear in this new setting of caring and active listening to each other" (Shepard, 1970, pp. 259-264).

In consciousness-raising groups, members begin to increase their awareness of sex-role stereotypes and the advantages and limitations of sex-roles. This process of identifying and unfreezing stereotyped attitudes, behaviors, and values is accomplished primarily through the members' detailing of their own socialization and sharing these experiences with others in the context of the group. Sharing is the primary process, for it is through sharing that members are able to develop a common understanding of what has influenced them as individuals and what has affected them as women or men:

We always stay in touch with our feelings . . . we assume that our feelings . . . mean something worth analyzing. . . . In our groups, let's share our feelings and pool them. Let's let ourselves go and see where our feelings lead us. Our feelings will lead us to ideas and then to action. . . . Our primary task now is to awaken "class" consciousness in ourselves and others on a mass scale. . . (Sarachild, 1971, p. 131).

All group members are regarded as experts, since expertise is defined in terms of personal feelings and experience. Although literature may be used to provide additional information, individual and group experiences are considered the essential ingredients in understanding problems: "We've learned that those experiences are *not* our private hang-ups. They are shared by every woman, and are therefore political. The theory then comes out of human feeling, not out of textbook rhetoric" (Morgan, 1970, pp. xvii-xviii).

Discussion generally begins with a focus on what it means to be a man or a woman. People talk about how they acquired their sex differences and which sex-linked behaviors would most benefit from change. Topics frequently include the models presented by parents; early childhood behaviors that were encouraged, ignored, and/or forbidden; feelings about one's body; and feelings and expectations about marriage, work, competence, affection, child rearing, and aging. During such discussions, there may recollections of youthful goals that have lost out to adult roles of "rescuer," "responsible protector," "nurturant mother or father," "clever witch," or "competitive achiever." Stereotypic assumptions concerning role-related behaviors are often exposed in discussions of husbands and wives, mothers and fathers, housewives and breadwinners.

In addition to increased awareness of sex-linked and role-related behaviors, the consciousness-raising group offers a setting in which members can explore new behaviors, and ways of relating. For women, emphasis is placed on valuing qualities that have been devalued as feminine as well as on validation and support for adoption of traditionally "nonfemale" behaviors such as assertiveness and competence in work. Men discuss their role constraints around being dependent or passive and the pressures they feel regarding status, power, and success. Problems which arise from norms promoting male competition and dominance are analyzed, and sensitivity and caring are encouraged as significant traits:

> . . . among some, the acceptable male role is changing in the direction of less emphasis on instrumental and organization involvements to a greater emphasis on expressivity. This has major implications for men's relationships to women, fatherhood, male affiliation, and work.[2]

Institutional structures and social norms are also important elements of the discussions in these groups. Personal attitudes and behaviors as well as legal, economic, and social policies are analyzed and evaluated. For example, a woman who has defined herself in terms of the needs of her husband and children will be helped to identify her own desires and goals. In discussing how to achieve change the group will explore the degree of personal support she is receiving from colleagues or her husband or children and how various social factors may inhibit change. In such analysis, significant change in the structure of her family, her work setting, and community may come to be viewed as prerequisites for personal change.

Consciousness-raising groups facilitate change through a self-consciousness about group behavior. For example, the group may discuss competition among women and decide how to avoid it. Men may

[2]Joseph H. Pleck and Jack Sawyer, *Men and Masculinity*, © 1974, p. 30, Reprinted by permission of Prentice-Hall, Inc., Englewood Cliffs, New Jersey.

decide to create a climate in which they are able to try to express feelings of caring to other men. Group norms are discussed and assessed before they are adopted so that the group may decide whether to accept a familiar societal norm or to develop new ways of relating.

A primary example of social norms being re-evaluated and modified is illustrated in leadership norms that have evolved in many consciousness-raising groups. Many in the Women's Movement believe hierarchies should not be allowed to develop, and further, that all women should learn leadership behaviors; therefore, many women's groups formally state that leadership must be assumed by as many members of the group aHpossible. This approach is explained in the *MS* article, ''A Guide to Consciousness-Raising'': ''The consciousness-raising group is specifically designed to eliminate preexisting habits of passivity, dominance, the need for outside instruction, or a hierarchy (July, 1972, p. 22). In these consciousness-raising groups, no one person is designated as leader. Dominance by any member will be identified, with discussion focusing on ways to share leadership responsibilities. To help these groups work better, several recent books and magazines offer formats and topics for discussion in ''leaderless'' groups.*

Some women's organizations have abandoned conceptions of leaderlessness and have developed models for structured, goal-oriented consciousness-raising groups. Workshops to train leaders for such groups are being offered. The Los Angeles chapter of NOW has developed a ten-session, structured consciousness-raising group and sponsors a leadership training program. An increasing number of university-based women's centers, such as Everywoman's Center at the University of Massachusetts, and various mental health clinics are organizing consciousness-raising groups along with leadership training programs.

In same-sex groups, other factors contribute to exploration and change of sex-role behaviors. Status rankings which the members have in the external world do not necessarily transfer to the culture of a consciousness-raising group and the system of rewards and punishments is open to the group for defining and redefining. Participants find that behavior for which they have been previously rewarded, such as dominance for men or submission for women, is no longer routinely accepted. As in other growth groups, the members benefit from the

*Guidelines for consciousness-raising can be found in:

Consciousness-raising handbook-Project of the Los Angeles NOW Consciousness-Raising Committee, 1974; Guidelines by Women's Action Alliance, 375 Lexington Ave., New York, New York 10017; Letty C. Pogrebin, ''Rap Groups, The Feminist Connection,'' in *MS*, March, 1973; ''Consciousness-Raising,'' in *Voices from women's liberation*, Leslie B. Tanner (Ed.) (New York: Signet, 1970); ''The do-it-yourself guide to consciousness-raising,'' in *Woman's fate*, Claudia Dreifus (New York: Bantam, 1973); Warren Farrell, ''Guidelines for consciousness-raising,'' in *MS*, July 19, 1972; Warren Farrell, *The liberated man: Beyond masculinity*, (New York: Random House, 1974).

process of feedback of the reactions of others to their behavior. Group members may also free themselves of programmed behaviors, such as flirting, that they have tended to use in the presence of the other sex but which has objectified the other. Men may choose to rely less and less on women's social skills, while women become more goal-oriented and self-reliant.

From shared experiences in the group, women and men come to see how little they have been using their personal resources and begin to define areas for change:

The changes which women attempt to implement usually begin with altering attitudes and interactions in relationships with husband, boyfriend, employer, co-workers, and female friends, with the goal of seeing oneself, and being seen, as an equal in interpersonal relationships. This change is perhaps the most difficult and the most fundamental for the Women's Liberation Movement. For, to change interactions, a woman must begin to change her entire concept of herself and begin to present a self-image which deviates from the accepted norms of the society (Polk, 1972, p. 324).[3]

This statement is also applicable for men, for they too must face social pressures as they attempt to deviate from the dominant masculine role.

Women are likely to emerge from consciousness-raising experiences emphasizing their own identity independent of men and children. Cherniss found that women in these groups developed "an active outgoing approach to the world . . . accompanied by a high degree of achievement striving and a strong valuation of autonomy and independence." As compared with nonmovement women, he found that women in the Movement had "higher self-esteem and a greater sense of self-acceptance" (Cherniss, 1972, pp. 113-114).

In her study, Eastman found members of a consciousness-raising group to have increased autonomy, self-confidence, and self-knowledge. The members noted that as a result of the group experience, they were able to overcome passivity and achieve a growing sense of identity with other women. "The respondent's sense of personal enrichment, of growth in awareness of both individual potentialities and vulnerabilities, and the evidences of shifts in active pursuit of ego aims and skills seemed genuine and impressive. Indeed, the results achieved by this leaderless, self-initiated group might well raise the envy of professional group therapists" (Eastman, 1973, pp. 180-181).

Newton and Walton report five changes for individuals involved in these groups:

First, the women experienced an altered world view in which they perceived

[3]*Women's Liberation: Movement of Equality,* by Barbara B. Polk, in *Toward A Sociology of Women,* C. Safilios-Rothchild (Ed.). Copyright © 1972 by John Wiley & Sons, Inc. Reprinted by permission of John Wiley & Sons, Inc.

"women as a group with definite characteristics" and society as divided into two major groups, males and females. Identity changes occurred, including different feelings about body image. For example, there were changes in clothing and cosmetics; more significantly, the women felt comfortable and accepting of their bodies, more physically and sexually competent. There were changes in reference groups and interpersonal relationships: feminist women became the primary reference group and relationships with men turned more egalitarian. There were changes in job-career orientation; many women felt ambivalent toward professionalism and male-dominated institutions, and made efforts to work for movement-oriented activities. Finally, the group members felt "an enhanced sense of self-acceptance and worth, and a lessening of guilt and self-doubt" (Newton & Walton, 1974, pp. 348-349).

A major outcome of consciousness-raising groups is that women learn to trust and respect other women. Historically, women have been socialized to compete with other women for the attention of men. Only through men could women attain important social resources, such as power, money, and social recognition. In this competitive marketplace, women learned to distrust one another—to consider other women unintelligent and unimportant. Under these conditions, it is difficult for women, on some fundamental level, to view themselves as intelligent, important, and deserving of respect. In consciousness-raising groups, women discover they can enjoy being with women as well as with men. They learn to share intellectually and to care for each other in a deeply satisfying way. Women come to know, trust and respect other women and thereby learn to trust and respect themselves.

Correspondingly, in men's groups, men begin to trust and share with one another as equals:

Being a master has its burdens. It is not really possible for two persons to have a free relation when one holds the balance of power over the other. The more powerful person can never be sure of full candor from the other, though he may receive the kind of respect that comes from dependence. . . . Persons bent on maintaining dominance are inhibited from developing themselves" (Sawyer, 1970, p. 170).

In consciousness-raising, men attempt to change the forms of male relationships, which are traditionally based on occupational status and physical and/or intellectual competition. One man in a consciousness-raising group said, "For some of us the most untrustworthy people in our lives were males of our own age . . . the most important thing that's happened . . . is that we're beginning to let down our defenses against the other men." In these groups men learn to talk about themselves, to share their feelings, to share their experiences with their children, and to request advice for problems at work or with their spouse-partners.

Finally, in these groups, women and men learn to observe and understand many of the social, political, and economic factors that affect their lives. Community and national policies that promote sexism and discrimination become personal concerns. In response to these concerns, members of consciousness-raising groups often participate in political activities aimed toward changing these conditions:

Sisters who thought themselves abnormal or neurotic because they were unhappy with the feminine role discover the normalcy of their discontent. CR (consciousness-raising) fosters self-confidence among its participants. Often self-confidence leads to action—action against the institutions that oppress women (Dreifus, 1973, p. 5).[4]

In work organizations, women are joining together to reduce competition with one another and to influence the organization to become more responsive to their particular needs. For these women, the consciousness-raising group also serves as a support system for political actions outside of the group. Recently, men and women have begun to join together in mixed groups in organizations to explore the myths and stereotypes they hold with respect to each other; to alter the patterns of dominance and submission that have existed in male-female relationships; and to look directly at other issues such as sexuality that arise as more and more women join the work force.

For growing numbers of women and men, discussions of the effects of sex-role stereotyping and discrimination have become essential to their personal change efforts. Yet, while coping strategies and behavior change by individuals are necessary, they are not sufficient for personal liberation. To increase the options and opportunities for men and women as equal members of society, awareness, personal change, and social change must take place. As such changes are slow and occur at an uneven rate, the consciousness-raising group enables women and men to build a free space where they have opportunity to share doubts, dreams, fears, and visions and begin to work toward significant personal, interpersonal, and social change.

references

Cherniss, C. Personality and ideology: A personalogical study of women's liberation. *Psychiatry*, 1972, *35*,113-114.

Dreifus, C. *Woman's fate*. New York: Bantam, 1973.

Eastman, P. Consciousness-raising as a resocialization process for women. *Smith College Studies in Social Work*, 1973, *43*, 180-181. A guide to consciousness-raising. *MS*, 1972, *1* (1), 22.

Morgan, R. (Ed.). Introduction: The women's revolution. In *Sisterhood is powerful*. New York: Vintage, 1970.

Newton, E., & Walton, S. The personal is political: Consciousness-raising and personal change in the women's liberation movement, as cited in B. Kirsh,

Consciousness-raising groups as therapy for women. In V. Franks & V. Burtle (Eds.), *Women in therapy*. New York: Brunner-Mazel, 1974.

Pleck, J. Psychological frontiers for men. *Rough Times*, June-July, 1973, *3* (6).

Pleck, J., & Sawyer, J. On male liberation. *Men and masculinity*. Englewood Cliffs, New Jersey: Prentice-Hall, 1974.

Polk, B. Women's liberation: Movement for equality. In C. Safilios-Rothschild (Ed.), *Toward a sociology of women*. Lexington, Massachusetts: Xerox Publishing Company, 1972.

Rueger, R. Seeking freedom from the male myth. *Human Behavior*, April 1973, *2* (4), 75.

Sarachild, K. A program for feminist consciousness-raising. In J. Hole & E. Levine, *Rebirth of feminism*. New York: Quadrangle Books, 1971.

Shepard, H. Personal growth laboratories: Toward an alternative culture. *Journal of Applied Behavioral Science*, 1970, *3*, 259-264.

Unbecoming men: A men's consciousness-raising group writes on oppression and themselves. Washington, New Jersey: Times Change Press, 1971.

innate factors in
sex differences

Norma L. McCoy _____

What makes the male male and the female female? Rather than assuming that sex differences in behavior are the result of social and cultural forces, we need to consider to what extent sex differences are determined by biological factors. By this I mean we need to consider to what extent sex differences in body and in behavior arise out of the genetic differences between human males and females. Is there something inherent in being a girl or boy, man or woman, that predisposes the individual to behave in certain ways? We know that human behavior, more than that of any other species, is plastic and dependent on experience and learning processes. Thus, any sex-related innate or hereditary factors will necessarily be viewed as predisposing rather than as determining.

But what are these innate factors? Anyone can tell whether an infant is male or female—look at the sex organs! But in order to determine how these physical differences, as well as other sex-related physical and behavioral differences, come about, we have to start back at the beginning with the biological building blocks—that is, the hereditary material—the chromosomes.

A normal human organism has 23 pairs of chromosomes in each of the cells of his body. One of the 23 pairs is the sex chromosome pair. If the sex chromosome pair consists of two X chromosomes, the individual is female; if the sex chromosome pair consists of an X and a Y chromosome, the individual is male. The egg and sperm each carry half of the normal chromosome complement. The egg normally carries 22 chromosomes and an X chromosome; and the sperm carries 22 chromosomes and an X or a Y chromosome. With fertilization, the 23 chromosomes in the nucleus of the mother's ovum and the 23 chromosomes in the nucleus of the father's sperm join, resulting in an individual with 23 pairs of chromosomes or 46 in all. If the ovum is fertilized by an X-bearing sperm, the individual is female and if by a Y-bearing sperm, the individual is male.

Chromosomes vary in size; the X chromosome is a fairly large one, while the Y chromosome is a small one and carries very little, if any, genetic information (genes). One result of the fact that men have only this small Y chromosome, instead of a second X chromosome, is that the genes on the X chromosome are unpaired with genes on the Y chromosome. This means that when the male has a defective gene on the X chromosome he will show that defect. This explains the high incidence in males of such conditions as hemophilia (a bleeder disease) and red-green color blindness, two among many undesirable conditions carried by the X chromosome.

In females, just before or just following the implantation of the female embryo in the uterus, one of the X's in each of the several hundred existing cells curls up, becomes what is called a "Barr body," and is thought to be inactive. Which X becomes a "Barr body" is a matter of chance. Thus, while all the cells in a normal man's body bear exactly the same chromosomes, a woman's cells differ in that some of them will have a functioning X from the mother and some will have a functioning X from the father. Even if a woman has a defective gene on one of her X chromosomes, chances are good that in approximately half of her cells the other X, bearing a normal gene, will be active and she will not show the defect.

Using hemophilia as an example, the male with an X chromosome carrying this defect will be a hemophiliac (bleeder); the woman with one normal X and one X with the defect will have slower blood clotting time but will not suffer from hemophilia. The extent to which her blood clotting time will be lowered will depend on the proportion of her cells in which the X with the defect is active. This generally accepted theory of a single-active-X is known as the Lyon Hypothesis, after Mary Lyon, who first suggested it (Stern, 1973). Related in some manner to these sex chromosome differences is the fact that more males than females die at all stages of development from conception through old age. The average life expectancy of females (74.9) is seven-and-one-half years greater than that of males (67.4).

Aside from all this, the subject of greatest interest to us is not what the Y chromosome doesn't do, but what it *does* do. The latest evidence suggests that it does little more than cause an embryo to develop into a male. In fact, it is known on the basis of individuals who are born with abnormal sex chromosome constitutions that the mammalian Y chromosome is strongly male determining. Given the presence of a Y chromosome, the human embryo will develop as a male even if there are two, three, or four X chromosomes. Conversely, in the absence of a Y, the body of a developing human will appear to be female even if only a single X chromosome is present. This fact has led some (Sherfey, 1972) to the position that the human embryo is innately feminine. However, John Money, a leading authority in this area, insists that progression in each stage of sexual differentiation is from an undifferentiated or bi-potential (either sex) state to a differentiated one (Money and Athanasiou, 1973). This statement is based on what is known about the process of sexual differentiation in the developing embryo and should be self-evident to the reader after becoming familiar with the process of sexual differentiation which follows.

Considerable experimentation was required in order to learn about the process of sexual differentiation in human beings. Because of the nature of such research, experiments were conducted largely with rabbits, guinea pigs, rats and subhuman primates. Subsequently, much of what has been learned in animal research has proved consistent with data obtained from the study of human beings with various clinical syndromes.

At present, the process of human sexual differentiation is thought to occur in the following manner:* After fertilization, the developing organism is normally differentiated according to whether it is either male (XY) or female (XX), genetically. At about the fifth week in gestation, the underlying structure or genital ridge which is destined to differentiate into ovaries or into testes appears. During this period, the embryo also has the beginnings of both male and female ducts. At the sixth week the presence of the Y chromosome, in some manner not yet understood, causes the genital ridge to begin sex development into testes. The testes produce male hormone (testosterone), which causes the male ducts to develop (vas deferens, seminal vesicles, ejaculatory ducts), and a second substance (Mullerian-inhibiting substance) which causes the female ducts to regress. In the absence of testosterone, female ducts develop (uterus, fallopian tubes, upper vagina) and the male ducts regress. The first indication that the underlying structures will develop into ovaries is that by the sixth week they have not begun to develop as testes.

As in the case of the gonads (ovaries or testes), the external sex organs of the two sexes also differentiate from identical underlying structures. Until the eighth week of gestation these structures are identical in both males and females. Then, some time between the second and third month of pregnancy, the presence of male sex hormones causes male external sex organs (urethral tube, scrotum, penis) to begin developing. In the absence of such male hormones these same structures will develop as female external organs (labia minora, labia majora, clitoris).

The presence of testosterone in the developing male not only causes the development of male sex organs but acts on a region deep in the brain, the hypothalamus, and directs it to function in a masculine rhythm and style. In the absence of testosterone, the hypothalamus is feminine in cycle and style of functioning. At puberty, this region of the brain will act on the pituitary, a gland attached by a stalk to the hy-

*After Money & Ehrhardt, 1972.

pothalamus, and cause it to act on the ovaries (female) or testes (male) to produce either cyclic hormonal activity resulting in ovulation and menstruation in the female or acyclic hormonal activity resulting in the relatively regular production of sperm in the male.

While the presence or absence of hormonal events during gestation causes distinct differences in the male and female brain, it is at puberty that these differences in the brain become fully operative. Puberty is thought to be triggered by the maturation of the hypothalamus, which then acts through the pituitary to bring about sexual maturation. Sex differences in the brain are responsible for male (ejaculation, etc.) as compared with female (menstruation, lactation, etc.) sexual behavior. The presence of such brain differences suggests the possibility of others, as yet undiscovered, which could be responsible for additional sex differences in behavior.

If the cyclic versus acyclic hormonal activity in women and men, respectively, exerts a general effect upon the nervous system, then one can hypothesize that women are predisposed to certain cyclic biologically based changes in behavior, while men undergo neither cyclic changes in blood hormone levels nor resultant changes in behavioral predispositions. Bardwick (1974) has summarized the research on this and concludes that there is substantial evidence of hormonally related mood swings in women. Bardwick speculates that self-assertiveness, self-esteem, and competitiveness are all highest at midcycle and that anxiety, tenseness, and depression are highest premenstrually and menstrually. These states are related to hormone levels through an hormonally linked enzyme (monoamine oxidase) which affects brain activity. Considerable correlation between the level of this enzyme and depression has been found; low levels of estrogen are associated with high levels of this enzyme, and high levels of this enzyme are associated with depression. As is always true, there is undoubtedly wide individual variation among women.

While many sex differences appear at puberty, physical differences in addition to those of the sex organs already exist prior to puberty (Tanner, 1972). Full-term male babies are slightly larger in all body dimensions than females, including height and weight, although female infants at birth have a wider pelvic outlet. Females develop faster than males, beginning in the fetal period and continuing throughout the course of development. There are many differences due to this differential growth rate, only one of which is the greater length and breadth of the male's forearm when compared with whole arm length or whole body length.

At all ages, the body composition of girls and boys differs, with girls having more fat and less water than boys, and boys having more muscle tissue than girls. Physical growth in girls is less variable than that of boys, such that the range of growth in a group of girls at a specific age is narrower than that in a group of boys. Thus, the number of teeth in two-year-old girls will show less variation than the number of teeth possessed by boys of that age.

On the average, girls reach puberty two years earlier than boys. For both sexes, puberty brings about a considerable increase in the length of bones and the thickness of cortex, and girls have a smaller loss of fat. The wider shoulders of the male and the broader hips of the female become striking differences. The "sexy" hip-swinging gait of women can be attributed, at least partly, to the structure of the female pelvis, which is such that for any given length of stride a woman must rotate her pelvis through a greater angle than men do. The proportion of the female pelvis appears to be a compromise between a pelvis suited for walking and one suited for childbearing (Napier, 1967). According to J. M. Tanner (1972), a leading authority on physical growth and development:

Before adolescence, boys and girls are similar in strength and shape; after, boys are much stronger, probably due to developing more force per gram of muscle as well as absolutely larger muscles. They also develop larger hearts and lungs relative to their size, a higher systolic blood pressure, a lower resting heart rate, a greater capacity for carrying oxygen in the blood, and a greater power for neutralizing the chemical products of muscular exercise, such as lactic acid (p. 911).

At the end of puberty, each is sexually and reproductively mature and shows all the secondary sex characteristics of the mature male or female. These apparent physical differences between mature men and women may be the result of a long period of evolution in which the male had to hunt, fight, and protect and the female had to bear and nurture young. Perhaps a man who was physically strong and who recovered quickly from physical fatigue was more apt to survive and reproduce, while a woman survived and reproduced who bore a child easily.

Up to this point we have considered physical differences between male and female human beings, both in terms of development and maturity. A more interesting and by far more difficult question is, to what extent do these differences in body and brain relate to, underlie, or predispose to sex differences in behavior? For human beings, one of the most fertile sources of information that we have as to possible biological bases of behaviors is the study of males and females who have developed in abnormal hormonal environments because of unusual genetic or environmental circumstances.

Psychologists John Money and Anke Ehrhardt (1972) have studied girls who were exposed to male hormones during gestation (androgenized females). Those studies include ten females whose mothers were given hormones during pregnancy in order to prevent abortion, and fifteen females who were exposed to male hormones during gestation due to a genetic defect (andrenogenital syndrome). These girls ranged in age from four to sixteen years, the majority being in middle childhood.

Compared with twenty-five normal (nonandrogenized) girls matched with them on the basis of age, I.Q., socioeconomic background, and race, these psychologists found that the girls exposed to male hormones during gestation differed from the nonandrogenized girls in several ways. Twenty out of the twenty-five androgenized girls termed themselves tomboys, a significant difference from the nonandrogenized girls. Both groups of androgenized girls showed significantly more athletic energy expenditure and skills, greater preference for male versus female playmates, slacks versus dresses, and toy cars and guns versus dolls. They showed significantly more concern with a career rather than marriage.

Of these findings, the activity level and tomboy tendencies are particularly interesting. These are consistent with the results of other experiments where female monkeys were exposed to male hormones in utero. Androgenized female monkeys subsequently resembled normal male monkeys in that they showed considerable rough and tumble play—much more than normal female monkeys display (Goy, 1970).

Money and Ehrhardt (1972) hypothesize that the masculinization in androgenized girls involves masculinization of part of the brain which mediates "dominance assertion (possibly in association with assertion of exploratory and territorial rights) and manifests itself in competitive energy expenditure" (p. 103). They hypothesize that these androgenized girls differ from normal girls in dominance assertion and, therefore, may find boys more compatible as playmates. The differences they found in toy and dress preferences may develop as a result of the girls' close companionship with boys rather than reflect sex differences in the brain. Money and Ehrhardt's findings should be viewed as suggestive rather than conclusive, since genital ambiguity is present in these girls at birth and is known to their parents. This knowledge could well have affected the parents' treatment of them; that is, parents may have tolerated more masculine activity in these girls than they would have normally; or the knowledge that a daughter was masculinized at birth may have made her parents *less* tolerant of masculine behavior.

When we put aside studies of human clinical syndromes like those of Money and Ehrhardt, we are really left with the task of looking at all known sex differences and trying to separate those with a substantial innate basis from those more social in origin. A summary of reported sex differences in behavior is presented in Tables 1 and 2. A more detailed presentation of such differences can be found in Maccoby (1966) and in Maccoby and Jacklin (1974).

One approach to the task of determining which of these sex differences are most likely to have a substantial innate basis is to assume that those differences that show up in infancy are less likely to reflect socialization, and, thus, more likely to be innately based. However, the fact that newborn female infants have slightly more mature skeletons and nervous systems than newborn males (Tanner, 1972) makes it necessary in each case to determine whether maturation level alone is responsible for sex differences in infants.

It is also possible to reason that puberty is the time that biologically based sex differences will appear. It can be argued that because it is at puberty that both males and females experience high levels of hormones which transform boys and girls into sexually mature men and women, sex differences in behavior appearing at this time are very likely to have a considerable biological component. One of the weaknesses of this argument is that both adolescent males and females encounter intense pressure at this time to conform to adult sex-role stereotypes, which could be largely responsible for such sex differences.

Another approach is to assume that sex differences which are evident in subhuman primates or cross-culturally in humans must have an innate basis. Although each alone is a substantial rationale, when a sex difference is found both in primates and cross-culturally, the case for an innate basis is a rather strong one.

Still another tack is to argue that sex differences in behavior which can be related to systematic differences in the behavior of parents or other socializing agents must be social in origin and, therefore, not innately based. This rationale is weak, since innately based sex differences in human behavior are just as likely to give rise to differential treatment by caretakers as differential treatment by caretakers is to produce sex differences.

A final rationale, which is the mirror image of the one just presented, is to suggest that those sex differences in behavior not clearly related to differential socialization of the two sexes must have an innate basis. However, here one cannot rule out the possibility that such sex differences are somehow *indirectly* related to differential socialization of the two sexes.

In general, the greater the number of rationales that support a biological basis for a specific sex difference in behavior, the more strongly psychologists hold the hypothesis that such a basis exists. The case has been easier to make in some areas than in others. Nurturance behavior in human females and aggressive behavior in human males are two such instances. In most subhuman primates, as well as cross-culturally in humans, females show more nurturance behavior than males, and males show more aggressive behavior than females (see Table 1) (Maccoby and Jacklin, 1974).

Rather than viewing these differences as directly related to sex differences in the brain, it is possible that the greater nurturance behavior seen in females comes about because it is the female—not the male—who gestates and lactates. The fact that she can bear an infant and is provided with a means for feeding it causes her to be nurturant. Similarly, it has also been suggested that the higher incidence of aggression in males is only indirectly related to differences in the brain

Table 1.   *summary table of sex differences in social and personality dimensions** ** †

	Age of Subjects			
	0-6	*6-12*	*12-Adult*	*Adult*
Aggression	Boys; strong effect	Boys; strong effect	Boys	Men
Aggression anxiety	No data	No data	Girls (one study)	Women
Dependency on others	Mixed; probably none	No good data	No good data; girls by self-report	
Activity level	Probably none	No good data	No good data	No good data
Nurturance (not very good measure)	Maybe girls	Girls	Girls	Women
Conformity and suggestibility	Probably none	Probably none	Girls (not good data)	Women
Anxiety, particularly test anxiety	No good data	Girls usually	Girls usually	Women usually
Fear of success	No data	No data	No data	Women

*Data from Maccoby: *The development of sex differences*, Stanford Univ. Press, 1966 and Maccoby & Jacklin, unpublished paper, 1972. (Tables 1 and 2.)

**From *Social Issues in Developmental Psychology* by Helen L. Bee: Table 1 (p. 5) "Summary Table of Sex Differences in Social and Personality Dimensions." (Harper & Row, 1974).

†The entries in this table and in Table 2 indicate whether consistent significant differences have been found; the sex named is the one significantly higher on that behavioral dimension.

which mediate dominance-assertion (Money and Ehrhardt, 1972) or in bodily structure and available physical energy (Tanner, 1972). Thus, not only is there little agreement as to which sex differences have an innate basis, but even when there is agreement, the exact nature of such a basis is still unclear. Other sex differences commonly thought to have a considerable innate component are verbal fluency and articulation in females and spatial abilities in males (see Table 2). The major argument is that these differences appear consistently and do not seem to be the product of socialization. Further discussion of sex differences and their relationship to biology can be found in Reinisch (1974), Hutt (1972), and Bee (1974).

Table 2.   *summary table of sex differences in cognitive functioning**

Observed difference	Age of Subjects			
	0-6	6-12	12-Adult	Adult
Verbal abilities				
articulation	Weak effect; girls	Weak effect; girls; more boys with speech defects	No data	No data
verbal fluency	Maybe girls	Probably none	Girls	Women
vocabulary	Probably none	Probably none	None	Women
grammatical development in speech	Probably none	No data	No data	No data
grammatical skill, analyzing sentences	Not relevant	Probably none	Girls	Women
spelling	Not relevant	Maybe girls	Girls	Women
verbal reasoning	No good data	Mixed; maybe boys	Mixed; can't tell	Maybe women
reading	Not relevant	Girls	Probably none	Probably none
Mathematical ability				
counting	Maybe girls	Probably none	No data	No data
computation	Not relevant	Probably girls	None	Probably no difference
mathematical reasoning	None	Maybe boys	Boys	Men
conservation	None	None	No data	No data
Spatial ability	None	Maybe boys	Boys	Men
Breaking set	No data	Probably boys	Probably boys	Men
Field independence	None	Maybe boys	Boys	Men
"Analytic" style	Probably none	Boys	Boys	No data
Total I.Q.	None	None	None	None
School grades	Not relevant	Girls	Girls	Not relevant

*From *Social Issues in Developmental Psychology* by Helen L. Bee: Table 2 (p. 7) "Summary Table of Sex Differences in Cognitive Functioning." (Harper & Row, 1974).

Even if we knew with certainty, many people question whether anything good could come from identifying those sex differences that are largely innate. Isn't it possible that such knowledge would cause men and women to be restricted to those realms where each has an innately based advantage? Not necessarily so! It might just as well be that as a result of such knowledge we could develop special training procedures to improve performance in the less-achieving sex even in those areas of cognitive functioning in which innately based sex differences appear to exist. Thus, no boy or girl, man or woman, would have restricted opportunities simply because of his or her biology.

In concluding this discussion, it seems important to consider clinical reports of individuals who have undergone early sex reassignment or have been reared as male when in fact they are genetically female and vice versa. As reported in Money and Ehrhardt (1972), it is the sex of assignment and rearing which is the critical factor in the development of sexual identity—not genetic sex or sex of the genitals.

A case in point (Money and Ehrhardt, 1972) is that of identical male twins in which one of the twins lost his penis due to a surgical mishap. A circumcision was being performed using electrocautery and the current, being too strong, burned the entire tissue of the penis, which then died and dropped off. The parents agonized over what to do. When sex reassignment was suggested by a plastic surgeon the parents decided to follow his advice. Medically such reassignment involves both genital reconstruction and hormone replacement therapy; however, it is the social outcome of such reassignment which is of greatest interest. In the case of the male twins, not only did the parents change the name, dress, and hairstyle of the reassigned twin, but they found themselves responding quite differently in their interactions with their "daughter" and their son. Six years following such reassignment the girl is not at all confused about what sex she is and in no way behaves inappropriately. Although genetically identical, the twins have developed quite differently—the one as a boy, and the other as a girl.

Money and Ehrhardt (1972) also report several clinical cases where at puberty the body began to mature in a manner inconsistent with the sex of assignment and rearing. In these cases the individuals responded with distress and wished to get rid of the offending organs.

Additional case studies that illustrate the importance of socialization and sex of assignment and rearing in the development of sexual identity can be found in Money and Ehrhardt (1972). The clear message here is that even if biologically based sex differences in behavorial predispositions exist, social factors such as the sex which the child is assigned and in which the child is reared can substantially override and obscure them.

references

Bardwick, J. M. The sex hormones, the central nervous system and affect variability in humans. In V. Bertle and V. Franks (Eds.), *Women in therapy.* New York: Bruner-Mazel, 1974.

Bee, H. *Social issues in developmental psychology.* New York: Harper & Row, 1974.

Goy, R. W. Early hormonal influence on the development of sexual and sex-related behavior. In G. C. Quarton, T. Melanchuk, and F. O. Schmitt (Eds.), *Neuro-Sciences: A study program.* New York: Rockefeller University Press, 1970, pp. 196-207.

Hutt, C. Sex differences in human development. *Human Development,* 1972, *15,* 153-170.

Maccoby, E. E. *The development of sex differences.* Stanford, Calif.: Stanford University Press, 1966.

Maccoby, E. E., and Jacklin, C. N. *The psychology of sex differences.* Stanford, Calif.: Stanford University Press, 1974.

Money, J., and Athanasiou, R. Eve first, or Adam? *Comtemporary Psychology,* 1973, *18,* 593-594.

Money, J., and Ehrhardt, A. *Man & woman, boy & girl: The differentiation and dimorphism of gender identity from conception to maturity.* Baltimore: John Hopkins University Press, 1972.

Mussen, P. H., Conger, J. J., and Kagan, J. *Child development and personality.* New York: Harper & Row, 1974. (4th ed.)

Napier, J. The antiquity of human walking. *Scientific American,* 1967, *216*(4), 56-66.

Reinisch, J. M. Fetal hormones, the brain, and human sex differences; A heuristic integrative review of the recent literature. *Archives of Sexual Behavior,* 1974, *3,* 51-90.

Sherfey, M. J. *The nature and evolution of female sexuality.* New York: Random House, 1972.

Stern, C. *Principles of human genetics.* San Francisco: W. H. Freeman, 1973.

Tanner, J. M. Sequence, tempo, and individual variation in the growth and development of boys and girls aged twelve to sixteen. In J. Kagan and R. Coles (Eds.), *Twelve to sixteen: Early adolescence.* New York: Norton, 1972, pp. 907-930.

psychological theories
of sex differences

Leonard D. Goodstein
Alice G. Sargent

The previous chapter presented an overview of our current knowledge of biological factors involved in sex differences. Psychologists, however, were interested in explaining sex differences long before such biological data was available. Their theories of sex typing vary in the degree to which they emphasize the biological basis of sex differences. Some theories, such as Freud's, place heavy emphasis on such biological factors as etiology in the development of sex-linked behavior. Others, such as Kohlberg's cognitive theory, tend to pay little or no attention to biology. We do not currently have a comprehensive, coherent theory that integrates what is known of the biology, psychology, and sociology of sex differences. When we consider the recency of our interest in this field, however, this state of affairs should not be surprising.

Each of us has some implicit theory about why the observed differences between men and women occur. You can determine this by asking yourself to what degree you hold that "biology is destiny" versus to what extent you believe that behavior is learned. Since most of us believe that it is more difficult to change biologically based behavior than learned behavior, the extent to which we feel sex-linked behavior can be changed is related to our theory of gender development. It is important to understand your own theories about sex typing before you can meaningfully change role-related behaviors. In order to facilitate the self-examination of your theory, you need to be familiar with three of the better known theorists on the development of sex-typed behavior—Sigmund Freud, Walter Mischel, and Lawrence Kohlberg. Their theories have had considerable impact upon professional psychology and have also influenced popular thought as well. We will first examine the oldest and the most biological position.

Reading Assign.

a freudian psychoanalytic theory of sex typing

Freud's ideas about sex roles are part of his more general theory of psycho-sexual development and cannot be understood without reference to the theory. Freud believed that there was an innate biological sequence of human development and that this pattern was universal for men and women alike. It is somewhat difficult to describe Freud's theory simply and briefly because it changed over the fifty years in which Freud wrote, and any brief presentation can deal only with portions of the theory.

Freud postulated a kind of sexual energy, *libido*, as the underlying force of human behavior. In some ways one can think of libido as the raw, unfocused energy that would be present in a stream, river, or machine that cannot be stopped but only channelled or directed. This psychological energy, or libido, is present at birth and is quite diffuse but shortly thereafter is channelled into the first of the three stages that comprise the psycho-sexual pattern of development. Again, it is important to note that both this energy and its pattern of development during the early years of life are governed by the biological nature of the human organism and are quite invariant.

Freud thought that the three major orifices of the body, the oral, anal, and genital, could be erogenized by the libido; for him there seemed to be a fixed order of development of these three structures. Initially, the libido becomes fixated in the mouth, the primary organ of pleasure for the newborn. The mother's breast or a bottle is the first source of gratification and the child's most important contact with the external world. The nurturance and satisfaction derived from this *oral stage* are crucial in learning the development of trust and dependency.

Towards the end of the first year, the focus of the libido shifts to the anal zone and involves the retention and expulsion of feces. It involves the child's first opportunity for defying and submitting to the parents and is thus the source of the developing feelings of power. The child learns that his/her control of feces can arouse concern in those who care for him/her. By withholding his/her feces, by choosing his/her own time of expulsion, he/she can upset the parents. The child also learns that acquiescing to the parents' wishes can be powerfully rewarding. Freud believed that the tendency to assume either an active or a passive attitude towards life was developed during this *anal stage.*

The third stage of development according to this theory is the *phallic stage* and represents the first clear differentiations of the sexes. At about the age of four, the penis becomes the center of erotic pleasure for the male and the clitoris "being its substitute" for the female becomes the new focus of libidinal energy. This early development of sexuality, which does not lead to any real gratification, is termed the phallic stage to differentiate it from the genital maturity which does not occur until adolescence. Not only is the phallus the focus of the libido, but, in some unspecified way, the penis becomes a highly valued organ for both the male and the female. At least for the little girl there is the sense that she is missing something by not having one. Freud has not made clear how this sense develops. Thus, the fear of loss of the phallus in boys—castration anxiety—and the sense of loss in girls—penis envy—are potent sources for much neurotic behavior in later life.

As we have noted, the first love object for the child is the mother. Her breast provides nurturance and satisfaction. This object relationship continues through the anal stage into the phallic stage. While the child is initially auto-erotic in the phallic stage, the phallic excitement begins to become directed towards the mother—the first love object. Freud gave the name *Oedipus complex* to these early sexual impulses of the child, especially the male child, towards the mother. These desires place the son in direct rivalry with his father for his mother's attention. Because of these rivalrous feelings toward his father and his taboo love for his mother, he expects to be punished, and castration is the feared punishment.

While male children have this fear of castration, the female, who has already "lost" her penis, has nothing more to lose. Girls love their fathers and hate their mothers because the mother is a rival for the father's love, but this fear, according to Freud, is less intense than the castration fear developed in the boy.

Here is an interesting complication of this part of Freud's theory: the little girl must somehow change the object of her initial attachment from the mother (whom she loves in the same way as the little boy) to the father. The little boy, on the other hand, needs only to continue his early attachment to the mother. Of course his attachment does become more specifically sexualized and he developes more focused rivalry with the father, but there is no necessity for him to change the object of his libidinal attachment.

The shift from the mother to the father occurs in the little girl as a consequence of the awareness of "penis loss." The little girl discovers that she lacks a penis and blames the mother for this loss. Indeed, she comes to depreciate all women. Thus, she turns her libidinal energies to her father, the most available man with the coveted penis.

Freud elaborates on the implications for the little girl's "discovery of her castration" and the following development of penis envy. She wishes to regain a penis through a male, and the most suitable and available male is her father. One way to do this is by having a child which she equates with regaining the lost penis. Thus, having her father's child will restore her penis! She gives up her initial clitoral masturbation, which only produces inadequate orgasm, and becomes dominated by the "passive aims" of the vagina in the development of normal femininity.

The guilt and anxiety produced by these incestuous desires leads to a denial and rejection of these taboo impulses coupled with an identification of the child with like-sexed parents. This identification with the aggressor represents a resolution of the Oedipal relationship and a termination of the phallic period. For the next eight to ten years the child denies sexual impulses in the so-called latency period and the libido is "desexualized" until it becomes recusitated by the flowing hormones of adolescence.

When puberty occurs, the two sexes respond rather differently. The boy maintains his interest in his penis and resumes his development. along the same pattern as during the phallic stage, although his mother is no longer the primary object of his attention. The girl, however, takes a different course of development, since up to this time she has been unaware of her vagina as a potential source of pleasure. Her earlier interest was in her clitoris and, at puberty, she must renounce her clitoris and accept the passive, feminine role demanded by her vagina. If she still has strong penis envy or strong constitutional "masculine trends," her adjustment will be difficult, and she will become resentful of being a woman.

We want to reemphasize that Freud believed that this pattern of psychosexual development, and the development of sex roles, was the normal innate, instinctual, biologically determined sequence. While many of Freud's students and critics have argued against this strong biological basis for psychosexual development, it clearly was an integral and important part of Freud's conceptualization of human nature and sex role.

a social-learning theory of sex typing

As we have seen, Freud's theory of sex difference is strongly anchored in biology, but other psychologists have looked at the same phenomena of sex-linked behaviors with far less recourse to biological influences. The social-learning theories of such psychologists as Mischel (1970) and Bandura and Walters (1963) are good examples of an approach which deemphasizes biology. Before we can examine social-learning theory, however, we need to make a brief review of learning theory, especially the role of reinforcement in learning.

Most theories of learning emphasize that the learner engages in some direct behaviors, typically of a trial-and-error type. The behavior of the rat in the Skinner box is a prototype of this kind of learning. The animal is placed in a special experimental box equipped with a device that when triggered, automatically gives a reward or reinforcement. The rat moves around the box, exploring his/her environment and eventually accidentally presses the lever which leads to a food pellet being released. Since the food pellet serves as a reward or reinforcement to the hungry rat, the rat rather quickly learns to press the lever in order to receive food pellets. The basic axiom of laboratory psychology is that all organisms, including humans, tend to repeat those behaviors which have been reinforced, that is, those responses having positive consequences. Much of our behavior is thus acquired by direct, trial-and-error behavior and by direct reinforcement of certain responses. But there are other kinds of learning as well.

The basic explanatory concept of social learning theory is that of modeling, or imitation. We have just noted the powerful consequences of direct positive reinforcement; the singular contribution of social-learning theory has been the demonstration that this reinforcement can occur indirectly or vicariously. Thus a child who observes another child receiving candy or praise for approaching a dog is more likely to approach a dog later than would otherwise be the case. While studies of vicarious reinforcements of this type show that the power of this technique may depend upon the similarities between the child and the model as well as a number of other experimental factors, there is virtually no question among psychologists that such vicarious reinforcement is a powerful modifier of behavior. In other words, we learn not only on the basis of the consequences of our own behavior but also by observing the consequences of the behavior of others.

Let us examine how vicarious reinforcement is used as a concept to explain sex typing. When a little boy sees a classmate ridiculed for behaving like a sissy, or when a little girl is commended for her neat picture and her tidy appearance, these actions vicariously reinforce the child's understanding of appropriate sex-typed behavior.

One carefully conducted piece of research illuminates how modelling helps explain the development of sex-linked behavior. Bandura (1965) showed boys and girls a film of a model exhibiting verbal and physical aggression. In the first treatment the model was severely punished following the aggressive behavior; in the second, the model was generously rewarded with treats and praise; in the third, there were neither rewards nor punishments given to the model. Subsequently, the children were asked to imitate what the model did. They were in a nursery school setting with Bobo dolls (the life-size blow-up clown). Both boys and girls imitated a significantly greater variety of responses after watching the rewarded model and the no-consequence model. Boys imitated the model's aggression more than girls under all three conditions, and the girls showed the least aggression after watching the model being punished.

Following this performance test, the children in all three groups were offered incentives if they would act as the model did. The introduction of the incentives eliminated the previous performance differences. An equivalent amount of learning had taken place under all three conditions: model rewarded, model punished, and no-consequences. The most significant finding for our purposes is that the initially large sex differential was virtually eliminated when incentives were given. Bandura's interpretation of this study is that it disproves that there is a "deficit in masculine-role identification by girls." In other words, girls have learned the behavior of boys; they simply do not practice it for fear of punishment!

When we talk about vicarious reinforcement, there are a number of characteristics of the model that need to be understood. Models vary in their capacity for influence. Bandura (1969) lists the factors which determine the degree of the model's influence: if the model has high power or control over the person's life, as does a teacher; if the model is a potentially highly nurturant or affiliative person; if there is similarity between model and observer, for example when the model is the same sex.

Thus is should be clear that parents, especially same-sex parents, are very important models for children. Since we differentiate the sexes at birth, the same-sex parent provides the earliest and most constant role model for the child's gender development. As the child attempts to master developmental tasks, he/she observes the behavior of the nurturant, seemingly all-knowing parent, who performs these tasks with apparent expertise. Indeed, for many years this is the child's most salient model. What adult has not observed a young child imitating the same-sex parent attempting to shave or apply make-up? The six-year-old daughter of one of the authors of this chapter claims that all pictures she produces are in fact for Mommy's book. The intensity and scope of these behaviors cannot be underestimated. In fact, the consequences of this modeling—this wanting to be like Mommy and Daddy—is called *identification*. Not only is there vicarious reinforcement of this behavior, there is much direct reinforcement as both parents praise and reinforce the child for behaving like the same-sexed parent.

While we have emphasized the singular importance of the same-sexed parent as an agent for socialization, we should not ignore the role of the other models who also affect the developing sexual identity of the child. As we will see in the next chapter, parents, teachers, the media (such as T.V. and the movies), and teaching aids such as textbooks, all vicariously reinforce consistent stereotypes for "appropriate" sex-role behavior. Consider how television teaches role behavior. Aggressive roles are almost always portrayed by men and nurturant roles by women. Recent research clearly demonstrates how children's aggressive behavior is increased by the observation of television violence. Increasing data is available to substantiate the impact of television role models, from Sesame Street to The Waltons, on shaping sex-role behavior (Isber & Cantor, 1975; Miles, 1975).

It is important to note the consistency of these stereotypes: the sex-role models initially presented by the parents are the same shown in the media, presented in the textbooks, and experienced in the classroom. Thus, in the socialization process, relatively specific behaviors are clearly differentiated as more appropriate for males or for females. The child is in turn both directly and vicariously reinforced for behaving according to sex.

**a cognitive
theory of
sex typing**

Social learning theory does not deal explicitly with the cognitive development individuals, that is, with the things people say to themselves about their sex roles. We will now explore the work of Lawrence Kohlberg who has developed a theory of sex-typing based on cognitive development. As with the social-learning theorists, Kohlberg's approach is non-biological.

Kohlberg (1966), influenced by Piaget, said that self-categorizations of gender become the fundamental organizers of sex role. According to Kohlberg, recent research indicates that:

Children develop a conception of themselves as having an unchangeable sexual identity at the same age and through the same processes that they develop conceptions of the invariable identity of physical objects. The child's sexual identity is maintained by a motivated adaptation to physical-social reality and by the need to preserve a stable and positive self-image (p. 95).

Kohlberg suggests five ways in which the child's sex-role concepts develop into masculine-feminine values:

1) The tendency to schematize interests and respond to new interests that are consistent with the old ones. 2) The tendency to make value judgments consistent with a self-conceptual identity. 3) The tendency for prestige, competence, or goodness values to be closely and intrinsically associated with sex-role stereotypes, e.g., the association of masculinity with values of strength and power. 4) The tendency to view basic uniformity to one's own role as moral, as part of conformity to a general socio-moral order. 5) The tendency to imitate or model persons who are valued because of prestige and competence, and who are perceived as like the self. (Kolhberg, 1966, p. 111).

In other words, the individual tells himself/herself: I am a girl or a boy. I will watch other girls or boys behave, and I will behave in like manner. This selection of behavior from sex-role stereotypes leads to the development of masculine/feminine values in children. Yet sex typing is taking place prior to the point where the child learns these concepts.

While Kohlberg very clearly describes how boys and girls cognitively categorize their behavior as appropriate or not for their sex, he suggests that the person also strives to be relatively self-consistent. Consider the vastness of the categories, *male* and *female:* there must be endless ways of being consistently a boy or a girl. Kohlberg's only allowance of additional causes for being made within categories is to say that, of course, a child's sex role may be influenced by certain environmental variables. He does not value the importance of the same-sex parent in shaping sex roles. He even goes so far as to say, "It is not at all clear whether certain parental attitudes can create appropriate sex-role attitudes. In fact, certain parental attitudes may create conflict and anxieties inhibiting the development of appropriate sex-role attitudes."

Kohlberg says that after masculine/feminine values are acquired, the child tends to identify with same-sex figures. This process is the reverse of the sequence in social-learning theory in which identification occurs first, followed by modeling, and then the development of masculine/feminine values. While cognitive-consistency theory does serve to explain how individuals select new sex-linked behavior after they have reached the stage of concept formation, it still does not deal sufficiently with the effects of the rewards and punishments which are directly administered in the environment and all of the development of sex typing that takes place before concept formation.

Another question concerns the relationship between these concepts—often called attitudes by psychologists—and other behaviors. To clarify this relationship, Zimbardo and Ebbesen (1969) suggest an attitude has three components: affect, cognition, and behavior. The affective component is an individual's emotional response to some object or person; the cognitive component is an individual's beliefs about, or factual knowledge of, the object or person; the behavioral component is the individual's overt behavior toward the object or person. The three components can be measured differently. The affective component can be measured by physiological responses or verbal statements of likes and dislikes. The cognitive component can be measured by self-ratings of beliefs or self-reports of knowledge about the topic. The behavioral component can be measured by direct observation of behavior.

It should be clear that for most attitudes or cognitions, the measures of the three components will differ in a given individual and, further, these three components are differentially changeable. In a classic study, Asch (1946) was able to show that subjects would shift their cognitive attitudes about the length of lines fairly dramatically if their reports were discrepant from those of the others in the group. On the other hand, there is much evidence to show that overt behaviors are much more difficult to change. Thus, for example, it is much easier to change an adult's attitude to "I think it is fine to combine motherhood and work," than to change the behavior so that a woman becomes a working mother or the spouse of a working wife supports her work wholeheartedly through behavior change. Brody (1965) studied the relation between maternal attitudes and child-rearing styles. Only seven out of fifteen constructs espoused by mothers correlated with their actual behavior. Hence, there was only a one-out-of-two relationship between expressed maternal attitudes towards child rearing and direct observation measures of the mother's behavior toward the child.

When we discuss or think of the functions of attitudes or cognitions, we must avoid considering attitudes or changing attitudes as leading directly to changing overt behaviors. We began the discussion with a consideration of the degree to which biological factors are important in the development of sex roles. Clearly, if sex roles are determined by

Mother Nature or Father Time, and if our current sex roles represent the natural order of things, then one should be very pessimistic about change. If, on the other hand, sex roles are primarily a function of social learning or cognitive development, then all that is required is restructuring of the social order—changes in child rearing, educational institutions, and so on!

All three positions—psychoanalytic theory, cognitive theory, and social learning theory—hold that much in the development of sex roles is learned behavior which starts at a very early age. However, psychoanalytic theory is deeply grounded in biological bases for differences in gender identity. The cognitive theorists claim that sex typing begins when the child tells himself/herself, "I am a girl" or "I am a boy" and therefore, "I must behave in a certain way." In contrast, psychoanalytic theorists and social-learning theorists hold that sextyping commences at birth when the child begins to imitate highly rewarding and nurturant role models, primarily the parents. Some of the imitated behaviors are reinforced and others are punished, depending upon the sex of the child. The constellation of behaviors which relate quite heavily to sex roles are those surrounding dependency and aggression. Dependency, passivity, showing vulnerability and pain all tend to be allowed to girls and denied to boys. On the other hand, aggression, negative attention-getting, physical strength, toughness, tend to be allowed for boys and denied to girls. Social-learning theorists differ from psychoanalytic theorists in contending that a number of significant models who influence the child's behavior besides the mother and father, including the media, teachers, and friends. In addition, social learning theorists hold that children of either sex are quite familiar with the behaviors allowed to the other sex and need only to be in a situation where these behaviors are rewarded in order to exhibit them.

There is a new emphasis on nonsexist child-rearing which stems from a cognitive, social-learning theory view of child development. In many homes now, little girls are being given trucks to play with and boys dolls or a pet to nurture. Children's literature is changing. There are books which depict a woman installing telephone equipment or a father baking a birthday cake.[1] There are an increasing number of male elementary teachers and a few female university presidents. These shifts in roles clearly follow the tenets of vicarious reinforcement, observational learning, and modeling theories. The impact on the cultural norms will be measurable within a few years. It remains for psychologists and sociologists to provide data which confirms that sex differences are not immutable or absolute, but are indeed normative.

Lollipop Power Press P.O. Box 1711, Chapel Hill, North Carolina 27514. Sadker, D. and Sadker, M. *Now Upon A Time: A Contemporary Approach to Children's Literature.* New York: Harper & Row, 1977.

references

Asch, S. E. Forming impressions of personality. *Journal of Social Psychology,* 1946, *41,* 258-265.

Bandura, A., & Walters, R. H. *Social learning and personality development.* New York: Holt, Rinehart & Winston, 1963.

Bandura, A. *Principles of behavior modification.* Stanford: Stanford University Press, 1969.

Bandura, A. Influence of the model's reinforcement contingencies on the acquisition of imitative responses. *Journal of Personality and Social Psychology,* 1965, *1,* 589-595.

Brody, G. F. Relationships between maternal attitudes and behavior. *Journal of Personality and Social Psychology,* 1965, *2,* 317-323.

Freud, S. *New introductory lectures in psychoanalysis.* New York: Norton, 1933.

Freud, S. Some psychological consequences of the anatomical distinction between the sexes. In *The Collected Papers* (Vol. 5). London: Hogarth, 1957.

Isber, C., & Cantor, M. *Report of the task force on women in public broadcasting.* Washington: Corporation for Public Broadcasting, 1975.

Kohlberg, L. A cognitive developmental analysis of children's sex role concept and attitudes. In E. E. Maccoby (Ed.), *The development of sex differences.* Stanford: Stanford University Press, 1966.

Miles, B. *Channeling children: sex stereotyping on prime time T.V.* Princeton: Women on Words and Images, 1975.

Mischel, W. *Personality and assessment.* Stanford: Stanford University Press, 1970.

Sadker, M., & Saker, D. Now upon a time: A comtemporary approach to children's literature. New York: Harper & Row, in press.

Zimbardo, P., & Ebbesen, E. *Influencing attitudes and changing behavior.* Reading, Mass.: Addison Wesley, 1969.

stereotypes, socialization, and sexism

Carol Tavris

Like polluted air, stereotypes surround us. Like polluted air, they are invisible; we tend to be unconscious of them, and there is a critical point at which they become dangerous.

To be sure, people in every society share expectations of how various groups will behave and think, and quite often those expectations are based on actual group differences. In most cases, the stereotypes we carry around are trivial and harmless, a means of condensing the extraordinary amount of new information we acquire daily. We have stereotypes about car owners (we expect people who buy Porsches to differ from people who buy Volkswagons), fraternities (men in Pi Phi aren't like men in Epsilon Omega), cities (New Yorkers are surly, San Franciscans are friendly). When I was in college I had stereotypes that stood me in good stead about every group of male students within a 100-mile radius. And they had stereotypes about us.

In recent years we have all become aware of the stereotypes that we hold about men and women, and the ways that those stereotypes affect the ways we rear children, select friends, choose a doctor, hire an employee, and so on. We think of the concepts of masculinity and femininity as polar opposites—women should be soft and nurturant, men must be strong and self-reliant. If women are passive and incompetent at everything but raising babies, men must be active and competent at everything but raising babies. If a woman's place is in the home, man's place must be at work. The "polar opposite" concept has been reflected in psychology for years, for virtually every test of masculinity-femininity assumes a continuum of characteristics: "very aggressive" is masculine, "not at all aggressive" is feminine. Inge Broverman and her colleagues have shown that the traits we associate with men—strong, competent, independent, rational, logical, and direct—are the exact opposite of those we associate with women—weak, incompetent, dependent, irrational, emotional, and sneaky.

The important question is what is wrong with having stereotypes about men and women, and defining some jobs as appropriate to one sex rather then the other? Why not raise boys to be firefighters and politicians, and girls to be wives and mothers? There are, I think, at least three wrong reasons.

First, the stereotypes are now socially dysfunctional. The actual behavior of men and women in this country today no longer fits the expectations we hold. Consider the old adage, "A woman's place is in the home." American women have not spent their whole lives in the home for generations. With the decline in the birth rate, the average woman sees her last child off to school when she is in her early thirties. The average family now has only 1.9 children, and when Zero Population Growth is achieved, that age can be expected to decrease. So women have thirty-five years or more of their lives to work, play, enter politics, or school after they have had children.

*"I want a book about a woman that starts out happy,
stays happy, and ends happy."*

Drawing by Stevenson; © 1974 The New Yorker Magazine, Inc.

This is contrary to the image of women portrayed in children's readers and most history or social studies texts, television commercials, movies, and novels. The myth maintains that most women want to stay home, still do stay home, and are miserable if they leave home. The truth is just the opposite. The proportion of women in the labor force increases yearly (42 percent in 1974); two in every five working women are economically independent of men; nine of every ten girls born today will work. Today the average working woman is 43 years old and married, and she works for as many diverse reasons as men do—satisfaction, economic need, interest, independence.

These economic facts, along with the lengthened life-span and the decrease in the number of children, mean that being a wife and mother is no longer, for most women, a full-time, lifetime job. Stereotypes do not recognize the extraordinary implications of this fact.

Second, stereotypes make discrimination against a group seem legitimate. If women are vain, emotional, passive, and incompetent, they are best kept at home. If they have simple minds, give them simple jobs. If they have "high manual dexterity" and "low mental ability" keep them at the factories and typewriters. Stereotypes, in short, justify putting women in low status, lesser-paying jobs. A national survey conducted at the University of Michigan's Institute for Social Research found that 95 percent of all American working women earn an average of $3,458 less than men with the same qualifications and education (Levitin, Quinn, & Staines, 1973). These women were no more likely than men to want dull, unchallenging jobs, but they were significantly more likely than men to have them.

Third, sex-role stereotypes have become psychologically stifling. They brand a whole group of people with the same label, admitting no individual differences, and they linger on even when they have become inaccurate. It doesn't really hurt a rich man in any significant way to drive a Volkswagen (thereby breaking the stereotype of VW owners); but many women who choose to step out of the bounds of traditional "feminine" behavior worry for a time that they may be "sick," or "neurotic," or doomed to a life of grief. Actually, the psychological evidence at present is that the traditional roles breed more illness, mental and physical, than untraditional life-styles.

Data from admissions to mental hospitals, from outpatient clinics, from private psychiatrists and physicians, from community surveys of mental health, all indicate that more women than men suffer from anxiety, depression, neurosis, and psychosis. This evidence is consistent, holding up across voluntary and involuntary visits to doctors and mental hospitals, and also in assessments of health in various communities and among people who have not sought therapy. This consistency counters the argument that women are not more likely than men to suffer these problems, simply more likely to report them (Gove & Tudor, 1973).

More married women than married men are dissatisfied with marriage and experience psychological problems (see Bernard, 1972). This finding runs counter to what one would expect since girls learn from infancy that their main ambition should be marriage and children. Perhaps the contrast between their expectations of the institution and the reality accounts for their dissatisfaction; after all, no one tells them what happens *after* marriage.

Bernard's careful analysis of marriage and mental health finds that single women and married men are the best off, both psychologically and physically. Men, for all the jokes and complaints they make about marriage, have trouble surviving without it; single men have higher suicide and sickness rates, and divorced men remarry, on the average, within two years of their separation. Why is this finding reversed for women? Perhaps, Bernard suggests, because women, when they marry, end up with several jobs: caring in all emotional and practical ways for the husband and children; most likely working outside the home; having sole responsibility for housework, cooking, and general chores. Husbands are cared for; wives are expected to care for themselves.

Because sex-role stereotypes are psychologically damaging and sociologically irrelevant, I believe that we can no longer justify rearing children to join a world that went out of date one hundred years ago. Yet socialization proceeds according to our often unconscious assumptions about the sexes: what our children are "naturally" like and what we want them to become. Many parents state vociferously that they treat their sons and daughters alike, but objective observers disagree with them. From the moment a parent puts a football shirt on a boy and a pink ruffled diaper on a girl, the cues are set for how the child will be treated.

Michael Lewis reports, for example, that parents talk to their infant daughters more than to their infant sons but give the boys more physical contact. When the boy is about six months old, however, the mother starts to push the boy out of the nest, cuddling him less. By the time the children in Lewis's study were one year old, sex differences were already apparent; boys looked for their mothers less than girls did, and could stay away from them for longer periods of time. Many have theorized that the greater independence of males is "biologically" determined, but it could also result from treatment by parents who believe, says Lewis, that "boys should be encouraged to explore and master their world." In short, parents expect boys to be more aggressive and independent, treat them accordingly, and lo! that's how they turn out.

More recently, Jeff Rubin and his colleagues at Tufts (1974) found that parents perceive male infants to be different in "personality" from female infants in the first twenty-four hours of the baby's life—even when doctors reported no significant objective differences in size, activity level, health, and so on. Both mothers and fathers agreed on the sex differences, disagreeing with each other on only one trait: fathers thought the girls were more cuddly, and mothers thought the boys were more cuddly (the researchers called this finding the Oedipus Effect).

In *The Psychology of Sex Differences*, Eleanor Maccoby and Carol Jacklin have carefully reviewed hundreds of studies of sex differences in childhood, to see what we know, what we thought we knew, and what remains uncertain. They report that it is not true that girls are more "social," "empathic," or "suggestible" than boys, or that girls have lower self-esteem. Boys are not more analytic than girls, or better at higher-level cognitive functioning, or even more achievement-motivated. Maccoby and Jacklin did find some differences that have been well-established: girls have greater verbal ability than boys, and boys excel in visual-spatial ability, math, and aggressiveness. But they found no conclusive evidence for differences in so-called nurturing ability, degree of anxiety and fear, activity levels, competitiveness, dominance, or compliance—psychological characteristics that have commonly been attributed to one sex or the other.

Maccoby and Jacklin conclude, after their exhaustive work, that the most likely explanation for the perpetuation of sex-role myths, even when study after study disproved them, was the powerful nature of stereotypes. "If a generalization about a group of people is believed, whenever a member of that group behaves in the expected way, the observer notes it and his belief is confirmed and strengthened. When a member of the group behaves in a way that is not consistent with the observer's expectations, the instance is likely to pass unnoticed" (Maccoby & Jacklin, 1974, p. 355).

Indeed, our expectations of how we think people should behave can often overcome our observations of how they do behave. People tend to label the same behaviors differently, depending on who is acting them out, in accordance with a stereotype. For example, a man and a woman may behave the same way on the job, but people will interpret their actions differently. The man is competitive but the woman is aggressive; the man is aggressive but a woman is a castrating bitch. If a man gets angry and screams at his coworkers, they decide he is legitimately upset because he lost the Merriweather account. If a woman gets angry and screams at her coworkers, they decide it must be her time-of-the-month, or that, like all women, she is hysterical. Same actions, different labels.

Our expectations of how people should behave do not stop at labeling. They are communicated to those we interact with and may actually influence what they do. Robert Rosenthal (1973) calls this the Pygmalion effect, after the unhappy artist who fell in love with his sculpture of the ideal woman. The force of Pygmalion's love eventually gave life to his creation, courtesy of Venus (who was much more agreeable about granting favors in those days). Rosenthal has amply documented the effect across a wide variety of experimental and field situations. He finds that we may unconsciously transmit to others our expectations of how they should behave, and they pick up our cues. Even if the exchange is purely nonverbal, the cues can still be strong.

Rosenthal and Jacobson (1969) launched the most controversial test of their hypothesis in the sixties, in a lower-class elementary school. They told the teachers that certain randomly selected children would become "intellectual bloomers" during the coming year on the basis of tests they had given the students. In fact, they had no evidence on which to rest such a prediction; but many of the supposed bloomers actually showed an increase in I.Q. at the end of the school year. The teachers *expected* these children to improve, and they did.

Several hundred similar studies have now been completed, and a significant proportion of them demonstrate the Pygmalion effect. Albert King (1973), for example, looked at the effects of supervisor expectations on the job performance of minority workers. He randomly picked names of certain trainees—nurse's aides, presser-machine operators, assemblers of electronic equipment—and told the supervisors that these trainees showed particular aptitude for their work. In four of his five experiments, King found that his planted, and unfounded, suggestion worked. He collected objective measures of the workers' performances on the job—tests, peer ratings, absenteeism, and so on—and found that trainees whose supervisors had expected high performance did better than the control groups.

Rosenthal and his colleagues are now working on measures to determine the nature of the nonverbal communication that seems to account for the effect. They found, for instance, that teachers who thought they were dealing with a bright child were more likely to smile at him, nod their heads approvingly, look him in the eye for longer periods, and make other supportive gestures (Rosenthal, 1973).

The Pygmalion effect would suggest that our stereotypes about sex-role differences are transmitted to children, to employees, and to lovers alike. Serbin, O'Leary, Kent, and Tonick (1973) observed teachers unconsciously producing a Pygmalion effect in the classroom. These fifteen nursery school teachers, the observers documented, paid more attention to boys than to girls, regardless of whether the boys were misbehaving or not. When the boys asked questions, the teachers responded with longer answers and more detailed directions than they gave the girls. The girls, in fact, received attention primarily when they sidled up to the teacher or behaved dependently. Then the teachers responded with pats on the head and other affectionate rewards.

In this same study Serbin and her colleagues found that when a boy was disruptive or aggressive—whenever he hit someone or something or refused to obey the teacher—the teacher almost inevitably reacted by speaking to him, usually with a reprimand or further directions.

When a girl was disruptive, typically the teacher did not react at all, or reprimanded her softly and forgot the episode. In short, boys received rewards and attention for disruptive behavior—exactly the teacher reaction that will cause the behavior to continue. Serbin also noted that teachers gave boys equal amounts of attention regardless of whether the boys were within arm's reach or on the other side of the room; but they gave attention mostly to the girls who were hovering near them, that is, dependently. The teachers gave the boys directions for doing things on their own, and hugged and praised them when they complied; but more often than not they showed the girls what to do instead of letting them experiment on their own. For example, in one classroom, when the teacher showed the boys how to staple the handles to the party baskets they were making, she showed them how to use the stapler themselves. Whereas with the girls she took the basket and did the stapling herself.

The teachers reported that they were completely unaware that they were treating boys differently from girls. But clearly and consistently, they were rewarding boys for independence and activity, behaviors they discouraged in girls.

The ultimate justification for sex-role stereotypes, of course, is that males and females are anatomically different. Personality differences rest on those ultimate physiological differences. We cannot change the sex roles, even if we try.

We have come a long way since Freud's anatomy-is-destiny theory, but the controversy still rages. It will continue so long as there is one person who justifies keeping women out of public office because they are subject to hormonal influences. It is to be hoped that just as we are moving toward a middle ground on the question of personality differences between men and women, so we will recognize that while nature and nurture play a role in human development, there is an extraordinary plasticity to the human being's ability to learn from his or her environment.

A good illustration of the interface between biology and learning is the correlation between menstruation and mood swings. Judith Bardwick has documented the correlation between phases of the menstrual cycle and emotions; the young women in her study were the happiest and most optimistic at ovulation (midcycle), when estrogen is at its peak, and the most depressed and anxious at premenstruation, when estrogen and progesterone are at their lowest. "Aha!" shout the sexists, "evidence to keep women out of office!" They ignore the fact that men, too, undergo changes of mood on a cyclic level, and the male sex hormone, testosterone, has been shown to correlate with aggressiveness in various animals and in men. Logically, if women are to be kept out of the Presidency because estrogen makes them anxious, men should be kept out of all public offices because testosterone makes them violent. (But few men are logical on this matter.) The point is simply that we are all influenced by our moods, our bodies, our states of physiological arousal. But we learn how to deal with those mood swings and physical states; parents, institutions, and culture all teach us appropriate reactions to and interpretations of those states.

Karen Paige (1973) has discovered some cultural influences for the way women react to menstruation. She argues that menstrual symptoms and moodiness may be a social response to menstruation itself, which is considered unclean, taboo, disgusting by many people in almost every society, rather than a response to changes in hormone levels. If hormones determine a woman's reaction to menstruation, all women should respond to it in approximately the same way. In fact, they do not. The Protestants in her study did not show much of a jump in anxiety levels between midcycle and menstruation, but the Catholics did; in fact, the Catholics were anxious about many sexual matters. And Orthodox Jews, to whom the menstruating woman is "unclean," had a consistently high anxiety level all month. Paige thinks that women's negative reactions to menstruation are socially, not hormonally, determined. "It is no mere coincidence," she writes, "that women get the blue meanies along with an event they consider embarrassing, unclean—and a curse" (Paige, 1973).

John Money and Anke Ehrhardt (1972) of the Johns Hopkins University were convinced for many years that hormones play a major role in the formation of gender identity. They observed fifteen girls who had received accidental high doses of the male hormone prenatally, and found that virtually all of them became tomboys. They didn't have maternal fantasies, they liked to roughhouse and were very active, and they liked "male" games and sports. But all considered themselves female. Now Money and Ehrhardt have reversed their views and argue for the extraordinary impact of environment and expectation on the child's gender identity. Learning can even overcome chromosomes. They describe the cases of four genetically female babies (all had a pair of XX chromosomes) who had received such high doses of prenatal androgen that they were born hermaphrodites: their internal reproductive systems were female, but they had penises.

In one case, the attending physician performed corrective surgery and the parents reared the child as a girl. In one case, they assigned the baby to the male sex, and reared him as a boy. In two cases, the parents and physicians waited to make a decision, because they weren't sure of the right choice. What happened? The girl who was treated as a girl formed the appropriate gender identity; the "boy" came to think of himself as a boy. But the children who were treated ambivalently were ambivalent about their sexual identity. The parents waited in vain for genetics to make the decision for them.

The time has come, it would appear, for us to drop the tired cliches we share about the sexes. Whatever the contribution of anatomy and biology to human personality, we cannot use hormones as an excuse for discrimination or to limit women's potential; a quick look at women's roles around the world shows that anything men can do, women have done too. Every day another woman in the United States crashes a formerly male-only profession. Women are becoming truck drivers, railway workers, jockeys, firemen, telephone linemen, executives, politicians and so on.

Yet so long as the stereotypes persist, they will wreak havoc on a person's self-concept. So long as achievement motivation, intelligence, and competitiveness are thought of as exclusively masculine, women with those traits feel less feminine. So long as the desire to be nurturant, emotional, and caring are thought of as exclusively feminine, men with those traits feel less masculine. So long as we think of sex-role traits in polar extremes, people in the middle will feel psychologically pinched. They do not need to be; most of us are in the middle.

That is why current research in psychology and physiology is moving away from the polarized view of male and female to an appreciation of the fact that most of us live with elements of each sex. Physicians used to think that only women had female hormones, and that only men had male hormones; now they realize that both sexes have, in different proportions, estrogen, progesterone, and androgens. Analogously, the concept of androgyny (from *andro*, male, and *gyne*, female) maintains that the traits we define as good, such as independence, gentleness, competence, strength, and sensitivity, should be as desirable for one sex as for the other, and the traits we do not admire, such as sneakiness, passivity, vanity, should be equally disparaged in both sexes. Some people argue that children who grow up thinking that men and women can work in the same jobs and act in the same ways will become confused as to their self-identity, and turn homosexual at worst. Sandra Bem's (1975) work, now on-going, dispels such fears. She is finding that androgynous people are more creative, flexible, and less anxious than either extremely masculine or extremely feminine persons. Bem's ideas offer a more fruitful direction for research than concentrating on sex differences. In psychology, as in biology, there is increasing awareness of sex similarities.

Balzac once commented on his view of liberated women: "A woman who is guided by the head and not by the heart is a social pestilence. She has all the defects of a passionate woman and none of her compensations. She is without pity, without love, without virtue, without sex." The day is coming in psychology and society when we can recognize that it is necessary and desirable that both sexes be guided by the head and the heart.

references

Bardwick, J. M. *Psychology of women.* New York: Harper & Row, 1971.

Bernard, J. *The future of marriage.* New York: World, 1972, Bantam, 1973.

Bernard, J. *The future of motherhood.* New York: Dial, 1974, Penguin, 1975.

Bem, S. Sex-role adaptability: One consequence of psychological androgyny. *Journal of Personality and Social Psychology,* 1975, *31* (4), 634-643.

Crowley, J. E., Levitin, T. E., & Quinn, R. P. Seven deadly half-truths about women. *Psychology Today,* 1973, 6 (10), 94-96.

Gove, W. R., & Tudor, J. F. Adult sex roles and mental illness. *American Journal of Sociology,* 1973, *78* (4), 812-832.

King, A. *In* R. Rosenthal, The Pygmalion effect lives. *Psychology Today,* 1973, *7* (4), 41-46.

Levitin, T. E., Quinn, R. P., & Staines, G. A woman is 58% of a man. *Psychology Today,* March 1973, 6 (10), 89-91. *See* also, The female experience. A special publication of *Psychology Today.* New York: Ziff-Davis, 1973.

Maccoby, E. E., & Jacklin, C. N. *The psychology of sex differences.* Stanford: Stanford University Press, 1975.

Money, J., & Ehrhardt, A. *Man & woman, boy & girl: The differentiation and dimorphism of gender identity from conception to maturity.* Baltimore: Johns Hopkins University Press, 1972.

Paige, K. Women learn to sing the menstrual blues. *Psychology Today,* 1973, *7* (4), 41-46. *See* also, The female experience. A special publication of *Psychology Today.* New York: Ziff-Davis, 1973.

Rosenthal, R., & Jacobson, L. *Pygmalion in the classroom.* New York: Holt, Rinehart & Winston, 1969.

Rubin, J., Provenzano, F., & Luria, Z. The eye of the beholder: Parents' view of sex of new borns. *American Journal of Orthopsychiatry,* 1974, *44* (4).

Serbin, L. A., O'Leary, K. D., Kent, R. N., & Tonick, I. J. A comparison of teacher response to the preacademic and problem behavior of boys and girls. *Child Development,* 1973, *44* 796-804.

Tavris, C. (Ed.). The female experience. A special publication of *Psychology Today.* New York: Ziff-Davis, 1973.

examining the
nature of masculinity

Robert A. Fein _____

American culture has clear ideas about what feelings, actions, and activities are appropriate for males. From his earliest years, a little boy
is presented with images and expectations concerning "masculinity"
and male roles: how a man should feel and behave, how he should relate to women, other men, and children, how he should perform as husband, father, and worker. Nowhere is masculinity defined concretely
for him. Never is he told that if he performs this or that action he will
once and forever become masculine. Rather, masculinity in the United
States is held up as a vague and critical essence for males, something
which must be pursued, fought for, and acquired, a label accorded to
boys and men who "measure up" to standards of toughness, coolness,
and competence.

The pressures to achieve masculinity create problems for men. Pleck
and Sawyer, two of a growing number of men who talk about their experiences growing up under male sex-role pressures, note: "Our
restriction of emotionality compounds the stress put upon us by our
striving to get ahead; we are often unable to acknowledge fully how the
striving makes us feel. We suffer in many ways that may relate to the
strain our emotional denial places upon our physical body. Compared
with women, we die younger, have more heart attacks, and contract
more stress diseases" (Pleck & Sawyer, 1974).

Many males learn early in life that "soft" feelings are not seen as
manly, and in later years do not allow themselves to express tender or
nurturant or gentle or sad feelings. Many men take jobs that do not suit
them, acting with false bravado out of fear of being considered less
than fully manly. Others, working in fields traditionally considered "female," such as nursing or early childhood education, suffer doubts and
opprobrium from crossing sex role boundaries.

Rewards for some men ensconced in traditional male roles have
been great: power, prestige, and wealth. But for many men, the costs of

masculinity are high: male suicides greatly outnumber female. The great majority of persons arrested are male (of the five million persons arrested in 1966, 88 percent were male). Almost all felons in state prisons are male (in 1960, 97 percent). Men are more likely than women to develop almost every major disease. And on the average, women live about 11 years longer than men (Sexton, 1969; Stoll, 1974).

That the problems of masculinity are not restricted to the United States is suggested by a comment from an observer in Sweden: "The stronger demand on the boy/man to assert himself, to push forward, to be hard and aggressive and not to show his feelings, creates problems of adjustment that emerge in a relatively higher rate of criminality, higher mortality, a greater risk of stress and certain symptoms of overstrain, and a higher suicide rate" (Dahlstrom, 1967).

In 1964, McClelland pointed out that psychological *continua* have often been converted into psychological *polarities:* "Women are perceived to be the opposite of men. This is possibly the psychologists' fault because if a judge wants to describe a woman as 'not strong,' he must place a check mark closer to its polar opposite, *weak*. In fact the strong-weak dimension may simply not apply to her at all" (McClelland, 1964). Since masculinity-femininity is seen as a polarity, the slightest chink in the masculine armor is reason for anxiety. For example, Hacker observed, "it was only after several months of counselling that a skilled mechanic developed the courage to dust off some old Caruso records he had stored in the attic, and find that listening to them was no threat to his manhood" (Hacker, 1957).

In recent years a "men's liberation" movement has begun to develop in the United States, as many men question and challenge notions presented to them of what it means to be a man. Accompanying and supporting this movement are attempts to analyze male roles and masculinity (Farrell, 1974; Fasteau, 1974; Harrison, 1974; Levine, 1976; Pleck & Sawyer, 1974; Pleck in press). While it is too soon to tell what effects analyses of masculinity and male roles may have on sex role norms in the United States, interest in the examination of masculinity appears to be growing.

In discussing masculinity and male roles, it is important to distinguish between the feelings and behaviors expected of males and the ways boys and men actually feel and behave. Although limited data on males' life experiences with regard to sex roles exist, currently it is far easier to describe the configurations of roles and expectations presented to males in the United States than it is to speak validly about the ways they respond to these role demands. It is to be hoped that in the next few years researchers will gather data that allow us to better understand the tolls exacted by traditional male roles as well as their benefits.

stereotypes of masculinity

Irene Josselyn has painted an outline of traditional masculine ideals:

Man is physically strong, courageous, objective and unswayed by emotions other than anger; tenderness is permissible only within the framework of husbandry. Personal physical or emotional pain must be born by him with stoicism and without the support of others; meaningful relationships with others can be tolerated only if disguised by superficial social relationships and bravely abandoned without evidence of remorse. *Man* must always be as independent of others as was the lone hunter of the past, caught in a blizzard many miles from his camping site. When *Man* weeps at the new grave of his beloved wife or child, others accept his right to do so but shyly turn away as if to acknowledge that *even Man* can be weak, although he deserves privacy when his strength fails (Josselyn, 1970, p. 86).

This portrait presents several major components of traditional masculinity: 1) suppression of almost all feeling; 2) physical presence and mastery; 3) minimization of the importance of personal relationships. These characteristics may be found in the male stereotypes described by Balswick and Peek: "The cowboy who feels but cannot express his emotions, and the playboy who has no emotions to express." (Balswick & Peek, 1971) These authors suggest that taboos against males recognizing and expressing their feelings ("he manfully held back his tears") are increasingly dysfunctional in a modern society which values the need for companionship at home and at work.

Aberle and Naegele, writing in 1952, described a stereotype of the middle-class male. This man has an occupational position with responsibility and is cool-headed, aggressive, independent, competent, hard-driving, rational, and self-restrained, adjectives frequently used to denote masculinity.

Whether these and other "masculine" characteristics or behaviors accurately describe most men (they probably do not), is not crucial. The key point in discussion of male stereotypes is that these character traits are consistently presented to boys and men as images to aspire to, as ideal types of manhood. When boys are told from their first years that "real" men should be aggressive, or independent, or inexpressive, and/or tough, many spend much of their lives striving and straining to achieve an intangible masculinity, often paying the prices of an undercurrent of anxiety and self-hatred and needless shallowness in their interpersonal relationships.

four major male roles: husband, father, friend, and worker

husband

In the United States men have been seen as the bridges between the occupational world and the family. While most societies, primitive and modern, have developed divisions of labor between males and females (D'Andrade, 1966), the split between home and work in the United States is a product of industrialization in the late nineteenth and twentieth centuries. With the growth of industrialism in the nineteenth century, American men began to leave their work on the family farm for factory and corporate employment. By the mid-twentieth century, men who did not leave their homes for paid employment were part of a small and dwindling minority (Rowe, 1973).

With women tied to hearth and home by biology (methods of birth control were so unreliable that the average woman might have as many as ten to fifteen pregnancies), men assumed a role as family breadwinner. The most popular social science concept used to describe this role is the instrumental-expressive dichotomy developed by Talcott Parsons: "This is to say that externally the husband has the primary adaptive responsibilities, relative to outside situations, and that internally he is in the first instance 'giver of care,' or pleasure, and secondarily the giver of love, whereas the wife is primarily the giver of love and secondarily the giver of care or pleasure" (Parsons & Bales, 1955).

The idea that a man should be instrumental pervades images of husbandhood. According to male stereotypes, a man should be the "head" of the household, responsible for major financial decisions, skilled in minor repair work and in the execution of certain household tasks: mowing the lawn, raking leaves, shovelling the walk. In relationship to his wife, a man should be rational and independent, strong enough for her to cry on his shoulder, strong enough not to burden her with the worries he brings home from the office or factory.

Though masculine stereotypes appear to die slowly, changes in society may have undermined the stereotype of the husband-provider role. In 1974 over 38 percent of the United States labor force was composed of women, with over 40 percent of the husband-wife families having both adults in the labor force. With millions of women bringing home paychecks, the idea that the husband should be the sole family breadwinner is rapidly becoming anachronistic.

At home, prompted and encouraged by the feminist movement, many women are negotiating agreements with their men which cross traditional male-female divisions of household labor. Articles on househusbands have made their way into the popular press (Davidson, 1973; Powledge, 1974), and some social scientists have published critical reviews of the husband-provider role (Gronseth, 1971). Although time-budget data suggests that few men have increased the number of hours they spend on housework and homemaking in relation to their wives' entrance into the paid labor force (Rowe, 1973), it seems likely that many men and women are reassessing the degree to which they want their marriages to conform to traditional husband-wife sex-role stereotypes.

father

Close to but distinct from the role of husband is father, a role currently under active reexamination. Although for years fathers were ignored in both social science and popular literature (English, 1952; Nash, 1955; Howells, 1969), roles for fathers in the United States have been, until recently, relatively well-defined. The traditional father role is as patriarch: distant, severe head of the family, instiller of moral values and self-discipline, distributor of punishment. In the traditional father role, men do not take responsibility for daily infant and young child care. Significant interaction between man and child begins when the child is ready to enter school and is preparing to share the symbols and meaning of the adult world.

In the last twenty years a counterimage to the patriarchal father has emerged and been popularized in American society, an image that probably serves to further confuse actual fathers about their possible roles and responsibilities. While in the traditional view, father is seen as strong and dominant in the family, in the counterimage he is perceived as bumbling, helpless, and ineffectual. The husband, tied to his wife's apron strings, the good-natured, passive, jelly-father appears often in media presentations of the family, particularly on prime-time television comedy shows. Such portrayals as Dagwood Bumstead in the comics and the "Life of Riley" on television during the 1950s, Danny Thomas and Dick Van Dyke in the 1960s, and the popular non-hero of the 1970s, Archie Bunker, have removed fathers from their distant pedestals and depict a comic image. Although in each of these portraits, the man is primary breadwinner and "wearer of the pants" in his family, none of these fathers controls his family in the manner of the stereotypical patriarch. Neither the comic image of "dad" nor the traditional stereotype of "father" portrays man as responsible for the nurturance of his children or as likely to share his emotional inner life with them.

In these stereotyped images of fatherhood, men are instrumental and breadwinners and do not participate in the expressive and nurturant core of life with children, hence there is some confusion about how men should fit in with their families. For example, Hacker noted in 1957, "That father is hard put to find his rightful place in the home is starkly summarized in the comment of the comic strip character, Penny, on the ambiguity of the father role, 'We always try to make Father feel he is part of the family.' "

Stereotypes about father must be examined in the context of limited information about the feelings and behavior of actual fathers. Social scientists do not know how most men experience becoming and being fathers. For example, a search of *Psychological Abstracts* from 1955 to 1959 revealed 202 listings under "mother" and 42 under "father." Of the 42, more than half were either theoretical essays or limited exploratory presentations of clinical material (Layman, 1961). In child development literature, the term "parent" usually has meant mother.

Frequently, when data on fathers was collected, the fathers themselves were ignored. An author of "Father Participation in Infancy" apologized, "It causes me great embarrassment to report that the actual data on fathers' participation was secured by interviewing the mothers" (Pederson & Robson, 1969).

There is some data that suggests that most American fathers spend little time with their young children, especially in feeding, cleaning, and general caretaking tasks (Kotelchuck, 1972; Leibowitz, 1972). A 1961 study on the resistances of working-class fathers treated in a child psychiatric clinic illuminates the inner deals that some fathers make with themselves and with their families that keep them away from their children. The fathers in the study regarded child care as "woman's work" in which they should not be expected to take part. Their role, as they saw it, was to "bring home the bacon." The identity of these men as masculine was "based upon their being able to minimize contact with these feminine concerns and maintain segregated roles."

In the course of treatment, fathers came to realize how they had been excluded from the heart of family life. But when they attempted to shift the balance of caretaking, disturbing the segregation of roles, "the mothers often reacted to the danger by urging the fathers to earn more and to leave the children alone because they were 'nervous' and the fathers did not understand them. The result frequently was that the fathers' involvement with their children became further circumscribed." The study suggests that these parents were so locked into their roles as fathers and mothers, that redefining the roles proved extremely difficult for them, even though the fathers wanted to be closer emotionally to their children (Bell, Treischman, & Vogel, 1961).

Recently several studies have suggested that many men are choosing to become more involved with the care and rearing of their children. For example, Greenberg and Morris (1974) pointed to the phenomenon of "engrossment." Men who were allowed to hold their infants soon after birth seemed to develop emotional bonds with their babies. Another study suggested that some men choose to be deeply involved in pregnancy, labor and delivery, and postpartum infant care, with apparently beneficial effect to themselves, their wives, and their babies (Fein, 1974). Levine interviewed men across the United States who were caring for children and found that stereotypes implying that men can not or ought not to nurture are unnecessary and out of date (Levine, in press).

A comment from Sweden perhaps suggests the direction in which male roles and men's lives in the United States are moving with respect to fathering. Said one man:

Nothing irritates me more than to be praised by well-meaning persons for "helping" my wife look after our children. Patiently, I try to explain that it isn't a question of "lending a hand," and that one could just as well praise my wife for "helping" me. We devote ourselves to the children equally, and cannot possibly find any sensible reason why we shouldn't. To our ears it sounds almost like an insult that anyone should assume that my wife looks after the children alone: as if I were negligent, didn't like my own children, weren't competent, or something equally offensive (Leijon, 1968, p. 37).

friend

Another major male role now receiving scrutiny is "friend." In the words of Ruth Useem, men are taught to be "friendly but not friends" (Useem, 1960). Prevalent masculine stereotypes of men as "pals" and "buddies" to other men imply that many men regularly experience the companionship of other men. Analyses like Tiger's *Men in Groups* (1969) argue that "male bonding" is a universal social fact and note that most societies have developed institutions in which men gather together without women—the men's hut, the men's bar, the locker room. Men in organizations are evaluated on their ability to be a member of the "team" or to get along with others (Whyte, 1956; Fasteau, 1974), and stories are common about men banding together to fight a common enemy (as in community defense or war) or to help a comrade in need (as in painting the home of an injured fellow worker).

At the same time as male sex-role stereotypes promote images of male-male friendship, increasing numbers of men are writing about the loneliness they experience and about their wishes to build closer relationships with other men (Pleck & Sawyer, 1974). They describe pressures that prohibit sharing of deep feelings or intimate experiences with other men and tell about the ways they learned to keep relationships with other men "cool" and superficial. Some men note ways in which sex-role pressures on them to be emotionally close to women inhibit or facilitate their friendships with other men. For example, Michael C. (in Pleck and Sawyer, 1974), writes:

As long as it was just the two of us, two men, we remained distant. We were unable to put out much energy, or attention, or emotion to each other. We were unwilling to expose ourselves in much of a real way. We were unable to put enough of ourselves into an interaction to really feel each other's presence. But then, when the woman was present we both changed our whole way of being. We became involved in what we said. We were committed. I could feel his presence. I could see him much more clearly (p. 76-7).

There are two distinctions in analysis of male-male relationships that may clarify the apparent contradictions between male stereotypes that emphasize friendship, on the one hand, and the alienated and lonely experiences of many men, on the other. First, in terms of both male role stereotypes and male experience, male-male bonds are more likely to be expressed in male groups than in dyads. Images of the "team" and a night out "with the boys" reflect stereotypes of male-male relationships much more often than do images of two men having a long walk together or talking intimately over a meal. That much male-male interaction occures in groups and not in twosomes is discussed and analyzed in Douvan and Adelson's study of adolescence (1966).

Second, as Pleck (1975) suggests, males in the United States are socialized more for sociability than for intimacy. Little boys learn how to get along with others, how to be a member of a team, and not how to build enduring friendships. Much interaction between boys centers on task completion (with competition usually a motivating factor) or on response to common threat. Boys are rarely taught the interpersonal and emotional skills that allow for the gradual unfolding and deepening of emotional ties.

Central to the discomfort that many men experience with regard to their friendships with other men is the prohibition of male-male touching put forth by male role norms and stereotypes. Only at times of crisis or joy or in sports are men permitted to embrace each other without risking pejorative judgments as "queer." Taboos against male-male touching and against homosexuality work to keep men distanced from each other, yet these taboos are increasingly being challenged by both gay and straight males (Weinberg, 1972; Altman, 1973; Pleck & Sawyer, 1974).

Anecdotal evidence suggests that many men are venturing forth into often scary areas of male-male friendship. "Men's groups" have been formed in most areas of the United States and provide opportunities for men to talk with each other about their wishes, hopes, doubts, fears, and needs: topics rarely explored at work or on social occasions (Cottle, 1974). More and more frequently men who have found themselves constrained by the male sex-role norms for "sociability," are challenging barriers to emotional closeness and are exploring what it means to them to share special feelings and experiences with other men.

worker   Male roles and masculine values prescribe that a man should have a paid job. Benson, writing about fathers, commented that a man's "activity as breadwinner has long been established as the chief embodiment of his masculinity: his success in this role is the cornerstone of his self-esteem" (Benson, 1968). Employment is the arena where men compete against each other for society's rewards: riches, status, and power. Employment, as observed by Aberle and Naegele, is distinct from family life: "The occupational world is one of clearly delimited responsibility and authority of judgment of individuals on the basis of what they can do, rather than who they are, of initiative and persistence, usually of competition and a world where aggressiveness—in the layman's sense—pays off" (Aberle & Naegele, 1952).

In masculine values, certain kinds of work are seen as more manly than others. Traditionally, outdoor work and rugged work with the hands have been regarded as highly masculine. This kind of occupation usually involves some element of risk or danger. Nineteenth century images of woodsmen and whalers convey a sense of manliness, while more recently, jobs in highrise construction have symbolized masculine endeavor.

In the past seventy years, as the economy of the United States has grown increasingly organizational, a series of "indoor" masculine work roles has developed. These include work that involves power over others (corporation president), work with major fiscal responsibility (at the Harvard Graduate School of Business Administration, for example, study of "finance" is viewed as high status and as manly), and to some extent, work involving professionalism (lawyer, surgeon, science or social science professor—see Silverstein, 1972).

While men have been barred from relatively few employment areas, masculine values have limited employment opportunities for many males by labeling some jobs as "unmanly." For example, according to the 1973 Economic Report of the President, only 3 percent of all stenographers and secretaries, 3 percent of the registered nurses, 5 percent of the telephone operators, 14 percent of the elementary school teachers, and 18 percent of the librarians were male. Men entering fields seen as traditionally female are not infrequently questioned about their masculinity (if mainly covertly—"I know he wants to work with young children, but really, what's his, you know, orientation?") And since jobs sex-stereotyped for females usually have lower salaries than jobs typed for males, men entering these fields pay a price in both social support and in income.

While the number of jobs in the service sector of the economy continues to grow (Riessman & Gartner, 1974), the male role values work done in the goods sector of the economy. This disparity between changes in numbers of jobs and masculine values seems likely to encourage changes in male roles in the coming years. Work that involves service to others may not continue to be seen as "stripping" a man of his manhood.

As yet, little attention has focussed on analyses of male roles in discussions of "blue collar blues" and "white collar woes." Connections, however, between aspects of work alienation and restrictions imposed by male roles appear to be promising areas for future inquiry. Writing in 1966, Brenton implicitly pointed to relationships between men's employment and their dissatisfactions with male roles: "Many of the men I talked to, business and professional men, as well as men who worked in factories, conveyed the idea that they felt something was missing, something that—although they didn't define it quite so precisely—could be summed up as a lack of primitive contact with life, with themselves."

conclusion   As long ago as 1887, the Swedish dramatist August Strindberg wrote
(in *The Father*):

Yes—I am crying, even though I am a man. But has a man not eyes? Has a man
not hands, limbs, likes, dislikes, passions? Is he not kept alive by the same
nourishment, is he not wounded by the same weapons, is he not warmed by the
same summer, cooled by the same winter as a woman? If you prick us, do we
not bleed—if you tickle us, do we not burst into laughter? If you poison us, do
we not die? Then why should not a man complain, a soldier cry? Because it is
not manly? Why is it not manly? (Strindberg, 1960, p. 39).

Strindberg's passion highlights the intensity which some men are
bringing to the examination of masculinity and male roles. Starting
from the premise that psychological and social development and adult
life are unnecessarily problematic for boys and men because of restrictive notions of masculinity, men (and women) are choosing to scrutinize
previously accepted conventional wisdom about manliness.

In relationships with women, men are negotiating agreements based
on mutual inclination and ability rather than arbitrary sex roles. Some
men are reassessing the nature and quality of their relationships with
children, realizing that sharing their lives with younger generations
matters more to them than traditional male roles indicate. Aware that
they are lonely, some men seek to build friendships with other men, establishing patterns of sharing with other males that hearken back to
their childhoods, or may be entirely new.

In relation to paid employment, unstated but deeply held connections
between holding a job and one's sense of manhood are being examined
by men to see to what extent pressures for masculinity add to the often
already considerable stress they experience in the world of work.

Examinations of masculinity and male roles, as I suggested earlier,
transcend limitations of personal experience. Researchers like Levinson et al. (see article in this volume) try to understand male midlife
changes. The area of male psychological development and socialization
is receiving renewed attention (see articles by Goodstein and Sargent
and by Tavris in this volume). Nonsexist curricula, designed to free
little boys as well as little girls from society's sexism, are making their
way into nursery school, day care, and elementary school classrooms.
Political decision making and public policy are being subjected to analyses that take masculine values and male roles into account (Fasteau,
1974). Even in legal circles, questions of maleness and masculinity are
emerging as major issues (Davidson, Ginsburg, & Kay, 1974).

In the late 1960s, perhaps heralding the future for other advanced
industrial nations, the Swedish government enacted a series of reforms
designed to encourage women to participate equally in employment
outside the home. Sweden taxes each individual's income separately,
thereby keeping a married woman's income in a lower bracket than it

would be in a joint declaration. If a married woman stays home, a special tax is put on her because she is a luxury—she is a "drudge on society" according to the Minister of Family Affairs. The action is designed to recognize, according to Prime Minister Olaf Palme, that all people are "economically independent individuals" (quoted in Herman, 1972). Building on a decision of the early 1960s, the government grants househusbands' insurance, money to pay for men who want to stay home to care for their young children while their wives work outside the home. Sweden is also experimenting with part-time work options for fathers as well as mothers of young children.

Speaking in Washington, D.C., in 1970, Prime Minister Palme articulated the goal of Swedish policy in the sex role area: "The greatest gain of increased equality between the sexes would be, of course, that nobody should be forced into a predetermined role on account of sex, but should be given better possibilities to develop his or her personal talents" (Palme 1970). Examinations of the nature of masculinity and male roles that are beginning or are underway may move society in the United States further toward a desired sex role equality.

references

Aberle, D. F. & Naegele, K. D. Father's occupational role and attitude toward children. *American Journal of Orthopsychiatry*, 1952, *22* (2), 366-378.

Altman, D. *Homosexual*. New York: Avon, 1973.

Balswick, J. O. & Peek, C. W. The inexpressive male: a tragedy of American society. *The Family Coordinator*, 1971, *20* (4), 363-368.

Bell, N., Treischman, A., & Vogel, E. A sociocultural analysis of the resistances of working-class fathers treated in a child psychiatric clinic. *American Journal of Orthopsychiatry*, 1961, *31* (2) 388-405.

Benson, L. *Fatherhood: A sociological perspective*. New York: Random House, 1968.

Brenton, M. *The American male*. New York: Fawcett, 1966.

Cottle, T. Men's consciousness raising groups. *Win*, 1974, *10*, 39.

Dahlstrom, E. (Ed.). *The changing roles of men and women*. London: Duckworth, 1967.

D'Andrade, R. G. Sex differences and cultural institutions. In E. Maccoby (Ed.) *Development of sex differences*. Stanford, Calif.: Stanford Univer. Press, 1966, pp. 174-204.

Davidson, K., Ginsburg, R., & H. Kay. *Sex-based discrimination*. St. Paul, Minn.: West, 1974.

Douvan, E. & Adelson, J. *Adolescent experience*. New York: Wiley, 1966.

English, O. S. The psychological role of the father in the family. *Social Casework*, 1954, *35*, 323-329.

Farrell, W. *The liberated man*. New York: Random House, 1974.

Fasteau, M. *The male machine*. New York: McGraw-Hill, 1974.

Fein, R. *Men's experiences before and after the birth of a first child: Dependence, marital sharing, and anxiety*. Unpublished doctoral dissertation, Harvard University, 1974.

Greenberg, M. & N. Morris. Engrossment: the newborn's impact upon the father. *American Journal of Orthopsychiatry*, 1974, *44* (4), 520-531.

Gronseth, E. The husband provider role: A critical appraisal, *In family issues of employed women.* Leiden, Netherlands: Brill, 1971.

Hartley, R. E. Sex role pressures and the socialization of the male child. *Psychological Reports,* 1959, *5,* 457-468.

Hacker, H. The new burdens of masculinity. *Marriage and Family Living,* 1957, *3,* 227-233.

Harrison, J. *A critical evaluation of research on "Masculinity/Femininity" and a proposal for an alternative paradigm for research on psychological differences and similarities between the sexes.* Unpublished doctoral dissertation, New York Univer., 1975.

Herman, S. R. Sex roles and sexual attitudes in Sweden: the new phase. *The Massachusetts Rev.,* 1972, *13,* 45-64.

Howells, J. G. Fathering. In J. G. Howells (Ed.), *Modern perspectives in international child psychiatry.* Vol. 3. London, 1969. New York: Bruner-Mazel, 1971.

Josselyn, I. M. Sexual identity crises in the life cycle. In G. H. Seward & R. C. Williamson (Eds.), *Sex roles in changing society.* New York: Random House, 1970.

Kotelchuck, M. *The nature of the child's tie to his father.* Unpublished doctoral dissertation, Harvard University, 1972.

Layman, E. H. Discussion: The influence of father in the family setting. *Merrill-Palmer quart.,* 1961, *7* (2) 107-111.

Leibowitz, A. Education and allocation of women's time. Unpublished mimeographed paper, 1972.

Leijon, A. *Swedish women — Swedish men.* Sweden: Swedish Institute, 1968.

Levine, J. *Who will raise the children? New options for fathers (and mothers).* New York: Lippincott, 1976.

Liljestron, R. The Swedish model. In G. H. Seward & R. C. Williamson (Eds.), *Sex roles in changing society.* New York: Random House, 1970.

McClelland, D. C. Wanted: A new self-image for women. In R. J. Lifton (Ed.), *The women in America.* Boston: Houghton Mifflin Co., 1965.

Nash, J. The father in contemporary culture and current psychological literature. *Child development,* 1965, *36,* 261-289.

Palme, O. The emancipation of man. Address before Women's National Democratic Club, Washington, D. C., June 8, 1970.

Parsons, T. & Bales, R. F. *Family, socialization, and interaction process.* Glencoe, Ill.: Free Press, 1955.

Pederson, F. A. & Robson, K. S. Father participation in infancy. *Amer. J. Orthopsychiat.,* 1969, *39* (3), 466-472.

Pleck, J. Is brotherhood possible? In N. Glazer-Malbin, (Ed.), *Old family new family: Interpersonal relationships.* New York: Van Nostrand-Reinhold, 1975.

Pleck, J., R. *Male sex role and personality.* Cambridge, Mass.: M.I.T. Press, in press.

Pleck, J. & Sawyer, J. *Men and Masculinity.* Englewood Cliffs, N.J. Prentice-Hall, 1974.

Powledge, F. Memoirs of a househusband. *Playboy,* Sept., 1974.

Reissman, F. & Gartner, A. *The service society and the consumer vanguard.* New York: Harper & Row, 1974.

Rowe, M. Finding the way to love and to work. Unpublished address, Office of the President, MIT, Cambridge, Mass., 1973.

Sexton, P. C. *The feminized male: Classrooms, white collars, and the decline of maleness.* New York: Random House, 1969.

Silverstein, M. The history of a short, unsuccessful academic career. *Insurgent sociologist, 3,* 1, Fall, 1972. Reprinted in Pleck and Sawyer, 1974.

Stoll, C. *Female & male: Socialization, social roles and social structure.* New York: Brown, 1974.

Strindberg, A. The father. In *Seven plays by August Strindberg.* New York: Bantam, 1960.

Tiger, L. *Men in groups.* New York: Random House, 1969.

Useem, R. Functions of neighboring for the middle class male. *Human Organizations,* 1969, *19,* 68-76.

Weinberg, G. *Society and the healthy homosexual.* New York: St. Martin's Press, 1972.

Whyte, W. H. *Organization man.* Garden City, New York: Anchor Books, 1957.

womanspeak and manspeak: sex differences and sexism in communication, verbal and nonverbal[1]

Nancy Henley

Barrie Thorne

A woman starts to speak but stops when a man begins to talk at the same time; two men find that a simple conversation is escalating into full-scale competition; a junior high girl finds it hard to relate to her schoolbooks, which are phrased in the terminology of a male culture, and refer to people as "men"; a woman finds that when she uses the gestures men use for attention and influence, she is responded to sexually; a female college student from an all-girl high school finds a touch or glance from males in class intimidating.

What is happening? Each sex has its own style of speaking, and each is spoken about in a different way. Male nonverbal communication is distinct from female and it has different effects. Moreover, females and males move in a context of sexual inequality and of strongly differentiated behavioral expectations. Because interaction with others always involves communication of some sort, verbal and nonverbal, it is through this communication that much of our pattern of sexist interaction is learned and perpetuated. Our ideas of how this happens are vague and sometimes misinformed. Do women talk more than men? Contrary to popular opinion, they do not. Is it "natural" for female voices to be high-pitched and to sound less authoritative than male? In actuality, female voices are pitched higher, and male voices lower, than their vocal cords would determine, even as children. Are the generic *he* and the frequent reference to humans in male terms ("mankind," "the common man") innocuous linguistic conventions? Does referring to females as *Ms.* really make any difference? Research has

[1]The research surveyed for this article can not all be cited here; but for those interested, all original sources are listed and described in N. Henley and B. Thorne, *She said/he said: An annotated bibliography of sex differences in language, speech, and nonverbal communication* (Pittsburgh: KNOW, Inc., 1975). This bibliography is also available in B. Thorne and N. Henley (Eds.), *Language and sex: Difference and dominance* (Rowley, Mass.: Newbury House, 1975).

201

shown that sexist language does indeed affect people's reactions.

These are a few examples of questions raised in the study of sexism and sex differences in language. These "trivia" of everyday interaction play an important part in determining the larger structure of our lives; they belong to the micropolitical structure that helps maintain and defend it (Henley, 1973-1974). The social status quo is left unruffled by the patterns of interaction which define and declare a person's status, role, value, and expectations. The minutiae of interaction are the first line of defense for the political and economic system, and they deserve our attention and serious investigation, despite any nagging feelings that they can't possibly affect us.

Most of us are largely unaware of the nuances of expression and gesture that identify and stereotype sex; but recent studies, inspired to a great extent by the resurgence of feminism, now make it possible to examine the nature of male and female communicative interaction and to consider ways to change it if need be. However, most of this research, reflecting the biases of our society, ignores the effects of race and class at the juncture of sex and language, so this survey largely focuses on details of white, middle-class life. We will start by examining sexism and sex differences in verbal communication, for which there is much more information than there is for nonverbal communication.

There are two aspects of language we can examine: how the sexes use language differently, and how language uses the sexes differently (though the two aspects also interact with each other). This latter topic, how the English language treats women—the sexism in our language—is one for which there is growing awareness in all segments of our population. To understand the importance of linguistic sexism, we must understand the important role language plays in influencing our thoughts and acts through naming, defining, describing, and ignoring. Language has been used in the past, and still is, to dehumanize a people into submission—it both reflects and shapes the culture in which it is embedded.

**the sexist bias
of English**

Sexism in the English language takes three main forms: it ignores; it defines; it deprecates.

ignoring

Most of us are familiar with ways in which the language ignores females. The paramount example of this is the so-called generic *he,* that is, the use of the male to refer to human beings in general. We find it in such common terms as *spokesman* and *chairman,* such phrases as "the man for the job," "the man in the street," "the working man," "men of good will," "the black man," and in names for familiar objects such as the "six-man tent" and "two-man boat." Some claim that the pronoun *he* is used so often mainly because of this generic usage, which, it is said, implicitly includes women. But one study (Graham, 1973) of children's schoolbooks found that of 940 uses of the word *he*, 97 percent referred to male human beings, male animals, or male-linked occupations; only 3 percent referred to sex-unspecified persons. In this study, male pronouns outnumbered female ones by about four to one and the mention of men over women was about seven to one. Females are, in short, largely ignored in the world of schoolbooks. Even when the male *is* used generically, its interpretation may not be generic, but biased toward the male (Schneider & Hacker, 1973).

We are taught to use *he* to refer to someone whose sex is unspecified, as in the sentence, "Each entrant should do his best," or "Everyone should now take his seat." We are told that the use of *they* in such a case ("Everyone should now take their seat") is ungrammatical; however, Bodine (1975) has found that prior to the eighteenth century, *they* was widely used in this way. Grammarians who insist that we use *he* to have agreement with the antecedent in number overlook the fact that such usage may entail a lack of agreement in gender. Current grammars condemn *he or she* as clumsy, and the singular they, as in "Who lost their glove?" as inaccurate. "Then," as Bodine writes, "the pupils are taught to achieve both elegance of expression and accuracy by referring to women as *he*!" In fact, the use of *they* to refer to the singular is quite common in everyday conversation, though it is still taboo in formal speech. We can also note that many people who claim they are referring to both males and females when they use the word *he* switch to the feminine pronoun when they begin to speak of someone in a traditionally feminine occupation, such as a homemaker or schoolteacher or nurse.

defining

Language reflects and helps maintain women's secondary status in our society by defining her and her "place." The male power to define through naming is seen in the tradition of woman's losing her own name upon marriage and taking the husband's name; the children of the marriage also have their father's name, showing that they too are his possessions. Seeing females as possessions is further evidenced by the common practice of giving female names and applying female pronouns to possessions such as one's car ("Fill 'er up!"), various machines, ships, and so on.

While men are often referred to in occupational terms, women are more often referred to in relational terms; that is they are named in terms relative to the males who own them. The usual titles of respect for females (*Miss, Mrs.*) denote whether or not they have a sanctified relationship to the male, that is, whether they are a male possession; the title of respect for a male (*Mister*) does not denote anything about his relationship to a female. In the study of children's school books, although references to men outnumbered references to women by seven to one, the frequency of the word *mother* was greater than that of the word *father*, and the word *wife* appeared about three times as often as the word *husband*.

Woman are also defined by the groupings that we put them in: the phrase "women and children" veritably rolls off the tongue. Women are also frequently classified with the infirmed and the incompetent (on women in groupings, see Key, 1972). When grouped with males, females are clearly the second sex. People almost universally mention males first, as in "men and women," "his and hers," "he or she," rather than "women and men," "hers and his," "she and he." The fact that the language generally ignores women means, too, that when it does take note of them it often defines their status. Thus, "lady doctor," "lady judge", "lady professor," "lady pilot," all indicate exceptions to the rule. On the other side of the coin, we have expressions like "male nurse"; however, these are much less common, because many more occupations are typed as male. Even in cases where a particular field is female-typed, males who enter it often have a term of their own, such as *chef* or *couturier*. Such a pattern of usage, of course, subtly reinforces our occupational stereotypes; deeper undertones further reinforce stereotypes around propriety and competency.

deprecating

The deprecation of women in the English language is seen in the connotations and meanings of words applied to male and female things. The very word *virtue* comes from an old root meaning *man*; to be *virtuous* is literally, to be "manly." Different adjectives are applied to the actions or productions of the different sexes: women's work may be referred to as *pretty* or *nice*; men's work will more often have adjectives like *masterful, brilliant*. Words for leadership and power are often derived from terms referring to males, while words referring to females more often connote unpredictability or treachery (as with female names applied to weather phenomena). While words such as *king, prince, lord, father* have all maintained their stately meanings, the similar words *queen, madam*, and *dame* have acquired debased meanings.

A woman's sex is treated as if it is the most salient characteristic of her being; this is not the case for males. This fact is the basis of much of the defining of women, and it underlies much of the deprecation. Sexual insult is overwhelmingly applied to women; one investigator researching terms for sexual promiscuity found 220 terms for a sexually promiscuous woman, and only 22 terms for a sexually promiscuous male. Furthermore, trivialization accompanies many terms applied to females. While male-based terms suggest concerns of importance, like *fraternalism* and *mastermind*, female-related terms tend to refer to unimportant and/or small things, such as *ladyfingers, ladybird, maidenhair fern* (Nilsen, 1973). The feminine endings -ess and

-*ette* are added to many words which are not in actuality male-limited, just as the female prefix "lady" is similarly added. Thus we have the trivialized terms *poetess, authoress, aviatrix, majorette, usherette.* Male sports teams are given names of strength and fearfulness: "Rams," "Bears," "Jets." Women's sport teams often have cute names like "Rayettes," "Rockettes." As Alleen Nilsen (1972) has put it,

The chicken metaphor tells the whole story of a girl's life. In her youth she is a *chick*, then she marries and begins feeling *cooped up*, so she goes to *hen parties* where she *cackles* with her friends. Then she has her *brood* and begins to *hen-peck* her husband. Finally she turns into an *old biddy* (p. 109).

how can we break out of sexist language?

Identifying linquistic sexism is easier than eliminating it. The Women's Movement has already developed or brought into increasing popularity such terms as *Ms., Chairperson,* and *spokesperson,* as well as the use of *he or she* and *her or his,* in place of the generic male pronoun. Several new pronoun systems have been suggested to take the place of "he, him, his" and "she, her, hers." Among them are "co, co, cos," "she, herm, heris," and "tey, tem, ter (s)." While such a dramatic change in our language would require a concerted program of action, it is not completely out of the question. However, for the time being there are a number of changes we can make in our own usage. There is no need to use male terms; if we wish to speak of human beings we can call them human beings rather than *man, mankind,* and so on. We can use both pronouns together, as "she/he," "he or she," or if we find that awkward, we can use *they* as a singular pronoun. Sentences can be reworded in the plural "We all remember our first day at school," rather than "Everybody remembers his first day at school." We can remember to refer to both sexes when we're speaking about *people,* and we can break down some expectations by referring to them in female-male order, rather than vice versa. We can watch ourselves so that we don't refer to women as possessions, relations, or appendages to males, nor as individuals whose sexuality is primary.

sex differences in speech

Sex differences in the use of language are so pervasive that even pre-kindergarten children are apparently aware of them. One researcher found that nursery school children could, on the basis of certain cues from vocabulary and sentence structure, attribute an utterance to a doll of the same sex to whom linguists would attribute the utterance. Before we talk about vocabulary and sentence structure differences, however, it would be helpful to confront two particularly widespread myths about sex differences in language.

myths—do women talk too much?

The first myth is that women speak more and longer than men. This is simply not so. In study after study, men have been found to speak more often and at greater length than women, and to interrupt other speakers more than women do. This finding applies to people in all kinds of social situations—alone, in single-sex or mixed-sex pairs, and in groups. In a laboratory study of married couples, for example, in 52 percent of the cases, the husband did most or more of the talking; for the rest of the couples, the time was either equally divided or the wives did more talking (Kenkel, 1963). Hilpert, Kramer, and Clark (1975) report a study of male-female dyads in which males spoke more than 59 percent of the time. Another study that set up husband-wife discussions found that the husband talked more in 19 cases, and the wives more in 15 cases (Strodtbeck, 1951). In an investigation that used mock jury deliberations, men constituted two-thirds of the juries but they contributed almost four-fifths of the talk (Strodtbeck & Mann, 1956). In a similar study of mock juries, it was found that in all occupational levels, males talked more than females (Strodtbeck, James, & Hawkins, 1957). A different sort of laboratory study, in which individuals were asked to describe a stimulus picture with no time limitations, females took an average of around three minutes, and males averaged 13 minutes—in fact, some of the males talked beyond the half hour that the researcher had of recording tape, and could only be counted as talking a half hour (Swacker, 1975).

Sociologist Jessie Bernard observed (1972) that on TV panel discussions males out-talked females by a considerable margin, and that as a general conversational pattern, women have a harder time getting the floor in groups and are more often interrupted than men. Several other studies have found that males interrupt more than females. The best research in this area, based on conversations of same-sex and mixed sex pairs taped in natural settings, found that 98 percent of the interruptions and 100 percent of the overlaps in conversation were by male speakers (Zimmerman & West, 1975). There is another type of male vocal intrusion on female activity: the voice-overs which appear on TV commercials picturing women doing tasks around the house. A study sponsored by NOW found that about 89 percent of voice-overs in television commercials are male.

how males and females sound

The second myth attributes the high pitch of women's speech to anatomical differences alone. While it is true that there are anatomical differences between males and females that produce a slightly higher pitch in females' voices, the difference is nowhere near so great as to produce the variance that is heard. Recent investigators have concluded that at least some of these differences are learned and constitute a linguistic convention. *Males and females talk at greatly different pitches because that is the requirement of their social role*, a requirement so strong that the differences in pitch outstrip the anatomical differences even in children, before the male voice change of puberty (see Sachs, 1975). There is such a universal expectation that male voices should be low and female voices high that any deviation from this expectation produces a powerful effect on other people's impressions of one's personality. Men with high-pitched voices may be taken for women in phone conversations (and treated accordingly), disregarded in group conversation, and ridiculed behind their backs. But female newscasters with lower pitch are preferred and are hired; since lower pitch is associated with males, who have more authority in our society, it carries more authority in a female also (Hennessee, 1974).

There are other sex differences in speech sounds. For boys in our culture, masculinity and toughness are projected by a slightly nasal speech; girls and "gentlemanly" boys have nonnasal, or oral, speech. Males also speak with greater intensity than females. There are differences in the intonation patterns used by each sex; women have more variable intonations, or more contrastive levels, than men do. Women are said to have more extremes of high and low intonation, and one linguist has proposed that while most men have three contrasting levels of intonation, many women have four such levels. This variability in women's speech sounds is said to produce unsure intonation patterns, ones of whining, questioning, and helplessness. It may also indicate greater emotional expressiveness of a more positive sort.

words and sentences

In the area of vocabulary and sentence structure, many descriptions of sex differences have tended to follow stereotypic conceptions of male and female roles. We should, therefore, look at them quite critically, remembering that many have little, if any, empirical grounding; those that are based on data may be overinterpretive of the findings. One researcher concluded that, in what they talk about, women are synthetic and man analytic; that women are other-oriented, concerned with internal states and integrating others into their world; while men are self-oriented, concerned with action and the projection of themselves into the environment (Barron, 1971). According to other researchers, males used more words implying time, space, quantity and destructive action, while females used more words related to feeling, emotion, and motivation and more self-references, auxiliaries, and negations (Gleser, Gottschalk, & Watkins, 1959). It is clear that such findings, and often the assumptions on which such research is based, reflect obvious sex stereotypes.

Women have often been said to be euphemistic and to "prefer" refined, veiled, and indirect expressions. Of course, linquistic taboos have made such usage more a necessity than a preference. Women are said to have a particular type of "feminine" vocabulary which uses abbreviations, diminutives (such as *hanky, nighty, meanie*) and extravagant adjectives (such as *heavenly, divine*). A number of linguists have attributed to women a greater use of intensifiers like *so, such, vastly, awfully,* and *quite,* and expressions like *goodness, gracious,* and *dear me.* In the absense of linguistic data on the matter, it is impossible to know whether or not these usages exist in real life. But such language is the basis for much ridicule of females in sexist comedy and cartoons and in everyday conversation. The pattern of word choice attributed to female speech connotes triviality, as do the domains of vocabulary that are associated with women (because "women's work" is considered unimportant). Women are more likely than men to have elaborate terminology in the areas of sewing, cooking, child care, and colors. Men's elaborated vocabularies center around such areas as sports, autos, and mechanical things. Several researchers have found terms of hostility to be more associated with men, for example, a greater use of hostile verbs, and a greater use of slang which contains many hostile sexual references.

Lakoff (1973) associates two forms of sentence structure with the uncertainty described in women's speech—the use of the tag question and of requests. A tag question takes the form, "This is the place, isn't it?" rather than an affirmative statement or, "Is this the place?" It is neither a flat statement nor a yes-no question, but allows the speaker to avoid full commitment to the statement. To express similar wishes, men are said to use *commands* while women use *requests*.

We should again recall that the research evidence for all these attributed differences is spotty. There may well be fewer actual differences in the speech of the sexes than our stereotypes would suggest. Kramer (1974) in fact failed to find such differences in written paragraphs obtained from males and females. Obviously, more work and more sophisticated research must be done in this area.

class, sex and propriety

There are, of course, differences in language associated with socio-economic status, as well as those associated with sex, and the two types of difference interact. The prestigious or "proper" form of speech, that associated with high-status persons, involves such niceties as pronouncing the "g" in running, rather than dropping it and saying runnin'; or in pronouncing *th* "correctly" rather than *d, t,* or *f* (e.g., in with); or pronouncing a final consonant cluster (as in strengths) or the *r* that follows a vowel at the end of a word (as in mirror). A number of detailed studies of how people choose among these patterns have found that females tend to use the "proper" form more often than males. This pattern has been found among black and white, young and old, in England and in the U.S., in North Carolina, Detroit, New York, and Chicago. Women's greater use of prestige patterns has been attributed to their insecure social position which has made them more status-conscious, and to males' valuing of "nonstandard" speech because of its association with masculinity (Trudgill, 1972).

conversing

There are differences in the conversational patterns of males and females in addition to the tendency of males to talk more and to interrupt. Again however, most of the differences noted are impressionistic. Jessie Bernard (1972) describes the flavor of the differences in these conversational styles: "Traditionally, the cultural norms for femininity and womanliness have prescribed appreciatively expressive talk or stroking for women . . . they were to raise the status of the other, relieve tension, agree, concur, comply, understand, accept" (p. 137). "Instrumental" talk, more associated with males, orients and conveys information, and may be argumentative and competitive.

In a study of interaction in a mixed sex group, men were observed to make many more jokes than women, while women participated by extensive laughing. Hirschman (1973, 1974) reports the impression that women talking to each other tend to elaborate on each other's utterances, while men in conversation tend to dispute or ignore what the other says. She found that females tended to use the expression "mm-hmm" much more than males did, as a nonobstrusive but supportive utterance.

The tendency to hesitate, to apologize, and to disparage one's own statement are examples of conversational patterns associated with females and with subordinate persons in general. How one person addresses another also reveals their relative status. Higher-status people must be addressed in our society by a title and last name, for example, *Mister* Jackson, *Professor* Smith. Lower-status persons may be addressed by only their first names.

Several linguists and psychologists have observed that women are more readily addressed by their first names than men are, but there are not yet any hard data to support this observation.

self-disclosure
Self-disclosure is another variable that involves language but goes beyond it. Research studies have found that women disclose more personal information to others then men do; subordinates in work situations are also more likely to self-disclose than superiors. People in positions of power do not have to reveal information about themselves, perhaps the ultimate exemplars of this principle being Howard Hughes and the fictional Big Brother. Closer to home we have the example of psychiatrists (usually male) to whom much is disclosed (by their predominantly female clientele), but who classically maintain a reserved and detached attitude, revealing nothing of themselves (Haley, 1962). This is the "cool" of the professional, the executive, the poker player, and the street-wise operator. Smart men, those in power, those who manipulate others keep their cool, maintain an unruffled exterior.

Women who obtain authoritative positions do likewise, but most women have been socialized to display their emotions, their thoughts and ideas. Giving out this information about themselves, especially in a context of inequality, is giving others power over them. Women may not be more emotionally variable than men, but their emotional variability is more visible. This display of emotional variability, like that of variability of intonation, contributes to the stereotype of instability in women. Self-disclosure is not in itself a weakness or negative behavior trait; like other gestures of intimacy, it has positive aspects—such as sharing of oneself and allowing others to open up—when it is voluntary and reciprocal.

topics of conversation

Conversational topics vary with the sexes. An observational study of conversations (Landis & Burtt, 1924) found that among men, business and money were the main topics (49 percent of conversations), with sports and amusements (15 percent), and other men (13 percent) following behind. Among women, men were the largest topic of conversation (22 percent), followed by clothing and decoration (19 percent), and other women (15 percent). This study was made in 1924; one wonders if choice of topics has changed since then.

A study of speech in the classroom in sixth and eleventh grades also found that both male and female teachers talked more about men. Just as men are more often written about, they are more often talked about.

In examining conversation between the sexes, we should note who controls the conversation's direction. Partly because men tend to interrupt and women to support and agree, control of conversational topics generally rests with the men, and women may find it difficult or impossible to initiate a topic when conversing with men.

males as the standard

We should remember that, as in other fields, there has been much study of male speech as the norm and as illustrative of the speech of people in general. Many studies are done on all-male groups without the realization that they are selected samples. When sex differences are found, the clear implication is usually that "women speak differently," not that "men and women speak differently." Anthropological reports of cultures which have sex-differentiated languages have often referred to "women's languages" in the cultures as the deviation, assuming that the "men's language" is *the* language. On the contrary, we must insist whenever this practice arises that women's speech forms are every bit as "standard" as men's.

ability and performance

In the area of language ability, women have often been thought to have the edge. Not only are they said to talk more but their speech is said to be more fluent, to flow more freely (despite their attributed hesitancy and false starts). There is a higher incidence of stuttering and other speech defects among males than among females; this fact has been interpreted both from a social and biological standpoint. (Socially, it may result from greater pressures on males to achieve.) A number of early studies pointed to greater verbal abilities of various sorts among female children, but these studies are currently being called into question. In the area of public speaking, studies have shown women to be superior to men in such areas as vocabulary, sentence structure, and grammar, and less fidgety and better integrated than men. On the other hand, male public speakers have been observed to be less withdrawn, more animated, and to have greater confidence and more useful physical activity.

speech differences — should we change them and how?

What general implications do these speech differences have for male and female interaction patterns? Some women think that female patterns reflect a slave status—the shuffling, insecurity, and "nobodyness" of being a woman. It follows from this line of analysis that in the search for equality women should adopt male speech—drop the politeness and tag questions, the intensifying adverbs and "cutesy" nouns, and use more direct statements, slang and taboo, with lower pitch and less variability in intonation. Indeed, many women already do some or all of these things. Does this mean women should also begin to interrupt, to gain and keep control of conversational topics, talk more and longer, be self-oriented and object-oriented, and engage in competitive and aggressive conversational styles? Obviously there are values attached to this behavior which override those of prestige and status. If women simply adopt male forms, they not only run the risk of losing valued female forms, but they themselves may overvalue maleness in "imitating the oppressor." Males can obviously gain by adopting certain "female" patterns, such as supportive listening, and should be encouraged to, in order to become better, less oppressive conversationalists. Women can benefit from exploring the positive side of their speaking culture, as well as from eliminating those forms which are self-deprecating and self-limiting. To "speak like a man" may command authority and be valued at this time, but we should work towards that time when all speakers will be attended to and valued.

nonverbal communication

Although we are taught to think of communication in terms of spoken and written language, *nonverbal* communication has much more impact on our actions and reactions. One psychological study concluded, on the basis of a laboratory study, that nonverbal messages carry over four times the weight of verbal messages when both are used in interaction (Argyle et. al., 1970). However, since verbal communication is emphasized and taught in our culture, there is much ignorance and confusion surrounding the subtler nonverbal form. This leaves nonverbal communication as a perfect avenue for the unconscious manipulation of others. Nonverbal behavior is of particular importance to women because, for one thing, their socialization to docility and passivity makes them particularly likely targets for this subtle form of social control. Also, their close contact with men, for example as wives and secretaries, entails frequent verbal and nonverbal interaction with those in power. This physical integration with the more powerful is not generally the experience of other subordinate groups (e.g., those whose subordination is defined by class or race). Finally, women have repeatedly been found to be more sensitive than men to nonverbal cues, perhaps because their survival depends upon it. Black people have also been shown to be better than whites at interpreting nonverbal signals.

Analogous to the myth that women's higher vocal pitch is innate is a common belief that much nonverbal communication—gestures, postures, body movement, etc.—are not learned but result from anatomical differences. While there certainly are physical differences between males and females that contribute to differences in their nonverbal behavior, their contribution is miniscule compared to that of learning. A renowned kinesicist has pointed out, that, compared to other animals, human beings do not differ greatly by gender. We are a "weakly dimorphic (two-sexed) species" and therefore organize much of our gender display in such learned behaviors as body positioning and movement (Birdwhistell, 1970).

In addition to communicating gender, body language communicates status and power; it is through this avenue that many gestures of dominance and submission are exchanged. Certain nonverbal behaviors are associated with subordinate position for either sex; and many of these same behaviors are associated with females (Henley, 1973-1974). Because females often occupy subordinate positions in our society, the status aspect and the sex aspect are frequently confounded. If we ask whether women avert their eyes (a gesture of submission) because they're status subordinates or because they're women, the answer might as well be "both": either way, they are powerless.

demeanor Persons of higher status have certain privileges of demeanor that their subordinates do not: the boss can put his feet on the desk and loosen his tie, but the workers must be more careful in their behavior. Also, the boss had better not put *her* feet on the desk; women in general are restricted in their demeanor. Goffman (1956) observed that in hospital staff meetings the doctors (usually male) had the privilege of swearing, changing the topic of conversation, and sitting in undignified positions; they could lounge on the (mostly female) nurses' counter and initiate joking sessions. Attendants and nurses had to be more circumspect in their demeanor. Women, too, are denied privileges of swearing and sitting in undignified positions which are allowed to men, and are explicitly required to be more cautious than men by all standards, including the well-known double one. This requirement of propriety is similar to women's use of more proper speech forms, but the requirement is much more compelling for nonverbal behavior.

Body tension is another sex-differentiated aspect of demeanor. In conversation, communicators are more relaxed with lower-status addressees than with higher status ones, and they are more relaxed with females than with males. Also, males are generally more relaxed than females; females' somewhat tenser postures are said to convey submissive attitudes (Mehrabian, 1972).

use of space

Women's general bodily demeanor must be restrained and restricted; their femininity is gauged, in fact, by how little space they take up, while masculinity is judged by males' expansiveness and the strength of their flamboyant gestures. Males control greater territory and personal space, a property associated with dominance and high status in both human beings and animals. Both observational field studies and laboratory studies have found that people tend to approach females more closely than males, to seat themselves closer to females and otherwise intrude on their territory, and to cut across their paths (Evans & Howard, 1973). One psychologist observed male-female pairs approaching each other on the street and found that generally women moved out of men's way (Silveira, 1972). In the larger aspect of space, women are also less likely to have their own room or other private space in the home.

looking and staring— eye contact

Eye contact is greatly influenced by sex. It has been repeatedly found that in interactions women look more at the other person than men do, and maintain more mutual looking. Some researchers have interpreted this finding in terms of women's traditional orientation toward the social and towards interpersonal relations. However, it has been demonstrated that people maintain more eye contact with those from whom they want approval. Women may depend on this social approval for survival (since they are often economically dependent) and may use this looking to obtain cues from others about the appropriateness of their behavior (Rubin, 1970). Also, it is a common finding that in conversations the listener tends to look at the speaker, while the speaker tends to look away. Since men generally talk more than women, in male-female pairs we would expect women to look at the other more than men do. Other writers have observed that women tend to avert the gaze, especially when stared at by men. Although there has not been research specifically on this pattern, there are several reports supporting the notion that the stare is a dominant and aggressive gesture in human beings, as it is in animals (Exline, 1971). Even if we do not have research evidence that women are more stared at and reciprocate by averting their gaze, we have the overwhelming personal reports of women who are stared at in public. Our language even has specific words—such as *ogling* and *leering*—for this phenomenon. This public staring, along with clothing which is designed to reveal the contours of the body, and public advertising which lavishly flashes women across billboards and through magazines, makes females a highly visible sex. Visual information about women is readily available, just as their personal information is available through greater self-disclosure.

smiling

The smile is women's badge of appeasement. Many feminists have pointed out that women engage in more smiling than men do, whether they are truly happy or not. The smile is a requirement of women's social position and is used as a gesture of submission. Monkeys and apes also smile to indicate submission; the smile is generally thought to signal to an aggressor that the subordinate individual intends no harm. In many women, and other subordinate persons, it has reached the status of a nervous habit. There is a type of smile, the coy smile, attributed to women, which one psychologist claims implies a feeling of subordination on the smiler's part (Nierenberg & Calero, 1971). However, a survey of seven recent books on nonverbal communication (all of them by men), as well as articles reporting research on smiling failed to turn up any statistics on the relative frequency of smiling by males and females.

touching

Touching is another gesture of dominance, and cuddling to the touch is its corresponding gesture of submission. Touching is reportedly used by primates to maintain a dominance order, and it is likely that it is used by human beings in the same way. Just as the boss can put a hand on the worker, the master on the servant, the teacher on the student, the businessman on the secretary, so men more frequently put their hands on women, despite a folk mythology to the contrary. Both questionnaire and observational studies (see Henley, 1973) have found that females are touched by others more than males are, even from the age of six months on. Much of this touching goes unnoticed because it is expected and taken for granted, as when men steer women across the street, through doorways, around a corner, into elevators and so on. The male doctor or lawyer who holds his female client's hand overlong, and the male boss who puts his hand on the female secretary's arm or shoulder when giving her instructions, are easily recognizable examples of such everyday touch from men to women. There is also the more obtrusive touching, the "pawing" by sexually aggressive males and the pinching of waitresses and female factory workers.

Many interpret this pattern of greater touching by males as a reflection of sexual interest, based on a greater level of sexuality among men than women. This explanation, first of all, ignores the fact that touching is a status and dominance signal for other groups, and not just between males and females. It also ignores the findings of sexual research, which give us no reason to expect any greater sexuality in males than in females (see Sherfey, 1966). Rather, there is more freedom in our culture for males to express their sexuality, and they are also accorded more freedom to touch others. Touching carries the connotation of possession when used with objects, and the wholesale touching of women carries the message that women are community property. They are tactually accessible just as they are visually and informationally accessible.

intimacy and status in nonverbal gestures

There is another side to touching, one which is much better understood: touching symbolizes friendship and intimacy. To speak of the power dimension of touching is not to rule out the intimacy dimension. A particular touch may have both components and more, but it is the pattern of touching between two individuals that tells us the most about their relationship. When touching is symmetrical, that is when both parties have equal touch privileges, we have information about the intimacy dimension of the relationship: much touching indicates closeness and little touching indicates distance. When one party is free to touch the other but not vice versa, we have information about the *status* or power dimension: that person with greater touch privileges is of higher status or has more power. (Even when there is mutual touching between two people, it is most likely to be initiated by the higher status person. In a dating relationship it is usually the male who first puts an arm around or begins holding hands with the female.)

There are other gestures which have meaning on both these levels, intimacy and status (Henley, 1973). Staring, intruding on personal space, and loosening of demeanor are all practiced between intimates, and are also privileges accorded more freely to men. When used by women with regard to men, these gestures are likely to be taken as sexual invitation, as is the initiation of touching by women. These are gestures of power and are out of context when used by the powerless. Their interpretation in sexual terms is possible because of the duality of the gestures—in another context they do symbolize intimacy. Furthermore, the attribution of sexual aggressiveness to a woman both compliments the man and disarms the woman, and places her back in her familiar unthreatening role as a sex object (as in "You're so cute when you're mad, baby").

gestures of dominance and submission

We have named several gestures of dominance—invasion of personal space, touching, and staring, and gestures of submission—cuddling to the touch, averting the eyes, and smiling. Pointing may be interpreted as another gesture of dominance, and the corresponding submissive action is to stop talking or to stop action. In conversation, interruption often functions as a gesture of dominance, and allowing interruption signifies submission. There is often mock play between males and females which also carries strong physical overtones of dominance: squeezing too hard, "pretending" to twist the arm, playful lifting and tossing about from man to man, chasing women and picking them up, and spanking them. This type of play is also frequently used to control children and to maintain a status hierarchy among friends of the same sex.

breaking the mold—a first step

Women can reverse these nonverbal interaction patterns with probably greater effect than with deliberate efforts to alter speech patterns. Women can stop smiling unless they are happy, stop lowering their eyes, getting out of men's way on the street, and letting themselves be interrupted. They can stare people in the eye, address someone by first name who has used their first name, be more relaxed in demeanor (when they realize it reflects more on one's status than on one's morality), and touch when they feel it is appropriate. Men can likewise begin to become aware of what they are signifying nonverbally. They can restrain their invasions of personal space, touching (if it is not by mutual consent), and interrupting. They may also benefit by losing their cool and feeling free to display some of their emotions. Males and females who have responsibility for socializing the next generation—that is, parents and teachers particularly—should be especially aware of what they are teaching children in terms of dominance, power, and privilege through nonverbal communication.

Manipulating the *indicators* of power in our society will not be enough in itself to change the fundamental power structure, but it can have profound effects on power relationships. How far these effects can reach we have no way of knowing at this point. At the very least, the knowledge of how we are affected by these patterns gives us the tools to resist them, tools that women can put to use in gaining control over their lives and creating new structures. We have no doubt that someday the language of a free and equal society will shed its vestiges of patriarchy and express its speakers' ideas and emotions directly and without nuances of inferiority.

references

Argyle, M., Salter, V., Nicholson, H., Williams, M., & Burgess, P. The communication of inferior and superior attitudes by verbal and nonverbal signals. *British Journal of Social and Clinical psychology*, 1970, *9*, 222-231.

Barron, N. Sex-typed language: The production of grammatical cases. *Acta Sociologica*, 1971, *14*, 24-72.

Bernard, J. *The sex game.* New York: Atheneum, 1972.

Birdwhistell, R. Masculinity and femininity as display. In *Kinesics and context.* Philadelphia University of Penn. Press, 1970.

Bodine, A. Androcentrism in prescriptive grammar: Singular "they," sex-indefinite "he," and "he or she." *Language in Society*, 1975, *4*, 129-146.

Evans, G. W., & Howard, R. B. Personal space. *Psychological Bulletin*, 1973, *80*, 334-344.

Exline, R. V. Visual interaction: The glances of power and preference. In J. K. Cole (Ed.), *Nebraska symposium on motivation, 1971.* Lincoln, Neb.: University of Nebraska Press, 1971.

Gleser, G. C., Gottschalk, L. A., & Watkins, J. The relationship of sex and intelligence to choice of words: A normative study of verbal behavior. *Journal of Clinical Psychol,* 1959, *15,* 182-191.

Goffman, E. The nature of deference and demeanor. *American Anthropologist,* 1956, *58,* 473-502. Reprinted in E. Goffman. *Interaction ritual.* New York: Anchor, 1967.

Graham, A. The making of a nonsexist dictionary. *Ms.,* Dec., 1973, *2,* 12-16. Reprinted in B. Thorne & N. Henley (Eds.), *Language and sex: Difference and dominance.* Rowley, Mass.: Newbury House, 1975.

Haley, J. The art of psychoanalysis. In S. I. Hayakawa (Ed.), *The use and misuse of language.* Greenwich, Conn.: Fawcett, 1962. pp. 207-218.

Henley, N. Power, sex, and nonverbal communication. *Berkeley Journal of Sociology,* 1973-1974, *18,* 1-26. Reprinted in B. Thorne & N. Henley (Eds.), *Language and sex: Difference and dominance.* Rowley, Mass.: Newbury House, 1975.

Henley, N. (1973). Status and sex: Some touching observations. *Bulletin of the Psychonomic Society,* 1973, *2,* 91-93.

Hennessee, J. Some news is good news. *Ms.,* July, 1974, *3,* 25-29.

Hilpert, F., Kramer, C., & Clark, R. A. Participants' perceptions of self and partner in mixed-sex dyads. *Central States Speech Journal,* Spring, 1975, *26,* 52-56.

Hirschman, L. Female-male differences in conversational interaction. Paper presented at Linguistic Society of America, San Diego, Calif., December, 1973.

Hirschman, L. Analysis of supportive and assertive behavior in conversations. Paper presented at Linguistic Society of America, Amherst, Mass., July, 1974.

Kenkel, W. F. Observational studies of husband-wife interaction in family decision-making. In M. Sussmen (Ed.), *Sourcebook in marriage and the family.* Boston: Houghton Mifflin, 1963.

Key, M. R. Linguistic behavior of male and female. *Linguistics,* Aug. 15, 1972, *88,* 15-31.

Kramer, C. Folklinguistics. *Psychology Today,* June, 1974, *8,* 82-85.

Lakoff, R. Language and woman's place. *Language in Society,* 1973, *2,* 45-79.

Landis, M. & Burtt, H. A study of conversations. *Journal of Comparative Psychol.,* 1924, *4,* 81-89.

Mehrabian, A. *Nonverbal communication.* Chicago: Aldine-Atherton, 1972.

Nierenberg, G. I., & Calero, H. H. *How to read a person like a book.* New York: Hawthorn, 1971.

Nilsen, A. P. Sexism in English: A feminist view. In N. Hoffman, C. Secor, & A. Tinsley (Eds.), *Female studies VI.* Old Westbury, N. Y.: The Feminist Press, 1972.

Nilsen, A. P. The correlation between gender and other semantic features in American English. Paper presented at Linguistic Society of America, San Diego, Calif., December, 1973.

Rubin, Z. Measurement of romantic love. *Journal of Personality and Social Psychol.,* 1970, *16,* 265-273.

Sachs, J. Cues to the identification of sex in children's speech. In B. Thorne & N. Henley (Eds.), *Language and sex: Difference and dominance.* Rowley, Mass.: Newbury House, 1975.

Schneider, J. W. & Hacker, S. L. Sex role imagery and the use of the generic 'man' in introductory texts. *American Sociologist,* 1973, *8* (8), 12-18.

Sherfey, M. J. The evolution and nature of female sexuality in relation to psychoanalytic theory. *Journal of the American Psychoanalytic Association,* 1966, *14,* 28-128.

Silveira, J. Thoughts on the politics of touch. *Women's Press* (Eugene, Ore.), 1972, *1* (13), 13.

Strodtbeck, F. L. Husband-wife interaction over revealed differences. *American Sociological Review,* 1951, *16,* 468-473.

Strodtbeck, F. L., James, R. M., & Hawkins, C. Social status in jury deliberations. *American Sociological Review,* 1957, *22,* 713-719.

Strodtbeck, F. L. & Mann, R. D. Sex role differentiation in jury deliberations. *Sociometry,* 1956, *19,* 3-11.

Swacker, M. The sex of the speaker as a sociolinguistic variable. In B. Thorne & N. Henley (Eds.), *Language and sex: Difference and dominance.* Rowley, Mass.: Newbury House, 1975.

Trudgill, P. Sex, covert prestige, and linguistic change in the urban British English of Norwich. *Language in Society,* 1972, *1,* 179-195. Reprinted in B. Thorne & N. Henley (Eds.), *Language and sex: Difference and dominance.* Rowley, Mass.: Newbury House, 1972.

Zimmerman, D. H. & West, C. Sex roles, interruptions and silences in conversation. In B. Thorne & N. Henley (Eds.) *Language and sex: Difference and dominance.* Rowley, Mass.: Newbury House, 1975.

sexual identity:
an unknown

Elizabeth Wales

"How do you think of your sexual identity?" When asked such a question, men and women usually react with puzzled looks and blank stares. The fact is we seldom think about our sexuality as a part of our self-identity. Too often our sexuality simply tags along with other aspects of our conditioning to the sex roles of men or women. Today many men and women are re-examining and rejecting some of the assumptions and behaviors that are assigned to them solely on the basis of gender. However, the area of sexuality is frequently neglected in the re-examination.

One reason why sexuality has been overlooked as part of self-identity is that in the past sexuality was assumed to follow rigidly sex-role identity. This is not to say that in the past people never deviated sexually from what was considered appropriate for their sex role. Rather, the deviation happened so often society developed ways of coping with it without examining its meaning. When behavior was expressed that was at variance with what was considered appropriate to their sex roles, people either 1) ignored the incongruence, which allowed for a good deal of hypocrisy around sexual behavior, 2) disowned the behavior, (i.e. "I must have been stoned/drunk"), or 3) believed their behavior to be deviant or sick and kept it to themselves in shamed silence.

Our society has assigned overt, publicly sanctioned sexual behavior to male and female sex roles. More insidiously, people's idealized concepts of masculinity and femininity affect the way they express their sexuality. Now, however, the very concept of appropriate and inappropriate sex-role behaviors is being challenged, and sexuality must be considered for itself. To be fully aware, independent, and responsible sexual beings, people need help to sort through the implications sex-role stereotypes have had on sexuality. The Dutch philosopher Hendrik Ruitenbeek has said, "The integration of his or her sexuality into a person's identity cannot be restricted to preconceived notions about what sexuality constitutes."

some effects of sex-role stereotypes on sexuality

It is generally agreed that our society has a puritanical, commercial preoccupation with sex (Slater, 1971; Fromm, 1963). This attitude is supported by and in turn supports our traditional sex-role stereotypes. Myron Brenton in his book *The American Male* discusses at length the dilemma men face today in trying to reconcile the traditional masculine image with contemporary values. He describes the masculine image in part as the provider, the protector, and the possessor, as well as "sexually virile and attentive . . . making love freely and spontaneously . . . the dominant figure in sexual relationships." An unverbalized but important aspect of this masculine ideal is physical bigness, with which many other positive characteristics are associated. This emphasis on a physical characteristic, over which no one has voluntary control, not only can make life miserable for short men, but frequently is a prime determinant in male/female relationships. Regardless of the given height of any one man, it is unusual for him to relate romantically to a woman who is taller than himself. Movies, television, or advertisements never show a tall woman with a shorter man except for comic effect. Being shorter than a woman may in no way effect how a man feels about her, but it can affect how he feels about his own masculinity. In turn, how a man feels about his own masculinity is important in any romantic or sexual relationship. Women also, often participate in emphasizing the importance of physical size for sexual functioning. Being smaller than a man makes some women claim to feel more feminine. Sadly many strategies may be employed to emphasize that valuable difference in height, such as low heeled shoes and flat hair styles.

This emphasis on size also facilitates anxiousness about penis size. The range of variability in penis size is less than the variability in size in any other member of the human body, such as torso, arms, or legs (Ford & Beech, 1951); yet the anxiety with which the comparisons are made is worthy only of something that has profound effect on either self-concept and/or functioning. In the case of penis size it is obvious that the concern has to do with self-concept rather than functioning. Despite the oft-repeated maxim that it is not how much you have, but what you do with what you have that counts, a man can remain unreassured. In a group discussing sexuality one man shared his continuing concern about the size of his penis. He was fearful about his adequacy, despite the fact that his penis functioned normally and none of his partners had ever commented on its size nor complained of any lack of satisfaction or pleasure.

Another aspect of our societal masculine ideal has to do with sexual confidence and assertiveness, that is, being "cool," "smooth," "bad."

This promotes the concept of the stud, always ready, always looking, and willing to "hit on" anything that moves. Although admittedly exaggerated, some part of that concept is present in most men's own desired masculine image. For example, in one group a man shared his increasing concern over his sexual adequacy. He and his wife had a marital agreement that included outside sexual relationships. As a result he was involved in a relationship with another woman whom he admired and cared for a great deal. Circumstances were such, however, that they could meet only once a week. His concern about himself arose when he found himself frequently impotent in these encounters. As he explored his feelings about the situation, he stated that a real man, given such limited opportunity, would hardly be able to wait for the time to come each week when he could begin sexual activity. He was ashamed of the fact (and didn't want to admit to the woman) that he often did not want sex at all, but preferred simply to talk and enjoy her company.

After further discussion he revealed that for him, sexual desire often arose as a consequence of sharing and talking which established warmth and intimacy, another fact that he considered unmasculine. His honesty allowed other men in the group to admit to having similar feelings on occasions. They too, were afraid these were unusual feelings, representing some sort of inadequacy. Because of that discussion, the man was able to realize consciously what standards he was comparing himself against and was able to accept his own feelings and desires as legitimately masculine. He later reported his impotency disappeared.

Women are no better off in this regard than men. Masters and Johnson (1970) recognized the cultural role of women as a major cause of female sexual dysfunction. They state, "Socio-cultural influence more often than not places women in a position in which she must adapt, sublimate, inhibit or even distort her natural capacity to function sexually in order to fulfill her genetically assigned role. *Herein lies a major source of woman's sexual dysfunction.*" (Italics theirs). Just as boys are trained to the masculine ideal, girls are trained to the feminine ideal, to be clean, neat, passive, and pleasant. An important, but unverbalized aspect of this feminine ideal has to do with romanticism. Basic physical sexuality does not fit with the feminine stereotype, but romanticism does. It fits comfortably in our minds to think of a woman being in love, but is slightly shocking to think of a woman being horny. As a result girls are taught both overtly and covertly to sublimate their sexuality into romanticism. From fairy tales through *True Confessions*, girls are fed a steady diet of romance as a model. Romanticism focuses on attraction and courtship rather than consummation. It is clean and pretty and more appropriate to the feminine image than sweaty, lusty sex.

Romanticism, with its emphasis on attraction and courtship, reinforces the undue stress given to female physical beauty. Certainly attracting a man and obtaining a marriage partner are heavily influenced by attractiveness. But our society generally values women in accordance with the degree of attractiveness they possess as determined by the standards set by Hollywood and *Playboy*. It has been well documented that attractiveness influences hiring and promotion even in skilled professions (Wiback, Dipboye, & Fromkin, 1973; Seidenberg, 1973). Unfortunately many women, observing the value and attentiveness paid to physical beauty, equate the ability to lure or attract with sexuality, an erroneous assumption that leads to a preoccupation with surface signals.

The passive and pleasant aspects of the feminine ideal lead many women to fake orgasm. The orgasm is staged to please their mates, to assure them that everything is fine, even though it is not. Many women feel that to admit they have not had an orgasm implies something wrong with them. So to keep their partners happy and cover up their inadequacy, they fake it. It is difficult for women to feel that meeting their own sexual needs is important enough to warrant making a fuss. "It takes me so long," they say, or "He will get tired or bored." Obviously such a woman believes that a man's feelings and pleasure are more important than hers. It seems easier to do one's duty and fake an orgasm, than to work for a truly reciprocal relationship in which both partners' needs are valued enough to make the effort required for satisfaction. The idea that a woman's sexual needs are negligible and that passive sexual acceptance is her duty to her mate is still so prevalent that, as Kaplan (1974) points out, if a woman complains of being nonorgasmic to her doctor or clergyman, it is not uncommon for her to be reassured by those male authorities that such a state is perfectly normal and that she should relax and not worry about it.

Sadly, many women have been known to state proudly that they feel like a woman only when a man is around. Certainly the presence of a man may enhance or heighten feelings of femininity, but a woman who feels neuter without the stimulation of the opposite sex bears an uncomfortable resemblance to a wind-up toy. A man is necessary to make such a woman feel sexual. Sexuality is not a part of herself that surges and ebbs like anger, boredom, love, or curiosity. It lies dormant and quiescent until a man releases it. To feel sexual when she is by herself is often embarrassing to a woman or considered a sign of pathology (being over-sexed). The inability of some women to see themselves as appropriately having sexual feelings and desires other than those resulting from male initiation makes it difficult for them to be the initiators of the sex act. Women who during the sex act are quite active and creative partners can still find it difficult to be the instigator of explicit sexual activity. To be the instigator and therefore risk rejection is difficult for both males and females, but it is, according to societal roles, particularly demeaning for a woman. After all, if we believe that males are always ready for sex, for a woman to be turned down can make her feel that there is something wrong with her. When a man is turned down, he is more likely to assume there is something wrong with the woman.

The common pattern of taking contraceptive precautions further reflects women's tendency to place responsibility for their own sexuality on men. Many men carry a condom in their wallets or brief-cases routinely, "just in case," regardless of whether or not they are having sexual relations with anyone. Such behavior is perfectly appropriate to the stud image. Some women, on the other hand, are uncomfortable about using a contraceptive until they are in a committed relationship. The number of unwanted pregnancies despite multiple and easily available forms of contraception testifies to how abhorrent such a thought is to many women. "It makes it all so cold-blooded," they say, or "It makes me look so eager," or "What kind of woman will he think I am?" This type of woman prefers the sexual encounter as spontaneous, which certainly fits the feminine ideal, but also makes the man responsible for filling her with uncontrollable passion. The issue is complicated because, to date, women's choices about forms of contraception have been limited and require a difficult decision.

The lack of feelings for their own sexuality, the lack of valuing their sexuality for its own sake and their own pleasure, leads many women to regard sex as something they "give" to men. Rather than being able to feel that the sex act is something they give to themselves, they focus on their sexuality as only valued by a man. Such an attitude is exemplified by a wife who complains that her husband expects her to make love after they have had a fight. "How can he," she says indignantly, "expect me to make love after treating me like that." If a woman can appreciate the comfort and pleasure to be obtained from the sex act per se—in other words, can enjoy the sex act for itself—the act is not only possible but often goes a long way towards easing the distress she feels from the argument. Implicit in the wife's feeling of indignation is the attitude that her husband not expect to get pleasure from her while she is upset. Surely it is possible for a woman to feel that *she* deserves some physical pleasure because she has been upset. Schwab (1974) says, "When this attitude is taken to an extreme, women truly regard their sexuality as a commodity which they barter with their mates to obtain services or reward good behavior" (p. 146). Regrettably, for a woman to use her sexuality as a commodity is an inherent consequence of what society has taught women regarding their sexual function. It is inherent in the notion that a woman needs to decide whether or not she should "give" herself to the man.

Since all of us, male and female alike, are brought up in the same culture with exposure to the same stereotypes, we are not only aware of the behavior expected from us, but from the opposite sex as well, As a result, a form of collusion takes place that reinforces the old traditional behaviors and makes it more difficult to change to new behaviors. One of the most striking examples of the reciprocal effects of expected sexual behavior was seen in a young man from South America who was briefly studying in this country. Like many Latin Americans he came from an area where the double standard was culturally institutionalized. Whorehouses were more like men's clubs, where it was respectable and expected for men to gather to drink, socialize, and enjoy themselves. "Good" girls came from respectable families, were well educated, well dressed, and also rigidly supervised. Men met with them only on formal occasions and under careful chaperonage. When he came to this country the South American student found himself consistently impotent. The problem was that he could not decide if the American women he met were "good" or "bad" girls. They were well educated, well dressed, and came from respectable families like good girls; yet they drank, associated with men and enjoyed themselves without supervision like bad girls. Not being able to decide which sexual behavior.pattern was appropriate, he found himself literally immobilized.

Similar problems are experienced by others. Ginsberg, Frosch, and Shapiro, at New York University School of Medicine, have reported (1972) a dysfunction which they term "the new impotence," where complaints of impotency are increasing in young men in their sexual prime. Investigation of the phenomenon revealed that these men were under pressure from their liberated sexual partners, who actively sought and expected orgasmic release. The authors state, "By breaking the former ecologic balance in society, a disequalibrium has been created, leaving its mark on the male partners of these new women."

Given the interrelatedness of males and females in sexual activity, change in one must produce change in the other. Therefore, when one partner's activity is at variance with traditional expectations, a disturbance may be created in the partner of the opposite sex. For example, men who reject the stud image and follow their own inclinations to be less assertive and active may find traditional, female partners turned off and regarding them as less than men. Likewise, women who follow their own inclinations may find traditional partners impotent and regarding them as truly castrating women.

Arbitrary sex-role stereotyping and the accompanying assumptions about appropriate sexual behavior are detrimental to both sexes, limiting the range of expressiveness, the depth of intimacy, and enjoyment that is possible for both men and women. The unconscious assimilation of these stereotyped expectations has imposed narrowness and inhibitions on our own sexuality. To change this requires both an awareness of the effect of culture on our sexual attitudes and behaviors and an effort to get in touch with our own sexual preferences and needs.

**developing
a personal
sexual
identity**

Sexuality and sensuality are body-based. This statement may seem simpleminded, but ignoring this truth leads to much of the distortion of our personal sexual experiences. As a general rule, men can increase their total sexual experience and enjoyment by becoming more sensual. And generally, women can increase their total sexual experience and pleasure by becoming more sexual. In other words, many men need to become more diffuse in their sexuality and women need to become more focused.

Men, in keeping with the traditional masculine image, tend to focus too narrowly on orgasm; they equate orgasm with the meaning of the whole sexual experience. "Scoring" is an example of language that reflects this preoccupation. The intensity of focus on the end point of the sexual act causes other aspects of the sexual experience to be neglected, overlooked, or valued less. "Fore" play becomes just that, a prelude for the main event. This attitude makes the sex act a highly goal-directed activity. An appreciation of the simple pleasures of non goal-directed sensuality broadens the whole sexual experience, both in sensation and in meaning.

Women, in keeping with the traditional feminine image, tend to stay too diffuse and are more aroused by romance than sex. A man once complained that the only time his wife really felt sexually excited was when they dressed up and went out for dinner with wine, candlelight, and elegant service. Unfortunately, many women are more turned on to mood and atmosphere than they are to physical stimulation. An increased ability to attend to and enjoy the purely physical sensations attached to sexual activity would broaden the sexual experience for them.

For different reasons then, both men and women need to open themselves up to experiencing physical stimulation. We may be unaware that we are preventing ourselves from experiencing various sensations. Consider, for example, the fact that our bodies are constantly bombarded by tactile stimulation. The clothes we wear have texture and move against our skin. Various parts of our bodies are exposed to different temperatures; furniture or other bodies press against us accidentally. We manage all this stimulation by ignoring it. We know there is no "message" in this type of stimulation, so we turn off these incoming physical stimuli by attending to what we consider important.

Men often masturbate and pay attention to the pleasurable and erotic feelings associated with the genitalia. This is obviously a conscious sexual activity with a clear end point, and it usually is appreciated and interpreted as such. On the other hand, men seldom pay attention to the erotic or pleasurable aspects of general body manipulation. Even when the body is stimulated, the sensations are ignored or interpreted as relating to cleanliness (a quick shower), health (a massage), or sports (bodily contact), The failure of some men to appreciate these sensations as sensual/sexual reinforces their attitude that orgasm is the sole end of sex. This in turn prescribes further behavior which validates their original attitude. Thus, a vicious cycle is created.

In contrast women often appreciate the sensuous luxury of long baths and the use of oils, perfumes, and powders applied to the body; but in keeping with their training, they frequently deny to themselves the sexuality inherent in such pleasure. Because of the emphasis on feminine physical beauty, most of these activities are viewed as efforts to improve or maintain attractiveness. In their efforts to mold themselves into the American stereotype of attractiveness, some women may become preoccupied with their bodies as if they were products to be improved for greatest marketability; and in this process they may lose the sense of their bodies as being a source of pleasure for themselves. Conversely, some women avoid such pleasurable grooming activities to demonstrate their superiority to such concerns. Either way, the ability to appreciate, value, and cherish the body as a source of sexual pleasure is diminished.

references

Barclay, A. M. Sexual fantasies in men and women. *Medical Aspects of Human Sexuality*, 1973, *567*(5), 205-216.

Brenton, M. *The American male*. Greenwich, Conn.: Fawcett, 1970.

Deutsch, N. *The psychology of women*. New York: Grune & Stratton, 1944.

Ford, C. S., & Beech, F. A. *Patterns of sexual behavior*. Harpers & Brothers, 1951.

Fromm, E. *The art of loving*. New York: Bantam, 1963.

Ginsberg, G., Frosch, W. A., & Shapiro, T. The new impotence. *Archives of General Psychiatry*, 1972, *26*, 218-220.

Hollender, M. H. Women's fanfasies during sexual intercourse. *Archives of General Psychiatry*, 1963, *8*, 86-90.

Honney, K. *Feminine psychology*. New York: Norton, 1967.

Kaplan, H. S. *The new sex therapy*. New York: Brunner-Mazel, 1974.

Masters, W. H., & Johnson, V. E. *Human sexual inadequacy*. Boston: Little, Brown, 1970.

Otto, H. A. The new sexuality: An introduction. In H. A. Otto (Ed.), *The new sexuality*. Palo Alto, Calif.: Science & Behavior Books, 1971.

Reich, W. *The discovery of the orgon: The function of the orgasm*. New York: Noonday, 1942.

Reik, T. *Of love and lust: On the psychoanalysis of romantic and sexual emotions*. New York: Farrar, Straus & Cudahy, 1957.

Ruitenbeck, H. *Sexuality and identity*. New York: Dell, 1971.

Schwab, J. J. The difficulties of being wife, mistress and mother. *Medical Aspects of Human Sexuality*, 1974, *8*(5), 146.

Seidenberg, R. Psycho-sexual adjustment of the unattractive woman. *Medical Aspects of Human Sexuality*, 1973, *7*(5), 60.

Shainess, N., & Greenwald, H. Debate: Are fantasies during sexual relations a sign of difficulty? *Sexual Behavior*, 1971, *1*(2) 38-54.

Slater, P. *The pursuit of loneliness*. Boston: Beacon, 1970.

Sullivan, P. R. What is the role of fantasy in sex? *Medical Aspects of Human Sexuality*, 1969, *3*, 79-89.

Wiback K., Dipboye, R. F., & Fromkin, H. *Experimental studies of discrimination in the evaluation of job applicants' resumes: 1. Relative importance of sex, attractiveness, and scholastic standing.* Paper no. 430, Institute for Research in the Behavioral, Economic and Management Sciences, November, 1973. Purdue University, West Lafayette, Indiana.

the competitive male as loser

R. C. Townsend

In trying to come to terms with ourselves, all of us think back to moments in the past that separately and cumulatively helped make us what we are. "Each of us," the poet Wordsworth writes, "is a memory unto himself." Though we know that out of an almost infinite number of recollections we select only a few, those few we dwell on as if they would yield the answers, the explanations we are looking for.

Four months ago I separated from my wife. I have not the distance, nor the novelist's or analyst's talent to discover and set down in clear sentences why our relationship failed, but I can look into myself, look into my own past and ask what it was that might explain *my* failure in the relationship. What I want to explore is how my experience over the years with men and women, boys and girls, shaped my expectations and behavior in what should be the culmination of a male-female relationship—a marriage. Only in the negative sense was it a culmination for me. What was distorting and stultifying in moments and situations in my early life bore sour fruit in my marriage. Looking at some of those moments and situations may help me understand why I failed, why my relations with my wife were not open, vital, life-affirming.

I am an only child, yet more—as an only child I was set off against the children of my parents' previous marriages. I had come late—my mother was thirty-seven, my father fourty-five—but I would still make up for the failures of previous marriages. (And as if it might help my imposed cause, as if it were worth another year's delay even at so late a date, my parents gave up smoking and drinking for a year before conceiving me.) I saw very little of my father's children, but I sensed even from that limited contact the kind of load my parents would have children bear. One brother I met only once but to me he lives most sharply in a letter he wrote my mother when our father died. Since he was the only one of all the children who didn't go to college, and only held the position of head of a car agency in Kansas, he took the occasion to express condolences, but mostly to apologise for having been a disappointment to my father all his life. My mother's children—a boy thirteen, and a girl eleven at the time of my birth—lived with us. Of all my half-siblings I came to know my sister best. The men were to succeed (and all, even the car agent, succeeded); whether the women succeeded or not was not important. My father's daughter made it through medical school, became the mother of six children, and never practiced. My mother's daughter lived with us and suffered continually in unfair comparisons with me. She was sick and didn't go to the good college where she was accepted. She stayed at home instead, tried commuting to school, until, at age twenty-five, she escaped into a marriage that eventually failed. If she played the radio and I was having trouble getting to sleep, I could call out in complaint and my parents would see to it that the radio went off. If she wanted to sleep late and mother wanted her up, I could go into her room, whack her sleeping head with a pillow, and get off scot free.

First vague memories are seemingly unrelated to my own marriage, but they are indicative of the atmosphere in which I—a boy and an only child—was first groomed for success. And being groomed for success can, I think, deprive one of the natural ability to give in a relationship. Out for oneself, one doesn't give; fearing failure, loath to admit to failure, one cannot receive. The memories that crowd upon me are of striving to succeed and of doing so in an atmosphere that was consequently lacking in opportunities to give, to fail, to take, to experience the mutual love in which a marriage must be grounded.

I was to vindicate my parents and I was to do so most obviously in school, that place, as Jules Henry points out, where the young are prepared to meet the tests of survival in competitive America. I was an exemplary boy around the house, my mother claimed, and my father said that his colleagues envied his having a son who called him "Sir," but in school my model behavior could be most widely appreciated. My two memories of nursery school are of figuring out that if I got up more slowly than my teacher as we sat around in a circle I could manage to look up her dress, and of my playing the west wind in a play. The first may suggest a precociousness that bears on my subject, but the second brings back images of running back and forth on stage going "Whoosh." For neither talent, but for some reason, I was put ahead a grade, and there began nine years of my being much the youngest, often the smallest, usually the best gradegetter in my class. I can only assume—as I assume in similar circumstances when I see them now—that what was at issue was not my superior intellect and the school's ability to spot and foster it but my parents' desire to have me singled out.

My parents were motivated not only by their marital history but also by living in wealthy New York suburbs. It was in Rye, New York that I was catapaulted into first grade; it was in Fairfield, Connecticut that I finished my elementary school education, in the Country Day Schools of both towns. The Depression figured prominently in the little of my parents' conversation that I heard. My father spoke of how a corrupt partner left him to pay off thousands of dollars worth of debts; he could always stun me with the story of how he knew the Depression had come when, sitting in a Wall Street office, he saw a body on its way to death below. More immediately, I knew that we rented a house for one hundred dollars a month in Fairfield; whereas my classmates owned their own houses, more than likely, swimming pools, and, in the case of an heir to the Reynolds tobacco fortune, a bowling alley. My mother might brag that when a friend of mine came for the night we used to fight for the honor of sleeping on the floor, but what I knew was that my friends very seldom came for the night. We had no extra bed; I usually did the visiting. My parents were older, poorer, and my mother was Armenian in a totally WASP community. She would take ritual swipes at the Turks and she would point to the fact that the first Christian church was established in Armenia, but she felt no pride. Mostly she wanted it known that Armenians were not Semitic. She wanted it known—when the warning went out to my future brother-in-law, for example—that there was no "Jewish blood" in the family. And I would have to succeed to the extent of wiping out any thought that there was.

Intended or not, I felt the pressure to defend us against a younger, more stable, wealthier, purer community. It was easy enough to get A's. It took a little more energy to stay on the honor roll while home in bed with pneumonia, but I did, and was praised. It was easy enough to play school sports. It took a lot more energy—primarily my mother's—to try out for and eventually play on the Pee Wee Rangers' hockey team. That required an hour's commute to New York City three times a week, and when Grantland Rice made a movie short of the team, some fast talking on my mother's part was necessary to get me a starring role. But she was the only mother there (the other boys knew the subways; I had to be driven in from the country), and she managed to have it that I was the representative Pee Wee, going through the paces with the Ranger's star center, Buddy O'Connor, for all the world to see. She wanted me to be a Quiz Kid and had the school fill out a recommendation; she wanted me to be a movie star. A lot of A's and a star role in a twenty-minute short were all I got, but that was a great deal and I was praised.

I was not praised enough by others for my mother's satisfaction, though: she never did forgive the school for giving the Outstanding Boy Award to someone else. I had to wait four years for that. Then I would win the Deerfield Cup, awarded "to that boy who most nearly represents the Deerfield ideal." At Deerfield I lived with boys my own age but still went to classes with boys a year older. It was not until my last year that, inevitably, I "caught up." I was, as the inscription would

have it anyway, an ideal student and though my parents were miles
away, I kept in touch, complying with their wish that I write once a day
on one of the self-addressed postcards they gave me at the beginning of
the year. And so it went; "A on the algebra test, scored three goals in
practice today. All's well. Your loving son." At the ivy-league college I
did the same, the difference being that my parents made it to most of
the home games. And I assume that their pride, the sense that their boy
was succeeding, only increased. It must have. When I was about
twelve, I can remember my father positioning guests in front of a portrait of me, asking them to admire not only the face—"look especially
at the eyes"—but also the prizes won up to that point. After I had graduated from college, my wife and I fended off my embarrassment and
her aggravation over my father's chatter about me by referring to me
as "Phi Beta Kappa, Summa Cum Laude," the terms in which he referred to me—reward, as it were, for my having called him "Sir" all
those years.

The success story goes on—scholarships, graduate school, a profes-
sorship—but God knows it is not in my pride that I write. First, I write
in order to bring out the tremendous pressure for success under which
I labored. Dr. Johnson speaks poignantly of what it was like to be
hauled out for display by older parents wishing to live through their
only child:

That is the great misery of late marriages. The unhappy produce of them becomes the plaything of dotage—an old man's child leads much such a life as a
little boy's dog, teased with awkward tenderness, and forced . . . to sit up and
beg . . . to divert a company, who at last go away complaining of their disagree-
able entertainment.

I felt the pressure keenly and I felt it long. Indeed, one may never get
out from under it; or at least it may always be there. When I told my
mother about my separation, beginning an uncharacteristically long
and searching letter with the uncharacteristic opening, "all is *not*
well," she answered in pain: "Oh, Kim (author's nickname). I always
thought of you as on a pedestal!" I might have found a better place to
stand: I might have realized that posing for others' momentary delight
(and being encouraged to strike poses by others) is soul-destroying. But
she only saw marriage as one more achievement—or, in my case, a
separation as grounds for being stripped of all one's hard-earned
honors.

Such was the pressure; it was only one kind of pressure, the most
obvious. It was, perhaps, extreme, but most young men feel it and they
exert it—and the attendant pressure created by the fear of failure—on
each other. Having given some indication of the pressure my parents
put on me, I must go on to explore what is inelegantly called "peer
pressure" and ask regarding both parental and peer pressure: What

are the implications for anyone trying to establish a mature male-female relationship? What relations must one have had while trying to make one's way? What relations to other young men? What relations to young women? What did those relations do to me? How did they prepare me for my marriage?

Anyone reading this will have known about peer pressure in school. The sixties produced a rash of criticism of the competitiveness of the American educational system, but it has always been there and, in spite of new names, new programs, sliding walls, and open classrooms, will continue to be there until the larger systems that produce it somehow change. All of us recognize ourselves in Jules Henry's (1963) searing portrait of little Boris—or, worse, in his depiction of the pack that pursues him:

Boris had trouble reducing "12/16" to the lowest terms, and could only get as far as "6/8." The teacher asked him quietly if that was as far as he could reduce it. She suggested he "think." Much heaving up and down and waving of hands by the other children, all frantic to correct him. Boris pretty unhappy, probably mentally paralyzed. The teacher, quiet, patient, ignores the others and concentrates with look and voice on Boris. She says, "Is there a bigger number than two you can divide into the two parts of the fraction?" After a minute or two, she becomes more urgent, but there is no response from Boris. She then turns to the class and says, "Well, who can tell Boris what the number is?" A forest of hands appears, and the teacher calls Peggy (p. 295-96).

In such an atmosphere it is unlikely that young men and women will learn much that could help them understand and care for anything about each other, and because my hand was among the first out, my face among those that strained hardest for recognition, it is likely that I learned less than most. But in this respect, as I say, we are all handicapped, men and women alike. We have all had to engage in the grade-grubbing, teacher-conning activities that constitute so much that passes for learning in American schools.

Furthermore, in my own case, because I attended nothing but elitist institutions, the pressure was not so intense. Country day schools, prep schools, ivy league college in the forties and fifties. Even now, in such institutions, one can allow oneself the feeling that in spite of the competition or the state of the economy, one has somehow made it. My father sent me off to college with advice that I suppose has been given before: See if you can't meet people with money! Think about some kind of partnership! Ashamed, a little horrified that my father would give such advice, I tossed it off, but I could still share in what was a common and unconscious sense that we students need never know deprivation, need never have to scramble over each other in desperate flight from real financial and social failure. For reasons I have cited, I was in more active pursuit of success than my classmates, but none of us was putting crippling pressure on anyone else for fear of failure. We assumed that none of us could go very far wrong.

In the classroom, at first at least, I was with young women, but at whichever institution, we were all protected from competition in its rawest forms. But it was not in the classroom that we (boys at least) were most seriously ourselves anyway. It was not there that I was most damagingly miseducated for marital life. There was—there always is—recognition of the fact that education is in part a game. Ironically, it was in games on the playing fields, and, of course, in the dormitories, that real damage could be done.

The serious business of education is soon turned into a game; in games one's life is often on the line. I was always good at sports, played successfully on many successful teams, but I always sensed that as was the case at home, one could never be quite good enough. Coaches are unrelenting parents.

I never have learned to love the violent in sport, but this was not for having been underexposed. My first memory of having failed at violence was in day school, in about the fifth grade, at football practice. Our colors were orange and black, but my parents, having seen the possibility of saving a little money, had found a cheaper version of the jerseys, something closer to yellow and black. I got into one of the few fights I have ever been in for a reason I cannot now imagine, especially as the boy I fought was one with whom I played, a boy with whom I sang in choir, a boy for whom I had vague sympathies because he was an orphan. Fights were rare at such a school. They were an educational opportunity. A group gathered; it seemed to be under the aegis of the coach, who made no attempt to stop us. I can remember being amazed

WHEN YOU'RE A CHILD GIRLS ARE THINGS TO HATE.

WHEN YOU'RE A TEEN-AGER GIRLS ARE THINGS TO LIE TO YOUR FRIENDS ABOUT.

WHEN YOU'RE A YOUNG MAN GIRLS ARE THINGS TO PLAY AROUND WITH AND GET AWAY FROM FAST.

WHEN YOU'RE A GROWN MAN GIRLS ARE THINGS TO SETTLE DOWN WITH SO YOU CAN HAVE A CAREER.

WHEN YOU'RE A MIDDLE-AGED MAN GIRLS ARE THINGS TO TRY TO FORGET BUT YOU CAN'T.

BECAUSE YOU'RE TOO ROMANTIC.

Dist. Publishers-Hall Syndicate

©1974 JULES FEIFFER

by the energies that welled up in me—the confusion, the loss of bearings—and suddenly I was seated on top of the boy. He was down. I saw him there and quickly jumped off, partly in bewilderment over why this kind of thing was going on, partly in fear of what had been unleashed in me and what, therefore, might be unleashed *on* me, partly, rationalizing my fears, assuming that my position proclaimed me the victor. And so I jumped off, though a winner, feeling myself somehow a failure. At least that is the lesson the coach would have had everyone learn: "You see Kim has a yellow streak," he announced.

One should fight through to the end, even though one does not know why one is fighting or what the end might be. It is a lesson in manhood in our culture. I could look as if I had learned it. I continued to play well. Though avoiding fights, I looked as if I was hell-bent on winning and, for the most part, I was. But I still held back and junior year in prep school I drove another coach to public comment on the virtues of manhood. This time it was my hockey coach. I knew him for the four years I was in school. I had infuriated him once by quietly questioning the worth of serving in the military, but it is unlikely that he was vendictive about it. Again, I was someone who would rather not fight without a reason. (Years later, when the question was being asked more loudly about Vietnam, I saw him and angered him so much, that without even raising the issue he grabbed my respectably longish hair in such a way as clearly to tell me that it represented values he would continue to fight.) But it was actually on the ice, during a game, that I enraged him (and thus he scared me) most. I cannot remember the game, can only imagine I was not skating my heart out, but down out of the players' box he came, grabbing me to steady himself on the ice, grabbing me, though, in fury over my lack of aggression, muttering through clenched teeth, "Move! Go! Fight!"

The lesson was shouted at me for years, most impressively, of course, by coaches, but also continually by teammates. And I shouted it at them. No need to cite examples, so pervasive is the competitive ethos of so-called "sports" in American life. Being a participant sharpens one's sense of the costs, but they may be felt as keenly by the spectator, as keenly even by the nonspectator who tries in vain to escape out of earshot of the calls "Win! Hit! Fight! Kill!"

Other human beings become the Enemy, far more than they do in the classroom. Thomas Hardy's famous soldier, musing what it would have been like to have a casual drink with "the man he killed" might—without too great a stretch of the imagination—have been an athlete. It was not until I played club sports in England (without coaches, incidentally) that I had any contact with an opponent. In America, after a game, you file sullenly or raucously back on the bus.

The first great cost I paid, that any "sportsman" pays, that a culture pays if it lets "sports" be so pervasive and penetrating a ritual, is that you may never relate to other men. And what followed, in my case at least, is that I could relate even less successfully to women. There was plenty of noise and contact. We were a team, pounded each other on the back, embraced each other after goals. We did what pros do on television, the kind of patting and hugging that you would get beaten up for if you tried it on the streets. But we never shared feelings. By senior year in college, I had tired of the same dirty jokes on every trip, of dropping water bombs out of hotel windows, and I took to reading. I cut myself off with some sense of the rightness of my cause, but I had also cut myself off because I had not been elected captain, because I had lost in the competition. I was, for bad as well as good reasons, "a poor sport."

Naturally, instinctively, I had tried to share thoughts and feelings with my "friends," my fellow sportsmen, all through the years, but the kind of competitive atmosphere I wandered in, the kind of *machismo* code I knew we all had to pay more than lip service to, made it impossible. It has been only recently—what with a separation and the attendant feelings of depression and loss—that I have been able to stop running, to share, to help and be helped. Up until now that had been made to seem weak, effeminate.

One learns to hide one's feelings early. My parents took pride in never admitting to being sick: my father collapsed rather than let on that the toilet bowl was filling up with blood from his ulcer; when he was discovered and the doctor called for an ambulance, my mother sent it back, insisting that she could get him to the hospital just as well. My parents were a great partnership, a devoted cheering section, but I never saw them touch (or fight), nor did they lavish caresses on me. When I went off to school my father informed me that from then on we would have to shake hands. Supposedly at fourteen I was a man and that was the way men expressed emotions.

There was little or no intimacy with my contemporaries either. Inevitably I was introduced to homosexual intimacy—not surprisingly by a fellow athlete, ironically by the eventual Outstanding Boy of Fairfield Country Day School. My memory of the physical side of it is that it was pleasing, involving, as it did, my first orgasm. Indeed, it was so pleasing that I tried to transform the occasion into my first mounting of a woman, which made it awkward as well. But it was, above all, embarrassing. We certainly had no words to understand what we sought. The embarrassment was so intense on my friend's part that he told another member of our grade school backfield, and told him a version that had me as the perverse instigator of the whole affair. In that form it came back to me, an intimacy too hard for my friend to live with, too much to accept as part of young men's attempts at growing up, feared and then scorned. None of us young men could imagine or tolerate the possibility that we were attracted to each other.

At Deerfield there was only one "case" of homosexuality and the two boys involved were isolated, exiled, with the name "Cold Creme Kids." By then, I was firmly established as a member of whatever clique it was good to be a member of and would not possibly have made any gestures of physical intimacy. I knew without knowing that being "one of the boys" meant guarding yourself against other boys, extending towards them only the cool gestures they extended towards you, speaking primarily in the same cool and ironic tones you heard. We had a classmate who was shy, ashamed of his body, who used to come into the shower with his face to the wall—all of which earned him the nickname "Both" (uttered with a kind of vomiting roar), a reference to a possible confusion of sexes in him. The title and the sound were enough to put him beyond our ken; we never imagined that in us might be "both," delicacy as well as physical prowess, grace as well as force, passivity as well as aggressiveness.

Gestures of physical intimacy were strictly out; those of emotional intimacy were almost impossible. Upon graduation, I drove to Mexico with a friend and the school's most popular teacher. My friend and I had been co-captains of the hockey team and had played on the lacrosse team together. Our teacher was a sensitive man, somewhat frail, a lover of literature and, in the Platonic tradition, a lover of his students as well. His is the type that humanizes such grimly male institutions as Deerfield—he was not afraid to emote over a sunset, able to put an arm around a student without embarrassment. I was a favorite of his, like him, unabashedly looking to literature for answers to basic questions on how to live. He gave me all of Francois Mauriac to read one winter, during a particularly difficult period of trying to adjust my sexual urges to the stern dictates of my parents and my society. It was not until years later, when the disparity between our ages narrowed, that a real friendship could develop out of the shared concerns of school days, but there was tenderness and a meeting of minds even then.

As our trip wore on I imagined that something like the same kind of relationship could exist between my contemporary and myself. I had some dysentary on the trip; I was a bit homesick perhaps; I was happy being with my friend, hail fellows, fellow class officers, headed for the same prestigious college. I look for causes, but that in itself is indicative of the kind of cultural taboo that curbs the simple desire for something more than the guarded relationships that characterize life at a prep school, or, I think, no less among boys in high school. I wanted more. One day, walking along the street, I put my arm around my friend, having seen Mexicans do it and having seen in the gesture a sign of ease and delight. I started to probe feelings, feelings about women, about his girl whom I knew and admired. What that produced was a curt exchange: "You're always making things so complicated!" "And you would never understand!" The physical gesture was no more successful. His body stiffened; he said not to do that.

Shortly before the trip was over, and by accident, we went into a section of town that tourists did not penetrate and there, in a grimey bar, we drank tequila. A middle-aged man found my friend attractive, bought him a drink, and when it became clear what was happening we left. The man followed us up one street and then another, until breaking into a run, we reached our hotel. And then it was I who turned on intimacy. I cavorted around the room, made remarks about his girl—what would she think!? Having had my overtures to intimacy rebuffed, I took refuge in the culture and its cliches about what made a man.

I tried again quite recently with a colleague, a former college friend, and again, an athlete. We were off to play squash and on the way, knowing his wife had been upset about whether or not to take a part-time job, I said that I knew, that surely this was hard on him too, that having experienced trouble in my own home I might be of some help. At the very least, I hoped he knew I was a person he could come to if he ever wanted to talk about something other than what as colleagues we regularly talked about—literature, college politics, sports. I went so far as to extend my arm out to touch his. It was all over in a moment: he drew back, eyes rivetted on the road, and said that all she really needed was to accept the job that was being offered and get to work. I might have persisted but I joined the retreat from intimacy.

My competitive atmosphere that envelopes men in America is unlikely to make for intimate relationships among men themselves and, as I have suggested, even less likely to engender them between men and women. Holed away in male institutions for eight years, how could I, or anyone else in my position, learn to respect and love a woman? (And are co-educational schools in the larger male institution that is America different in kind?) Our very language (as is students' now) was filled with proof that we viewed women as we viewed each other, as strangers somehow pitted against each other, only more so. What we did was "score" against women or, as such claims were almost always false, we got to first or second or third base. A frequent question after a vacation or a date was, "Did you get much?" Women were commodities, fields on which we played, or so we assumed, never imagining how sad and foolish we might have seemed in their eyes.

We were born too soon to try to take advantage of a liberated era; we were of an age that had to frequent whore houses. It started in prep school. I never made it to Florida where most of the clique had their first such experience, but I am sure I would have remained in the car, in bewilderment, in fear, as did one friend of mine, and I would have been derided as he was. Nor did I make the New York trip from college: a run in, armed with lust and notebooks, the latter for studying purposes while one waited one's turn to satisfy the former.

But I listened with envy as well as with disgust. After one Deerfield vacation I got a ride back to school with two friends who lived in New

York. I went in, spent the night in the Park Avenue apartment of one of them, and in the morning we set out, we three in the back of his car, a chauffeur driving. At our lunch stop, the chauffeur having tactfully disappeared, my two friends talked of a girl they knew in common, not only knew but, as it turned out, had successfully dated on the last two nights of vacation. How far did each get? We all had to know, but neither would say. And so it was decided that each would write down his achievement on a napkin and I, an impartial judge, would declare the winner. But it was a tie, a tie over which we could all three laugh with a sense of conquest and relief: both had written "Finger Fuck."

A woman had been almost conquered and both men had won. That was ideal, for as was not the case in the classroom or on the playing fields, we did not want to win out over each other. We only wanted it known that we were "men" on the same team. For years stories were told, exploits shared. There was this girl who let every member of one fraternity do it to her on the pool table; there was this one suite of men who had it rigged so they could watch their dates relieve themselves, so honorable a group that they vowed never to go near their mirrors when one of their mothers was involved. Occasionally, there was trouble with real people: one fraternity group refused to pay up so the lady from New Haven leapt out a window and went right to the police; another club group was visited by a version of the Mafia when they lost the blue movie they had rented.

But reality seldom intruded. Or is it that it never intruded on my illusions? I recount a bit of the lore. I myself perceived the world and other people in the fantastic terms of the lore, but perhaps others saw beyond, could imagine what a girl felt like there on the pool table or could dismiss the tale altogether and build up a relationship with another human being physically, emotionally, intellectually, even spiritually. In thinking back on those years, I can only recall that somehow we knew there was a better way to live and that many of us started out to find that way. I cannot say that then and there we found a way out of the male-dominated, competitive world I have described. Indeed, our record of affairs and separations and divorces does not suggest that many of us did find a way. Of eight relatively close friends with whom I went both to school and college, two never married, six did, and of them two remain married.

Still, it is my own progress I am recounting. As I have warned, I cannot speak very searchingly to the particular dynamics of my own relationship with my wife, but I can say something about that relationship in the context of the history I have traced. I can see how what I perceived to be parental and peer pressures prompted me, forced me (who can assess the degree of influence?) to find a certain kind of mate and a certain kind of job.

During my school and early college years I had correspondences and relations with many women. This one I necked with, that one I wrote

longing letters to. I had no way whatsoever of bringing body and
soul—sensuality and tenderness, as Freud would have it—together. I
can think back on two women who loved me in a way that indicated
that they were reaching some maturity themselves, but before long
they simply scared me. I knew in those cases that passionate but un-
consummated groping could never be the basis for any lasting relationship, but that was all I could manage. I was not up to anything else;
those I idealized and longed for must have understood this because
they rejected me.

What I sought was someone with whom I could remain competitive
and successful on my own woefully limited terms, the terms in which I
had defined so much of my life up until then. I had to remain intellectually and physically superior, or to be able to maintain the illusion
that I was. Also, I had to find someone who was socially acceptable. In
the past I had liked one girl of Italian descent, one with a Polish name,
and been made to feel by my parents and peers that that would not do.
The Italian girl's name was Vito, and in my school yearbook my friends
wrote about smells, there being a deodorant out with a similar name.
But my parents dealt that relationship its final blow simply by refusing
to pick Anna up for a dance to which I had invited her. They did not
have to expose themselves to break up my relationship with Sally Os-
trowski but still I was told how Catholics tend to take over—first me,
then maybe the Papacy would move in on Washington!

The woman I was to marry was a WASP, went to good private
schools, and lived in a nice country house. And I sensed that my parents approved. (When I asked my mother recently if the sight of such
respectable money had impressed her, she scorned the notion, saying
she'd seen much more magnificent estates, which hardly contradicted
my sense of my parents' stake in the matter.) They did not care, but I
found security in the fact that although Susan was well-schooled, she
was not in the intellectual race, as it was set up by her college, at least.
By the time I met her (our sophomore year), she was just getting off
academic probation, and when she took courses in English in an
attempt to understand what I was interested in, she did poorly. No
competition there, nor, I thought, was any there in our sexual relationship. Susan was boyish, short-haired, slight, almost waiflike, and
without much guilt we did everything allowed by the Victorian belief in
virginity that we shared.

On the narrow grounds on which I had played up until then, there
was no competition. But neither was there any voicing of our doubts
and fears, so little time had been spent in warm human relationships.
We were about to graduate, everyone else was getting married, our
parents were clearly satisfied, and somehow it would work out.
Susan's roommate announced her engagement a few months before
ours and at a house dinner her fiancé got up and toasted the two of us
for planning to follow suit. I did not know our plans were so definite but

I said nothing. Susan allowed her deep reservations about our relationship to surface only once but I quickly buried them. The occasion was grimly appropriate: an idle hour before the final hockey game against Harvard. Our training rules were lax enough to allow for visitors and while I thought of the approaching game she started to cry and said she didn't think she could go through with the marriage. But I was never to learn why, for once I knew that she had doubts, I brought to bear the pressure I felt from thoughts about the engagement party the previous December, about the wedding in June, and—not least—about the game that was soon to start. Ours was not a relationship in which we could help each other express doubts and needs.

But we were married. That summer I responded to the disorientation of living in Susan's house, of playing on her family's court, as it were, by vomiting everything I ate and losing ten pounds. In the fall we were off to England where I had won a scholarship, and once again the conditions were familiar, a home game. I was back to winning prizes and to my normal weight. What with scholarships and some parental support, both in England and in graduate school back in America, we had no financial worries, so I had a clear track in my race to the doctorate. Not even Susan got in my way. She had a part-time job and I was there to read, which I did day in and day out, touring or at home. When news came that my scholarship was renewed, my parents were in England visiting us and to celebrate, at my prompting, they bought me Trevelyn's social history of England. My mother inscribed my parent's congratulations in each of the four volumes. Susan let out a howl of protest against the life we were leading by writing in bold letters in each volume, "ME TOO," but it went unheard.

In England there was little status a student's wife could derive from her husband's position; back in America there was not much more. But we started having children—one, because everyone wants children, two because nobody wants an only child, and three, six years later, because we were trying to cement up the cracks in our relationship.

When I took a job teaching college I was returning to even more familiar turf, literally, because Deerfield was only fifteen miles away, but most important, socially. The atmosphere could be summed up in the words of a therapist whom two colleagues of mine visited in an effort to cope with the pressures of our department. The first went on at length about the overbearing presence of the then "old man" of the department and about the ways his staff competed with, yet supported each other. When the second came, he started in on the same story, only to be interrupted by the therapist's saying, "Yes, I know—rigid informality." It was a phrase that characterized not only the department but the institution, not only this particular all-male institution, but the others I had attended as well, another place where men worked and played and competed against each other, while women played the unrespected, often unrecognized roles of grader, librarian, home-maker, mother. It was, like those institutions, a place where men, like the students they taught, like the students I imagine them to have been themselves, fended off exposure and intimacy with irony and the pose of stoic self-sufficiency.

I thought Susan would be a perfect mother, a willing hostess, an effi-cient homemaker, but she turned out to be a human being, an indi-vidual, a woman who would not simply fit into the roles I had imagined for her. Obviously if she were only what I had to make her out to be, we would have remained married. We would not have been two human beings, mutually respecting and loving each other, but we would have been content. As it was, she resisted the work required to entertain and run a home, she continued to cry out ME TOO!

Having been an "ideal" student, on my way to being a professor, I knew the importance of filling out one more role, that of being the model husband. Those who watched and judged demanded it. I de-manded it of myself because I didn't want to repeat my parents' mis-takes, more immediately because, ironically, I sensed the model was a bad one (and I was certainly made to feel it was a bad one by Susan), and I wanted to do something about it. Though at one level I would have liked Susan to be a glorified maid, I knew that it was deadly to expect that of anyone and in my guilt I did much more than my colleagues to lighten the load at home. So our household appeared all the more serene.

In the process of being a model husband I was a model father too, spending time with the children, working with them in the yard, teach-ing them to play tennis, dragging them to cultural events. With them there were moments of tenderness and delight such as I could not find with Susan and that made it easier to maintain the facade, even to ignore the fact that it was a facade we were maintaining. There were precious few moments of tenderness and delight with Susan for the simple reason that I was not in competition with my children and was, though I did not know it at the time, in competition with her.

As had been the case from my earliest years, competition precluded intimacy. While getting A's, making teams, winning prizes, I kept my distance from my schoolmates and they kept theirs from me. While be-coming what my parents and what I thought society wanted me to be, I deprived myself or was deprived of intimate relationships with boys and girls, men and women. I looked on marriage as a refuge from the competitive world I had known. In choosing a mate I tried to avoid com-petitiveness, tried to be best from the start so that finally, in marriage, I could find intimacy.

Such was the meager legacy of my earlier years. Nothing in it would help me recognize the real competition I had entered nor build on what intimacy existed in spite of that legacy. Rather than avoid competition,

I ran into more than I could handle, or, what is sadder, given all the waste, I didn't really know that Susan and I were in competition. We never fought but we continually struggled: who would do the shopping? who the cleaning? who would sleep late? who would nap? who would take care of the children? Always, who would take care of the children? The facade was maintained but the struggle went on. If Susan was victorious—got a nap, say—I would begrudge her her success. If I succeeded—particulary out there, in the "real world"— Susan would be resentful. To overturn the old terms of endearment, we couldn't do enough for each other. And all the while we could not admit to our real needs, to our deep needs for pleasure and love, nor, of course, could we meet those needs in each other, not even with a counsellor's help. We could not even see, we were not mature enough to realize, the predicament we were in. As the struggle wore on I wore out and began to look for intimacy elsewhere. Eventually the competition ended. This time everybody lost.

references Henry, J. *Culture against man.* New York: Random House, 1963. Vintage, 1965.

family renewal

Luanne Lynch

Jerry Lynch

We are moving from a rigidly role oriented family in which we ate at separate tables from the children to a family where everyone is accepted as a first class citizen.

This new direction in our lives began with an awareness of our stifling behavior and the efforts we took to change. It took drastic action on our part, even living in a camper for two years where we shared the same table and bedroom.

In this chapter we want to share some personal experiences that led to our awareness and thus our family renewal. We have written in the first person, speaking as Luanne and Jerry.

Following the anecdotes are a series of activities that we have developed in our Loving Family workshops.

Jerry

Each of us has mingled elements of masculine and feminine personality. It was in Spain that I discovered the feminine part of myself. Luanne and I were living and working as teachers in Spain. We lived there for six years during which time our four children were born.

I had mirrored my Spanish counterparts almost too well as far as adopting a masculine role. Added to my already well-developed roles of sole provider and hunter were male vanity and an intolerance of weakness, both in myself and in others.

A rapid succession of births all four of the children were born in just over three years shook my false, overly masculine stance to the core. The demands to participate fully in an almost overwhelmingly infant-oriented home grated against me terribly. I roared and complained and became intolerable at times, even to myself, but I found an escape. I became a hunter. I lived to fish and took on the role of the provider, fishing for my family's daily fare. The problem, of course, was that I was needed as a living social presence in the family, not just as a stereotype, a provider.

243

Luanne

One night, we were sitting on the rug looking at some family photographs. We all were sharing the tranquility in the moment, smiling as we passed the pictures around.

The photographs shuffling between us suggested a game. "Let's put Mommy's picture and my picture at either end of the rug," Jerry suggested. "Everyone else place their picture where they want to." Cathy, age 5, without hesitation placed her picture right next to mine. Cindy, her twin, and Danny, 4, followed suit. Elisa, 7, paused and looked at Jerry, then placed her picture right in the middle of the rug.

After an uncomfortable silence, Jerry said that he felt left out. Elisa responded, "Well, it's just that Mommy is more with us." I explained that I sometimes felt like the picture on the rug—smothered with the children on top of me. Although Jerry had made great strides in helping with the care of the children, I felt that I was carrying the emotional burden of the family.

One afternoon, after moving back to San Diego, I was standing in the living room overlooking the front yard and could see that the children were wearing a hole in the lawn underneath the swing where the grass had been. Now they were flooding the place with water and using it to make mud pies. My first reaction was to tell Jerry about it. I knew that he would probably get angry with them and settle with the children once and for all, but something familiar about the situation stopped me from calling him. I could see that if Jerry was to get closer to the children, I was going to have to stop making him carry the entire anger burden in the family. I went out of doors and began to deal with the children when Jerry also came out and began to scold. He seemed to have taken over the situation out of habit, with his loud voice and forceful presence.

This has happened before. In past situations, I had just begun to assert myself when Jerry had taken over. The result was that I usually backed down and gave up my power, and thus a part of myself, feeling that both of us expressing our anger was too much. I could see now that it was not enough for me to assert myself in the children's situation, but that I must also take responsibility for my feelings with Jerry.

After the children had adapted to the new mud hole I had provided for them, I shared with Jerry my feelings of impotence caused by his anger. In order to be openly angry myself, I needed his support, and I welcomed his feedback, but not his taking over. We agreed that we would allow each other the freedom to handle our own feelings and interactions with the children. Once we began, to share the emotional load of the family, I had to learn to carry my own anger, Jerry learned to be more gentle and explored new ways to show his caring.

Jerry

"I'll play with you in a while—I'm busy right now," I promised Cathy, our five year old. Her face dropped and she looked at the ground silently. I saw in her face the disappointment of the many broken or forgotten promises that she had endured from me. I was putting her off again. I decided that this time I had better carry through.

"Want to play a game with me?"

"O.K., what is it?" She answered.

"The game is, I'll meet you in your room in five minutes."

She may have been skeptical that I'd meet her, but in exactly five minutes I was there. We played for awhile and then I made another commitment to meet her in ten minutes. She suggested meeting in the playhouse.

Cathy was already there when I arrived and was radiant, since it was the first time I had visited her in the playhouse. She made me a cup of "tea." While we sat quietly she began to open up about herself. Cathy said that she felt lonely sometimes because she has no one to be with. "Mommy is with you, Daddy. Elisa is with Cindy, and Danny—well, Danny just likes to be with himself. I'm the only one who's all alone."

We invited Luanne to join us and she also listened as Cathy told her how she felt.

"I hear you, Cathy—you really feel alone," Luanne said.

Cathy's eyes were intense and penetrating now. "I feel like no one really hears me."

"Do we?"

"Sometimes, not very much. But I guess I'm getting better now."

"Better at what?" I asked.

"I must be getting better at talking, because you can hear me now."

I started out by listening and I found that my five year old daughter understood things on a deeper level than I had ever suspected. Cathy was under the impression that it was entirely her fault that we couldn't hear her, she was isolated from the rest of the family from not having been listened to or having had her feelings taken seriously. She had shown this in many nonverbal ways but I hadn't known how to reach her.

The challenge was clear; at the time we were learning what it means to be "honest" in Educational Counseling classes in San Diego and encounter groups with adults, but if we were ever to become autonomous, congruent individuals, we knew we must begin at home with our own family.

We found that although we were learning to listen and to relate to people on a better level, it was with our own children that we had the most difficulty making meaningful contact. We seemed often to catch ourselves talking at them rather than with them. And yet, it was they who needed us most to be accurate mirrors with them.

We began by sharing our feelings with our children and each other. We got in touch with the subtle, sometimes powerful effect we have on each other.

Luanne

We were fortunate to have had extensive exposure to the Harold Bessell-Uvaldo Palomares Magic Circle Program as consultants. The Magic Circle is a short, daily group, which is practiced widely in elementary schools, that promotes social and emotional growth in children.

We decided to try having Magic Circles at home. They would take place after dinner, two or three times a week, with a time limit of about twenty minutes for each meeting. During these sessions, we practiced the techniques we had learned—listening to each other by making good eye contact, by trying to repeat some of the exact words a speaker used to show that we really had heard, and by using the feeling words they expressed. We asked as few questions as possible, feeling that these put others on the spot. Instead, we tried to use statements to convey our understanding.

At our first meeting, everyone sat on kitchen chairs in a circle in the living room. Our children were small then and we thought they would be less restless on chairs. A covered box was in the center of the circle with a sweet hidden inside for each person.

We began with, "We're going to imagine that this is a very special magic box. It's magic because inside is anything that you could wish for. It can be anything, any size." Elisa said that the box had a dolly that was real. Jerry's box had a sailboat. I shared after Cindy, then Cathy and Elisa had their turns. Danny was only two then, so he left the circle shortly to play with clay in the kitchen. He returned to his chair for the opening of the box.

Everyone was delighted with the treat and the attention. We had a new family ritual. We all decided that it would be nice to read our bedtime story while we were still sitting in the circle.

We repeated the magic circle several times during the following weeks. Danny began to stay with us longer and longer, and soon began telling what he would like in the box before he left for the kitchen, and returning before it was time to open the box. We began to explore other themes. Our favorite was, "Someone here made me feel good." "You made me feel good when you played with me today," was an often-heard response in our circles. After a number of meetings we explored themes that dealt with unresolved feelings, such as, "Someone here made me feel bad," and "I made someone here feel bad."

The circle found a place in our family ritual. Everyone knew that he could speak up and would be listened to when we sat down for the circle. After awhile it didn't take long to make such contact in other situations—a minute or two was usually enough. The secret we found, is to touch base often and try to clarify or resolve the points of conflict between us. There were times when we became conscious of our total communication with each other, our body language, and what our eyes were saying.

We were making contact as a family now and as we learned to listen, we found that we had become much more interesting to each other. By focusing on feelings, we had somehow become more genuine. We began to discuss subjects that were forbidden to us in the past, such as the family roles we had become locked into.

Jerry   We felt that we needed a change: Elisa, 8, wore dresses exclusively and didn't like to risk child-like behavior around adults. We wanted her to be able to tap into more spontaneous behavior. Cathy, 6, felt alone and separate from the family. She wanted to make a bigger place for herself in the group and needed lots of listening to. Cindy, Cathy's twin, needed to be more than a twin. She was ready to begin standing out as a person herself. Luanne, 36, felt oppressed by the domestic duties we all threw her way. She wanted more sharing—not just help with the dishes and laundry. She didn't want to be in charge all of the time. And I at age 35, didn't like being away from the family on workshop trips. It was difficult to reconnect upon returning.

Although two of our children were of beginning school age, we felt that what they needed more than school was to become aware of themselves and their power. We wanted to see them develop self-confidence and enjoy themselves in the out of doors.

Since we are teachers ourselves, we decided to try something risky: we would take on the responsibility of their education for a few years. We wanted to teach them what we and they considered important to learn and to provide them with challenging experiences by coming face to face with nature.

We would have to give up living in a house in order to do this, but it fit in with our long-standing dream, to explore and develop ourselves not just talking about it but by acting. Now seemed the time to act.

After months of preparation and sometimes painful process of selling our belongings and leaving our home and friends, we were finally on the road in our camper heading south toward warm Mexican beaches.

Luanne   That evening, as we sat around the camper table at our first beach stop, we tried yet another "Magic Box Circle," but our conditions had changed so, no one felt much enthusiasm for it. The circle was finished quickly, and we began sharing "Something I did that made me feel good." Everyone talked animatedly about what they had done on the beach that day, happy to be staying where they were. As the sharing drew to a close, Elisa said that something also made her feel bad—"It's that we have to leave tomorrow." There was a silence, then Danny spoke up close to tears, "Daddy when are we leaving?" When Jerry answered that we were leaving tomorrow, Danny blurted out, "I thought we were going to get to go fishing." The others expressed disappointment because they wanted to slide down the sand dunes, since they had only gotten a taste of it that day.

Everyone looked at Jerry, it seemed that he had already made up his mind that beaches were better further south. "We'll have plenty of time then to fish and play on sand dunes."

"But there are sand dunes and fishing here," the children pleaded.

I said to Jerry, "It looks like you and I are still waiting for this trip to begin but the kids are already on the trip. They are enjoying where they are now and have been ever since we left home."

Jerry laughed with me, "Maybe we can learn how to be "on the trip" from them."

Even though we had all sacrificed equally to be here on this remote beach together, Jerry and I had somehow considered this to be our trip with the kids coming along with us. It became clear that they were as involved as we were, the trip belonged to us all. They were here to have fun and wanted us to have fun too. That night they shared with us their hopes and dreams and we shared ours.

The next day we remember as the day we learned to play again. It was as though we were retrieving a lost part of ourselves. We slid down the sand dunes on our bellies and the children collected firewood to cook the fish Jerry and Danny caught for our dinner that night. We were developing the spirit of play in us and now we were playing our trip together.

Jerry

Our children had been doing things well all along, but we hadn't really noticed. We were beginning to stop and watch; our pace had slowed down enough for us to see who and what was in front of us. Danny could spot fish swimming in the waves; Cindy had an eye for finding tiny things, as she said, "I'm close to the ground so I can see them better." Cathy overcame her fear of making new friends, addressing people with, "Hi, do you want to play?" for openers. Elisa was good at building little houses with whatever materials were at hand.

We knew that the children had a lot to learn but we hadn't realized that it was we ourselves who had the most to learn. The children came to know and were understanding when we didn't always have the right answers or the best judgement.

The lessons were sometimes harsh but we learned together things we hadn't been aware of before—about listening to warnings, about the closeness of death, and our responsibility to ourselves and each other. It became important to all of us that we each learn to walk as solidly as possible on the earth. It was necessary for the well-being and security of us all that each of us learn to use his own good judgment.

Luanne

After a few months of being around others on beaches we felt we needed to be alone as a family. Our journey became a search for somewhere to stop and relax, in a way, I guess we were looking for a home. We found our place at the end of a long rocky road, in a green, moist oasis next to a wide river. After a few days of feeling truly isolated and away from people I began to feel oppressive. I felt lonely and needed someone to talk to besides Jerry. I wandered outside the camper and saw Elisa (8). "Gosh, Elisa, I sure wish I had a friend to talk to, I sure do feel lonely."

"Why don't you talk to me?" she asked as she looked up into my eyes.

"Well, I meant a grownup—but maybe you could understand how I'm feeling now." We sat down to talk, she listened to me as I shared my feeling with her. I told her that I had never lived right out in nature like this before with nowhere to go and nothing to do. I felt scared about being alone with myself.

Elisa said, "Yes, we really are alone here. I'm alone too, we all are, but we're alone together." We smiled at each other, we were indeed alone together, how freeing to know that we could be alone and together at the same time.

There on the edge of the desert each of us became less dependent on the others, we began to allow each other enough space so that we each found our own place and rhythm. We began to enjoy each other in new ways.

Jerry

Our new found independence gave us the freedom to range farther and farther from camp, alone and in pairs. One day, after lunch, Elisa and Danny left for an alone-time together in the desert. When they had been gone for quite awhile, I began wondering if they were okay.

Forcing my eyes to adjust, I looked from our shady oasis across the deep green alfalfa field to the cactus-studded desert hills beyond. They should be back soon, I thought. The tall organ pipe cactus formed a frame around the rim of our little valley. A hawk, circling overhead cried out. Still no sign of the children.

"I'm going to see if I can spot them."

"Don't let them see you."

"Don't worry, I won't." Luanne understood—Elisa and Danny were proving they could handle themselves in the desert.

I climbed into the desert from the valley, avoiding the main trail, listening for them. The hawk, outlined by a cloud against the sky, called out.

I looked back and saw Luanne moving between the trees on the other side of the valley. The old mill, hidden by the trees, was barely visible from here. The sound of the waterfall by its side filled the valley—not quite spilling over into the dry desert at its edge. Turning again, I now saw two hats bobbing along silently on the other side of a rock wall. Danny and Elisa were winding their way carefully and soundlessly through the desert. They stopped to pick "chilito" berries from a barrel cactus, then began moving down the slope again, the clear dry air carrying their voices now. Danny spotted a lizard. Elisa showed him a rock, then a flower. Their words rose and fell with the wind, the sounds blending naturally with the buzzing, chirping background of desert sounds.

Elisa, her back straight and her movement graceful, was leading now. She seemed to be sharing her power and confidence with Danny, and he was teaching her what he knew of the desert. I was moved by the competence I saw in them. At that moment, they stood out as self-sufficient, autonomous persons—quite separate from us.

activities

The following activities were developed in our "Loving Family" workshops. The first set of activities may be done with a single parent and child. The second set needs a larger group and someone who can act as a director.

listening to a child

We found that listening to a child is the first step to making contact. Too often, we block communication with children by trying to lower ourselves to their level and talk babytalk to them; at the other extreme we fire overly complex questions at young children. There is a middle ground where we can let go of our masks and listen, actively and attentively. Asking no questions, not judging or approving, we respond with our eyes, faces and gestures to what the child is telling us and when it is our turn to speak, we begin by paraphrasing something the child has said to show we are really listening. We focus on feelings, using the emotional language the child has just used. As we begin to flow and share the affection that is our bond, we find ourselves touching more often and making better eye contact.

Try listening to a child today for five minutes. Try not to ask questions, and avoid interpretations. First, be the child's mirror and reflect the feelings that come through to you. After awhile, repeat something the child has said. Focus on the *feeling* words you hear. Be as open as you can allow yourself to be and let your feelings be seen by the child.

observing

Observing a child for a few minutes and making an anecdotal record of a child's actions can help us break out of old habits of perception and develop a more detached viewpoint. The longer term developmental viewpoint is one of our goals.

Try watching someone for five minutes. Write down objectively what you observe. Do not include your feelings, just the child's actions. "She feels angry" is subjective, whereas "Her face is scowling, her voice is loud," is more objective. Now observe the child's interaction with another child. Observe how she/he initiates, holds back, shows dependency or shows anger. To what extent does the child act as a boy or as a girl "should" act.

one-to-one time

A good way to show a person he is special to you is through one-to-one time. It allows for the intimacy necessary to see without masks or roles.

Plan an activity with another member of the family for this week. Make an appointment with someone you haven't spent much time with lately. Share equally in planning what you will do. Make it a special time by practicing good listening and sharing your own feelings. Going out to lunch or having a picnic together are good choices.

giving appreciation

When we appreciate someone, we make them feel good about something they have done.

It is especially rewarding at bedtime, when you're tucking the child into bed, to tell the child something he did during the day that you appreciate. Be specific about the behavior—such as, "I appreciate the way you included your brother in the game." You may find that soon the child will also be able to tell you about something that you did that was appreciated. When you have established comfortable, positive contact with each other, you might talk of something one of you did that the other still feels bad about. When confronted with something you've done that your child resents, admit it—"Yes, I did that."

completing circles

This activity reinforces the habit of taking responsibility for completing circles once begun.

If I make a peanutbutter and jelly sandwich, it means I will not only eat it, but make sure that I've washed the plate and put away the fixings. I then have a feeling of circular accomplishments in my day, a feeling of completion.

These circular accomplishments are sometimes rewarded symbolically by drawing a circle on a piece of paper. The rewards for finishing circles are intrinsic. Do this record keeping of circles completed for only a few days at a time.

favorite place activity

The following exercises were developed for family workshops.
This activity encourages intimacy and trust. By sharing with others how we feel in our favorite places, we let them know something of our private lives.

Have someone take you to a favorite place around the house or neighborhood. Listen to them tell about it and how they feel there. This is where they're really able to be themselves. Take that someone to your favorite place and share it with that person. Tell them about your feelings.

This activity can also be done as a whole family project. Each member takes the rest of the family to his favorite place. Try a family meeting at the end where everyone who wants to shares his feelings.

family collage

One way of building family unity is to do something fun together. Making a family collage communicates feelings and perceptions on an unspoken level.

The materials you will need are simple: magazines, glue, scissors, and a posterboard large enough for everyone to work on.

Search through magazines and cut out pictures or words that convey your feelings about you and your family. Put the posterboard in the center of a circle formed by family members. Everyone involved in the activity may paste his/her pictures on the poster. To assure that no one gets to feeling like he/she owns the collage, turn the poster from time to time by calling out "change." Anyone can call out "change" anytime. No one person can decide when the collage is finished—the project is completed when the last person stops working on it.

Various topics provide themes:

What does being a girl mean in our family?
What does being a boy mean in our family?
What does mother do in our family?
What does father do in our family?
How do we feel about school?

teasing

We've found that brothers and sisters often like to be with each other, but sometimes excessive teasing can get in the way of their having a really good relationship.

Try forming a group with the children, or a family meeting where you talk about the difference between mean teasing and friendly teasing. Mean teasing can make someone feel bad. Friendly teasing can be a way of making contact.

When The family has labelled a behavior and talked about it together. It then becomes easier to identify the problem with each other when someone steps over the line between positive attention and making someone feel bad.

hand signals

This exercise came about as a result of an experience within our family.

Cathy was crying, standing in a circle of her friends. "Nobody is nice to me," she said. They listened to Cathy as she expressed her feelings.

Finally, Michelle spoke out. "I haven't been very nice to you, but you haven't been very nice to me either." Michelle told Cathy how she had made her feel bad.

Cathy wailed, "I don't know why I keep saying those mean things—I forget how to be nice."

Luanne

Later, Cathy and I explored together how it feels to act like a critical parent. "When I'm mean, it feels like being a pushy thumb," she said. "People don't like to be around a thumb," she observed. Cathy admitted that she had been feeling like a victim herself, and had been saying bad things to herself, like "you're bad." "It's not a pushy thumb I feel like now, but a weak pinkie finger," she said. "I'm tired of being a thumb or a pinkie," she said clearly.

"But, you're not being a thumb or a pinkie right now," I observed. "You're being more like an index finger. An index finger is strong." We pushed on our index fingers to feel its strength.

"I feel like a strong index finger now because I'm talking about it," Cathy said.

The children like the imagery we had discovered for naming our behavior. In adult language, thumb symbolizes the critical parent in each of us. Pinkie stands for the adaptive, defensive child, and index finger stands for the assertive, happy adult in all of us.

One day I realized that I had been very much of a thumb recently, but I didn't know how to get out of it. I asked Cathy if she knew of a good way to stop since she had just recently made such a breakthrough. She said, "Imagine yourself in all the different ways you can act. Then you can choose whichever one is the best."

We made a bulletin board and filled in our behaviors as they occurred to us: *This is me as a pinkie; this is me as an index; this is me as a thumb.*

role-playing

We've gained knowledge of ourselves and each other by naming the behavior we see. Once we name it, it is easier to recognize and deal with it when it reoccurs. Sometimes we role-play hypothetical or real situations as an awareness exercise. One of the benefits of acting out a role we don't ordinarily assume is that it enables us to separate ourselves from the role we are playing. In a artificial situation, it is often easier to detach ourselves and see the choices we make that involve us in that role. A father might play the part of his daughter, or a boy his mother.

This activity can be an enjoyable and effective way to see ourselves reflected as others play roles familiar to us. Many situations in our daily lives can lend themselves to role-playing situations. If you wish, start with one of the following—then you might want to invent your own.

1. There are five of you in your family and you are moving to a house with three bedrooms.

2. You are all at a summer camp and there is one boy's bicycle in a family of two boys and two girls. The boys claim it.
3. You are a family with three young children, two girls and a boy. Grandma has sent a ball to the boy and dolls to the girls. The girls want to trade presents.
4. A sixteen year old girl announces at supper that she wants a **motorcycle**.

Start the role-play, sit in a circle facing each other and decide which part each of you is going to enact. Try being a member of the opposite sex or someone not your own age.

   One of you will have to be a director. The director presents the situation and stops the action after five minutes, then leads a short discussion covering one or more of the following topics:

1. What type of behavior did each person assume? Who was a "thumb" or aggressive person? Who was a "pinkie" or defensive person, and who was an "index finger" or adultlike person?
2. How did each of you feel in your role?
3. Did you arrive at a solution? How?

If, after discussing it, you don't feel finished, begin the role play again, this time trying to deal with each other without being either a domineering "thumb" or a poor me "pinkie finger." Each role-playing topic should not exceed fifteen minutes. It is not necessary to arrive at a commonly agreed-on solution. The value of this exercise is in the insight gained by seeing how many alternatives are presented. Each person's ideas and input should be welcomed.

equal citizenship

One of the most compelling goals we strive toward in our own family is to allow everyone equal emotional time and space. Each of us should be a first-class citizen, regardless of age or sex. We set out to change the way we related to each other. We had a long way to go, and at times indulged in self congratulation when we appeared to have made a breakthrough only to have our old conditioned behavior betray us again. We've learned that it takes repeated action to bring about a noticeable difference in negative behavior. Whatever progress we have made, our goals of autonomy, intimacy, and equal citizenship have been the result of these repeated positive actions by all of us.

We practice making good daily contact with each other.
Permission is not needed to call each other's behavior.
Playing and creating together have become rituals with us.
We try to plan alone-times with each member of the family.
And conversely, after living so closely in a camper for 2 years, we've
    learned that it is important to be separate from time to time from
    each other.
We share in small decisions.
We camp together.

A good friend in Mexico once said, "Love is not just a feeling—it is
an action." Love must be demonstrated and exercised to thrive.

minority women's issues

introduction*

Minority women are the victims of double discrimination—racism and sexism. They are discriminated against in the areas of education, housing, and earnings, being underemployed, and underpaid more than any other segment of the population.

Like white women, minority women hold essentially none of the top jobs in America. In 1974, while 12 percent of minority women and 15 percent of Anglo women held professional positions or were technical workers, minority women, even more than white women, were involved in an economic struggle for employment opportunities and purchasing power. Within that 12 percent the breakdown is as follows: Chicana, 6 percent; American Indian, 9 percent; Black, 11 percent; Japanese, 15 percent; Chinese, 21 percent; Korean, 23 percent; Filipino, 27 percent.

Before minority women can deal significantly with questions of self-actualization and identity as women, issues of employment need to be confronted. Moreover, all women need to be concerned with the issues of minority women.

Since 1970, little evidence exists of any advance in the relative earnings of black females:

Black females held none of the top jobs in 1960 and essentially none in 1973. (Thurow, 1976; Craig, p. 5)
Black women with degrees equivalent to those held by men and white women have been unable to obtain equivalent jobs.
The gap between the salaries of black men and women has widened.
Both black and white women with some college education earn less than a black male who has only eight years of education (1975 Census).

*The data for this introduction was compiled by Donna Hart, George Washington University, School of Education.

economic facts of minority women

	Median income	% Working	% Female heads of hse.*	% Earning under $5000	Yr. Education completed	Complete H.S.
Black	$2,810	49	$4,465/35			75
American Indian	1,697	35		86%	10.5	35
Chicana	2,682		**4,800/14	76	9.4	23
Puerto Rican	3,889	17	**4,800/31	68	9.5	25
Filipino	3,513	55	6,322/8%		12.2	
Chinese	2,686	49	8,085/6%	75	12.4	
Japanese	3,236	49	7,706		12.5	75

*Should also be titled Median Income for Female Heads of Household.
**Female head of family of *Spanish* origin.

Black women earn less than white women (a median income of $2,810), are employed in greater numbers (about 60% between the ages of 20 and 54), and hold a greater percent of low-paying, low-status jobs (54% are employed as operatives, or service workers). (1975 Census) In 1975, 35% of black families were headed by women who earned a median income of only $4,465 (Milius, 1975). The high levels of labor force attachment among black women reflect in considerable degree their continuing obligation to supply a substantial proportion of family income and the fact that educational attainments, no matter how small, raise participation rates more for blacks than for white women.

A comparison of the labor force status of women shows that a larger percentage of Asian American women (50%) work outside the home than do black (48%) or white women (41%). (Sung, 1975) A little over 55 percent of Filipino women and 42% of Korean women work. Japanese and Chinese women occupy an intermediate position with 49 percent taking jobs.

Differences in earnings between Asian American and white women are relatively small. At most educational levels, Japanese women average about 10 percent higher earnings than white women. The earnings of Chinese women are higher than for white women only for high school graduates and those with some college. Filipino women with some college also earn slightly more than white women, but as college graduates they earn less than whites. In contrast, the earnings of Korean women are quite consistently lower than for whites at all educational levels (Wilber, 1975). In 1969, the median personal incomes of Asian-American women ranged from $2,686 for Chinese, $2,741 for Korean, $3,236 for Japanese and $3,513 for Filipino women in the United States.

The proportion of Asian American females gainfully employed is higher than the national average and this does not take into account the unpaid Asian women in family-operated businesses since many of these women do not classify themselves as "employed" (Wilbur, 1975).

The annual income of Chincanas in 1974 demonstrates the cycle of poverty with respect to minority women. A drastic 76 percent of all Chicanas earned less than $5,000 in 1974 (1975 Census). The Chicana is at the bottom in terms of earning power as compared to all other Spanish origin women, earning a median annual income of $2,682. Chicanas are increasingly in the labor force because of economic need and responsibility as heads of households. Fourteen percent of Chicano households are supported by Chicanas, and one half of these families are below the poverty level (1975 Census).

The 1975 Census reports that there are 1.7 million Puerto Ricans in the United States, of which 906,000 are female. Although only 17 percent have jobs, over one half of Puerto Rican women participating in the labor force are operative or service workers. In 1975, 68 percent of working Puerto Rican women earned incomes below $5,000; 31 percent of Puerto Rican households in the United States are headed by women who earn a median income of $3,889 (1975 Census).

Employment participation and opportunities for American Indian women are affected by the level and quality of their educational background. Indians "stand in a class by themselves when it comes to economic deprivation." (Thurow, 1976: pgs. 3-7) More Indian women than any other group (86%) earn less than $5,000 per year. Thirty-five percent of Indian women participated in the labor force in 1970; they earned a median annual income of $1,697. Seventy percent were in the powerless and vulnerable positions of clerks, operatives and domestic service workers (U.S. Census, 1970). Although there were two wage earners in almost one-half of Indian households in 1969, their median family income was $3,300.

references

American Indians, Bureau of the Census, PC (2)-1F, June 1973.

Japanese, Chinese, and Filipinos in the United States. Bureau of the Census, PC (2)-1G, July 1973.

Persons of Spanish Origin in the United States: March 1975. Bureau of the Census, Series P-20, No. 290, February, 1976.

The Social and Economic Status of the Black Population in the United States, 1974. Bureau of the Census, Series P-23, No. 54, July 1975.

Sung, Betty Lee, *Chinese American Manpower and Employment.* Report to the Manpower Administration, Department of Labor, 1975.

Thurow, Lester C. "The Economic Status of Minorities and Women." *Civil Rights Digest,* Vol. 8 (2-3), 1976.

Wilber, George; Jaco, Daniel, Hagan, Robert; and de Fierro, Alfonso, *Orientals in the American Labor Market.* Vol. II, Social Welfare Research Institute, University of Kentucky, 1975.

sisterhood is complicated

Michele Russell

It is 1976 in America: the age of technological marvels, space travel, microwave ovens, liberated life-styles, new careers, *Ms.* and *VIVA!* magazines. And precisely because it is, we must remind ourselves of some things. We are not a homogenous "middle class" nation moving toward an equalization of opportunity, power, and participation. Nor is our technology necessarily liberating.

Ask a black woman tenant farmer in the rural South how things have changed since 1876. Technology has made it harder for her to live.

Five miles south of Greenville, Mississippi, close to the Mississippi River, is a big flat cotton field owned by a white family. Under a blazing sun, a group of Negro women and children are hoeing the weeds between the rows. Fifty yards away stands a row of wooden shacks, warping in the heat, alongside a sluggish creek, the only sanitary facility. "The man pays but $3.00 a day," said one woman, hoeing as she spoke. "No, I don't know how much the children will get, but he said something. Maybe 60 cents the day, maybe more. It don't do no good to press him. We need the work and he pays more than some people. Across there (she pointed toward a plantation on the far side of the highway) the man pays $2.50 a day." She goes on, "There used to be a whole lot more people on the plantation than there are now. The machines started long back in '50, '53, '54. Then every year they begin to get more and more, more and more, and that begin to cut people down out of the pickin', you know." Poisons sprayed from crop-dusting planes have ended the demand for cotton choppers. Mechanical cotton pickers, looking insect-like with their large awkward bins angling out above their tiny wheel base, have replaced hand pickers, except at the ends of the rows where the picker makes its turn and cannot reap cleanly for a stretch about 15 feet deep in the row. Here the women can still get a few sacks.[1]

[1] *Regulating the Poor*, Frances Piven & Richard Cloward, Vintage Books, 1971, pp. 201-2.

259

Or ask a young white woman office worker how things have changed from the 1920's when entry into white collar employment was regarded by women as an escape from home-centered drudgery. A receptionist in a large midwestern business establishment says: "You're there just to filter people and filter telephone calls. You're there just to handle the equipment. You're treated like a piece of equipment, like the telephone. You come in at nine, you open the door, you look at the piece of machinery, you plug in the headpiece. You tremble when you hear the first ring. After that, it's sort of downhill—unless there's someone on the phone who's either kind or nasty. The rest of the people are just non, they don't exist. . . . The machine dictates. This crummy little machine with buttons on it—you've got to be there to answer it. You can walk away from it and pretend you don't hear it, but it pulls you. Your job doesn't mean anything. Because you're just a little machine. A monkey could do what I do."

An airline reservationist adds these comments:

"They brought in a computer called Sabre. It's like an electric typewriter. It has a memory drum and you can retrieve that information forever. Sabre was so expensive, everything was geared to it. With Sabre being so valuable, you were allowed no more than three minutes on the telephone. You had twenty seconds, busy-out time it was called, to put the information into Sabre. Then you had to be available for another phone call. It was almost like a production line. We adjusted to the machine. They monitored you and listened to your conversations. If you were a minute late for work, it went into your file. I had a horrible attendance record—ten letters in my file for lateness, a total of ten minutes. . . . I was taking eight tranquilizers a day."[2]

Boredom, atomization and depersonalization, bureaucratic surveillance and rigidity, invasions of privacy. Progress.

Or think of the industries where women predominate like the garment industry. Still tied to the piece-work system, seasonally employed, often nonunionized, Puerto Rican and Filipino women are trapped in the same jobs today that Eastern European women entered at the turn of the century to be followed in turn by Asians and blacks. One's hope for individual security is tied to retirement benefits, not advancement.

And remember the millions of women still at home whose primary social and economic function is reproduction: the bearing and nurturing of future generations of workers. Preoccupied with deciding the superiority of liquid over powder detergents and roused into momentary titillation by the game shows and soap operas they can watch on TV while ironing, finding satisfaction vicariously in caring for others, how have things changed for them?

It's all still happening: the disorganization, the conditions of life, and the range of consciousness each situation creates. Collisions are inevit-

[2]*Working*, Studs Terkel, Pantheon Books, 1974, pp. 29, 49.

able as we each learn in our own circumstances what it means not to be free and to rage against our bondage.

The recent movement that has tried to bridge this range of consciousness and condition originated from a narrow social base and has, in turn, experienced extensive fragmentation. Only the most reformist organizations, emphasizing equal treatment under law, have avoided the deep schisms attending more ambitious programmatic efforts and ideological perspectives.

In the period of Southern organizing spearheaded by SNCC, thousands of young white women took the existential step of breaking through the insulation, racism, and moral taboos of fifties communities to stand with grass roots black folk in their struggle for voting rights. Rosa Parks and Fannie Lou Hamer became for them what Sojourner Truth and Harriet Tubman were to nineteenth century Abolitionists and Suffragists. A few of these women found lasting community and rewarding work among poor whites in those same and other locales. Many more, unsure of everything except an intuition of injustice and their own hunger for a fuller life, naively hoped to absorb politics by association. They clothed themselves in the accessories of struggle. They "bore witness" to the wrongs experienced by others. For those to whom Freedom Summers were adventurous safaris, the urge to become collectors proved overwhelming. Commodity culture triumphed. And they returned with their trophies: slogans, songs, souveniers, emotional attachments to black men (who were often reduced to fetishes, too), and the hatred of black women who viewed their behavior as more white thievery.

Then back North: the campus Free Speech Movements, the revolt against America's aggression in Southeast Asia, the rhetoric of participatory democracy and communalism all the time the Movement was becoming more and more a collection of mass demonstrations. Black and white women learned bitter lessons in that crucible of activism and partially realized idealism. And separatist tendencies blossomed from the unevenly plowed fields of the Movement's racism and male chauvinism. Both white and black women temporarily retreated from the unprecedented and complex difficulties of giving leadership to a racially, culturally, economically, and sexually divided constituency. Black women cleaved to race and white women to gender as the most all-embracing and rewarding context in which to continue their struggle for self-actualization and collective freedom.

It would be unproductive and diversionary to scrutinize in these pages the varied and sometimes rarified paths that many black and white sisters pursued during this period. More important is a review of the activity and consciousness currently in evidence among masses of black and white women which the political climate of the sixties shaped. Above all, the sixties produced a mass of people sophisticated enough to agree to the following statements:

1. Many forms of discrimination against women are similar to forms of discrimination against racial minorities, especially blacks: confinement to low-skilled, low-pay jobs, wage differentials for similar work, separate lines of seniority and progression on the job, use as a reserve labor force which can be enlisted in times of war and expansion and discharged in times of peace and recession, ghettoized in dual labor markets.
2. The whole of our national culture is permeated with stereotypes equating femininity with passivity, ignorance, docility, ineffectuality, and service to others above oneself.
3. The history of America is replete with examples of how those in power have played off women and racial minorities against one another to limit effective political participation, keep wages down, thwart unionization, and narrow the terms in which people think of "self interest."
4. History is also replete with examples of how women and racial minorities have come together to accomplish specific objectives in the face of heavy odds to the contrary. Recent successes include the 1973 strike for union recognition at Oneita Knitting Mills in South Carolina, where women are 85 percent of the workforce and 75 percent of the workers are black.

Yet all too often, when we who say we understand these things begin to act, we are confronted with undreamed of difficulties. Difficulties within our own ranks. What happens? What happens in situations where there should be functional solidarity among women across race lines but only discord reigns?

I have seen black women courageously attack the right of the government to define their children's socialization in schools. They demanded community control; they unmasked the racism of the curriculum and the bankruptcy of the whole credential system by proving their own ability to teach; they actually forced their own institutional access to the educational process through paraprofessionalism, and then wound up, in the words of one sister, as "teachers' maids, not teachers' aides"—pouring juice, cleaning classrooms, running errands, only accomplishing the further stratification of janitorial service. Reinforced in their children's eyes as domestics. They found themselves still under the supervision of white women often half their age whose "feminist" concerns surfaced primarily in striking for higher salaries for less work.

I have seen white women build on the corporate analysis of the sixties movement and develop sophisticated rationales and organizational strategies to break through the channeling system that feeds women into jobs that are the public extensions of housework such as, nurses, waitresses, seamstresses, cooks, and maids. I have watched them demand and achieve access to so-called "non-traditional" careers and in their escape, still give but scant attention to how work for sisters trapped in those other jobs could become just as political.

I have seen black and white women come to blows over the issue of birth control and abortion because for the white woman such reforms meant increased freedom of choice in a context of family-centered oppression. For blacks, however, the institutionalization of such prerogatives meant all the horrors of involuntary sterilization, the further extension of government control in their lives, the spectre of genocide, and the commitment by whites that blacks are and always shall be fifteen to twenty percent of the race.

What makes the black RN resist hospital unionization drives which the white Croatian orderly welcomes?

What perpetuates the tunnel vision with which white career women pressure their corporations to institute child care facilities to maximize their vocational options without regard to the wage scales or institutionalized values which will insure third world women being the primary workforce locked into doing the child care function?

What prompts black women to say "Please, Lord, let me have the luxury to stay at home and be a housewife"? And against what historical background should that cry be judged?

By what feminist criteria do white women celebrate token jobs as truck drivers when the racism of the trucking industry is legendary and the unemployment rate for the black community as a whole continues to be twice that in the white?

None of these are false issues. They all describe part of the problem. To resolve them, we must go beyond the framework of "change within the system." It was never organized to stretch that far.

Our problem is not just that the dominant patterns of socialization for white women in America have been home-centered, privatized, male dominated, and self-sacrificial. Although they have been all that and more.

It is not just that black women in America have been on the public auction block—meat for sale—from day one, and that slavery, tenant farming, and industrial labor left little room for bourgeois role differentiation between the sexes in the black community. Although that is demonstrably true.

It is not just that in the cultural mystification of our society black women, almost involuntarily, will associate white female existence with "cloisters" and "pedastals" and being "pampered" and white women will flash "sexual promiscuity", ADC, and "strength" in characterizing black women as a group.

It is not that in individualistic attempts to transcend historical roles black women will take pay-cuts in order to have white-collar jobs associated with gentility. Nor is it that white women will voluntarily submit themselves to severe psychological and physical hardships to break into the male preserves of assembly-line labor and the skilled trades, demonstrating their "strength under the lash" as well as enjoying higher wages.

In 1976 America, the black community is almost as socially and economically stratified as the white community. Black women have maids and white ADC mothers go hungry and know the reality of forced labor. Black women are still used by corporations as double statistics to substantiate the sham of progress and to avoid employing more black men. And white women, believing the corporate figures, continue to have faith that the economy will at least be able to provide them with ever-expanding personal and occupational opportunity. Never mind that general unemployment keeps rising.

We experience at least as many varieties of human alienation as there are job categories in the system. Often those of us who enjoy the most economic and vocational security and have the time to invest in creative personal exploration are also the most isolated from others and most narrow in social outlook.

Our immediate impulse as individuals in the fight for self-respect under capitalism is to legitimize our particular form of victimization. We unfurl the flag of our condition and make that our morality. Because we have been trained to survive in the context of capitalistic hierarchical relationships at home and on the job we tend to reproduce those values even as we organize for our "rights." We clutch fiercely to the status of our personally felt oppression (just as we sacrifice ourselves to the miniscule prerogatives provided by moving up the job ladder) because we are not yet ready to contend for fundamental power to end all forms of exploitation.

Granted, as women we each have our own range of personal needs which must find expression before we can enter as strong human beings into free association with others struggling for broad societal transformation. But those needs must be connected to the dominant political realities that divide active women today. Those in America who own and control the corporations, who "advise" the politicians, and who shape the contexts and terms of our participation in this society continue to rely primarily on race and class stratification within and across racial lines to maintain their power.

First we must get to the point of identifying their system as the one we want to replace. Then our behavior in daily life, hour by hour, is the only trustworthy bridge linking who we want to be as individuals to the community we must create at every step to sustain our new emerging selves. Sharpening the consciousness with which we live through the minutes, the small acts, the habits which are really decisions, should force all of us, black and white, to ask one another at least the following questions as we seriously contest for hegemony:

Do we find ourselves unconsciously capitulating to the commodity transformation of our best impulses? (For example, winning the right to wear slacks to work and then spending every coffee break comparing the latest pant-suit fashions.)

Do we recklessly revel in situational power as an individual before there is any collective context to give such expression meaning? (For example, threatening our boss with filing a Title VII discrimination suit and settling for a personal promotion rather than organizing a union of clerical workers.

Do we let ourselves relax into hard-won personal comfort in the face of mass hardship or expect others to take risks we shy away from in our own lives?

Ultimately, the questions are: What do we want to build? What are we willing to risk? What do we think we have to lose? And who do we need to help us?

This is the kind of scrutiny and judgment that creates political sisterhood. This is the relentless process that cannot be kept alive solely by organizational affiliation, ideology, nationality, or common gender. This is why Che Guevara said that to be a revolutionary, one must also be guided by feelings of great love. This is why sisterhood is complicated.

the Chicana as feminist

Cecilia Preciado de Burciaga

Viola Gonzales

Ruth A. Hepburn

To the larger American society, Chicana feminism is a part either of black power or is under the protection of the white feminist movement. For the most part, the term minority connotes black, and Chicana falls in the broad category of Spanish-speaking. Few people discuss Chicana feminism unless they are talking about women. However, Chicana feminism is neither an offshoot of one or the other, nor does it seek an identity from either one. It is an entity brought about by unique circumstances and distinctive needs.

Although the total experience of Chicanas is distinct from that of other women, they share many of the same patterns of gender, class and race oppression. Moreover, Chicanas have many of the same economic and social patterns as other working-class groups. Distinctions are to be found by elaborating specifics rather than by noting patterns.

employment

Contrary to the image of the Chicana who stays at home as a baby and *tortilla* maker, the 1970 California census indicated that 49 percent of all Chicanas over eighteen years of age are in the work force. During the peak child-bearing years, between twenty and twenty-one, 56 percent of all Chicanas are workers. In California, 53 percent of the Chicanas are employed as domestic workers, or in service industries and factories; thus they are relegated to the lowest status, lowest paying jobs.

Economic discrimination is common to all women. It is more severe, however, for ethnic minority women. Chicana earnings were at the bottom of a list of nine groups of workers in the 1970 census. Chicanas who worked 40 hours a week, according to the report, could expect an average wage of less than $1900 per year. Earning more than Chicanas were white men, black men, "other ethnic" men, white women, Japanese-American women, Filipino women, and black women. Only American Indian women earned less than Chicanas: an average of $1600 per year.

High unemployment or underemployment are common among women, but especially among Chicanas. In the state of California, white women comprise 41.5 percent of the white work force with an unemployment rate of 6.8 percent. The Chicano labor force, which is 40.5 percent women, has an unemployment rate of 9.6 percent throughout the state. In high density population areas, such as Los Angeles or San Jose, the unemployment rate for Chicanas ranges up to 14.5 percent.

Across the country, Chicanas have lower incomes and larger families as compared to white women. Table 1 indicates that 31.2 percent of Chicano families have incomes below $5,000 per year. As compared to white families, a larger percentage of Chicano families are headed by females.

Table 1.   *socioeconomic characteristics*

Indicators	White	Chicano
Total families (in 000's)	45,770	2,039
Percent with income less than $5,000 (annually)	16.2%	31.2%
Percent with female head	9.0%	12.8%
Percent with children under six years	25.5%	40.3%
Mean size of family	3.49	4.38
Birth rat′ (per 1,000 women, aged 35-44 years)	2.89	3.90

Source: Manpower Report of the President, March 1973.

Until very recently the Women's Bureau (U. S. Dept. of Labor) has failed to investigate Chicanas as a category of workers, depending instead on unreliable census statistics. Consequently, Chicanas have been forced to initiate, develop, and compile their own data. Many of the statistics on Chicanas in California in this discussion were made available by the East Los Angeles Chicana Service Action Center, a group that has spearheaded the development of employment data on Chicanas.

society and family

The institutions of family, school, and church socialize all women but the impact of these institutions reflect a different reality for Chicanas. For the Chicana, the *familia*, or family, evokes three levels of concern, awareness, and commitment. She is first concerned with the family nucleus for which she feels direct responsibility as mother, wife, sister, or daughter. Second, she is committed to an extended family, as the *familia* also encompasses grandparents, uncles, aunts, cousins, nephews, and nieces. Third, in *carnalismo* (sister or brotherhood) she is concerned about the progress and betterment of La Raza, or her people, as well. The Chicana's role within the *familia* is in constant evolution. She relates not only as a wife and mother but also as granddaughter, daughter, sister, aunt, worker, confidante, and sometimes political activist.

In the Chicano *familia* aged parents or grandparents are seldom left to fend for themselves. They form an essential part of family life and are taken into the homes of their sons or daughters. Frequently, young children are cared for by grandparents while both parents work outside the home. This commitment to family has lessened the generation gap within the Chicano household because there can be daily exchange between the very young and the very old.

An idealized, cohesive family is perhaps a more common Chicano family portrait demonstrating the mutual dependence and support of the family. Chicanas have acted as the conduit for the cultural preservation of family. It is impossible for the Chicana to consider her liberation in isolation. Her life is interwoven with the lives of a community and to detach herself from these concerns and commitments would negate an essential part of her being.

Against the background of a family that builds and reinforces a spirit of unity, young Chicanas enter an educational system that prizes constant competition. If a Chicana chooses not to compete openly against her friends in the classroom, the schools stereotype her as "shy and reticent."

In many instances, the values of a school system are in direct conflict with the values of Chicano parents for whom the concept of *educacion* is much broader than the mechanics of reading, writing, and learning arithmetic. For the Chicano family, an "educated" person is one who has developed personal integrity, a sense of self worth, and is concerned for others. These human qualities are seldom emphasized or reinforced in a typical curriculum or school activities.

Rigid sex-role stereotyping portraying women as mothers cheerfully baking cookies and cleaning house all day while fathers work in offices is damaging for all women. For Chicanas the damage is compounded by the fact that the "mothers" in the media stereotypes are almost always middle-class white women.

For Chicanas, role models in the schools are seldom teachers, principals, or school-board members but more often service workers in cafeterias. Chicanas have borne the brunt of the educational system's self-fulfilling prophecies. They have been traditionally counseled or tracked into vocational classes such as cosmetology and clerical skills because the school system operates under the misconception that this is what they are most interested in and best suited for. For example, a high school in South Texas provided Chicana students with what they termed "relevant" work-study experience by contracting with local hotels for "domestic maintenance courses." Chicanas learned how to clean hotel rooms properly and work in hotel kitchens. No doubt school officials believed that this was the proper role for Chicanas.

The Texas example is not exceptional. Chicanas constantly battle with their counselors to be in college preparatory classes. It must be recognized that the educational system is the microcosm of the larger society. Chicanas must organize to assert and delineate their needs in the school system.

Another major socializing agent to influence Chicanas has been the Roman Catholic Church. Women in the Church have been excluded from decision making; they are relegated to supportive roles. Nuns provide one model for women to emulate; they are people who devote their lives to Christ and selflessly spend their energies as teachers, nurses, and missionaries. They are the Church's service workers. In the Church, wives and mothers ar responsible for providing leadership as Catholic role-models in their homes. They are encouraged to be members of altar societies (which take care of the altar and church linens), teach catechism or join in other service-oriented organizations in their parishes. The Church has provided socialization for all women that emphasizes chastity, idealized in the image of the Virgin. Mary, as Mother of God, is venerated primarily because of her virginity. Nuestra Señora de Guadelupe (Our Lady of Guadalupe) is a strong figure for Chicanas to identify with because of her importance in Mexican history.

A traditional Chicana is socialized to protect her virginity at all costs. Many women saints are venerated because there were examples of chastity, and many were martyred in order to protect their virginity. The symbolism of white, for purity, predominates in the sacraments of Holy Communion and marriage. It is the woman who must wear the outward signs of purity while the man dresses in black or dark colors.

A Chicana, as a Catholic, is taught to believe that the greatest demonstration of love she can give on her wedding night is the surrendering of her virginity. The dual standard is in full operation because a Chicano is not socialized under the same norm. His virginity is not valued in the same light nor does he suffer from the same psychological guilt if he loses it.

Abortion is not always seen as a clearly moral alternative for traditional Chicanas. It is many times easier for a Chicana to mouth the words that all women must have the right to control their bodies than to actually choose the alternative of abortion for herself. Abortion carries with it all of the negative vestiges of murder or an immoral act. A traditional Chicana confronts psychological, spiritual, and emotional drain in the face of an abortion.

White women must understand that each Chicana differs from others in her religious, social, and emotional makeup, so that it is impossible to generalize about "all Chicanas." Too often, white women's assumptions about Chicanas have been based on quaint stereotypes that have gone unchallenged. White women and Chicanas must begin an open dialog without preconceived notions of what they will discover. The essential myth to destroy is the fact that Chicana feminism depends on the Women's Movement.

chicana feminism vs. white feminism

Chicana feminism is not new and must be understood in its own context. Historically, Chicanas have many role models from which to draw in Mexican history. Sor Juana Inez de la Cruz, a Mexican nun in the seventeenth century, can be considered one of the leading feminists of the Americas. Sister Juana recognized the oppression and limitations that women faced and chose to enter a Catholic cloister in lieu of living in a society that would force her to accept her fate passively. From her cloister cell came the earliest written proclamations in defense of women as intellectual equals with men. Unfortunately, she was looked upon as an exception in her own time. Her argument was that the powers, virtues, and strengths of women were not visible because society had not permitted them to express themselves.

La Adelita, or woman soldier, was seen as the very center of strength in the Mexican Revolution. There was not one but hundreds of *Adelitas* who were soldiers in the revolutionary effort; these women left their homes, families, and villages in order to fight alongside men. Many of the songs of the Revolution speak of *Adelita* and extol her fierce bravery in the line of fire. Yet, she had to face societal criticisms in her day and overcome the image of being a campfollower. Chicanas today continue to emulate the *Adelitas*, realizing they cannot be passive while being bombarded with injustices. Throughout the history of the Chicano movement, women can be singled out as leaders in labor, education, and community efforts.

Chicanas have developed a resentment because white women say that they sympathize with Chicanas because they "understand" the concept of *machismo*. All too often, their understanding is based on gross stereotypes and extremes that rarely exist or are a product of white anthropologists and sociologists. Positive attributes of *machismo* are rarely discussed by critics. A *macho* protects his family at all costs; he defends and supports the family with the help of the Chicana. White women who fail to evaluate their "understanding" of *machismo* advise Chicanas that "their men" are their oppressors, thus challenging the critical gender divisions in La Raza. Women who construct such an argument analyze oppression in narrow and incomplete terms. Predictably, Chicanas will reject alliances with these women.

It must also be recognized that Chicanas too often generalize that the "White Women's Movement" is coherent and unified, a microcosm of the dominant society. White feminists, thus narrowly categorized, are thought to be concerned exclusively with buying into the dominant society that systematically devalues and exploits Chicanos. This becomes another reason for Chicana feminists to have no interest in working with white feminists. However, white women are not alike in their personalities and beliefs and their feminist expressions differ. Chicanas rightly condemn and reject white feminists who are uncritical of the system in their frantic rush for entry into it. So do many white women.

White feminists range over a wide political spectrum. They include conservatives, who plug away at legislative reforms; liberals, who exaggerate gender differences and who aim for "humanization" and change by getting women into the system; "radical feminists" who define oppression exclusively in terms of gender; and feminists who understand and acknowledge that the exploitation of women follows other patterns in society.

Consequently, Chicanas must consider values, not race, as the bases for participating in alliances and coalitions with white women. Automatic rejection of the Movement on the basis of its association with the white race serves the dominant society and, in fact, is fostered by it. Tactically, women have been divided in their competition for crumbs. "We've got to stop comparing wounds," as Black feminist Florynce Kennedy has stated, "and go after the system that does the wounding."

If there are times when Chicanas and white women "work together against the injustices of the system, then Chicanas will want to establish some checkpoints with which to evaluate white feminists. The predominant consideration must be how white feminists define themselves by their actions. Does their analysis of the "oppression of women" encompass the experiences of Chicanas? Do they develop all the women in their group or do they imitate the dominant society by creating "leaders" and "stars." Do they value children and affirm the strengths of motherhood?

Three checkpoints are critical. How do white feminists function on the issues of racism and consumerism? Feminists must guard against accepting racist solutions to their problems. In the work place, for instance, white women are often put directly into competition with Chicanos. Rather than resist this division, white women should question their advancements at the expense of Chicanos and other Third World men.

Further, it is essential for white feminists to use their consumer power to combat racism. White women have the power not to buy—the economic boycott—and thus lend material support to some of the struggles of Chicanos; for example, the United Farm Workers boycotts of lettuce, grapes and Gallo wines.

A final checkpoint might be to what extent have white feminists assumed their responsibility to educate members of their own race about systematic oppression? If white feminists do not become active in this regard, there is no reason for them to expect Chicanas (or other Third World women) to be willing to form alliances or coalitions. White women must learn about their complicity in systematic oppression. They do not, by themselves, exploit Chicanas, but their acceptance of the status quo amounts to maintaining a system that oppresses all Raza people. While acceptance of the status quo is basic to its force and stability, many white women should beware of going beyond acceptance to active support of exploitive relationships.

Thus we note the curious phenomena that white women function simultaneously as both exploiters and exploited. To the extent that white feminists examine common sources of oppression—and structure their actions accordingly—Chicanas will be accessible to coalitions when interests and values are shared.

At present, the widest sharing of interests between Chicana and white feminists is in the context of women in the work force. Chicana and white women serve the same function of being "marginal" workers in the economy. Historically, they are brought into the work force during times of economic expansion and discarded when the economy contracts.

White women and Chicanas work at many of the same jobs. As clerical workers, for example, they often find themselves "subemployed," that is, working full time but earning less than a subsistence wage. Women can organize to secure more accurate compensation for efforts—wages that reflect the value of labor.

Many of women's on-the-job needs are the same. All races require cheap transportation to and from the workplace as well as desirable childcare facilities. Thus, together women can fight for free public transportation and community controlled child nurturing centers.

All women are coming to realize that the feminist demand of "equal pay for equal work" is outdated. The fundamental demand must be for access to equal work. For example, women can work to secure training in skilled trades—jobs valued highly in our society and an integral part of our economy.

All women and Third World men are the most vulnerable workers in a time of economic collapse—"last hired, first fired." Unity, mutual understanding and acknowledgment of common problems will be required for their survival. If women are ready to assert their power as workers, they will insure that many are not "traded off" in exchange for the continued employment of a few.

Chicana and white feminists will realize unity and understanding only to the extent that they commit themselves to difficult processes of communication and set aside preconceived notions about each other.

The difficulty of the task should not be underestimated; the two groups have been put into direct competition with each other too often for members easily to forget their mutual distrust. They have classified one another and, in the process, abstracted each other into categories: "bourgeois Anglos" and "*macho*-oppressed Chicanas." Each condemns the other for a failure of analysis. These categories are confining at times when situations demand critical evaluation of the specifics of other individuals and groups.

This rigid stereotyping effectively destroys opportunities to evaluate the possibility of creating coalitions that might benefit all women. In so doing, women perform the work of the dominant members of society whose interests are served by keeping them divided.

To overcome the societal forces of division women can commit themselves to a deliberate analysis of the ways in which forms of oppression are linked and the interests they share. The most basic requirement is for women to see each other in terms of their values. In this process, Chicanas can recognize the political spectrum of white feminists; white feminists can recognize that Chicanas can lead as well as follow.

A viable women's movement will encompass the experiences of all women and oppressed men, will refuse to be divided by racism, and in addressing common interests, will recognize that the first step in the process of liberation is survival.

references

Consuelo Avila, "Ecos de una Convencion," *Magazin:* 1 (9), September 1973, pp. 33-36.

Fidel Castro. *Address to the Confederation of American Women* (1966).

Evey Chapa, "Report from the National Women's Political Caucus," *Magazin:* 1 (9), September 1973, pp. 37-39.

Marta Cotera, "A Chicana Bibliography," *Magazin:* 1 (9), September 1973, p. 39.

"Mexicano Feminism," *Magazin:* 1 (9), September 1973, pp. 30-32.

Elena Hernandez, in *Chicanismo:* III (3), April 10, 1972.

Dolores Ibarruri. *They Will Not Pass: The Autobiography of La Pasionaria* (1966).

Enriquetta Longauex y Vaxquex, "The Mexican-American Woman" in Robin Morgin, ed. *Sisterhood is Powerful* (1970).

Miguel Montiel, "The Social Science Myth of the Mexican-American Family," *El Grito*, III (4), Summer 1970.

Chicana Service Action Center, "The CSAC Newsletter," "Regeneracion," and various publications on socio-economic statistics. 1226 S. Atlantic Blvd., Los Angeles, Ca. 90022.

"Women of the Barrio," *Los Angeles Times:* February 10, 1972: April 2, 1972: May 21-25, 1972.

"Women in Transition," *Cuba Review:* IV (2), September 1974.

personal
change

In education, in marriage, in religion, in
everything, disappointment is the lot of
women. It shall be the business of my life to
deepen this disappointment in every
women's heart until she bows down to it no
longer.

—**Lucy Stone - 1855**

There is a tacit assumption that somehow
we know the dictates of the real self, and
that we should live in terms of these rather
than of a romanticized self-image or of the
pseudo-self of others' expectation. But like
understanding of "reality," such a real self
is something to be discovered and created,
not a given but a lifelong endeavor.

—**Helen M. Lynd**

Women and men have essentially been
socialized in two different cultures. In
our society the division of labor has
allocated to women the responsibility
for intimacy and connectedness with
men, and to men the values of work,
power, and achievement. Women have been encouraged to meet the
socioemotional needs of other people, to pay attention to feedback in

relationships, to express emotions, to take feelings into account when making decisions, and to personalize what is being said. Men, on the other hand, have been taught to achieve, to be independent, to pay attention to feedback from tasks almost more than to feedback from people, to be logical rather than emotional, and to depersonalize situations.

Fulfillment for women has consisted in their marrying the kinds of men and obtaining the homes which would allow them joyful altruism and nurturance as they care for their families. The care of families remains critical, but, until the present, most of the responsibility has fallen unquestioningly upon one party, the wife. The cost to many women is that much of their daily life is lived in a world of children, homemaking, and other responsibilities which do not provide them with sufficient "open space" for self-exploration and self-actualization.

Fulfillment for men has consisted in achieving and being productive in the world of work and being a responsible provider at home. The cost to many men is that they do not enjoy a nurturant, involving relationship with their children which encourages their own growth and the expression of their tender feelings, nor do they have a clear sense of themselves apart from their work roles. Some men are aware of the costs of their position: a loss of contact with feelings, a loss of a sense of self, a loss of purpose other than to achieve and produce, a lack of intimacy with their children, a lack of ability to derive comfort from their relationships with their children, and the lack of opportunity to be dependent, to be afraid, and to hurt out loud. But many men have been seduced into the system which they did not create and whose costs they have only recently begun to assess. It would seem that if the skills of a woman and a man were to be combined they would be a complete person. If women and men are to self-actualize and to become independent, then they need to learn each other's skills.

As we have discussed at length in the first section of this book, the initial step in the change process is awareness of these sex-linked behaviors. In the next step, men and women begin to modify the behaviors which they have overlearned or underlearned.

Women need:

to learn how to be powerful and forthright;
to be entrepreneurial;
to have a direct, visible impact on others rather than functioning behind the scenes;
to state their own needs and not back down even if the immediate response is not acceptance;
to focus on a task and regard it as at least as important as they consider the relationships of the people doing the task;
to build support systems with other women and to share competence

with women rather than compete with them;

to build a sense of community among women instead of saying: "I pulled myself up by my bootstraps, why can't you";

to intellectualize and generalize from experience;

to behave "impersonally" rather than to personalize experience, thereby denying another's reality because it is different from one's own reality;

to stop being intrapunitive and turning anger, blame, and pain inward;

to stop feeling more comfortable with feelings of suffering and victimization;

to have the option of being invulnerable to feedback if the information does not come in a helpful way;

to stop being bitchy or passive-resistant about resentments and anger;

to respond directly with "I" statements rather than with blaming "you" statements;

to be effective problem solvers which means being analytical, systematic, and directive at times rather than fearful or dependent,

to stop self-limiting behaviors such as allowing oneself to be interrupted or laughing after making a serious statement;

to be risk takers, although it is particularly difficult at this time when each woman feels that she is regarded as representative of all womankind.

At the same time, men need to learn:

to become aware of feelings, rather than avoid or suppress them;

to accept and express feelings as a valid part of oneself, rather than as a part to be hidden and compartmentalized;

to regard feelings as a basic and essential part of life, as guides to authenticity and effectiveness as a fully functioning person, rather than as impediments to achievement;

to experience and own the vulnerability and imperfections which are part of all persons;

to assert the right to work for self-fulfillment rather than only to meet the obligations of the "provider" role;

to value an identity that is not defined totally by work;

to accept a share of responsibility for "providing," but to refuse total responsibility for it;

to learn how to fail at a task without feeling one has failed as a man;

to accept and express the need to be nurtured when feeling hurt, afraid, vulnerable, or helpless, rather than hide those feelings behind a mask of strength, rationality, and invulnerability;

to touch and be close to both men and women, with less inhibition over the presence or absence of sexuality in the contact;

to listen actively and emphatically without feeling responsible for solving others' problems;

to share feelings as the most meaningful and personal part of one's contact with others;

to accept the risk and vulnerability that the sharing of feelings implies;

to build support systems with other men, sharing competencies without competition, and feelings and needs without dissembling;

to personalize experience, rather than assuming that the only valid approach to life and interpersonal contact is "objective";

to give up performance-oriented sexuality for a more sensual, less goal-oriented, personalized sexuality;

that the emotional, spontaneous, and rational are valid parts of oneself to be explored and expressed as need be;

to nurture and actively support other men and women in their efforts to change.*

The articles in this section suggest ways to facilitate some of these behavior changes through workshops in which they can explore changing relationships among women and men and other planned change training programs in the sex-roles area. Androgyny is offered as a model for self-actualization which encourages the full expression of the feminine and masculine personality dimensions in each person.

*I am grateful to Vincent Ward, University of Connecticut, Department of Child Development and Family Relations, for helping to generate this list.

periods in the adult development of men: ages 18 to 45

Daniel J. Levinson
Charlotte M. Darrow
Edward B. Klein
Maria H. Levinson
Braxton McKee

This is a progress report on a study of forty men, all of whom are currently aged 35-45. There are ten men in each of four occupational groups: blue-collar and white-collar workers in industry; business executives; academic biologists; and novelists. Each man was seen six to ten times for a total of ten to twenty hours over a period of two to three months. We had a single follow-up interview with most of the men about two years after the initial interviews. Our aim is to construct a theory of adult male development over the age span of about 20-45.

developmental periods in the adult life course

We have found it convenient to distinguish several gross chronological periods in the adult life course: early adulthood, roughly ages 20-40; middle adulthood, ages 40-60; and late adulthood, age 60+. We are studying early adulthood and the "mid-life transition," that is, the several years on either side of 40 that constitute a transitional period between early and middle adulthood.

These are descriptive time units that we use to begin making developmental distinctions within adult life. Something even as simple as this is necessary because of the tremendous neglect of development

Note: The project is carried out by the Research Unit for Social Psychology and Psychiatry at the Connecticut Mental Health Center, and the Department of Psychiatry, Yale University. This is a slightly revised version of a paper by Daniel J. Levinson et al., "The Psychosocial Development of Men in Early Adulthood and Mid-Life Transition," in *Life History Research in Psychopathology*, Vol. 3, edited by David Ricks, Alexander Thomas & Merrill Roff. The University of Minnesota Press, Minneapolis. © Copyright 1974 by the University of Minnesota.

and socialization in the main adult years, roughly 20-65, in psychology, psychiatry, sociology, and so on. In the past, people have spoken as though development goes on to age 6, or perhaps to age 18; then there is a long plateau in which random things occur; and then at around 60 or 65 "aging" begins.

There is little work in sociology on adult socialization. In psychology there are the concepts and "psychohistorical" approach of Erikson and the extensive work of Jungian depth psychology, which is almost totally ignored by the academic disciplines. Like Jung and Erikson, we assume that there is something we can call adult development, that there is a psychosocial evolution just as in pre-adult life, and that we will not understand adults and the changes they go through in their lives if we do not have a conception of what is intrinsic to adulthood. We can then see how derivatives of childhood operate to facilitate or hinder certain kinds of development.

One of our chief theoretical aims is to formulate a sociopsychological conception of the life course and the various developmental periods, tasks, structures, and processes within it. There are, of course, wide individual and group differences in the concrete life course, as our findings show. At a more conceptual level, however, we are interested in generating and working with hypotheses concerning *relatively universal, genotypic, age-linked, adult developmental periods* within which variations occur. As we conceive of these periods, their origins lie both in the nature of the individual as a biosocial and biopsychological organism and in the nature of society as an enduring multigenerational form of collective life. The periods do not represent simply an unfolding of maturational potentials from within; they are thus different from the Freudian or Piagetan stages of childhood development, which are seen largely as an internal unfolding. Nor do they simply represent stages in a career sequence as shaped by an occupational, educational, or familial system. The periods are thus not simply a function of adult socializing systems, although these systems play an important part in defining timetables and in shaping one's course through them.

We are trying to develop an embracing sociopsychological conception of male adult development periods, within which a variety of biological, psychodynamic, cultural, social-structural, and other timetables operate in only partial synchronization. It is an important further step to do similar studies of women and to learn about similarities and differences between the sexes under various social conditions. The remaining sections of this paper set forth our theoretical conception of these periods from roughly age 20 to 45. Within the framework of this overall theory we shall show some illustrative concepts, findings, and areas of exploration. Again, we emphasize that this is a report of work in progress and by no means a final statement.

leaving the family (LF)

We conceive of Leaving the Family (LF) as a period of transition between adolescent life, centered in the family of origin, and entry into the adult world. In our sample, LF ordinarily occupies a span of some three to five years, starting at age 16-18 and ending at 20-24. It is a transitional period in the sense that the person is half in and half out of the family: he is making an effort to separate himself from the family, to develop a new home base, to reduce his dependence on familial support and authority, and to regard himself as an adult making his way in the adult world.

The separation from the family proceeds along many lines. In its external aspects, it involves changes such as moving out of the familial home, becoming financially less dependent, and getting into new roles and living arrangements in which one is more autonomous and responsible. In its internal aspects, it involves an increase in self-parent differentiation and in psychological distance from the family. Of course, these processes start earlier and continue well beyond the LF period. We say that someone is in this period when there is a roughly equal balance between "being in" the family and "moving out." From the point of view of ego development, the young man is in the stage that Erikson has identified as Identity versus Role Diffusion.

LF ordinarily begins around the end of high school (graduation or dropping out). Those who enter college or the military have a new, institutional life situation that is in many respects intermediate between the family and fully adult life in the community. The institution constitutes a home base providing some degree of structure, control, support, and maintenance. It also provides spheres of autonomy and privacy in which the young person is largely responsible for himself and can strike out on new paths. He has increasing opportunities to form relationships, as a compeer, with adults of various ages and thus to begin experiencing himself as an adult who is part of that world (rather than an adolescent standing reluctantly at the edge of it).

Those who move directly from high school into the labor force—and this is most often the case within the working-class population—have no institutional matrix to shape the transition into adult life. These young men do, nonetheless, go through the LF transition. They may continue to live at home for several years on a semi-boarder status, "leading their own lives" and yet remaining in some ways subject to parental authority and integrated within the family network. This is a common pattern among ethnic groups with strong communal and extended family bonds. Often the young man works with his father or relatives during this period. If he marries during LF, the couple may live for some time with one spouse's parents or relatives. The initial work history has the same transitional character. For several years (in some cases, permanently) the young man has no genuine occupation. He works at various jobs and acquires a variety of skills. But, lacking seniority, influence, and broader competence, he tends to be given the worst jobs on the worst shifts and to have the least job security. Even though a young man in this position may be economically self-sufficient and living on his own, he is still on the boundary between the family and the fully adult world; and getting across this boundary is his major developmental task.

The LF period ends when the balance shifts—when one has for the most part separated from the family (though further work on separation-connectedness in relation to family continues for many years, if not forever) and has begun to make a place for himself in the adult world.

**getting into
the adult
world (GIAW)**

The period we call Getting into the Adult World (GIAW) begins when the center of gravity of one's life shifts from the family of origin (or an equivalent authoritative-protective social matrix) to a new home base and an effort to form an adult life of one's own. This period ordinarily starts in the early 20's and extends until roughly age 27-29. It is a time of exploration and provisional commitment to adult roles, memberships, responsibilities, and relationships. The young man tries to establish an occupation, or an occupational direction, consistent with his interests, values, and sense of self. He begins to engage in more adult friendships and sexual relationships, and to work on what Erikson has termed the ego stage of Intimacy versus Aloneness.

The overall developmental task of the GIAW period is to explore the available possibilities of the adult world, to arrive at an initial definition of oneself as an adult, and *to fashion an initial life structure* that provides a viable link between the valued self and the wider adult world.

The concept of life structure is of central importance in our thinking. In its external aspects it refers to the individual's overall pattern of roles, memberships, interests, condition, and style of living, long-term goals, and the like—the particular ways in which he is plugged into society. In its internal aspects, life structure includes the personal meanings these have for the individual, as well as the inner identities, core values, fantasies, and psychodynamic qualities that shape and infuse one's engagement in the world and are to some degree fulfilled and changed by it. Traditional behavioristic and sociological approaches tend to emphasize the external aspects and to ignore the internal. Conversely, depth psychological approaches tend to emphasize the internal dynamics without taking sufficiently into account the nature of the sociocultural world and the individual's actual engagement in it. Our approach is to use concepts such as life structure to provide an initial focus on the *boundary between individual and society*; from this base, we can then move outward to a fuller examination of the social world and inward to a fuller examination of the personality.

GIAW is, like all entry periods, a time of exploration and initial choice. It involves, to varying degrees and in varying sequences, the processes of exploratory searching, of making provisional choices, of further exploratory testing through which the rightness of an initial choice is assessed and alternatives are considered, of increasing commitment to certain choices and the construction of a more integrated, stable life structure.

There are wide variations in the course, duration, and outcome of this period. These are a few of the patterned sequences we have found:

a.   Perhaps the most frequent pattern we find is that of the man who makes a provisional commitment to an occupation and goes through the initial stages of a career. During the 20's he is establishing a tentative structure, including an occupational choice and the beginnings of commitment to an occupational identity. Then, somewhere in the interval between age 28 and 32, he enters a transitional period in which he works on the questions: Shall I make a deeper commitment to this occupation and build a stable life structure around it? Or, I still have a chance to change shall I take it? There is a kind of bet that's being made here, at around age 30. Many of our subjects remain in the occupation initially chosen in their 20's; they get married or reaffirm the existing marriage, and they enter a new period, Settling Down.

b.   In some cases, the man at around 30 decides that his initial occupational choice was not the right one—that it is too constraining, or that it is a violation or betrayal of an early dream which now has to be pursued, or that he does not have the talent to succeed in it—and he makes a major shift in occupation and in life structure, sometimes including marriage. In this pattern the man makes a provisional structure in his 20's and then makes a moderate or drastic change at about 30.

c.   Still another variant is that of the man who during his 20's lives a rather transient, unsettled life. He then feels a desperate need at around 30 to get more order and stability into his life. It is our tentative hypothesis that if a man does not reach a significant start toward settling down by about age 34, his chances of forming a reasonably satisfying life structure, and one that can evolve in his further development, are quite small. A number of movies in the last few years have depicted this particular kind of age 30 crisis. One is *Five Easy Pieces.* Another is *Getting Straight,* which is about an ex-college radical who has been in a transient, wandering stage during his 20's. Around 30 his tentative occupational choice is to become a high school teacher, and he makes an effort which he and the educational estabishment collude to destroy.

A concept of great value in the anlysis of the GIAW period is the *dream.* Many men, though certainly not all, enter adulthood with a dream or vision of their own future. This dream is usually articulated within an occupational context—for example, becoming a great novelist, winning the Nobel Prize (a common dream of our biologists), contributing in some way to human welfare, and so on. Where such a dream exists, we are exploring its nature and vicissitudes over the life course. Major shifts in life direction at subsequent ages are often occasioned by a reactivation of the sense of betrayal or compromise of the dream. That is, very often in the crises that occur at age 30, 40, or later a major issue is the reactivation of a guiding dream, frequently one that goes back to adolescence or the early 20's, and the concern with its failure. We are also interested in the antecedents and consequences of not having a dream, because the dream can be such a vitalizing force for adult development.

A second crucial concept is that of the *transitional period.* The time around 28-32 seems to be a transitional period, a link between the termination of GIAW and the onset of the next period. We are trying to be very specific about age-linkages in order to counteract the strong tendency to assume that in adulthood very little is age-linked because development is not occurring. We pursue tenaciously the possibility that the age-linkages are stronger than has been recognized. The *Age 30 Transition,* and others like it at different points in the life course, may occasion considerable turmoil, confusion, and struggle with the environment and within oneself; or it may involve a more quiet reassessment and intensification of effort. But it is marked by important changes in life structure and internal commitments, and presages the next stage in development.

settling down (SD)

The next period is Settling Down (SD). As noted above, this period ordinarily begins in the early 30's. The individual now makes deeper commitments; invests more of himself in his work, family, and valued interests; and within the framework of this life structure, makes and pursues more long-range plans and goals.

The imagery and meaning of Settling Down are multifaceted. One aspect of this period involves *order,* stability, security, control. The man establishes his niche in society, digs in, builds a nest, and pursues his interests within the defined pattern. This aspect may be stronger or weaker in a given case. A second, contrasting aspect has more the quality of *making it.* This involves planning, striving, moving onward and upward, having an inner timetable that contains major goals and way stations and ages by which they must be reached. The executive has to get into the corporate structure by age 40 or has to be earning at least $50,000 by 40; the assistant professor has to get tenure by 40; and so on.

So these are two aspects of SD. One has more to do with *down, in, order;* the other has more to do with *up, mobility, ambition.* Antithetical to both of these is the disposition to be free, unfettered, not tied to any structure no matter how great its current satisfaction nor how alluring its future promise, always open to new possibilities, ready to soar, wander, quest in all directions as the spirit moves one. We see the surgence of this disposition in the present state of society. This disposition is usually not predominant during the early SD period, but this does not mean it is necessarily absent nor that it may not in time reassert itself. Indeed, it frequently reappears toward the end of SD.

The SD period lasts until the late 30's or early 40's, when various internal and external changes bring on new developments. We shall note just a few major characteristics of this period. In creating an integrated life structure, one can utilize only certain parts of one's self, and this means that important parts of the self are left out. A myth supported by most theories of pre-adult development is that at the end of adolescence you get yourself together and, as a normal, mature adult, you enter into a relatively stable, integrated life pattern that can continue more or less indefinitely. This is a rather cruel illusion since it leads people in early adulthood to believe that they are, or should be, fully adult and settled, and that there are no major crises or developmental changes ahead. The structure one creates in early adulthood cannot fulfill or reflect all of oneself. Parts of the self are repressed or simply left dormant. At some point the life structure must be enlarged, reformed, or radically restructured in order to express more of the self.

One reason the SD structure must change is that it is based to some degree upon illusions—illusions about the importance and meaning of achieving one's occupational goals, about one's relationships with significant others, about what it is one truly wants in life, and so on. A *de-illusioning* process—by which we mean the reduction or removal of illusions and not a cynical disillusionment—is an important aspect of post-SD development. For example, the man in the early SD period tends to regard himself as highly autonomous. He is making his own way, he is not a child anymore, his parents are not telling him what to do, he is on his own. One of his illusions is that he is, in fact, freed of what we would call tribal influences. In actuality, however, the ambitions and the goal-seeking of the 30's are very much tied in with tribal influences. We seek to a large extent what the institutions and reference groups important to us are helping us define. We may be more free of our parents, but we find or invent others who guide us, protect us, tell us what to do. Toward the end of SD, a new step is taken.

becoming one's own man (BOOM)

The next step is Becoming One's Own Man, BOOM. Calling this the BOOM time has a certain metaphorical rightness. We are now inclined to regard BOOM not as a separate period but as a time of peaking and culmination of the Settling Down period and a connecting link to the Mid-Life Transition.

BOOM tends to occur in the middle to late 30's, typically in our sample around 35-39. It represents the high point of early adulthood and the beginning of what lies beyond. A key element in this period is the man's feeling that, no matter what he has accomplished to date, he is not sufficiently his own man. He feels overly dependent upon and constrained by persons or groups who have authority over him or who, for various reasons, exert great influence upon him. The writer comes to recognize that he is unduly intimidated by his publisher or too vulnerable to the evaluations of certain critics. The man who has successfully risen through the managerial ranks with the support and encouragement of his superiors now finds that they control too much and delegate too little, and he impatiently awaits the time when he will have the authority to make his own decisions and to get the enterprise really going. The untenured faculty member imagines that once he has tenure he will be free of all the restraints and demands he's been acquiescing to since graduate school days. (The illusions die hard!)

The sense of constraint and oppression may occur not only in work but also in marriage and other relationships. We have been greatly impressed by the role of the mentor, and by developmental changes in relationships with mentors and in the capability to be a mentor. The word *mentor* is sometimes used in a primarily external sense—an adviser, teacher, protector—but we use the term in a more complex psychosocial sense. The presence or absence of mentors is, we find, an important component of the life course during the 20's and 30's. The absence of mentors is associated with various kinds of developmental impairments and with problems of individuation in mid-life.

The mentor is ordinarily 8 to 15 years older than the mentee. He is enough older to represent greater wisdom, authority, and paternal qualities, but near enough in age or attitudes to be in some respects a peer or older brother rather than in the image of the wise old man or distant father. He may be a teacher, boss, editor, or experienced co-worker. He takes the younger man under his wing, invites him into a new occupational world, shows him around, imparts his wisdom, cares, sponsors, criticizes, and bestows his blessing. The teacher and the sponsoring have their value, but the blessing is the crucial element.

The younger man, in turn, feels appreciation, admiration, respect, gratitude, love, and identification. The relationship is lovely for a time, then ends in separation arising from a quarrel, or death, or a change in circumstances. Following the separation, the personaity of the mentee is enriched further as he makes the valued qualities of the mentor more fully a part of himself. In some respects the main value of the relationship is created after it ends, but only if there was something there when it was happening. This is probably true of psychotherapy as well.

The number of mentor relationships in an individual's life does not vary widely. Few men have more than three or four, and perhaps the modal numbers are none and one. The duration of the intense mentor relationships is also not extremely variable, perhaps three to four years as an average and ten to twelve years as the upper limit. When this relationship ends, the pair may form a more modest friendship after a cooling-off period. The ending of the mentor relationship may take a rather peaceful form, with gradual loss of involvement. More often, however, and especially during the 30's, termination is brought about by increasing conflict or by forced separation, and brings in its wake intense feelings of bitterness, rancor, grief, abandonment, and rejuvenation in the mentee.

The final giving up of all mentors by those who have had them tends to occur in the middle or late 30's. One does not have mentors after 40. One may have friendships or significant working relationships after this, but the mentor relationship in its more developed form is rare, at least in our sample and in our life experience. It is given up as part of Becoming One's Own Man. The person who was formerly so loved and admired, and who was experienced as giving so much, comes now to be seen as hypercritical, oppressively controlling, seeking to make one over in his own image rather than fostering one's independence and individuality; in short, as a tyrannical and egocentric father rather than a loving, enabling mentor.

There are clearly irrational elements in this process, such as the reactivation and reworking of Oedipal conflicts, which have their origins in childhood. To focus solely on these, however, is to restrict our vision and to miss the adult developmental functions of the relationship and its termination. Whatever its Oedipal or early childhood-derived meanings, the relationship with the mentor has crucial adult meanings as well. It enables the young man to relate *as an adult* with another man who regards him as an adult and who welcomes him into the adult world on a relatively (but not completely) mutual basis.

The young man must in time reject this relationship, but this is largely because it has served its purpose. He is ready to take a further step in becoming his own man: to give up being a son in the little boy sense and a young man in the apprentice-disciple-mentee sense, and to move toward assuming more fully the functions of mentor, father, and peer in relation to other adults. This kind of developmental achievement is of the essence of adulthood and needs to be studied. It is probably impossible to become a mentor without first having been a mentee.

The importance of mentors in the adult development of women is just beginning to be recognized. To take but one example, Epstein has shown that the lack of a mentor has been a major obstacle in the professional development of women. It would serve crucial developmental functions, for male as well as female students, if there were more female faculty members in our graduate schools and professional schools. Among other things this would help to overcome the tremendous polarization of masculine and feminine that now exists in professional training and in our society generally. Men can certainly function in important respects as mentors to women students. However, there is much to be learned about the subtle ways in which conscious or unconscious sexism may lead the male teacher to regard his female student as a little girl or a mascot or a sex object, rather than welcoming her into a truly compeer relationship.

Mentor relationships probably are also of crucial importance in initiating and working on the ego stage of *generativity versus stagnation* and its attendant virtue, *caring* (for adults). Erikson has identified this stage as beginning at around 40 and as involving one's relationship to future generations in general and to the next generation of adults in particular. This goes beyond caring about one's small children, which one ordinarily has to learn in the 20's. The issue now is caring about adults, being generative in relation to adults, taking responsibility in the adult world, and getting over being a boy in the adult world. We are saying that one can't get very far with this before age 40 and that the BOOM time of the late 30's is the beginning of work on it.

During BOOM a man wants desperately to be affirmed by society in the roles that he values most. He is trying for that crucial promotion or other recognition. At about age 40—we would now say within the range of about 39 to 42—most of our subjects fix on some key event in their careers as carrying the ultimate message of their affirmation or devaluation by society. This event may be a promotion or new job—it's of crucial importance whether one gets to be vice-president of a company, or full professor in a department, or foreman or union steward. It may involve a particular form of symbolic success: writing a best seller or a prize-winning novel, being recognized as a scientist or executive or craftsman of the first rank, and so on. This event is given a magical quality. If the outcome is favorable, one imagines, then all is well and the future is assured. If it is unfavorable, the man feels that not only his work but he as a person has been found wanting and without value.

Since the course and outcome of this key event take several (perhaps three to six) years to unfold, many men at around 40 seem to be living, as one of our subjects put it, in a state of suspended animation. During the course of the waiting, the next period gets under way.

**the mid-life
transition (MLT)**

The next period we call the Mid-Life Transition. A *developmental transition,* as we use the term, is a turning point or boundary region between two periods of greater stability. A transition may go relatively smoothly or may involve considerable turmoil. The Mid-Life Transition occurs whether the individual succeeds or fails in his search for affirmation by society. At 38 he thinks that if he gains the deserved success, he'll be all set. The answer is, he will not. He is going to have a transition whether he is affirmed or not; it is only the form that varies.

The central issue is not whether he succeeds or fails in achieving his goals. The issue, rather, is what to do with the *experience of disparity* between what he has gained in an inner sense from living within a particular structure and what he wants for himself. The sense of disparity between "what I've reached at this point" and "what it is I really want" instigates a soul-searching for "what it is I really want."

To put it differently, it is not a matter of how many rewards one has obtained; it is a matter of the *goodness of fit between the life structure and the self*. A man may do extremely well in achieving his goals and yet find his success hollow or bittersweet. If, after failing in an important respect, he comes primarily to castigate himself for not being able to "make it," then he is having a rough time but he is not having a mid-life crisis. He just regrets failure. He is having a crisis to the extent that he questions his life structure and feels the stirrings of powerful forces within himself that lead him to modify or drastically to change the structure.

In making the choices out of which the Settling Down structure was built, he drew upon and lived out certain aspects of himself, fantasies, values, identities, conflicts, internal "object relationships," character traits, and the like. At the same time, other essential aspects of the self were consciously rejected, repressed, or left dormant. These excluded components of the self—"other voices in other rooms," in Capote's vivid image—now seek expression and clamor to be heard.

We shall note briefly some of the major issues within the Mid-Life Transition: a) The sense of *bodily decline* and the more vivid recognition of one's *mortality*. This brings the necessity to confront one's mortality and to deal in a new way with wounds to one's omnipotence fantasies, to overcome illusions and self-deceptions which relate to one's sense of omnipotence. It also brings greater freedom in experiencing and thinking about one's own and others' deaths and greater compassion in responding to another's distress about decline, deformity, death, loss and bereavement. b) The sense of *aging,* which means to be old rather than young. The Jungian concepts of puer and senex as archetypes that play a significant part in the mid-life individuation process are important here. c) The polarity of *masculine and feminine*. Ordinarily in man's Settling Down structure masculinity is predominant; the emergence and integration of the more feminine aspects of the self are more possible at mid-life. During the mid-life period there is often a flowering of fantasies about various kinds of women, especially the maternal (nurturing and/or destructive) figures and the younger, erotic figures. These fantasies do not represent simply a belated adolescence, a final surge of lasciviousness, or self-indulgence or dependence (though they may have these qualities in part). The changing relationships to women may also involve the beginnings of a developmental effort. The aim of this effort is to free oneself more completely from the hold of the boy-mother relationship and to utilize one's internal relationships with the erotic transformative feminine as a means of healing old psychic wounds and of learning to love formerly devalued aspects of the self. It is the changing relation to the self that is the crucial issue at mid-life.

restabilization and the beginning of middle adulthood

For most men the Mid-Life Transition reaches its peak sometime in the early 40's and in the middle 40's there is a period of Restabilization. There seems to be a three to four year period at around age 45 in which the Mid-Life Transition comes to an end and a new life structure begins to take shape and to provide a basis for living in middle adulthood.

We are not presenting this as the last developmental change or the one in which everything will be resolved. For many men little is resolved, and the chickens come home to roost later. But it is a time both of possibility for developmental advance and of great threat to the self. Men such as Freud, Jung, Eugene O'Neill, Frank Lloyd Wright, Goya, and Gandhi went through a profound crisis at around 40 and made tremendous creative gains through it. There are also men like Dylan Thomas and F. Scott Fitzgerald who could not manage this crisis and who destroyed themselves in it. Many men who do not have a crisis at 40 become terribly weighted down and lose the vitality that one needs to continue developing through adulthood. Arthur Miller's play *The Price* tells something of the crisis of a man at 50: the sense of stagnation he has because of what he did not do earlier, especially at 40 when he considered changing his life structure and did not; he is now sinking in it.

We regard the Restabilization, then, as an initial outcome of the Mid-Life Transition. We are examining various forms of Restabilization and considering their implications for an understanding of the possibilities and problems of middle adulthood.

references

Brim, O. G., & Wheeler, S. *Socialization after childhood.* New York: Wiley, 1966.

Buhler, C. The curve of life as studied in biographies. *Journal of Applied Psychology*, 1955, *19*, 405-409.

Cain, L. Life course and social structure. In R. E. L. Faris (Ed.), *Handbook of Modern Sociology.* Chicago: Rand McNally, 1964.

Campbell, H. Jr. (Ed.) *The Portable Jung.* New York: Viking, 1971.

Epstein, C. F. Encountering the male establishment: Sex-status limits on women's careers in the professions. *American Journal of Sociology*, 1970, *75*, 965-982.

Erikson, E. H. Identity and the life cycle. *Psychological Issues*, 1959, *1* (1).

Erikson, E. H. *Gandhi's Truth.* New York: Norton, 1969.

Jaques, E. Death and the mid-life crisis. *International Journal of Psycho-Analysis*, 1965, *46*, 502-514.

Jung, C. G. *Memories, dreams, reflections.* New York: Pantheon, 1963.

Neugarten, B. L. (Ed.) *Middle age and aging: A reader in social psychology.* Chicago: University of Chicago Press, 1968.

Riley, M. W., et. al., *Aging and society.* (3 vols.). New York: Russell Sage Foundation, 1968ff.

Note: There are excellent biographies and autobiographies of persons such as Sigmund Freud, Eugene O'Neill, Bertrand Russell, Henry James, James Joyce, and F. Scott Fitzgerald. There are also novels and plays about men in the mid-life transition, often written by men during or just following their own mid-life transition—for example, *The Iceman Cometh* (O'Nell), *Who's Afraid of Virginia Woolf?* (Albee), *The Tempest,* (Shakespeare), *The Man Who Cried I am* (Williams), *Chimera* (Barth), and *Herzog* (Bellow). Works of this kind are of great value, both in forming a theory of adult development and in testing and extending our present theory.

male-female interpersonal styles in all male, all female and mixed groups

Elizabeth Aries

People hold many stereotyped beliefs about the interpersonal styles of men and women. Women are supposed to be expressive, nurturant, and supportive while men are concerned with leadership, power, and influence in their interactions. Women are weak and have difficulty expressing their anger; they rely on intuition and are emotional in their reactions, while men reason analytically. Women are more socially oriented while men are more task-oriented. Many of these stereotypes have not been well documented by facts.

To begin, let us discuss whether men and women display the same interpersonal style with members of their own sex as they do with members of the opposite sex. What effect does the sex of the participants in an encounter have on their interaction style? Some research has shown that individuals are capable of a wide range of behavior(s) and select from their repertoire behavior(s) to fit the situation. High dominance women, for example, have been found to assume leadership over low dominance women, but not over low dominance men (Megargee, 1969). In a society where it is appropriate for men to dominate women, but not the reverse, high dominance women will not attempt to dominate men for fear of social rejection.

Women conform more to group pressure in mixed groups than in all-female groups (Tuddenham, MacBride, & Zahn, 1958; Reitan & Shaw, 1964). In a society where women are socialized to let the men direct and make decisions, they are less firm about their own beliefs in the presence of men and more likely to conform to the men's opinions. Women are more socio-emotional and men more task-oriented both in family interactions and in mixed-task groups (Parsons & Bales, 1955; Strodtbeck & Mann, 1956). However, a similar task/social-emotional role differentiation has been found to occur in all-male task groups (Slater, 1955; Bales & Slater, 1955). Thus, men are capable of both task behavior and social-emotional behavior. In a society where the woman's role is wife and mother and the man's role is having an occupation, their different socialization causes the sexes to show bias towards task or social-emotional roles in their interactions together.

From the above findings we can see that the interaction styles of men and women are affected by the sex-role demands of the situation, not just the capacities of the individual. There is a growing desire, now, on the part of men and women to achieve freedom from some of the restrictiveness of sex-role pressures, and to develop more variation in interpersonal style. Because of the current trend toward greater personal freedom, it is important to document the characteristics of social interaction that exist in single-sex and mixed-group settings. Once we are familiar with the existing interpersonal styles, we can develop techniques for breaking out of traditional restrictive patterns.

With this goal in mind, six experimental discussion groups were organized, two all-male, two all-female, and two mixed. Group members were volunteers, primarily undergraduates, from an Eastern Ivy League school. In each group were five to seven members who met in five 1½ hour sessions with task of getting to know one another. There were no formal topics for discussion; group members were free to discuss anything they wanted in getting acquainted. The groups were co-led by the author and a male co-leader, who were to make occasional observations about what was going on, but were not to provide discussion topics. The co-leaders were the lowest initiators and receivers of interaction in the groups, each initiating less than 4 percent and receiving less than 5 percent of the interaction.

The interaction styles of the group members were studied both for content (the members' topics of discussion) and interaction (who spoke to whom and how often). The sessions were tape recorded and the content of the interactions was analyzed by the General Inquiror, a computer-aided content-analysis system (Stone, Dunphy, Smith & Ogilvie, 1966). From the tapes, 5 minutes were transcribed every half hour to reduce the 45 hours of tape recordings to a more manageable amount, producing a sample of 70,000 words.

The interaction data was gathered by two observers who recorded each time a group member spoke, to whom the group member spoke, and whether an individual or the group at large was addressed (Bales, 1970). The observers scored a single speech as the unit of interaction; for every 15 seconds a speaker continued, the act was rescored. With this method, the number of scores for a person reflects the length of his participation.

the interaction patterns

Let us look at the interaction styles of men and women to discover who initiated and who received interaction in the groups. The rank order of speaking provides important information about the relative power of group members. Those who initiate the most interaction take up the most time and can be considered as leaders. In the mixed groups, males both initiated and received more interaction than females, assuming at least two of the top three ranks in every session. In a society where it is considered appropriate for women to be submissive to men, sex-role pressures led men to assume leadership in the mixed groups.

The rank order of speaking yields further information. We observed whether a similar rank order was maintained from session to session, with the same members holding either dominant or submissive positions over a period of time. The all-male groups established a more stable dominance order over a period of time than the all-female groups. In the male groups, the same men were the most active speakers in every session, and never missed sessions. The only men who missed sessions were inactive speakers, and they never assumed important positions in later sessions.

In the female groups, on the other hand, there was greater flexibility over time in the rank order of speaking. When a woman missed a session she was able to make up for lost time by being an active speaker in the following session. The active speakers said they felt uncomfortable in the leadership positions, and felt they were taking up too much of the groups time; in some sessions they drew out more silent members, and assumed lower ranks. This difference between all-male and all-female groups in dominance or leadership style shows men develop more ways to express competition and leadership in their social interaction with other men, while women develop more ways to express affection and concern in their social interaction with other women.

These differences are further supported by examining the amount of interaction addressed to the group as a whole. Talking to the group as a whole has been considered as an exercise of power or influence (Bales, 1970). It is a style where the speaker is less concerned with individuals than with being seen and heard by all. Significantly more interaction was addressed to the group as a whole in the all male groups than in the all female groups (36 percent and 30 percent for the male groups vs. 9 percent and 4 percent for the female groups).

This difference in style follows the same patterns that have been found in male and female adolescent friendships. Girls form close one-to-one relationships with other girls, developing an interpersonal style of intimacy and closeness. Boys form less intimate friendships in the groups or gangs which support them in their development of independence (Douvan & Adelson, 1966). The exercise of power and influence becomes an important part of the male style of relating to other men.

The mixed groups provide an important comparison to the single-sex groups, and demonstrate that the interpersonal styles of men and women are different in the single-sex and mixed-group settings. Men addressed significantly more of their remarks to the group as a whole in all-male groups than they did when interacting with women. We see then that men are capable of a more personal emphasis, but avoid it in all-male interactions. There are two possible explanations for this difference. Just as in their friendships males avoid close one-to-one contact, in all-male groups they may avoid the same closeness by addressing the group as a whole. Contact with one other is more attractive to the speakers in a mixed setting, and men are more interpersonal in both interaction patterns and discussion content when there are women present. Another explanation is that all-male groups create greater pressures for a man to establish himself and pose a greater threat to his identity than do the mixed-group setting. Thus, there are increasing attempts at power and influence in the all-male setting.

While the female style of addressing individuals remained constant in both all-female and mixed groups, an important pattern emerged for women in mixed groups. There was very little interaction between women in the mixed groups. In all groups there was an upward flow of communication from inactive speakers to active speakers, and under this pattern with males assuming the role of active speakers, there would be a low probability of female to female interaction. However, sessions where females initiated a more equal amount of interaction were marked by more cross-sex than same-sex interaction. Thus, while increased participation did increase male communication with women, it did not increase interaction between women. The social significance of women for each other in a mixed group was low, as women are trained conventionally to compete with each other to win the attention and affection of males, and to regard males as more important. Women's liberation is now making women aware of their lack of significant relationships with members of their own sex, and their need for support from other women.

the discussion content

Having looked at *how* men and women related to each other on an interaction level, we turn to the *content* of their conversations. Let us look first at what types of concerns men and women expressed with members of their own sex, and then bring in the mixed groups as a comparison.

The first major difference revolved around the issue of intimacy and openness, how close group members wanted to be, and how much they wanted to reveal about themselves. Men in the all-male groups talked very little of themselves, their feelings, or of their relationships with persons of significance to them. In the all-female groups, on the other hand, members shared a great deal of information about themselves, their feelings, their homes, and their relationships with family, friends, and lovers. The General Inquirer showed that women referred more frequently to self, feelings, affiliation, home, and family.[1]

The second area of difference was in regard to competition and aggression. One of the greatest concerns expressed by members of the all-male groups was where they stood in relation to each other. This initially took the form of brain picking, sizing up the competition in the group by finding out who was the best informed about movies, books, current events, politics, and travel. There were frequent references to practical joking, tricking someone out of something, into something, or simply being one up. This pattern of self-aggrandizement and sarcastic teasing was also found by Newman (1971) to be quite prevalent in all-male high school groups. If a member was not quick and clever, he became the target of joking.

The themes of superiority and aggression were often merged in the male groups. Stories were told of the riots between dormitories, and of the pranks played where participants humiliated, threatened, and terrorized others. The theme of victim or victimizer ran through most stories, often evoking themes of castration and fears of loss of masculinity and potency. The General Inquirer documents these differences between the all-male and all-female groups by showing more frequent male references in its categories for sports and amusements, physical hostility, action, and the category describing what someone may have seen, read, or heard.[2]

Stylistically the male and female groups differed; that is, males engaged in dramatizing and story telling, jumping from one anecdote to another, and achieving a comraderie and closeness through the sharing of stories and laughter. Females discussed one topic for a half hour or more, revealing more feelings, and gaining a closeness through more intimate self-revelation. The findings from the content analysis and who-to-whom scoring similarly reflect the themes of intimacy and interpersonal relations for women, and themes of competition and status for men. Males, unlike females, avoid a high degree of intimacy with members of their own sex and acknowledge warmth and friendship in the form of joking and laughter. The strength of the competitive and aggressive images is related not only to being a man but also to the developmental stage of the group members. Adolescence is a period when individuals face strong pressures of socialization in their sex role, and it is through aggressive play and competition, confronting and differentiating oneself from others that a male establishes his own potency, competence, and independence. The predominance in the female groups of themes of loving and being loved, of home and family, reflect the female socialization and concerns towards their future roles in conventional society as wife and mother.

[1]The technical names of the categories are: *first person singular, feel, affiliation,* and references to the word "home" within the category *place: social gathering.*
[2]*The technical names of the categories are: expressive, hostile, active: move-exert* and *communicate.*

The mixed groups provide an interesting comparison with the single sex groups. Members directed their attention more towards the group itself, expressing concerns about what to talk about and how group members felt about the proceedings. The General Inquirer documents the overall emphasis in the mixed groups on the group itself by the frequent references in the category for the communication taking place in the group.[3] For both sexes the mixed group setting brought more awkward silences and hesitations at first, and then lead to a point of excitement and nervousness evoked by the emphasis on the encounter itself and the possibilities for pairing. The General Inquirer revealed that for both males and females in the mixed groups there was greater use of emphatic, exaggerated words, and more doubtful, uncertain words, connecting a defensive style (Stone et al., 1966). There were also more frequent uses of qualifications (if, but, maybe, possibly, etc.) in the mixed groups than in the single-sex groups.[4]

Some of the themes that were very important in the one-sex groups played a less significant part in the mixed groups. The male themes of aggression, competition, victimization, and practical joking were no longer frequent. These gave way to talk by males of themselves and their feelings. The dramatic change in the behavior of males from the single-sex groups to mixed groups is revealed by more frequent references in categories for self and feelings, and decreased references in categories for sports and amusements.[5] We may conclude that the presence of women changes the all-male style of interacting, causing males to develop a more personal orientation, with increased one-to-one interaction, greater self-revelation, and a decrease in the aggressive, competitive aspects of the encounter.

For females the difference in interaction style from the single-sex to mixed-group setting is less dramatic. In the mixed groups The General Inquirer showed that women talked about home and family less.[6] This may reflect women's desire to present themselves as more competent and independent when males are present. However, there are certain costs to women in the mixed group setting. The presence of men causes women to speak less, initiating only 34 percent of the total interaction. Women spoke less than men of achievement, power, and the institutions of society, all traditionally male concerns.[7] The mixed-group setting seems to benefit men more than women by allowing men more variation in their interpersonal style, while for women it brings more restrictions in style.

[3]The technical name of the category is *communicate.*
[4]The technical names of the categories are: *overstate, understate* and *qualify.*
[5]The technical names of the categories are: *1st person singular, feel,* and *expressive.*
[6]The technical names of the categories are: references to the word "home" within the category *place: social-gathering,* and *kinship.*
[7]The technical names of the categories are: *achieve, power, academic, economic, expressive, legal, political, religious.*

conclusions   The research that has been described here documents some characteristics of the styles men and women display when interacting with members of their own sex and members of the opposite sex. We can see that
despite the new ideology developing about sex roles, the interpersonal
styles of the group members reflected the sex-role demands of conventional society. The subjects in this study were all white, middle-
class college students, and it would be important now to consider these
findings as hypotheses to be tested with groups differing in age, race,
or social class. The groups in this study were also experimentally
created, and the hypotheses should be tested with naturally occurring
groups in settings such as jobs, informal social occasions, clubs, or living units such as communes.

If the patterns discussed here are found to occur in many settings,
the challenge that faces us is to develop ways to ease the restrictiveness of sex-role pressures, in order to create environments where
individuals can achieve fuller, more complete expression of
themselves. It will take risks on the part of both men and women to
achieve a broader range of behavior; for example, for women to be
more forceful in expressing themselves in mixed groups, for men to
relate more personally and intimately to other men. But if individuals
desire sex-role change, and if they can establish less restricting norms
for their interactions, they can in time begin to relate more fully to one
another than now seems possible.

references   Bales, R. F. *Personality and interpersonal behavior*. New York: Holt, Rinehart
& Winston, 1970.

Bales, R. F., & Slater, R. E. Role differentiation in small decision making
groups. In T. Parsons & R. F. Bales, *Family, socialization and interaction
process*. Glencoe, Ill.: Free Press, 1955.

Douvan, E., & Adelson, J. *The adolescent experience*. New York: Wiley, 1966.

Megargee, E. I. Influence of sex roles on the manifestation of leadership. *Journal of Applied Psychology*, 1969, 53(5), 377-382.

Newman, B. M. *Interpersonal behavior and preferences for exploration in
adolescent boys: A small group study*. Unpublished doctoral dissertation,
University of Michigan, 1971.

Parsons, T., & Bales, R. F. *Family, socialization and interaction processes*.
Glencoe, Ill.: Free Press, 1955.

Reitan, H. T., & Shaw, M. E. Group membership, sex composition of the
group, and conformity behavior. *Journal of Social Psychology*, 1964, 64, 45-
47.

Slater, P. E. Role differentiation in small groups. *American Social Review*,
1955, 20, 300-310.

Stone, P. Dunphy, D., Smith, M. S., & Ogilvie, D. M. *The general inquirer: A
computer approach to content analysis*. Cambridge, Mass.: M.I.T. Press,
1966.

Strodtbeck, F. L., & Mann, R. D. Sex role differentiation in jury deliberations. *Sociometry*, 1956, *19*, 3-11.

Tuddenham, R. D., MacBride, P., & Zahn, V. The influence of the sex composition of the group upon yielding to a distorted norm. *Journal of Psychology*, 1958, *46*, 243-251.

the changing place of
work for women and men[1]

Dee G. Appley

What are some of the psychological and societal barriers in the choice of a career? Here we will deal largely with the issue of limitations in choice imposed on individuals simply by virtue of the sexual apparatus with which they are born; that is, whether they possess a penis or a womb (Freud, 1905). Obviously this is a universal condition, involving two groups of people of about equal numbers who have, in most societies, developed over time a hierarchical relationship with deeply ingrained psychological consequences for both (Rosaldo & Lamphere, 1974b). This is true for other stereotyping and imposed restrictions also: there are always serious psychological consequences for all. The same holds for restrictions put on people by virtue of religion, race, nationality, age, and for all the other ways that societies have for classifying people and keeping people in their roles. Inevitably such restrictions lead to decreased options.

Increasingly this has led to what has been called alienation. More recently, there has been a movement towards liberation, first identified as the women's movement and very recently the beginning of a men's movement. Let us try to clarify the dynamics of this process of moving from alienation to liberation in work by looking at some of the forces which stand in the way of increasing options, and some of the currents which suggest that the status quo can and must give way.

There are many perspectives from which to analyze how work and the individual have been and can be related. In order to emphasize the limits and negative sanctions put on people, we will examine various options for men and women to combine work and marriage. From the beginning this forces us to deal with the fact that, although the options

[1]Based on a paper, "Two-person careers and two-career persons," presented in Quebec City, August 1973, at the annual meeting of L'Association Internationale d'Orientation Scolaire et Professionelle; it was subsequently published in the *Actes* (Proceedings) of the Association, Quebec, 1973, 310-322.

for both men and women have been limited, the options for women are drastically more limited (Márkus, 1970). However, since a man and a woman in a marriage are a system, changing any part of that system must inevitably lead to changes in the whole system, and we must deal with the resistances to change which are often set off in the second person (Lewin, 1948). And since any two-person relationship is also part of a larger, societal system and has some effect on the total system, we will need to examine the resistances from the larger system to any change in its subsystems.

In other words, we shall have to deal with individual, interpersonal, and societal questions if we are to understand how to increase, for the individual, opportunities for liberation and decrease the problem of alienation. It will be assumed that liberation is the preferred mode of existence and that the quality of our lives would be enhanced by such a development.

For a long time, the most important decision a man has had to make has been the life work he would choose; for a woman, what man's offer of marriage she would accept. It has been accepted that, for a man, his work would take him out of the home; for a woman, her most important work would be in the home. Taking care of the house and the children are considered the most important concerns of any woman, no matter what her talents, inclinations, or education.

Men are supposed to be rational, competitive, aggressive, and successful in their work. Women are supposed to be emotional, passive, dependent, and nurture their families. Thus normally it takes two adults to maintain one career—the man's. And it is further required that the man support his private family and provide for all their material needs. This is the standard version of the two-person career.

As Epstein (1975) says:

Although working was the reality of many women's lives, certainly it did not constitute an ideal. American culture traditionally prized the family group in which the husband was the breadwinner and his wife the homemaker who cared for the children. The latter, in turn, were to be well educated and not enter the labor force during their adolescent years (p. 4).

Thus if the wife works outside the home (and as a matter of fact many women do work, most because of financial need), her work outside is always considered secondary to her responsibilities in the home (Rapaport & Rapaport, 1972). Even in professional dual career families, the two-career persons, it is almost invariably the woman who is responsible for making the provisions that make it possible for her to leave the house. She must hire the housekeeper, find a substitute if a sitter or housekeeper does not show up, and she continues to be responsible for the ongoing maintenance functions of the family such as planning birthdays, going to parent-teacher conferences, and in general facilitating the human relations in the family.

Furthermore, there is " . . . no indication that either men or women desire to see an equal sharing of both masculine and feminine role tasks in the family . . . *Wives are constrained by their own idea of ideal feminine roles"* (Poloma & Garland, 1971, p. 757).

As Safilios-Rothschild (1969) notes, ". . . the myth that the American family is equalitarian was probably born as an ideal congruent with major American values and has been perpetuated despite all research evidence to the contrary. Neither decision making nor the division of labor in the family has been found to be equalitarian, nor has the conception of marital roles by married people been reported as companionate or equal in any sense" (Poloma & Garland, 1971, p. 758).

It has been taken for granted that women, by nature, are better able to perform the menial and nonrewarding chores that are required in our lives. Particularly in a country like the United States, it is assumed that children must have their natural mother with them all of the time, and anything less than that leads to feelings of guilt for the mother should anything go wrong, now or in the future.

Thus the myths that keep women in their homes make them live vicariously through their husbands, and their children. And the woman/wife/mother becomes the guardian of the emotional life of the family. This both limits her development and makes her very powerful. She can give or withhold resources that make life meaningful and human (Janeway, 1971). Men, on the other hand, give up the emotional part of themselves and accept that it is the woman's role to supply expressive behavior, their role as men is to supply instrumental behavior as the sociologist Talcott Parsons (1955) has described it. Or, as Chodorow (1971) has said: woman's life is being, men's doing.

Thus both men and women are alienated from one part of themselves rather than recognizing "the duality of human existence" (Bakan, 1966). Both sexes possess what have been labeled feminine and masculine tendencies; that is, both can be intelligent and emotional, competitive and collaborative, aggressive and nurturant, autonomous and dependent, active and passive. Instead we have forced each sex to specialize and cultivate only one set of sex-role characteristics and deny the other. This leads to alienation within the individual, and polarizes the sexes which makes communication between them more difficult.

We have furthermore come to think that the way things are is a function of human nature, that this is the way things must be. But a look at history and anthropology would help rid us of this misconception. Recently, more and more information is finding its way into print to remind us and inform us that much of our understanding about the sexes is based on myths, not facts.

Increasingly there has also been speculation that up until five to eight thousand years ago, women were "the first sex," that matriarchy rather than patriarchy was the rule (Davis, 1972). Presumably this early society was classless, there was communal ownership of production, there was no coercive state apparatus, and the family was not the basic unit but rather the tribe and the clan. Sexually, women were free as were men, and children were cared for by all, not owned by their parents. As Bachofen (1967) wrote, the child-bearing function was the source of power, and as Briffault (1963) says, women were producers of goods as well. All activities but hunting and warring were carried on by women. No woman was dependent on one man; no child on one mother or father. All of this may or may not be true. Indeed it has more recently been suggested that "Contrary to some now popular assumptions, there is little reason to believe that there are, or ever were, societies of primitive matriarchs, societies in which women predominated in the same way that men predominate in the societies we actually know . . . (Rosaldo, 1974, p. 19).

In any case, beginning five to eight thousand years ago we began to move from tribal communes to separate clans to extended families (as on old time farms) to the nuclear family, the family as we know it which dates only from about the late seventeenth century (Ariès, 1962). Thus, with the accumulation of surplus wealth, patriarchal values developed to insure that wealth stayed "in the family" which required also monogamous marriages so that the father could be sure of the paternity of his children (Figes, 1970). Women went from producer to dependent. Law and religion both accepted it as a natural obligation and duty for the individual man to support his family.

With the industrial revolution came the further separation of house and work: men went out of the house to work, women stayed home to keep house, and the nuclear family further developed its hold on the breadwinner to support this unit. So communal membership and communal care of children were left behind with whatever matriarchal values there might once have been, and so was the family as a self-contained unit. Now production and consumption were separated, and the work that women did came to be seen as not valuable because it had no monetary value. And the man now owned his wife along with his children and slaves.

Whatever the origins, it came to be that particularly in industrialized society, the man was considered the breadwinner, and the woman the keeper of the house and children. Marriage, childbearing, and childrearing became woman's full-time work; running the world became man's work. Specialization of work and function became increasingly exaggerated (Sacks, 1974).

As Roszak and Roszak* (1969) describe it:

He is playing masculine. She is playing feminine.

*Roszak, B. & Roszak T. Foreword. In B. Roszak & T. Roszak (Eds.) *Masculine/feminine: Readings in sexual mythology and the liberation of women.* New York: Harper Colophon, 1969, vii-xii.

He is playing masculine *because* she is playing feminine. She is playing feminine *because* he is playing masculine.

He is playing the kind of man that she thinks the kind of woman she is playing ought to admire. She is playing the kind of woman that he thinks the kind of man he is playing ought to desire.

If he were not playing masculine, he might well be more feminine than she is—except when she is playing very feminine. If she were not playing feminine, she might well be more masculine than he is—except when he is playing very masculine.

So he plays harder. And she plays . . . softer.

He wants to make sure that she could never be more masculine than he. She wants to make sure that he could never be more feminine than she. He therefore seeks to destroy the femininity in himself. She therefore seeks to destroy the masculinity in herself.

She is supposed to admire him for the masculinity in him that she fears in herself. He is supposed to desire her for the femininity in her that he despises in himself.

He desires her for her femininity which is *his* femininity, but which he can never lay claim to. She admires him for his masculinity which is *her* masculinity, but which she can never lay claim to. Since he may only love his own femininity in her, he envies her her femininity. Since she may only love her own masculinity in him, she envies him his masculinity.

The envy poisons their love.

He, coveting her unattainable femininity, decides to punish her. She, coveting his unattainable masculinity, decides to punish him. He denigrates her femininity—which he is supposed to desire and which he really envies—and becomes more aggressively masculine. She feigns disgust at his masculinity—which she is supposed to admire and which she really envies—and becomes more fastidiously feminine. He is becoming less and less what he wants to be. She is becoming less and less what she wants to be. But now he is more manly than ever, and she is more womanly than ever.

Her femininity, growing more dependently supine, becomes contemptible. His masculinity, growing more oppressively domineering, becomes intolerable. At last she loathes what she has helped his masculinity to become. At last he loathes what he has helped her feminity to become.

So far, it has all been very symmetrical. But we have left one thing out.

The world belongs to what his masculinity has become.

The reward for what his masculinity has become is power. The reward for what her femininity has become is only the security which his power can bestow upon her. If he were to yield to what her femininity has become, he would be yielding to contemptible incompetence. If she were to acquire what his masculinity has become, she would participate in intolerable coerciveness.

She is stifling under the triviality of her femininity. The world is groaning beneath the terrors of his masculinity.

He is playing masculine. She is playing feminine.
How do we call off the game? (pp. vii-viii).

The changes that are needed cannot be brought about by individuals; there must be societal sanctions and supports. The most pervasive problem that we must deal with at the present time is the fact of sexual stereotyping; that is, the most important determinant of what an individual will learn, can become, and will be circumscribed by is the presence or absence of a penis or a womb, and what that signifies psychologically in terms of options and negative sanctions. For the one possessing the womb, getting married and having children represent the prescribed accomplishments; passivity and dependence, the accepted psychological characteristics. For the one possessing the penis, the requirements are finding an occupation, and being achievement oriented and aggressive. The psychological impications of this accidental fact of birth takes precedence over all other characteristics of the individual (Ortner, 1974).

Every day, children are socialized by their parents, by their schools, by the media, through the books they read—by all the socialization agents that have a stake in keeping people in their places by gender (Andreas, 1971). Instead of recognizing the duality of human existence, and using both one's so-called masculine and feminine possibilities[2], we have channeled people into sex-role behaviors, accomplishments, and lives. Thus most individuals are alienated from parts of themselves: women from their assertive, intellectual, rational, competitive, striving selves; men from their emotional, caring for others, acknowledging dependency, collaborative selves. Instead of a dialectic, there is polarization both within the self and between the self and the other. From the moment of birth, we begin to handle boys and girls differently: smile at one, bounce the other; dress one in pink and the other in blue to be sure that they are responded to properly by others. The end result is two categories of people: both accepting the limitations put on them; but for one, the male, the seeming rewards are more striking.

There are elaborate social science theories which explain the status quo such as Parson's (1955) theory of instrumental and expressive behavior being representative of males and females and Freud's theory of sexuality (1924). But as social learning theorists and others are beginning to demonstrate, it would appear that society invents the kind of human nature it needs for its purposes. *If maleness and femaleness are so natural, why are there so many sanctions to insure conformity?*

We must acknowledge that social scientists, like other human beings, exist in the context of their societies, and many so-called theoretical explanations are based on limited perspective, not on facts (Rosaldo & Lamphere, 1974a). Up until very recently, research had not been done that would begin to give us the answers we need (Hochschild, 1973). It seems abundantly clear that people are shaped by their cultures to be whatever the culture needs. Thus in time of war

[2]D. Bakan (1966) has suggested that we call these masculine and feminine impulses *agency* and *communion:* the former a tendency to overcome, the latter a tendency to join with.

and labor shortages, women are seen as able to work at many kinds of jobs; and day-care centers, wage incentives, and other supports are provided. When they are not needed, they are encouraged and indeed forced to return to their homes to do their womanly, anatomy-is-destiny jobs.

There are many ways that any two individuals can work out their marriage and work relationship, that two people can agree on an arrangement that is more or less satisfactory to both. But for most people, these arrangements are not choices; they are prescribed and accepted, however unwillingly.

Are men going to have to continue to meet these standards? Are women going to remain "the second sex"? Or is it no longer necessary to accept certain assumptions about men and women, and their separate spheres, so that there can be individual choice rather than sex role conformity to patterns of behavior that are taken as givens? Individuals must be freed from the restrictions of socialization which limit their options unnecessarily: limitations based on myth, on convenience, on fear, on social pressure and expectation. Is the division of labor based on biology as Freud, the church, Madison Avenue, and the media have been telling us, or is it based on mythology? Is it a form of oppression that, like all oppression, must be seen as political and dealt with as such?

Surely if it were a matter of being natural that men went out to work and women stayed home, there would scarcely need to be so many rules and regulations to ensure that this would happen. Rather it has been convenient for society, after a certain point in history, to set people up in their single unit families dependent on the man's earnings, and the man in turn dependent on the woman's emotional nurturance. The man's career choice has usually been left up to his talents and his training; the woman's has been determined for her when she is born. He has been destined to work; she has been destined to bear children and keep house.

But some men and women have begun to recognize that this is not a law of nature, but a rule of man. And they have begun to make changes in their life styles. Some men have begun to recognize that they enjoy being nurturant, and caring, and thoughtful of others, up until now considered the sphere of women; and some women have begun to recognize that they are persistent, and strong, and have ideas they would like to deal with in the real world outside the house, and they are finding ways to do that without having to consider themselves abnormal, masculine, or sick. In other words, we are beginning to see that sexism and sexual stereotyping, not nature, have set the rules by which people are living unhappily, and these things are beginning to be challenged.

We can be too easily misled by the exceptions—by the few men and women who are making it without conforming. The price is very high for both the individual exceptions, and for the society that places the restrictions. Always some members of a minority group, even a caste, have been able to make it in a system that excludes most of their members. This does not make the system acceptable, and indeed it is obviously not meeting the needs of many people. Signs that the system is not working include the abuse of drugs and alcohol, the rising rate of divorce, the many kinds of drop-outs and countercultures, runaway children, mental illness, the dissatisfaction of large numbers of workers, and so forth: these are all signs of alienation.

As a matter of fact, not only is it very difficult to overcome the restraints of the system; a "study—made in 1969 by Dean Knudsen, showed that generally women had lost ground, relative to men, by measure of occupation and income over the past twenty-five years" (Epstein, 1975, p. 8).

Not too long ago the lifespan was shorter, many children who were born did not reach adulthood, and many more people had to work long hours just to make a survival living. Now the need to limit population, and the fact that people live longer and do not have to work such long hours, all combine to mean that women no longer can be asked to commit their lives to raising children. Besides, since most paid work does not any longer provide the sense of self-worth that it is supposed to, men also are beginning to question their options and the restrictions and expectations placed on them (Brinton, 1966). Indeed many drop-outs from the system are successful men between the ages of 35 to 45. In addition

Since 1953, the labor force participation rate of married men declined gradually from 92 to 85 percent. Over the same period, the rate for married women rose persistently, from 26 to 42 percent. . . . A major reason why the men stopped working was health problems. Another was, and is, the relative lack of education of many men 55 through 64 years of age, which takes a heavy toll in an economy more and more in need of educated workers (Epstein, 1975, p. 6).

For men, the paid labor force has been dropping somewhat; for women, it has been rising somewhat; but for neither has there necessarily been increased satisfaction. A task force report to HEW tells us that work should not damage or degrade, but rather it should interest and satisfy, should use many skills and provide a chance to learn new skills, should enhance other life roles such as parenthood, and should provide goods and services (HEW, 1974). This is certainly not true for many jobs or even careers. Both men and women want more options and more satisfaction.

Women might like to be asked if they want a career; men might like to be asked if they would like to stay home. Given the variety of ways that work could be a part of one's life, there are many variations on the theme of two-person careers and two-career persons if psychological barriers can be taken away, and social supports provided. So a two-person career can mean—as it often does now—one person in paid employment, the other at home. But it could mean the woman going out to work, the man staying home. Or it could mean alternating over a period of years. Or it could be two people sharing one job, with all the benefits of a full-time job and only half the work for each.

As for two-career persons, it can mean dual career families with true sharing at home. Or it can mean that individuals, both men and women, will have two or more careers in a lifetime: just as now men retire early from business or the military and turn to a service profession; just as women go back to work after spending ten or more years at home with the children. Others could have a series of careers.

But the combinations are much greater than that. We need to recognize that, for different individuals, work can mean different things at different stages of life. So we need more flexibility, and we need to think of a lifetime as containing cycles of work-leisure-education. The rigidity of our traditional expectations must go.

All of this means changing our attitudes from *should* or *must* to *would like to* or *can*. Differences in choices would be encouraged, not punished. What fantasy do you have about what you would like to be doing five years from now? What is standing in your way: your own feelings? your spouse? society? What education or training opportunities are required? What permissions and support do you need?

Obviously there must be societal structures which will support social changes for women and men. At the same time, people will need to meet together to raise their consciousness and dare to change without feeling they will be condemned, chastised, punished, considered ill, insane, or irresponsible. This is the way to liberation; to put off these societal and group supports can only lead to further frustration and alienation.

Although there are now increased enrollments of women in law and medicine, "Any significant changes which would substantially increase the female professional labor force cannot occur so long as basic values and attitudes concerning the sexual division of labor in the society remains unchanged." (Theodore, 1971, p. 34). Even with support it will be difficult to overcome the attitudes we acquire even before we can speak: that mothers are soft and warm and always there; that fathers take care of us and protect us from the outside world. Truly terror strikes at many as these myths are challenged. Who will take care of the children, who will provide emotional support for the father; who will provide the money and the protection for the family?

Most social controls are informal. The messages, however, are clear. To women: be beautiful, be a mother, do not think, do not lead; to men: be strong, be brave, be responsible, work. From every source, both are urged to marry. For the woman, this means further restrictions about what she can do. If she does work, she must choose from limited "feminine" occupations and limited rewards. Even in Sweden, where many social supports are provided, still there are "women's" occupations; and "men's" occupations (Bande & Holmberg, 1971). An oft-cited statistic that in Russia four out of five physicians are women is misleading: of the prestigious positions among physicians, four out of five are men!

We can classify societies by the range of options offered to both sexes. We can look to see whether there are child-care facilities, paid maternity leaves, tax benefits for two-career families, alternative modes for hours of work, level and type of promotions, no differentiation between masculine and feminine occupations, and so on. We can also classify families according to how non sex-role related the functions are, and the range of options offered and allowed, without regard to sex, for the children as well as the parents. We will find then that there can be societal support with or without family support; and there can be family support with or without societal support for non sex-role related choices. *Real liberation would mean no imposed sex-role requirements* (Safilios-Rothschild, 1972, pp. 181-182.).

These social controls are so strong and so subtle that, even when there are no societal and family sanctions, and even when women can enter "masculine" occupations, they choose to specialize in the less prestigious areas of a profession and hardly ever reach the top levels. It is a vicious cycle: women have a lower level of aspiration, there is a poor support system, their level of aspiration is lowered further, and so on. And even if they escape this first set of socialization barriers, they are given the boring jobs or the most tedious tasks in the professions. If women do gain entry to a man's profession in large numbers, it loses status and becomes a woman's occupation, and thus provides lowered salaries. If men enter a woman's occupation, they are given the higher level, higher paying jobs.

It is possible to anticipate some of the consequences if all people could have all options. But it is almost impossible to foretell the possibilities: the synergistic and serendipitous benefits, that is, the changes that will be brought about by change itself. However, changes are both inevitable and necessary (Fairweather, 1972).

The strongest psychological attitudes to overcome are the belief that women are weak, passive, dependent, accommodating, and born to be mothers; and the belief that men are strong, aggressive, independent, competitive, and born to be breadwinners. We know from psychological testing that individual differences are greater than sex differences. In many cases, women must overcome the fear of success; men, fear of failure (Horner, 1970).

And we already know how to do many of the things that would make a difference. We know that if children get independence training and mastery training, they learn to think analytically. We know that differential treatment by the father is important in the way boys and girls differ and that often, if we find achievement-oriented women, they had encouraging fathers. We know that boys learn to shape the world; and girls to be shaped by it. (Weitzman, 1975).

We are learning to distinguish facts from fictions about "the American working woman." As Crowley, Levitin, and Quinn (1973) say, "Job related attitudes, unlike job rewards, could not be substantially predicted from the sex of the worker. There are, therefore, no objective grounds for justifying pay differentials on the basis of presumed differences in the styles of jobs workers want," (p. 26): that is both women and men have similar attitudes about having challenging work and the opportunity to make friends at work.

Also both the women's movement and the men's reactions to this changing consciousness are leading to a re-examination by men not only of their attitudes to work but of their relationships with other men as well as with women. Men are also beginning to examine their feelings and attitudes about fatherhood (Farrell, 1974; Fasteau, 1974; Nichols, 1975; Pleck & Sawyer, 1974).

So, besides getting over these restricting attitudes about males and females in relation to work, we must also recognize that there are other acceptable personal life styles besides the two-person marriage, with children, living in a single household, and responsible presumably for all of its own problems (Firestone, 1971). It will require legal changes as well so that women are recognized as individuals in their own right; so that tax benefits can be given; so that new style communal families can live together, and so forth (Dahlstrom, 1971).

In a study conducted in spring 1975 at the University of Massachusetts, 17 percent of the sample of women students (N=60) say they do not intend to marry: 10 percent say they do not plan to have children. But an additional 43 percent are not sure if they will have children or not. That is, only 47 percent say a clear yes to motherhood. All (100 percent) plan to be working five years from now; 87 percent plan to be working ten years from now. Those who do not plan to be working in ten years attribute this to child rearing. Furthermore, only 42 percent choose full-time work as their first choice whether married or unmarried, whether childless or with children (Appley & Kent, 1975).[3]

Where do we go from here? We have seen that there are psychological barriers to free choice of careers, and societal barriers. We have seen that this is not a law of human nature, but of man-made nature. And we have seen that there are both resistances to change, and dissatisfactions which presage change. Now let us go one step further.

[3]D. G. Appley, with the assistance of K. Kent, (1975): a report based on a study supported in part by the Carnegie Foundation through the award of a Gilman Fellowship to Prof. Appley for the spring semester, 1975.

Having looked at some of the barriers of free choice that have been put upon women and men, what can we say about the future of work if these sex-role barriers were to be overcome? Fred Best (1973) has edited a book which is an exciting collection of ideas by various individuals who deal with such provocative thoughts as the meaning of work throughout history, an emerging synthesis of work and education, the idea of guaranteed income so that we can move towards post-economic motivation, and the future meanings of work.

As we have seen before, we ought to expect and plan for diversity. We cannot of course foresee dramatic breakthroughs, but at least for now we can still think of work as part of the life of most individuals, and define it as goal-oriented human activity. Historically work has moved from a drudgery to a calling, and for economic man, an end in itself. Now Herman Kahn and Anthony Wiener (1973) tell us that we may look forward to a range of attitudes towards work with different basic values to be fulfilled by work:

Basic attitude toward work as:	Basic additional value fulfilled by work
1. Interruption	Short-run income
2. Job	Long-term income—some work-oriented values (one works to live)
3. Occupation	Exercise and mastery of gratifying skills—some satisfaction of achievement-oriented values
4. Career	Participating in an important activity or program. Much satisfaction of work-oriented, achievement-oriented, advancement-oriented values
5. Vocation (calling)	Self-identification and self-fulfillment
6. Mission	Near fanatic or single-minded focus on achievement or advancement (one lives to work) (p. 152).

They conclude that it will probably be difficult to get people to do demanding work that requires long and arduous training, or working under difficult, dangerous, and frustrating conditions although cutting the hours of work down drastically (e.g. a four-hour workday) may make up for this. Still they predict that

Yet, at the same time, skilled, personal services requiring irreducible quantities of human time, training, and talent would become both absolutely and relatively expensive. Thus there would probably still be a very strong demand for, and probably also a much expanded supply of expensive and skilled professionals, managers, enterpreneurs, artisans, technicians and artists—for the most part, the well-educated upper middle class. This group may well be much too busy and well rewarded to be alienated (p. 154).

So, while some people are demanding and will continue to demand the right to work at jobs, occupations, careers, vocations, and missions, which they have up until now been denied, others may now choose not to work for money, and certainly may choose a job over a career. Again we must remind ourselves that work can now be thought of as only one part of an individual's life, and for many not even a central part.

As more people get more education, still another development to take into consideration is the increase in "the reserve army of the under-employed." For a long time, women have belonged in this cate-gory—working at jobs beneath their educational qualifications. Increasingly, men may find themselves in this situation also so that satisfaction and self-esteem may have to come from nonpaid work in which people can channel their desires to be useful and creative (Appley, 1974; O'Toole, 1975).

As we have explored the factors involved in change, we have seen that resistance to change—both in the individual and his/her interper-sonal and societal supports—is a very important factor. Our habitual ways of behaving become very comfortable, and change, especially forced change, is seen as very threatening. The more basic the atti-tudes we are trying to change, the more threatening the change may be seen. We have seen also that one of the important factors making change necessary is that the present system does not meet the psychological needs of large numbers of people.

As long as each individual thought it was a personal problem, she/he suffered alone and accommodated, fled into illness, took out his/her aggressions on spouse and children, expected more from close rela-tionships like marriage than could be found, looked to one's career for satisfaction (but did not receive human, emotional rewards there), and increasingly felt alienated, dissatisfied, and often worthless.

We have seen how a combination of factors has coalesced to produce this time of great change. Now, along with accumulating knowledge and increasing affluence, there is increased awareness and ever larger numbers of people beginning to be a critical mass seeking change; a large enough concerned group to keep pressing for change and to become models of alternative ways of coping and living and working in less alienated, more liberated ways. It would be very mis-leading to write this off as "the woman's problem" and think that mov-ing towards "equal rights" meaning equal pay for equal work and such measures would solve the problem. It is rather a human liberation problem and demands qualitative not quantitative changes.

As the basic needs of human beings are met, so-called higher needs become prepotent and must be satisfied. So as survival becomes less a problem for human beings, growth needs become more important (Appley, 1974; Gorney, 1972; Maslow, 1973). People are no longer content to automatically pursue their jobs as their central concern; rather they begin to look for ways of increasing their consciousness, their awareness of those other parts of themselves which have for so long been neglected. Obviously retreat to the suburbs, escape through the abuse of drugs and alcohol, unlimited sex, spectator sports, and war have not been able to provide a lasting answer either. So we see that the old system does not work; and we cannot go back to any "golden age"; we must instead cope in the present and plan for the future. Trial and error experimentation has been providing us with some alternatives. Intentional changes through supports provided by society are also needed. This will include informal support of those individuals and small groups that are already prepared for change and trying to live out alternatives, as well as formal support through legislation and other societal changes.

All of us of course are embedded in our cultures and our experiences, and it requires rather remarkable feats to find ways to gain perspective on issues which concern us here: work, marriage, family; psychological factors in the choice of a career; alienation or liberation. There are, as Guerreiro-Ramos (1971) tells us, parenthetical people: those who managed to escape the repressive socialization which most people do not escape. And so, some people can get beyond the limitations imposed by having grown up and lived with the myths of their society, and the rewards and punishments which help to maintain the status quo, and meet the needs and expectations of those in power. Probably some of us would identify with these parenthetical people as we examine the options available to women and men in relation to their work plans.

It is on a note of limited optimism that I come to the end of this paper. I believe it is probably an inevitable development that societies will move towards more equalitarian based relationships among men and women, among people, with more equal opportunities for all and more personal freedom to select among options. That will be true for the long run. Nevertheless, in the short run, it will require active efforts to effect attitude changes that lead to cooperation between women and men, among people, to overcome the sex role barriers that have for so long existed. This requires individual and social change since it is both a personal problem and a social issue (Mills, 1959). We must avoid simply taking on and extending the values of men, the dominant group, but rather must integrate the best parts of women and men: collaboration and competition, passivity and activity, emotional expression and rational thinking, independence and dependence, and so forth—so that women and men are no longer alienated within themselves by denying parts of themselves, and are not alienated from each other by polarizing their differences.

Some people call this androgyny. Rowe (1973) builds a strong case for this kind of development, and also suggests some strategies for research to evaluate effects of parental employment on children, including when both parents are employed. Heilbrun (1973) writes: "I believe that our salvation lies in a movement away from sexual polarization and the prison of gender toward a world in which individual roles and modes of personal behavior can be freely chosen . . . best described by the term 'androgyny' (pp. ix-x)."

The life of human beings has been changing, at first very slowly, then more and more rapidly. From cave man to apartment dweller is a long way in changing life styles. We are well on our way from a life of labor to one of leisure, from a life of scarcity and survival to one of abundance, from a life of givens to one of options, periodic recessions notwithstanding. And we need to prepare ourselves psychologically to welcome instead of fear such change (Appley, 1974; Gorney, 1972).

In the midst of all this change, almost as a paradigm for the problems we all face, is the currently renewed question of the relation between the sexes of the human race, and all of its implications. Centuries of sexism are being reviewed as bearing of children as women's fundamental function is challenged which up until now has left the work of running the world to the men. Is this the last revolution? Because what is called for is certainly revolutionary: a re-examination of everything heretofore believed about the nature of women and men, their relationship to each other and to the world. This is a universal challenge with very profound implications for all human relations and activities.

This re-examination involves consciousness raising which is that process whereby all persons may begin to be in touch with ideas, feelings, experiences, and knowledge undistorted by mythology, tradition, propaganda, education, parental injunctions, and other instruments whereby society produces the people it needs. Socialization helps maintain the status quo. When re-examined, often "facts" prove not to be facts at all but systems of thinking that, though based on inappropriate methods of observation, have gradually gained social sanction.

In all areas of our lives, we are in the process of moving from role-related performances to non role-related participation. During this time, it is very difficult to avoid the discomfort arising out of uncertainty and confusion. For at least five thousand years, there appear to have been sex-related roles. Now that is changing. Whether we look at changing sex roles as cause and/or effect of social change, it is nevertheless very obvious why so much is at stake as these old roles change.

It has been said that the unexamined life is a wasted life. More and more people are agreeing with this injunction. Certainly it is no longer possible to think of consciousness raising as a strange activity that some freaky people engage in. It is no longer possible to label the people who are trying to raise questions as "sick," "maladjusted," "unusual," or just plain "wrong." It has come to be impossible to ignore the facts of sexism in our lives, our organizations and our institutions.

And it is no longer possible to stop at consciousness. A kind of inexorable process of change has been initiated, and it is only a matter of time now until those changes become the new standards. The rate of this development picks up momentum from a variety of sources, and the "tipping point" of certain kinds of change will be reached sooner or later. It is no longer a matter of individuals wanting to expand their consciousness for personal development. Rather the reality of the underlying social issues is becoming apparent to more and more individuals. Indeed society itself cannot survive with nonconscious participants.

As more individuals become aware that their personal problems are integrally related to these social issues, the need for choice and commitment become clearer. So these individuals feel not only the need for personal change but for societal changes. Meanwhile they feel the need for support systems to help them through these changes, and for ways of being more impactful and effective. Thus caring and collaboration become necessary ingredients in this change process.

It will take the efforts of all of us to counteract centuries of role-related behaviors which have come to be accepted as "natural" and to facilitate the liberation of individuals from the prescribed and proscribed options for work, love and play. We need to support diversity and flexibility; we need to see change as continuous and to know that there can be stability without rigidity. For the individual and for society, the fewer the options, the more the restrictions, the greater the alienation: people are shut off and shut out; the fewer the restrictions, the greater the options, the greater the likelihood of liberation. It is not easy to be in transition, but neither is it possible not to act. The problems are there; solutions must be found.

references

Andreas, C. *Sex and caste in America.* Englewood Cliffs, N. J.: Prentice-Hall, 1971.

Appley, D. G. Two-person careers and two-career persons. *Actes* (Proceedings), Quebec: L'Association Internationale d'Orientation Scolaire et Professionelle, 1973, 310-322.

Appley, D. G. *Work and the human condition.* Invited address, Annual Meeting of New York Personnel and Guidance Association, Rochester, N.Y., Nov. 1974. c/o author, Psychology Department, University of Massachusetts, Amherst, Mass. Report No. 74-2, 1974.

Appley, D. G. with Kent, K. *Women, work and marriage.* Report No. 75-3, c/o author, Psychology Department, University of Massachusetts, Amherst, Mass., 1975.

Ariès, P. *Centuries of childhood: A social history of family life.* New York: Knopf, 1962.

Bachofen, J. J. *Myth, religion and mother right: Selected writings of Jakob Bachofan,* trans. by Ralph Manheim. Princeton: Princeton University Press, 1967.

Bakan, D. *The duality of human existence: Isolation and communion in western man.* Boston: Rand-McNally, 1966.

Bande, A. & Holmberg, P. The positions of men and women in the labour market. In E. Dahlstrom (Ed.), *The changing roles of men and women.* Trans. by Gunilla and Steven Anderman. Boston, Beacon Press, 1971, 105-134.

Best, F., (Ed.), *The future of work.* Englewood Cliffs, N.J.: Prentice-Hall (Spectrum), 1973.

Briffault, R. *The mothers: The matriarchal theory of social origins,* abridged. G. R. Taylor (Ed.). New York: Universal Library, Grosset and Dunlop, 1963.

Brinton, M. *The American male.* Greenwich, Conn.: Fawcett Premier, 1966.

Chodorow, N. Being and doing: A cross-cultural examination of the socialization of males and females. In V. Gornick & B. K. Moran (Eds.), *Woman in a sexist society.* New York: Basic Books, 1971, 173-197.

Crowley, I. E., Levitan, T. E., & Quinn, R. P. *Facts and fiction about the American working woman.* Research report, 1973.

Dahlstrom, E. Analysis of the debate on sex roles. In E. Dahlstrom (Ed.), *The changing roles of men and women,* trans. by Gunilla and Steve Anderman. Boston: Beacon Press, 1971, 170-205.

Davis, E. G. *The first sex.* Baltimore, Md.: Penguin, 1972.

Engels, F. *The origin of the family, private property and the state.* Trans. by Unterman, Charles Kerr, 1902.

Epstein, C. *Reflections on the women's movement: Assessment of change and its limits.* New York: Institute of Life Insurance, 1975.

Fairweather, G. W. *Social change: The challenge to survival.* Morristown, N.J.: General Learning Press, 1972.

Farrell, W. *The liberated man.* New York: Bantam, 1974.

Fasteau, M. F. *The male machine.* New York: McGraw-Hill, 1974.

Figes, E. *Patriarchal attitudes.* Greenwich, Conn.: Fawcett, 1970.

Firestone, S. *The dialectic of sex.* New York: Bantam, 1971.

Freud, S. Some psychological consequences of the anatomical distinction between the sexes (1905). In D. L. Schaeffer (Ed.), *Sex differences in personality: Readings.* Belmont, Calif.: Brooks/Cole, 1971, 11-21.

Freud, S. *Three essays on the theory of sexuality.* (Vol. 7). (Standard Ed.). London: Hogarth, 1924.

Gorney, R. *The human agenda.* New York: Bantam, 1972.

Guerreiro-Ramos, A. The parenthetical man. *Journal of human relations,* 4th qtr., 1971, *19,* 463-487.

Heilbrun, C. G. *Toward a recognition of androgyny.* New York: Harper Colophon, 1973.

H.E.W. Task Force Report. *Work in America.* Cambridge, Mass.: MIT Press, 1974.

Hochschild, A. R. A review of sex role research. In J. Huber (Ed.), *Changing women in a changing society.* Chicago: University of Chicago Press, 1973, 249-267.

Horner, M. S. Femininity and successful achievement: A basic inconsistency. In J. M. Bardwick et al., *Feminine personality and conflict.* Belmont, Calif: Brooks/Cole,1970, 45-74.

Janeway, E. *Man's world, woman's place: A study in social mythology.* New York: Delta, 1971.

Kahn, H. & Wiener, A. The future meanings of work: Some "surprise-free" observations. In F. Best (Ed.) *The future of work.* Englewood Cliffs, N.J.: Prentice-Hall (Spectrum), 1973, 141-154.

Lewin, K. The background of conflict in marriage. In G. W. Lewin (Ed.), *Resolving social conflicts.* Harper and Brothers, 1948, 84-102.

Maslow, A. A theory of human motivation: The goals of work. In F. Best (Ed.), *The Future of work.* Englewood Cliffs, N.J.: Prentice-Hall (Spectrum), 1973, 17-31.

Márkus, M. Women and work: Emancipation at an impasse. *Impact of science on society* 1970, *20* (Jan.-Mar.), 61-72.

Mills, C. W. *The sociological imagination.* New York: Oxford University Press, 1959.

Nichols, J. *Men's liberation: A new definition of masculinity.* New York: Penguin, 1975.

Ortner, S. B. Is female to male as nature is to culture? In M. Z. Rosado & L. Lamphere (Eds.), *Woman, culture and society.* Stanford, Calif.: Stanford University Press, 1974, 67-88.

O'Toole, J. The reserve army of the underemployed: I. The world of work. *Change,* May 1975, 26-63.

Parsons, T. *Family, socialization and interaction process.* New York: Free Press, 1955.

Pleck, J. H. & Sawyer, J. (Eds.) *Men and masculinity.* Englewood Cliffs, N.J.: Prentice-Hall, 1974.

Poloma, M. M. & Garland, T. N. The myth of the egalitarian family: Familial roles and the professionally employed wife. In A. Theodore (Ed.), *The professional woman.* Cambridge, Mass.: Schenkman Publishing Co., 1971.

Rapoport, R. & Rapoport, R. N. The dual-career family: A variant pattern and social change. In C. Safilios-Rothschild (Ed.), *Toward a sociology of women.* Lexington, Mass.: Xerox Publishing Company, 1972, 216-244.

Rosaldo, M. Z. Woman, culture and society: A theoretical overview. In M. Z. Rosaldo and L. Lamphere (Eds.), *Woman, culture and society.* Stanford, Calif.: Stanford University Press, 1974, 17-42.

Rosaldo, M. Z. & Lamphere, L. (Eds.) *Woman, culture and society.* Stanford, Calif.: Stanford University Press, 1974 (a).

Rosaldo, M. Z. & Lamphere, L. Introduction. In M. Z. Rosaldo and L. Lamphere (Eds.), *Woman, culture and society.* Stanford, Calif.: Stanford University Press, 1974 (b), 1-15.

Roszak, B. & Roszak, T. Foreword. In B. Roszak & T. Roszak (Eds.), *Masculine/feminine: Readings in sexual mythology and the liberation of women.* New York: Harper Colophon, 1969, vii-xii.

Rowe, M. P. *That parents may work and love and children may thrive.* c/o author, M.I.T., Cambridge, Mass., 1973.

Sacks, K. Engels revisited: Women, the organization of production and private property. In M. Z. Rosaldo and L. Lamphere (Eds.), *Woman, culture and society.* Stanford, Calif.: Stanford University Press, 1974, 207-222.

Safilios-Rothschild, C. Marital expectations and marital experience: Why such a discrepancy? (Paper read at the ICOFA meeting in Rennes, France, April 3-7, 1969). Cited by M. M. Poloma and T. N. Garland. The myth of the egalitarian family: Familial role and the professionally employed wife. In A. Theodore (Ed.), *The professional woman.* Cambridge, Mass.: Schenkman, 1971, 758.

Safilios-Rothschild, C. (Ed.) *Toward a sociology of women*. Lexington, Mass.: Xerox, 1972.

Theodore, A. The professional woman: Trends and prospects. In A. Theodore (Ed.), *The professional woman*. Cambridge, Mass.: Schenkman, 1971, 1-35.

Weitzman, L. J. Sex role socialization. In J. Freeman (Ed.), *Women: A feminist perspective*. Palo Alto, Calif.: Mayfield, 1975, 105-144.

psychological androgyny

Sandra Lipsitz Bem

Both historically and cross-culturally, masculinity and femininity seem to have represented two complementary domains of *positive* traits and behaviors, behaviors which I believe to be essential for healthy and effective human functioning. Thus, in a modern complex society like ours, an adult clearly has to be able to look out for himself/herself and to get things done. This would seem to require the ability to be assertive, independent, and self-reliant, all commendable human qualities. But traditional concepts of femininity inhibits these behaviors in many women. On the other hand, an adult also needs to be able to relate to other human beings as people, to be sensitive to their needs and to be concerned about their welfare, as well as to be able to depend on them for emotional support—again, all commendable human qualities. But traditional concepts of masculinity inhibit these behaviors in many men.

In contrast, psychological androgyny (Andros, male and Gyne, female) allows men and women to be *both* independent and tender, *both* assertive and yielding, *both* masculine and feminine. In other words, psychological androgyny expands the range of behaviors available to everyone.

The Bem Sex Role Inventory (BSRI) was designed to measure the extent to which a person's self-definition is masculine, feminine, or androgynous. The BSRI consists of twenty masculine personality characteristics (e.g., ambitious, self-reliant, independent, assertive) and twenty feminine personality characteristics (e.g., affectionate, gentle, understanding, sympathetic, sensitive to the needs of others). The specific masculine characteristics were selected because they were judged by a large sample of undergraduates to be more desirable in American society for a man than for a woman, and the specific feminine characteristics were selected because they were judged to be more desirable in American society for a woman than for a man. In the

319

test itself, the masculine and feminine characteristics are interspersed with one another and with an additional group of twenty neutral characteristics, and the person is asked to indicate on a seven-point scale how well each of these various characteristics describes himself/herself. The scale ranges from 1 ("Never or almost never true") to 7 ("Always or almost always true"). The masculine, feminine, and neutral characteristics are all shown on page 321.

inventory

On the following page, you will be shown a large number of personality characteristics. We would like you to use those characteristics in order to describe yourself. That is, we would like you to indicate, on a scale from 1 to 7, how true of you these various characteristics are. Please do not leave any characteristic unmarked.

Example: sly

Mark a 1 if it is *NEVER OR ALMOST NEVER TRUE* that you are sly.

Mark a 2 if it is *USUALLY NOT TRUE* that you are sly.

Mark a 3 if it is *SOMETIMES BUT INFREQUENTLY TRUE* that you are sly.

Mark a 4 if it is *OCCASIONALLY TRUE* that you are sly.

Mark a 5 if it is *OFTEN TRUE* that you are sly.

Mark a 6 if it is *USUALLY TRUE* that you are sly.

Mark a 7 if it is *ALWAYS OR ALMOST ALWAYS TRUE* that you are sly.

Thus, if you feel it is *sometimes but infrequently true* that you are "sly," *never or almost never true* that you are "malicious," *always or almost always true* that you are "irresponsible," and *often true* that you are "carefree," then you would rate these characteristics as follows:

Sly	3	Irresponsible	7
Malicious	1	Carefree	5

describe yourself

1	2	3	4	5	6	7
Never or almost never true	Usually not true	Sometimes but infrequently true	Occasionally true	Often true	Usually true	Always or almost always true

Column 1

- Self reliant 6 6
- Yielding 4 4
- Helpful 6 6
- Defends own beliefs 7 6
- Cheerful 5 5
- Moody 3 5
- Independent 6 6
- Shy 4 4
- Conscientious 6 6
- Athletic 4 1
- Affectionate 7 6
- Theatrical 4 5
- Assertive 5 4
- Flatterable 3 5
- Happy 6 6
- Strong personality 6 6
- Loyal 7 6
- Unpredictable 3
- Forceful 3 3
- Feminine 5 6

Column 2

- Reliable 6
- Analytical 6 3
- Sympathetic 7 6
- Jealous 4
- Has leadership abilities 6 4
- Sensitive to the needs of others 6 5
- Truthful 7 6
- Willing to take risks 7 6
- Understanding 6 6
- Secretive 2
- Makes decisions easily 6 3
- Compassionate 6 6
- Sincere 6
- Self-sufficient 4 6
- Eager to soothe hurt feelings 6 5
- Conceited 4
- Dominant 5 4
- Soft-spoken 4 5
- Likable 5
- Masculine 4 1

Column 3

- Warm 7 6
- Solemn 4
- Willing to take a stand 6 5
- Tender 6 6
- Friendly 6
- Aggressive 5 3
- Gullible 3 6
- Inefficient 4
- Acts as a leader 5 4
- Childlike 3 4
- Adaptable 6
- Individualistic 7 6
- Does not use harsh language 4 3
- Unsystematic 3
- Competitive 5 4
- Loves children 7 7
- Tactful 3
- Ambitious 6 4
- Gentle 7 6
- Conventional 3

items on the masculinity, feminity, and social desirability scales of the BSRI

Masculine items		Feminine items		Neutral items	
49.	Acts as a leader	11.	Affectionate	51.	Adaptable
46.	Aggressive	5.	Cheerful	30.	Conceited
58.	Ambitious	50.	Childlike	9.	Conscientious
22.	Analytical	32.	Compassionate	60.	Conventional
13.	Assertive	53.	Does not use harsh language	45.	Friendly
10.	Athletic	35.	Eager to soothe hurt feelings	15.	Happy
55.	Competitive	20.	Feminine	3.	Helpful
4.	Defends own beliefs	14.	Flatterable	18.	Inefficient
37.	Dominant	59.	Gentle	24.	Jealous
19.	Forceful	47.	Gullible	39.	Likable
25.	Has leadership abilities	56.	Loves children	6.	Moody
7.	Independent	17.	Loyal	21.	Reliable
52.	Individualistic	26.	Sensitive to the needs of others	30.	Secretive
31.	Makes decisions easily	8.	Shy	33.	Sincere
40.	Masculine	38.	Soft-spoken	42.	Solemn
1.	Self-reliant	23.	Sympathetic	57.	Tactful
34.	Self-sufficient	44.	Tender	12.	Theatrical
16.	Strong personality	29.	Understanding	27.	Truthful
43.	Willing to take a stand	41.	Warm	18.	Unpredictable
28.	Willing to take risks	2.	Yielding	54.	Unsystematic

Note: The number preceding each item reflects the position of each adjective as it actually appears on the inventory.

**scoring
the test**

On the basis of his/her responses, each person receives three major scores: A Masculinity Score, a Femininity Score, and, most importantly, an Androgyny Score. To compute the Masculinity Score, add up all of the points assigned to the masculine adjectives and then divide that sum by the total number of masculine adjectives actually rated. To compute the Femininity Score, add up all of the points assigned to the feminine adjectives and then divide that sum by the total number of feminine adjectives actually rated. To compute the Androgyny Score, substract the Masculinity Score from the Femininity Score.

**discussion
of the
score**

The Masculinity and Femininity Scores indicate the extent to which a person endorses masculine and feminine personality characteristics as self-descriptive. As indicated above, the Masculinity and Femininity Scores are simply the means of each subject's ratings of the masculine and feminine adjectives on the BSRI. Both of these scores can range from 1 to 7. It should be noted that these two scores are logically independent. That is, the structure of the test does not constrain them in any way, and they are free to vary independently.

In contrast, the Androgyny Score (computed as Femininity minus Masculinity) reflects the relative amounts of masculinity and femininity that the person includes in his or her self-description, and, as such, it best characterizes the nature of the person's total sex role. Thus, if a person's Femininity Score is much higher than his or her Masculinity Score (that is, if a person describes himself as being much more feminine than masculine), then we think of that person as having a feminine sex role. Similarly, if a person's Masculinity Score is much higher than his or her Femininity Score, then we think of that person as having a masculine sex role. In contrast, if a person's Masculinity and Femininity Scores are approximately equal (that is, if there is really no difference in how masculine or feminine a person thinks he is), then we think of that person as having an androgynous sex role. A feminine sex role thus represents not only the endorsement of feminine attributes, but the simultaneous rejection of masculine attributes. Similarly, a masculine sex role represents not only the endorsement of masculine attributes, but the simultaneous rejection of feminine attributes. In contrast, an androgynous sex role represents the equal endorsement of both masculine and feminine attributes.

The Androgyny Score itself can range from -6 (Extremely Masculine) through 0 (Completely Androgynous) to +6 (Extremely Feminine). However, because individuals rarely score at the extremes, we suggest that the Androgyny Score (AS) be interpreted as follows:

Sex role	Androgyny score
Feminine	AS > +1
Near-feminine	AS > +.5 and < +1
Androgynous	AS > -.5 and < +.5
Near-Masculine	AS > -1 and < -.5
Masculine	AS < -1

As of this publication, the BSRI has been given to approximately fifteen hundred undergraduates at Stanford University. Semester after semester, we find that about 50 percent of the students are "appropriately" sex-typed, about 35 percent are androgynous, and about 15 percent are "cross" sex-typed. The norms are as follows:

	Stanford University		Foothill	
	Males (N = 444)	Females (N = 279)	Males (N = 117)	Females (N = 77)
% Feminine	5%	29%	8%	35%
% Near-feminine	5%	18%	7%	15%
% Androgynous	44%	39%	55%	41%
% Near-masculine	16%	8%	12%	5%
% Masculine	30%	7%	17%	4%

references

Barry, H., Bacon, M. K., & Child, I. L. A cross-cultural survey of some sex differences in socialization. *Journal of Abnormal and Social Psychology*, 1957, *55*, 327-332.

Bem, S. L. Beyond androgyny: Some presumptuous prescriptions for a liberated sexual identity. In A. G. Kaplan & J. P. Beene (Eds.), *Beyond sex role stereotypes: Readings toward a psychology of androgyny*. Boston: Little, Brown, 1976.

Bem, S. L. Sex-role adaptability: One consequence of psychological androgyny. *Journal of Personality and Social Psychology*, 1975, *31*, 634-643.

Bem, S. L., & Lenney, E. Sex-typing and the avoidance of cross-sex behavior. *Journal of Personality and Social Psychology*, 1976, *33*, 48-54.

Edwards, A. L. The measurement of human motives by means of personality scales. In D. Levine (Ed.), *Nebraska symposium of motivation, 1964*. Lincoln: University of Nebraska Press, 1964.

Eickson, E. H. Inner and outer space: Reflections of womanhood. In R. J. Litton (Ed.), *The woman in America*. Boston: Houghton Mifflin, 1964.

Gough, H. G. Manual for the *California Psychological Inventory*. Palo Alto, Calif.: Consulting Psychologist's Press, 1957.

Kagan, J. Acquisition and significance of sex-typing and sex-role identity. In M. L. Hoffman & L. W. Hoffman (Eds.), Review of child development research (Vol. 1). New York: Russell Sage Foundation, 1964.

Kohlberg, L. A. A cognitive-developmental analysis of children's sex-role concepts and attitudes. In E. E. Maccoby (Ed.), *The development of sex differences*. Stanford, Calif.: Stanford University Press, 1966.

Nunnally, J. C. *Psychometric theory*. New York: McGraw-Hill, 1967.

Parsons, T., & Bales, R. F. *Family, socialization and interaction process*. Glencoe, Ill.: Free Press, 1955.

some notes about power relationships between women

Judith M. Bardwick

The idea for this paper originated in experiences I had and observations I made during a five day lab, the Women's Development Program for the National Training Laboratories Institute summer program at Santa Cruz, California. Especially in sessions involving smaller groups I was startled to hear women participants say, "Don't interrupt me. Don't do that. You are taking my power away." The discussions usually involved familiar topics: how to be assertive, how to get husbands and children to cooperate when a woman returned to school or took a job, criticism from neighbors, uncertainty about goals, and guilt about leaving young children. These themes of needing to achieve, dealing with role conflict, and needing to be loved did not seem, however, to be the crucial variables affecting what was happening within the group. Instead, the interactions between the participants and between the leaders and the participants seemed to be grounded in issues of power: either getting power, wielding power, or attacking those who seemed to have power. That was a stunning insight for me. Psychologists never write about women and power. In this society we do not associate women with power; women in this culture do not think of themselves in reference to power. The women who came to the lab were a varied group of about fifty. Those who had been sent by their firms were generally employed at the level of executive secretary. Only a few of the particpants had unusually high levels of training such as a doctoral degree. Some of the women were students, many were housewives and mothers. The great majority of those who were employed were not especially successful. In general, women came or were sent to the lab in order to explore and share concerns which are of special interest to women today. The great majority of these women did not occupy roles with significant power and very few had unusual skill or personal power. Yet once the interpretation was made that power was the crucial variable, apparently inexplicable events became understandable.

There was one particular incident that especially jarred me and pushed me to reinterpret what was going on. There was a remarkable middle-aged woman in our group of twelve. She was a handsome women, widowed, now enjoying a relationship with a man she loved, a mother of two sons, one of whom had died, and a woman with a highly successful career. Mature, warm, integrated, intelligent, realistic, not hostile or threatening, she impressed me enormously as a marvelous person. Certainly everyone in our group seemed to respond to her in the same way; we talked about her as an admirable and likable person and role model. On the last day of the lab, group activities began where they had left off the day before and the women seemed to be basking in those earned feelings of mutual trust, intimacy, and self-affirmation. Rather suddenly and without any obvious reason one young woman, who had initially acted passive-aggressively but who had seemed to relax and become more spontaneous, direct, and honest, interrupted the discussion. She turned to the older woman, thrust her arm out, index finger accusing, and said, "I hate you." Others instantly joined her in this chorus of rage. The older woman listened, contained her anger and replied, "I am sorry that you bring this up so late because it is not possible to deal with it now. I do not know how you think I threaten you but I would have liked to have helped you if I could." Later I understood this to be a confrontation between one with and those without personal power.

This is a personal rather than a scientific paper. It is an interpretation of my impressions and is intended as an exploration of hypotheses rather than a presentation of firm conclusions. People who have read the draft have been in surprising agreement about the main ideas and some have told me that they have seen these dynamics operate in similar labs with mixed groups and with all-male groups. That may well be the case, but in this paper I will confine myself to speculations about what I observed.

After writing the draft of this paper, I chanced to reread Abraham Maslow's *Toward a Psychology of Being,* and was taken by some passages which had not made as much of an impression before:

There are certainly good and strong and successful men in the world—saints, sages, good leaders, responsibles, B-politicians, statesmen, strong men, winners rather than losers, constructors rather than destroyers, parents rather than children. . . . But it also remains true that there are so few of them even though there *could* be many more, and that they are often treated badly by their fellows. So this too must be studied, this fear of human goodness and greatness, this lack of knowledge of how to be good and strong, this inability to turn one's anger into productive activities, this fear of maturity and the god-likeness that comes with maturity, this fear of feeling virtuous, self-loving, love-worthy, respect-worthy. Especially must we learn how to transcend our foolish tendency to let our compassion for the weak generate hatred for the strong (Preface to 2nd ed. p. iv).

In a later passage Maslow wrote:

The commonly seen hatred or resentment of or jealousy of goodness, truth, beauty, health or intelligence ("counter-values") is largely (though not altogether) determined by threat of loss of self-esteem, as the liar is threatened by the honest man, the homely girl by the beautiful girl, or the coward by the hero. Every superior person confronts us with our own shortcomings (p. 196).

types of power

To begin, let us enumerate some different kinds of power. There is the power which comes from a role, is part of the role, and accrues to anyone who occupies that role. For example, in organizational hierarchies those who occupy positions at the top of the pyramid have a great deal of responsibility as well as enormous power in making decisions that affect people below them in the hierarchy. A second kind of power comes from skill, and with unusually high skill people tend to make decisions, even in the absence of a role which assigns them that responsibility, because their expertise leads others to look to them for leadership. For example, in a group of scientists, if one person is acknowledged as having greater scientific authority, when decisions involving scientific content have to be made, this person assumes the leadership of the group. A third kind of power is exercised for psychologically compensatory reasons. Here, people who are vulnerable manipulate and take power from others in order to protect themselves. The overbearing, overassertive, overintrusive, didactic leader comes to mind. When arrogant decisiveness and certainty are too great, the psychologist must suspect bluff and compensation.

There is yet another kind of power, which Maslow described and which I saw in the middle-aged woman. This is personal power, a feeling of power that resides within a person and comes from maturity, ego-integration. security in one's relationships with others, lack of need to gain from others, and confidence in one's impulses. These are strong people because they trust themselves. They hear others but their behaviors and judgments are not dominated by a need to conform, to be liked, or to lead, rebel, or manipulate others. They can be spontaneous and honest, being less coerced than most people are by their past, present, or future needs. Maslow calls these people "self-actualized"; in this paper I use the synonymous terms *strong* and *powerful*. Such women have high ego-strength, are relatively autonomous and decisive, and have a strong sense of responsibility. I am *not* referring to compensatory and aggressive manipulation by those who are not mature, not ego-integrated, not self-actualized.

The main question to be examined in this paper is, why are women who are personally powerful likely to be attacked by those who are not? The second question is, under what conditions is attack likely to take place? The third question is, what are the forms of the attack? Last, what are the likely responses of the personally powerful woman to those less powerful women who attack her? We may note that there is likely to be considerable overlap because those with personal power are also likely to occupy positions of role or skill power; those who lack personal power are less likely to occupy legitimized power positions. The individual's internal dynamics and real life situation tend to combine, with the result that a person tends to develop toward one extreme or the other.

reasons and conditions for attack on powerful women

Women who are personally powerful, self-actualized, and high in ego-strength and autonomy are simultaneously objects for emulation and hatred by other women. The self-actualized woman is certainly the very ideal of what a woman should want to be; thus it is easy to understand why she is a model. But why is she also an object of hatred? A reasonable hypothesis is as follows: Powerless women, being jealous, become uncomfortable in the presence of a self-actualized woman. Such a person makes it difficult for those without potency to attribute their powerlessness to external forces over which they had no control. The nature of the threat lies in the fact that the stronger woman has prevailed over the same external forces. Thus, denial mechanisms in the powerless, which absolve them of responsibility for their own development, are threatened by the reality of the other woman. The personality, the very being of the stronger woman is the threat to the weaker.

Insofar as the threat is experienced at the personal level and the needs of the powerless are at the personal rather than at the role or skill level, then those who are weaker will feel that they need emotional support and affirmation from the stronger woman. This is intrinsically an ambivalent situation. The needier women experience and acknowledge their feelings of dependence, their lack of secure self-esteem, their resentment of this emotional infantilism, and their pleasure in the personal affirmation that they receive from the stronger woman. There seems to be something especially threatening when power is the result of psychological integration rather than role or skill dominance—much less aggressive manipulation.

An additional reason for the resentment experienced by the weaker women might be in their concept of power. They seem to see power as being limited. Either one has it or not; and if one person has it, then another cannot. They experience the stronger woman as having a quantity of power and therefore blocking the possibility of their getting power and assuming leadership. Thus they can say, "You are taking my power away." Those who are personally powerful do not think of interpersonal relationships in terms of power. Most women are uncomfortable thinking of themselves as powerful. It also holds true that personally powerful women seldom experience the lack of power or helplessness. It is therefore difficult for powerful women to perceive themselves as either having power or withholding it from others. If this is true, then those with personal power are likely to be insensitive to power needs of others, since such needs are not a salient issue for them in most personal situations. In addition, powerful women are very likely to withhold the possibility of leadership power from the weak because the strong generally lead, without meaning to, by dint of personality. Thus, weaker women appropriately perceive more potent women as models to emulate and objects to fear.

Women who experience themselves as weak or impotent will naturally feel weak and vulnerable in relation to those who are strong. Confronted with the strong woman, those with fragile self-images are greatly threatened, and their anxiety becomes more poignant as they experience the gulf between their real self and their fantasied self. It is less likely that the weaker will be able to express the resentment directly because, in general, it takes a strong ego to confront a strong ego. It is much more probable that the weaker woman will express an exaggerated admiration, a pathologically exaggerated idealization, a kind of ingratiation that says, "Like me. Like me better than anyone." Especially among women we may observe the play of weakness that says, "I need your help. Help me."

I suggest that if we were to compare a male or mixed group with a female group, we would be more likely to see females acting overtly out of high dependence needs and a form of covert aggression involving dependence relations. This would occur because emotional dependence is more congruent with the stereotypic female than the male character. Acknowledgment of emotional dependence is therefore much easier for women than for men. Women tend to be more skilled in using others to promote their own emotional needs.

Under what conditions would we expect either a personal attack by the weaker women upon the stronger or the playing out of the dynamics of the emotional neediness by the weaker? While there is always the possibility of these dynamics occurring, they are more likely when it is easier to personalize the situation. That is, when the situation is not structured as it normally is in work or in organizations, where there are no assigned tasks, roles, or leadership specifications, when responsibilities are not specified, then the dynamics of the people involved are more likely to become personalized. Among women, the acting out of emotional dependency and passive-aggressive behavior also becomes more probable.

Imagine an organization where there are subordinates and a person in charge, and each has a specific job to do. In this case, if one of the group members feels anxious, aggressive, or resentful towards another member, he or she might attribute this feeling to how the group is organized. To relieve it, the person, may try to alter the structure of the organization. This becomes a threat from and an attack upon a relatively impersonal organizational structure. But suppose the set-up

of the organization is not clear or the situation is ambiguous and leaders have emerged on the basis of personality or skill rather than role.
Then power is not directly related to the role and anxiety, aggression,
or resentment can be experienced personally. In this instance,
attempts to make changes must be directed toward other persons.
Here, interactions are more totally personal. The encounter group, or
T-group, is a deliberately contrived situation where power is distributed as evenly as possible among participants and there is a maximum of emotional response. The encounter laboratory is an extreme
situation in which one is most likely to be able to observe these dynamics in an unmodified form.

When someone's personal style makes her emerge as a leader, but
that position is not voted on or acknowledged by group consensus or
task criterion, when her leadership cannot be perceived as the result
of an objective role position or some particular relevant expertise, then
leading and following are done on the basis of personality. Very simply,
when people become dominant and make decisions without there being
a specific and consensually understood role, then followers see these
leaders as powerful individuals. This is entirely different from the type
of authority that derives from a specific job that has limitations. When
an individual dominates, for example, not because she is chairperson,
but because she is forceful, then leadership is personalized. In the ambiguity of this situation, those who are led are more likely to feel
anxious and thus personally used if not abused. As a result, chances
are good that those who emerge in dominant positions will be attacked
for taking on the leader role. (This is especially true for those whose
personal style is more direct and assertive and may be less true for
those whose personal style is softer and more traditionally feminine.)

What difference does the role make? When power attaches to a role,
it is relatively impersonal; and there is the crucial stipulation that anyone who takes on the role assumes specific decision-making responsibilities and works within the role's limitations. That is, roles provide
specified, limited power and responsibility and they spell out the leader's responsibility to those led.

When the role is less clear, or does not specify limitations and obligations, then the powerless become anxious. This occurs because
they are vulnerable to the potentially unlimited manipulations of the
stronger. When someone is in a role which basically has no bargaining
position, that is, no power, then that individual has recourse only to
personal power. Sometimes the relatively powerless are protected by
custom or by the law. Such situations include that of pupil and teacher
where the law limits the teacher's ability to punish, or the relationship
of employee and employer, where the law protects the employee within
the working situation. But in more personal relationships, especially
now when roles are changing and areas of obligations and respon-

sibility are no longer traditional, then the role no longer has built-in constraints and the less personally powerful individual is dependent upon the beneficence of the more powerful. Such relationships would include that of child and parent, wife and husband, lover and lover. This means that when role definitions are more ambiguous, either because of the nature of the role or because the definition of that role is changing, then the less powerful lose the protection that comes from role constraints and they are indeed in greater danger of being engulfed by those who are more personally powerful.

forms of the attack and responses of the personally powerful woman
Those who are easily manipulated by others who have more powerful roles or especially by others with stronger personalities are not likely to use direct or overt forms of aggression. They are more likely to be overtly fawning or ingratiating but covertly and subtly aggressive. This form of attack makes it more difficult to label their intent as aggressive and to hold them responsible for their aggression. The ingratiating behavior both secures an emotional affirmation from the stronger woman and induces guilt in her because she is responding to the acknowledged needs of the weaker. Thus the more powerful woman is likely to act supportively rather than assertively and the weaker has inhibited the stronger. While this is an ego trip for the personally powerful woman it will probably result in the muting of her leadership, for she will tend to withhold direct contradictory opinion or chastisement. Since the emotional acting out is a plea for support by someone who shows her needs overtly, the needs are acknowledged but the aggressive manipulation is not and is, in fact, very difficult to see. After all, how many people are aware of the fact that when someone says, "I need you," they may also be saying, "I hate you." Not many.

If the group is without leadership, roles, or tasks and especially if it is set up to create as many emotional interactions as possible, it becomes quite possible for the emotionally demanding weaker women to dominate what occurs and thereby become the strongest members of the group. If the group does not confront these issues, then emotional needs instead of coping skills become the focus. Emotional dependence thus becomes a reinforced behavior and the tyranny of the weak is evident.

Those who are characteristically without power, either because they lack personal power or because their role does not call for the exercise of power, seem to be prone to perceive relationships and situations in terms of power. Their lack of decision-making responsibility and mature personality means that they are always a potential victim when others intrude into their real life or their psychological space. In the Catch-22 of their lives, when the stronger speaks only in neutral or positive ways, then it becomes appropriate for the powerless person to be hypersensitive to the possibility of negative feelings, scanning constantly for the subtlest of cues—"Her smile doesn't look so genuine today. She really doesn't like me." The powerless person suffers from a paranoia; she goes through life with antennae extended to sense even the most subtle acts, attempts, or thoughts of coercion or intrusion into her own lifespace.

This preoccupation with power by the powerless contrasts abruptly with the perceptions of the powerful woman. She seems relatively oblivious of power issues and indeed of her own power. Not being vulnerable to other's power, she is less sensitive. Power is still not a part of the idealized female character and even personally powerful women seem resistant to perceiving themselves as such: having power means having more responsibilities.

It seems that in some crucial ways the experience of power of the haves and the have-nots is fundamentally different. When they talk about power they mean different things. The powerless seem to imagine that having power is the opposite of being without it. They define it primarily in personal terms because it is in the personal sense that they are fundamentally vulnerable. They seem to imagine that having power means to be coercive, potent, and free; and for them, because they feel themselves to be coerced, impotent, and trapped, that is an understandable perception. Thus, in the many situations where power is a salient issue for the powerless, power is understood in personal terms and having power means not being vulnerable, not being impotent.

Those with personal power are much less likely to conceive of power in personal terms and are far more likely to think of power in relationship to tasks or roles. These people can take for granted the fact that others cannot intrude into their space—they have boundaries, they have some control over their vulnerability and certainly over their intimacy, which the powerless do not have. Those who do have power and who characteristically lead, talk about the power to make decisions and be responsible for the outcomes, to lead people and be responsible to them, to make policies, to influence, to guide—in every circumstance the result of having power is to increase the number or the breadth of responsibilities.

Those without power fantasize that having power means being freed from incursions into the self. They imagine that having power, some quantity of it, would protect them from coercion. Since the concepts and the experiences of the powerful and the powerless are fundamentally different, it is understandable why communication between them may totally break down. We can imagine a basic difference in behavior as well: to the extent that the powerful woman experiences the ambivalent feelings directed toward her and to the extent that she must decide whether she is willing to take on more responsibilities, she may well hesitate before acting as a leader. The powerless, unable to imagine the negative aspects of having power and eager to be powerful is likely to find the indecisiveness of the powerful woman stressful.

Confronted by overt aggression, one would expect the powerful woman to respond the same way. That did not happen in the lab, perhaps for the following reason. Along with the overt aggression there was an expression of acute emotional dependence similar to the manipulation of a mother by her child. Some of the succorance did take the form of holding, cuddling, and protecting, arousing in the more powerful woman responses that seemed to be maternal. It is hard to be the "bad mother." It arouses guilt. It seemed that the traditional feminine attributes, the habit of helping others, and the determination not to impose personal pain on people who are weak was operating. To nurture and help are not simply aspects of the feminine stereotype, they are also internalized values which are a central part of a woman's idealized self-image. It is also possible that women who are self-actualized have integrated this nurturing aspect of themselves more than those who are weaker because the weaker may experience emotional giving as depleting their own resources. Simultaneously, powerful women are not likely to be comfortable with their own power and may find it far more comfortable to act within the more congruent role of supportive mother.

The weaker group members act out their emotional dependence and arouse anxiety in the stronger about not imposing personal pain. When this happens they cause the stronger woman to withhold her assertiveness and leadership, and the dynamics of the group become particularly feminine. The phenomenon called the "Queen Bee Syndrome" may occur not only because women in leadership roles want to protect their position from competitors. In addition, the followers may keep the leader from acting on her strength because it is potentially destructive to them. In this case the leader must distance herself from the weaker, first because they cause her to blunt her behaviors, and second because the leader does not want to identify herself with weakness.

implications for role models and the women's liberation movement

There is a good deal of discussion within the Women's Movement about role models. Somehow the focus has been on the positive to the neglect of the threatening aspect. Surely those who are already somewhat confident but just a little timorous can respond to those who have achieved personal integration positively—but even here I begin to suspect an unacknowledged ambivalence. I discussed with a former Ph.D student of mine the nature of our relationship. We agreed that I was a combination of mentor, friend, sister, and mother. Perhaps the fact that the relationship was more than a mentor/apprentice one is partially because it was between two women, and women characteristically operate on affective personal levels even when there is an objective task to accomplish. Also, I suspect, it is because in the stress of the task situation the female mentor responds to the support needs of the younger woman. Emotional support is probably a necessary condition for competitive risk taking for many women, at least in the beginning of a career. While the psychodynamics of men may be similar, it seems that emotional needs are far less likely to be expressed by either man nor responded to by the mentor, since the stereotype of male ego-strength has characteristically precluded expressing anxiety and dependence. But if we take the model of this feminine mentor as including (objective) mentor, (peer) friend, (intimate) sister, and—(ambivalent) mother, then the relationship is operating on both a task-related objective level and a quite personalized, intimate, emotional one. It is then very likely that even when the younger woman is basically strong, she will necessarily respond to the older, stronger woman with many of the same affects she experiences with her own mother. And as in her relationship with her own mother she will have to introduce some level of distancing, some amount of ambivalence, some quantity of rejection of the more powerful figure, before she can experience herself as her own person. Of course, exactly the same dynamics can operate with men, but since they are more likely to avoid the overt expression of this more personal and emotional interaction, this kind of intimate relationship is more characteristic of women.

Who would be experienced as the strongest of the strong? Who is the greatest model and therefore the greatest threat? I suggest that it will be the woman who has personal power, who is confident, able to be assertive, who is likely to achieve, and who simultaneously conveys empathy, warmth, and caring. When might the threatening qualities of such a woman be lessened? Only when roles are specified, therefore, limiting power, and when all members of the group have a known task which contributes toward the group goal will the threat subside. Under which circumstances could the individuals in a group work without known roles and a given hierarchy of responsibilities? Perhaps when members of a group are peers in some sense relevant to the group goal or when the members have previously established trusting relationships with each other then, we will be able to work without role definement. When these conditions are not fulfilled, when trust has not been previously established, or when roles or responsibilities are not acknowledged, the probability is that power dynamics in the personal sense will dominate the group.

The organization of women's groups and especially the hidden hierarchy of leadership is an important issue in the Women's Movement because one of the objectives of the movement is to break down the traditional organizational pyramid which assigns leadership and power responsibilities only to the few who rise to the top.

The traditional values of women, in which the welfare of the people with whom they interact and for whom they have responsibility, might be able to modify the norm of organizational structure and the fairly unidirectional flow of power. In the literature of the Women's Movement there seems to be a naive and extreme point of view which is an emotional reaction to the coercion and manipulation of the traditional organizational pyramid. The solution proposed is the predictable reverse of the rigid role structure of the traditional organization. That is, the solution is to have no organization, to have no leadership, and to have no specified roles because specification is constraining. Leadership means hierarchy. When it exists, some people will exert the leverage of power over others. Since women have traditionally been the victim-recipients of that manipulation, the ethos is that women will or should not join in creating new organizations which perpetuate the same old destructive dynamics. Individuals are protected in roles where limitations on power are specified. There is too high a probability of anxiety and anger in the ambiguity of a real but unacknowledged differential in power or leadership. So the solution might be not to give up roles or leadership or organization even if they are heirarchal, but to modify those structures so that constraints on power are specified and the breadth of shared decision making is greatly increased.

assertiveness training for men and women[1]

Nancy Richardson

A woman executive who feels that her ideas are not taken seriously by her colleagues begins to withdraw during business meetings. A man who does not want to become sexually involved with a woman he has been dating feels compelled to make up excuses about his demanding work schedule for the next day. A wife whose husband makes all the decisions related to their lives has "headaches" when her husband is sexually aroused. A woman who goes out of her way to please nearly everyone without asking for anything in return loudly berates her friend for asking for a ride home.

passive-aggressive-assertive responses

The people who have such reactions to stressful situations are choosing *passive behaviors* to express negative feelings; the one exception is the woman who loudly berated her friend. Passive behavior is emotionally dishonest and self-denying and it is not likely to achieve a desired goal. Rather it will probably extract a certain amount of "revenge" from the recipient of the behavior, who may in turn act even more negatively. The woman executive will probably become less competent and her relationships with her colleagues will continue to deteriorate. The man who is avoiding any direct confrontation about his feelings concerning a sexual relationship may be establishing a pattern which puts a ceiling on the level of intimacy he might achieve. The wife may find that her relationship with her husband continues to grow more intolerable and may decide that her only option is to leave him.

The woman who loudly berated her friend, however, exhibited unreasonably hostile or *aggressive behavior*. Aggressive behavior is exaggerated action taken at the expense of another, who will usually feel hostile or humiliated. Consequently, the aggressor is not likely to

---

[1]The author wishes to thank Rita Whiteley and John Flowers for many hours of training and support, and Ted Fenton and Pat Perrin for their extensive editorial assistance.

achieve any desired goal but may instead succeed in damaging an important relationship. Aggressive behavior can be thought of as an angry form of "overkill." The woman involved in the angry interchange with her friend by her inability to assert herself, previously had allowed, even asked, people to use her. Her anger broke through in the form of inappropriate hostility in response to a reasonable request.

Knowledge of assertive behavior, or action taken in self-interest that does not violate another's rights, might have proved useful to each of the people in the previous examples. When we assert ourselves, we communicate our positive and negative feelings honestly and directly. We are aware of our rights and protect them appropriately. Assertive action does not guarantee that our goals will be achieved, but it underscores our self-respect and often improves our relationships with others by letting them know where we stand. Assertive actions communicate self-confidence and self-respect.

The same person may act assertively in one situation and be inappropriately passive or aggressive in another. Some people handle work situations assertively but cannot handle conflict at home. Unreasonable or reasonable fears in specific situations may block our normal abilities to cope effectively. A new situation requiring assertive abilities may also be baffling. While recognizing our negative feelings about difficult situations is a step in the right direction, it does not help us to dwell on these feelings. We need to find ways to reevaluate the experiences and a means to rechannel the energy without damage to ourselves and others. Assertiveness is one way to deal with repeated frustrating situations and emotions.

Assertiveness training is an educational experience which promotes self-confidence. It helps individuals to analyze problematic situations and offers techniques for the development of more effective behavior. Assertiveness training helps people to understand the effects of stereotypes on their behavior and works toward the establishment and implementation of goals for behavior change. It seeks to aid men and women who are in the process of becoming androgynous. Androgynous people usually are able to be strong, vulnerable, competent, open, and sensitive in appropriate situations.

An important application of assertiveness training has been in helping people to change stereotypic sex-role behaviors. In our society, it is generally more acceptable for men to act assertively than women. A manifestation of this societal norm is found in the interaction and speech patterns of women and men (Aries; Henley & Thorne, see chapters in this book). Women and men often speak differently in same-sex groups than in mixed-sex groups. Women tend to leave more sentences unfinished and make fewer statements of opinion, they often insert unnecessary qualifiers. Men tend to sound more definite than they feel, to talk in paragraphs, and to interrupt more often.

Due to the societal demand that men be cool, strong, and unemotional, it is often especially difficult for men to display feelings of doubt, tenderness, and strong emotion. Many men find that their ability to share feelings, dependency needs, perceived burdens and responsibilities, or so called weaknesses, can improve with practice. The ability to recognize and communicate feelings and needs is crucial for both assertive behavior and meaningful relationships.

In order to better understand passive, assertive, and aggressive behavior, let us examine a tense, emotional business situation. John Senior, a hard-pressed business executive, who has had a very difficult week, decides to raise his self-esteem by making a conquest of his office manager, Mary Bright. Leaving his wife and two children at home, John asks Mary out to dinner, making it clear that his intentions are "romantic." Mary, who is not sexually interested in John, but does value her job and has also asked for a raise, can answer him in several different ways.

She can accept, even though she has no romantic interest in John. She might do this if she were afraid of losing her job and raise, or possibly, she might be afraid of hurting his feelings if she said no. The problem with this passive response is that it may lead to the loss of her job if John's wife or boss were to discover the relationship. Also Mary would be allowing herself to be used unfairly. Her anger at this treatment might later emerge with possible negative consequences. In such passive behavior one's rights are violated by another person, with or without their knowledge.

If Mary feels threatened by John's proposal, she may reply with an angry, insulted refusal. This aggressive-defensive response would leave John feeling rejected, humiliated, and fearful that she might tell someone important about this invitation. If he feels threatened enough, he will try to get rid of Mary. Although Mary has won a short-term goal of enhancing her own prestige by righteously rejecting John, she has damaged this important relationship. This type of aggressive response is self-enhancing at another's expense. Often it may leave the other person hurt and the relationship will usually suffer.

What, then, can Mary do? The two obvious solutions, acceptance and refusal, both appear to mean disaster for Mary and John. Mary may calmly say something like, "John, I think we have a good working relationship and I'm not willing to jeopardize it by becoming sexually involved with you." If he maintains that it would not influence their working relationship, she should simply say, "I don't want to have a sexual relationship with you." *Assertive behavior* involves honest and direct communication of feelings and rights, as well as respect for the other person's rights and feelings. If Mary is a good listener, she may realize that John has had a very bad week and say something like, "John, this seems to have been a hard week for you. Is there anything wrong that you would like to talk about?" Even if John is embarrassed by her rapid perception of the real situation, he will be gratified to find that he has a friend.

It is sometimes difficult to develop an assertive response on cue, especially if strong feelings are involved or the stakes are high. Let's say Mary was so stunned by John's invitation that she didn't know what to say. It may be better for her to postpone a reply by asking John if she can have some time to think about it. Rather than denying her feelings, she should try to convey her confusion and surprise. Hence, she may want to say, "I'm not sure how to respond; you have really caught me by surprise and I need some time to think about this." Avoiding the confrontation can be interpreted as another form of nonassertive behavior, either passive or aggressive. John may leave, fearing Mary will "tell," or assume that she will accept as soon as possible. Hence, Mary should make a point of being direct whenever possible, and especially when the next situation occurs.

Most people have trouble formulating assertive responses in a tense, emotionally charged situation, especially if it is suddenly thrust upon them. For this reason, one will usually benefit from assertiveness practice or "role rehearsal," assertiveness training's principal tool. Through role rehearsal (the practicing of desired behavior) a person becomes less anxious and more able to devise assertive responses in previously difficult situations. Both role rehearsal (Friedman, 1971) and videotape feedback (Melnick, 1973) have been found to be highly effective in producing and refining assertive behavior.

Role playing, the acting out of a role which is not necessarily one that the person expects to assume, and role rehearsal are effectively practiced in a group. The use of tokens for facilitating the assertion training process, as designed by Shoemaker and Paulson (1973), can help members of the group to learn the differences between assertive, aggressive, and passive responses. Group members give each other tokens of a specific color for aggressive (red), passive (light blue), or assertive (white) responses in the various problematic situations which are role-played in the group. Lacking the group, it may be helpful for you to formulate an aggressive, passive, or assertive answer for each of the following situations.

1. Hi, I'd like to ask a favor. Since you're going to be out of town for a week, I wonder if I could borrow your car. (This person isn't a close friend and you don't know anything about his or her driving habits.) *Your reply:*
   Passive_____
   Aggressive _____
   Assertive _____

2. You are a member of a graduate seminar in which the men are addressed by their first names and the women are called "honey" or "dear." Your professor turns to you and says, "Well, dear, now

what was it you were saying?'' *Your reply:*

Passive _____

Aggressive _____

Assertive _____

3. You are standing in a long line at a movie theatre. When you are near the front of the line, a man approaches you and asks you to buy tickets for him. *Your reply:*

    Passive _____

    Aggressive _____

    Assertive _____

4. Your child is sick. Both you and your spouse have important work-related matters which must be accomplished that day. Your spouse tells you that he or she is leaving to handle the work task and asks you to take care of your child. *Your reply:*

    Passive _____

    Aggressive _____

    Assertive _____

5. You are attending a lecture. The person next to you is smoking and you find this very annoying and distracting. *Your reply:*

    Passive _____

    Aggressive _____

    Assertive _____

Some typical responses to these situations might be:

1. *Borrowing automobile*

    Passive—''I don't know why not. Come by and get the keys.''

    Aggressive—''Certainly not! You could be a reckless driver for all I know.''

    Assertive—''I don't feel I know you well enough to lend my car to you.''

2. *Graduate seminar*

    Passive—You simply repeat your idea.

    Aggressive—''You didn't hear me the first time, *sweetheart?*''

    Assertive—''Dr. Samuels, I would prefer that you address me by my name.'' Or, you may wish to comment on the process: ''I wonder if you are aware that you address all the men in class by their names and that you call the women 'dear' or 'honey.' I would prefer to be called by my first name.'' (Note: It is important to be sensitive to the embarrassment that the professor might feel. It may be much more effective to speak to him privately about this.)

3. *Theatre line*

    Passive—''I suppose so. Give me your money.''

    Aggressive—''You sure have some nerve, Mister.''

Assertive—"No. I think that it would be unfair for me to buy the tickets."

4. *Child care*

Passive—"I guess that's O.K. I'll call you if anything happens."

Aggressive—"Don't you have any sense of responsibility?"

Assertive—"I know we both have important commitments; let's work out a compromise. One of us could stay with Melissa in the morning and the other could be with her in the afternoon."

5. *Smoking*

Passive—Say nothing. Cough and wave one's program throughout the lecture.

Aggressive—Say loudly, "Smoking is a filthy habit."

Assertive—"I am bothered by your cigarette smoke."

Group interaction is especially helpful in role rehearsal for these and similar situations because often it is not what we say that matters but how we say it. Many times we are not aware of our own voice tones or body movements that may send authentic messages of hostility or fear, although the words do not. Situations that are highly anxious for us make our reactions especially difficult to control.

suds scale

The Subjective Units of Discomfort Scale (Wolpe, 1969; Flowers, 1974), commonly known as the SUDS scale, is designed to help you recognize situations that make you anxious and to aid in controlling the anxiety. The SUDS levels can be used as a guide for selecting personal areas for future role rehearsal and assertiveness training. To develop a SUDS scale, think of a general action you might take, or one that you might fail to take, which makes you anxious. For example, asking for favors, saying no to someone, attempting to establish a relationship, refusing to establish a relationship, expressing emotions, or being critical are some anxiety-provoking situations that can serve as a topic area. Suppose a person selects "asking for favors" as her/his general topic. Asking someone to pass the salt doesn't make her/him anxious at all; so she/he assigns that situation a 0. Asking her/his boss for a raise is the most stressful situation she/he can imagine; so she/he assigns it a 100. Next she/he would need to think of at least eight more situations that fall into order between 0 and 100; and then would examine each situation closely. What exactly makes her/him anxious? Is it a place? A person? What might she/he say? She/he should then write a description of these situations and then rank order them from 0 to 100. It is best to have each situation spaced about ten units apart on this discomfort scale. Finally, she/he should think how she/he could handle each situation in a positive, assertive manner. Sitting or lying down in a comfortable position and imagining each item of the hierarchy in sequential order will help to diffuse some of the anxiety around these behaviors. At first, some of the items may be too anxiety producing to even imagine them; hence, it is best to move up the hierarchy gradually if this occurs.

Now that the reader is more familiar with the differences between passive, assertive, and aggressive responses and is aware of how to determine an anxiety level in different situations, the following techniques may be useful in formulating assertive responses.

assertive responses

1. the minimally effective response

When we are angry, hurt, or want something, Rimm (1973) suggests expressing these sentiments with a minimally effective response. For example, you have an appointment with Mr. Miller and you have been standing for several minutes at a secretary's desk waiting for him to acknowledge your presence. He appears to be absorbed in some papers. Feeling that you have given him a reasonable opportunity to finish what he was doing and time to recognize your presence, you say, "Excuse, me, sir, I have a three o'clock appointment with Mr. Miller." If you still aren't acknowledged, you may escalate your responses: "I have an important appointment with Mr. Miller; would you tell him that I am here." If you are still ignored, you might say, "I am getting angry and will be late for my appointment with Mr. Miller." And if you are still ignored, you might walk past the secretary to Mr. Miller's office. By slowly escalating your demand for a response, you achieve your goal with the minimum effort required.

2. feedback

Feedback to others describes events or interactions that please or displease you. This is especially constructive if you follow two rules. First, feedback should always be specific rather than vague. Saying, "I'm upset that you are late for our date" is much more effective than saying, "I'm upset with you." Second, feedback should always refer to a recent incident, not something that happened last month. If these guidelines are observed, the information exchange is more likely to result in positive change and less defensiveness on the part of the recipient.

Jacobs, Jacobs, Cavior, and Feldman (1973) find that it is best to keep personal feelings out of negative feedback but include them in positive feedback. For example, a wife may say to her husband, "If you would like me to do something for you, I would prefer that you ask me directly rather than hinting about what you want" (statement of fact). For positive feedback, "I am really happy (statement of feeling) that you are reading that book; I am sure that it will raise a lot of ideas for us to talk about" (statement of fact).

3.   I-messages

Assertive statements and feedback can be phrased effectively as I-messages (Gordon, 1970).[2] When you take a position on some issue and wish to communicate it, I-messages are often the most appropriate form. An I-message states the effect another's behavior is having on you. In a nonhostile manner, the I-message should describe the problem behavior. For example, you might say to a spouse, "In the future I would appreciate it if you would not criticize my driving in front of other people." Or to a business associate, "I find it difficult to carry on a conversation with you because you are constantly interrupting me," rather than send a you-message, "You always interrupt me." An I-message that says, "I feel you interrupt me all the time" is really a you-message because it *doesn't state the effect the interruptions have had on you.* A you-message is a direct attack on another's behavior. An I-message describes the behavior and explains the effect a behavior has had on you.

The I-message is usually less likely to provoke resistance because it states your perception of a fact rather than an evaluative statement. The other person is not thrown immediately into a defensive position and is free to listen to your statement. Disclosing feelings involves risks, yet self-disclosure is necessary if we are to develop intimacy and meaningful friendships (Jourard, 1971). I-messages are also very effective when you want to communicate positive feelings.

The following situations can be resolved with I-messages. Read each situation and write down an I-message you think might be effective.

1.   A friend who means a lot to you will leave in the morning for a long trip. You say _____

_____

2.   Your spouse or roommate is not helping with the housework. You say_____

_____

3.   Someone dominates an important meeting with trivial matters. You say_____

_____

4.   A group of acquaintances always has lunch together. You have never been invited but would like to go. You say_____

_____

---

[2]The application of I-messages from Gordon's work was first introduced to me by Rita Whiteley.

Some possible I-messages for these situations are outlined below:

1. "I hope you decide to come back soon. I'll really miss you."
2. "Since I am doing the dishes, I would appreciate it if you could go to the store." It would also be appropriate to suggest a general discussion about this problem.
   Note: Gordon (1970) offers a helpful model for conflict resolution. Briefly, when two (or more) people encounter a conflict of needs situation, one person should suggest that they participate in a joint search for some solution acceptable to all. They then can critically evaluate the proposed solutions until they reach a final solution which is satisfactory.
3. "I find myself becoming distracted by the many side issues being brought up. I would appreciate it if we could all stick to the main topic of the meeting."
4. "I'd really like to have lunch with your group; would it be all right with you if I joined you one day this week?"
   Note: One of the difficulties which people often experience in asking to spend time with another person is that they make the request too specific. For example, "Anne, would you like to go to see *Scenes from a marriage* next Friday at 7:00?" If Anne says no, it may be for any number of reasons. She may have already seen the movie or might not be arriving home until 8:00. Unfortunately, her negative response is often assumed to be a rejection of the person making the request; particularly when this occurs across sex lines (male to female or female to male).

4. free information

New relationships are especially difficult to some of us. If we are especially anxious in a new situation, we may overlook free information, that is freely volunteered information not specifically requested by a question we have asked (Flowers, 1974). This is usually information about which the other person enjoys talking. For example, a person standing next to you at a bus stop may ask the time and add, "I'm afraid I'll be late for my appointment." (Free information.) You might say, "Oh, is it an important appointment?" The person might reply, "No, it's one I wish I didn't have to keep. It's a dentist's appointment." (Free information.) If you are a good listener, you may wish to offer some sympathy since dentists' appointments are usually stressful situations for most people. Watching for free information develops listening skills that are especially useful in anxious situations.

5. open-ended questions

An open-ended question requests additional general, rather than specific, information (Flowers, 1974). "How do you feel about your job?" is an open-ended question, while "You do like your job, don't you?" is a closed question. This is another device that helps us to listen more effectively. "You do like your job, don't you?" hints that the only possible answer is yes and that the questioner might not approve of a no answer. Open-ended questions are more likely to indicate genuine interest and leave more room for the other person to talk about areas of interest to him or her. Listen to some television talk shows to hear good open-ended questions and responses that contain free information.

6. broken record

You may find yourself in a situation where you are trying to make a point but the other party seems to be avoiding or ignoring your request or refusal. He or she may also be continually attempting to distract you with side issues. This is particularly common in sales transactions or family fights. You simply state your main point and continue to restate only that point, without becoming distracted by side issues and without offering free information the other person might use to argue with you (Flowers, 1974). You may even say, when presented with another side issue, "but the point is . . ." Faced with a child who makes a number of demands to avoid going to bed, a father might say over and over, "No, son, I will not read you another story (get you another drink of water, kiss you goodnight again). I want you to go to sleep."

7. disarming anger and criticism

When someone is too angry to talk to you effectively, it is usually more effective to address and acknowledge the emotion rather than attempt to deal with the content of the speech. (Flowers, 1974) Women often experience problems expressing anger or criticism; often when the anger is finally expressed, it is in the form of a highly emotional outburst. The intensity of the emotion usually makes it impossible to have a productive discussion. When one encounters this type of situation, either as the angry person or the recipient of the anger, it is usually best to postpone the discussion until some of the strong emotion feelings have subsided. An appropriate response would be, "I can see that you really have strong feelings about this issue; I'm finding it difficult to talk about it right now. I would like to talk about it in a few minutes." The person who is emotionally upset then understands that his or her feelings have been communicated but the message is being lost. A clear commitment to address this matter must be made.

This same technique, acknowledging the emotion or information, is also useful when we face criticism. It is basically a listening technique. For example, a mother says to her daughter. "I know your career is demanding, honey, but aren't you ashamed that your house is so messy?" "You are right, the house is a mess; David and I have very busy schedules. We both feel we would rather spend most of our free time with each other and the children than on housework." Acknowledging the criticism, agreeing with the statement when it is valid, and presenting one's own views in a nonthreatening manner, when you disagree with the criticism, will usually keep channels of communication open.

8. empathy

Empathy is also effective for responding to anger or strong emotions although it cannot be strictly defined as assertive (Lazarus, 1973). When someone abuses you for an incident beyond your control, you may wish to be empathic rather than assertive. Since the incident obviously has nothing to do with you, the emotionally distraught person before you may be merely working off steam caused by other unhappy events. A statement like "It sounds like you're really having a bad day" may bring forth a confession of troubles unrelated to your function. While empathic responses are often very effective, it is important to be aware that passive behaviors are often justified as being empathic in order to avoid difficult situations.

Now, supported by the definition of assertive behavior, the anxiety level indicator, and new behavior techniques, you might want to keep a log of various difficult situations you encounter over a week or month and begin practicing assertive responses. Record the time, date, place, and person with which the event occurred, and record your responses to the situation and yours SUDS anxiety level. Is there a pattern in any of the events? Do certain people cause you more problems than others? Are your responses typically passive, aggressive, or assertive? How could you have handled some of these situations differently or better?

You may want to select a situation to test your new assertive skills. Find one that is easy and offers a high probability for success. If your SUDS anxiety level rating is over 40, it may be wise to wait until a later time to try new behavior. Highly anxious situations are best saved until last and rehearsed in front of a mirror or role-played with a cooperative friend or group. You will want to examine all aspects of the situation before deciding on the appropriate behavior. Ask yourself the following questions:

1. What about the situation is making me uncomfortable?
2. What do I want to happen?
3. What behavior will I use?
4. Is it likely to be effective?
5. What will the other person's response be?

6. If I were the other person, what would I think and say?
7. How will I feel about myself after I do this?
8. How will I feel about the other person after I do this?

Flowers (1973) found that people who had clear goals were more often judged assertive by independent raters. He also found that the goal should be stated in a single sentence, otherwise you may have more than one goal. If you know precisely what you want, you'll be more likely to achieve your goal. However, take care that your goal focuses on your behavior rather than on the other person's. If you want to ask a friend to go to a play, your goal should be to assertively ask your friend to go with you, not to have your friend agree to go.

belief systems

Even after learning and applying all these new skills, in some situations you will undoubtedly have problems changing your behavior patterns because of underlying belief systems or partly successful past behavior systems. You may have learned these behaviors and belief systems as a child. If they've been with you for a long time they may be hard to unlearn. For example, in our society a "good" mother puts nearly every family member's demands before her own. She "should" care for her children, keep her house clean, and obey her husband. Similarly, our society believes in a specific role for men. They "should" be strong, authoritative, and unemotional. Consider how difficult assertive behavior can be if you are a mother who believes that taking a stand on something or putting your own needs first is basically unmotherly. And if you're a man who believes men should be unemotional, you might have a great deal of trouble expressing your love for a friend.

Examine the situations you find most anxiety-ridden and frustrating. Are underlying belief systems keeping you from being assertive? If so, you may want to question these belief systems and look around for exceptions or examples that prove them to be untrue. Exploring a particular belief in depth often helps to make it less powerful (Whiteley, 1975). The following chart will serve as a model to explore the ideas which may keep you acting in a nonassertive manner. Looks at the present behavior that you wish to change or are uncomfortable with and then at the belief that keeps you acting in this manner. Then record the new, desired behavior along with the new belief which would correspond to acting in this manner.

For example:

The old behavior: I don't mention my feelings of annoyance when you are consistently late in picking me up.
The old belief: It isn't nice to point out someone's faults; he'll think I'm petty; he was probably too busy to get away.

New behavior: To be able to tell him in a calm, constructive manner that I feel annoyed when he is late in picking me up.

New belief: My feelings are equally important, and I have the right to communicate both positive and negative feelings without feeling guilty in doing so.

Eventually, as you change your behavior, you may also be able to change the belief and act assertively much more successfully.

If your new assertive behavior does indeed challenge current norms or belief systems, you may find a notable lack of support and even discouragement for your new behavior. This is especially true in relationships where one person (usually the wife) must continue to be passive for the relationship to continue. This "nonassertive bargain," identified by Jackubowski-Spector (1973), may be challenged and destroyed by assertive behavior. Often, the passive partner must weigh the value of the relationship against the value of personal growth in pursuing assertive goals.

A common manifestation of unproductive belief systems which presents a roadblock to assertive behavior is called "gunny-sacking" (Bach, 1968) or "stamp collecting" (Berne, 1972). These terms refer to a person who collects injustices and develops a mounting rage that can be triggered by a very small incident. People who tend to be injustice collectors allow their rights to be violated until they eventually "explode" at a later date. These people often have difficulty even acknowledging their anger when their rights are violated. They may feel it is "wrong" to argue, feel guilty when they are angry, and so suppress angry feelings. If you do this, and we all do at one time or another, you can begin to get in touch with your feelings by recording incidents when you feel the slightest bit irritated or annoyed. Then ask yourself if your rights were violated. Did you react as you should have? Consider solutions like I-messages that allow you to blow off a little steam at a time rather than build to an explosion.

value assumptions of assertiveness training

Since assertiveness training offers an important framework for considering alternative behavior and quite powerful techniques for cognitive and behavioral change, it is crucial that the underlying value assumptions of assertiveness training are understood. In order to clarify these assumptions, several common misinterpretations must be contrasted with a more adequate conceptualization. First, some argue that assertiveness training is a form of verbal karate where the actor learns a new set of behaviors and from that day on will always be able to control situations for his/her own advantage. This position is an aggressive, egocentric interpretation. Second, some people seek assertiveness training thinking that they should make the lives of those around them more meaningful. That is, the most important justification for assertiveness is that it will benefit someone else. This conception misses the important assumption that assertiveness training seeks to raise the participant's level of self-confidence which usually has the effect of improving interpersonal relationships.

Finally, the most common characterization is of a process which involves a factual interpretation of the rights that were violated and the selection and refinement of behaviors to insure that the rights will be protected. While this last approach is often justifiable and correct in practice, an important central assumption is missed. That assumption: assertiveness training seeks to enhance and maintain the level of self-confidence of both the trainees and those that they will come into contact with. There is an important recognition of the rights of all those involved in the interaction, as well as an explicit acknowledgment that assertiveness in a purely "legalistic" manner of protecting one's rights (i.e., disagreeing just to disagree) may not always be the most appropriate response.

A major difficulty of the factual or "legalistic" interpretation of assertion training is that rights are not always easily defined. Also, the short-term protection of one's rights may have greater undesirable consequences, which when analyzed might cause the person to forgo an assertive response. For example, consider the person who has been consistently passive in a relationship but later finds this behavior unacceptable and is forced by the definition of the relationship to choose between self-growth and the friendship which often involves responsibilities to others (i.e., children and spouse). The assertiveness trainer has a responsibility to make explicit the value assumptions behind a particular technique, as well as any possible risks or value choices that should be decided by the participant.

In conclusion, assertiveness training can be an effective means for helping people to acquire androgynous behaviors. Basically, healthy relationships are established when both individuals are encouraged to experience and share their feelings and strengths in an open, honest manner. Assertiveness is a characteristic which is acquired through practice. When a person learns to analyze difficult situations and to comfortably incorporate the value assumptions and techniques of assertiveness training into one's personality and behavioral repertoire, then that person is truly assertive.

references

Bach, G., & Wyden, P. *The intimate enemy: How to fight fair in love and marriage.* New York: Avon, 1968.

Berne, E. *What do you say after you say hello?* New York: Bantam, 1972.

Flowers, J. V. Role playing and simulation methods in psychotherapy. In F. H. Kanfer, & A. D. Goldstein, *Helping people change: Methods and materials.* New York: Pergamon, 1974.

Flowers, J. V. *The function of goal clarity in assertive behavior.* Paper presented at the meeting of the Western Psychological Association, Anaheim,

California, 1973.

Friedman, P. H. The effects of modeling and role playing on assertive behavior. In R. D. Rubin, H. Fensterheim, A. A. Lazarus & C. M. Franks (Eds.), *Advance in Behavior Therapy, 1969.* New York: Academic Press, 1971.

Gordon, T. *P.E.T.: Parent effectiveness training.* New York: Wyden, 1970.

Jackubowkski-Spector, P. Facilitating the growth of women through assertive training. *The Counseling Psychologist,* 1973, 4(1), 75-86.

Jacobs, M., Jacobs, A., Cavior, N., & Feldman, G. Feedback II: The credibility gap: Delivery of positive and negative emotional and behavioral feedback in groups. *Journal of Consulting and Clinical Psychology,* 1973, 41(2), 215-223.

Jourard, S. M. *The transparent self.* New York: Van Nostrand, 1971.

Lazarus, A. A. On assertive behavior: A brief note. *Behavior Therapy,* 1973, 4, 697-699.

Melnick, J. A comparison of replication techniques in the modification of minimal dating behavior. *Journal of Abnormal Psychology,* 1973, 81(1), 51-59.

Rathus, S. A. A thirty-item schedule for assessing assertive behavior. *Behavior Therapy,* 1973, 4, 398-406.

Rehm, L. P., & Marston, A. R. Reduction of social anxiety through modification of self-reinforcement: An instigation therapy technique. *Journal of Consulting and Clinical Psychology,* 1968, *32,* 564-574.

Rimm, D. C., & Masters, J. C. *Behavior therapy: Method, research, and theory.* New York: Academic Press, 1973.

Shoemaker, M. E., & Paulson, T. L. *Group assertion training for mothers as a family intervention in a child out-patient setting.* Paper presented at the Western Psychological Association, Anaheim, California, 1973.

Whitely, R. *Belief system analysis in assertion training.* Paper presented at A.P.G.A. Annual Convention, New York City, March 26, 1975.

Wolpe, J. *The practice of behavior therapy.* Oxford, England: Pergamon, 1969.

social change

"You are either part of the problem or part of the solution" has become a standard by which to measure ourselves in the seventies. It also serves as an appropriate framework through which to view the third section of the book: Social Change. Where social change is concerned, none of us can be neutral: we either contribute to changing the status quo culture or we help maintain that culture's oppression. The earlier sections of the book discuss how the culture oppresses both men and women; our stringent role expectations constrain members of both sexes from being fully expressive persons. The change process begins with an awareness of the extent to which cultural expectations set limits for sex-linked behavior. The next step is the development of new skills—assertiveness, the ability to express feelings, and the desire and interpersonal competence to have intimate relationships. A third step, institutional change, is critical if options are no longer to be denied to individuals on the basis of their sex roles.

To a limited extent these social and institutional changes are being advanced by Affirmative Action orders, the Equal Employment Opportunity Commission, Title VI, and Title IX. Yet in order to open up access and opportunity in organizations, schools, and bureaucratic institutions, there need to be changes in attitudes, in behavior, and in the structure of the system. Individuals such as the readers of this book—students, faculty, homemakers, administrative staff, managers, people connected to social systems—can become change agents. What is required is that you have a commitment to a value system, skills in assessment, knowledge of how to organize, the know-how to plan for change, and access to decision makers.

As change agents, we must face a large number of inequities that extend far beyond the scope of our lifetime. Nonetheless, we must begin to work away at the slowmoving, grinding process so characteristic of change in our culture. The Women's Movement (and now the movement for sex-role liberation) seems to have selected, at least to date, legal change processes, the grass-roots consciousness raising, and information networks among women as methodology for change. The organized parts of the movement have chosen legislation as the way to change the system rather then the revolutionary tactics of the civil rights movement in the sixties. Minorities have taken political action and are organizing to win elected office. Now women, too, are seeking election and organizing through the National Women's Political Caucus.

You the reader face a question which cannot be avoided. When you finish the book, you need to ask yourself what is the next step you intend to take to contribute to the expansion of the options available to men and women regardless of sex role. If you are part of the problem, you will do nothing. If you are part of the solution your next step may be:

to join a consciousness raising group for men and women

to organize an assertion training program

to develop a support group in your life to encourage you to make change

to help elect a sympathetic political candidate

to ask your child's teacher what he/she is doing about sexism in the classroom

to ask what training programs are available to help teachers increase their awareness of sexism and racism in the schools

to work to have a woman principal or superintendent in your district

to talk to guidance counselors about how they are dealing with occupational stereotyping as they advise students

to see that the next person hired in your office or department is a minority member or a woman

to press for flex-time scheduling in your organization to increase employment opportunities for women and to make their work lives easier.

to ask for paternity leave for men

to try and change the norms of your organization: if management is working a twelve-hour day—8:00 a.m. to 8:00 p.m.—and hence unable to be home with families or lead personal lives

to collaborate at home, sharing equally in the fun as well as the routine tasks

to examine the extent to which managers and support staffs in your organization are collaborative rather then one-up, one-down (this includes looking at salary inequities)

to look at the interaction between your doctor and nurse to see if they are collaborative or engaged in a "superior-subordinate" relationship which denies the skills and resources of one party

to question the values of rationality and objectivity in contrast to the values of commitment and collaboration

You undoubtedly can generate your own list as you become committed to change.

The following will help you as a change agent: A knowledge of organizations or the social system in which you live and work; the ability to diagnose how an organization operates; a knowledge of the norms of a particular institution; an understanding of how social institutions (the schools, mental health organizations, businesses, and the like) are agents of socialization for the culture; an understanding of how power and influence are carried out in organizations; the ability to become influential; knowledge of the subgroups within the system and how to organize them. Several of the chapters in this section are intended to help you gain skills in diagnosing social systems and take steps to stop the collusion which tolerates underemployed women and minorities.

power, collusion, intimacy-sexuality, support: breaking the sex-role stereotypes in social and organizational settings

Barbara Benedict Bunker[1,2]
Edith Whitfield Seashore

Women are moving into new roles in their personal and organizational relationships. In organizations, they are moving into executive roles in which rational decision making and the exercise of power and authority are required. Personally they are experimenting with new forms of social relationships—for example, the dual-career family with a redistribution of the traditional sex-role behaviors (Rapoport, 1971)—or new living structures like communes, with roles redistributed in a variety of patterns (Kantor, 1972). These new roles call for new behaviors which may not be tied to the traditional female role. The focus of this paper is on the issues raised for the woman herself, and for the other men and women who relate to her, by her assumption of new behaviors.

The values surrounding sex-role behavior in our culture are such that women are more likely to be disapproved of if they adopt masculine behaviors than men are if they adopt feminine behaviors (Broverman, Vogel, Broverman, Clarkson, & Rosenkrantz, 1972). Women's increasing awareness of these overt and covert forms of discrimination has energized them to expand the roles they can occupy and the behaviors which are seen as acceptable in any role.

During the last several years these changes have received widespread attention both in the public press and in the informal conversations of men and women. As we, the authors, have worked within organizations and in training settings, issues which arise from the loosening of the grip of sex-role stereotypes, particularly on women's behavior, have confronted us constantly. This paper is a starting point for conceptualizing what men and women are experiencing as they

[1]The authors are named alphabetically and no seniority is intended in the order.
[2]The authors are grateful to Lee Bolman, Douglas Bunker, and Charles Seashore for comments on an earlier version of this article.

rearrange their relationships in response to this new situation. The issues which we have designated as power, collusion, intimacy-sexuality, and support are ones which in our experience were omnipresent in a wide variety of settings and are major sources of anxiety and confusion to those who are dealing with them.

As women move into new roles in organizations they are confronted with two tasks. First they have to be able to do a new job; this, as we have said, may require new behaviors. Second, they have to deal with the effects of the behaviors on their relationships. In this process several things happen. Their initial attempts at behavior change may be awkward. Others' reactions to the change may be partly due to that awkwardness and partly to the unexpectedness of the behavior. The previously quiet and responsive woman who becomes assertive, for example, may feel uncomfortable with her new behavior and may be responded to in that way. This situation increases the potential for confusion in existing relationships as well as for the development of productive new kinds of relationships.

To make an informed choice, however, one must understand the situation in which the choice is being made. The four issues, which we believe are crucial in this period when traditional sex-role behavior is open to negotiation, encourage the exploration of four questions. In the section on power we shall ask: What are the effects on men, women and institutions of women assuming positions of influence previously reserved for men? In discussing collusion we inquire: By what process do we become conscious of and begin to change the effects of sex-role socialization? Under intimacy-sexuality the question is: How do attraction and friendship, the personal relatinships of men and women, intersect the work setting? Finally, in a section on support we explore ways in which women can share common issues and help each other understand and deal either personal or externally caused dilemmas. Our major attention in all four sections will be devoted to women under the assumption that if women understand these issues, they are better able to engage in re-educative relationships.

power   We want to discuss two types of power, role power and personal power. The power that comes from occupying a particular role, that is acquired when one takes a position, has been called role power or legitimate power (French & Raven, 1959). It has traditionally been associated with men. The other type, personal power or influence power, is informal; that is, it is tied to the person and not to role. It has traditionally been associated with women. As more and more women acquire legitimate power through occupying roles which previously were denied them, they move into a world for which they were not socialized, a world that is hardly prepared to receive them.

The exercise of legitimate power requires behaviors that may not be well practiced by some women. It requires clear decision making, assertiveness, and accountability. It is sometimes a lonely task. Becoming more assertive, expressing her own views first rather than soliciting others', being pro-active rather than re-active, indicating clearly the degree to which she is willing to share power, being decisive, all these behaviors are less a part of the socialization of women than of men. For this reason women who are moving into executive positions often feel awkward. It may take a while to enjoy the pleasure of being assertive if earlier training labeled that behavior as unfeminine.

Some women have contained and overcontrolled their natural assertiveness. When at last it is let loose, those who are the recipients of the assertiveness find her to be aggressive, pushy. However, her intention may have been assertive but not aggressive. She may not have learned how to manage the expression of her assertiveness in a graduated manner. We have had similar experiences with both men and women who are newly in touch with anger which has long gone unexpressed. Time and practice are needed to be able to use this anger constructively. It is also important to differentiate the aggressiveness which is really an assertiveness management problem from the angry aggressiveness of women who are newly conscious of societal restrictions and are in a period of generalized anger. Though the behaviors may be indistinguishable, the motivation must be clarified and understood before the anger can have a productive outcome. A woman who has practice, the concern of others, and informative feedback can shape her aggressive-assertive behavior into highly effective functioning.

The assertive woman who knows her own mind and direction is so different from the female stereotype that a man may label her "unfeminine." Unfortunately, other women who are not conscious themselves of the effects of sex-role socialization may join in this reaction. Only a clear understanding of the sex-role stereotypes which we all share will prevent their being doled out as punishments in this period of renegotiation of male and female roles. Meanwhile, women who are testing out their own assertiveness need the support of other women who have been through the process and who can provide feedback on behavior as well as help to sift others' reactions. We will return to this notion of support systems later.

A second important issue for women with newly acquired role power is the climate in which that power is exercised. In our culture, the power of roles is usually played out in a competitive environment. Young men are early socialized to win, to be best, to compete. Young women are expected to do well until their adolescence when the socialization process reverses and we find them calibrating their achievements relative to males (Horner, 1969). Competition with men is not encouraged for young women; being desirable, receptive, and chosen is encouraged. When a woman passes from such an adolescence to the position of corporation executive, she walks a tight-rope of ambivalence. Women who have "made it" against the grain of the dominant socialization pattern in our culture have done so in the very competitive world of men.

Although competition is energizing, it has been repeatedly demonstrated that it does not always lead to the most efficient and productive problem-solving process (Deutsch, 1973). Moreover, shifting a normatively competitive work climate into a more collaborative one is not a one-person job, it involves the sustained work of most of the members of the organizational team. Many women experience great frustration when trying to participate in a very competitive climate; they need to understand why.

During their socialization, men usually acquire a whole range of behaviors which permit them to compete at moderate levels through banter, "zinging" each other, the repartée in which they take each other's measure. Women not only lack such behaviors, but they may have had experiences in which attempts to develop them were sanctioned as "unfeminine." To participate is often to collude in a content and context which are sexist. When most of the daily interchange of an organization is conducted in a competitive mode, women often feel ignored, invisible, and/or excluded (especially when they do not have the behaviors to participate). As they become frustrated and angry, they may explode into tears or show some other form of frustration-releasing behavior. Men are often incredulous at this situation. "No one was preventing this woman from participating, so why on earth is she blowing up like this?" He may feel guilty (did he do something?), angry (what's *her* problem?) or puzzled, depending on the way he handles inexplicable emotion.

Since women are socialized not to show anger openly, both men and women should realize that tears are more often manifestations of anger and frustration than of hurt. Many men, in our experience, translate a woman's tears into, "I have hurt her. What did I do? I didn't do anything! So what the hell is she crying about? I can't understand women." When the correct translation is more often, "She's crying, I wonder what that's about. Maybe she's mad or frustrated about something and can't express it. I guess I'll try to find out what she's feeling."

We are not suggesting that women are the only ones who may want to elaborate their behavioral repertoire. While competitive behavior or having a comfortable attitude in the presence of conflict will help women in many work settings, our experience in training managers and business executives is that men are also dissatisfied with their competitive job climate. When pressed, they express dissatisfaction with the grinding competition that cannot give way to other forms of interpersonal collaboration. Many feel trapped in known behavior patterns and dissatisfied with the relationships these patterns produce.

Women learn useful skills as part of their socialization: how to express feelings and how to develop relationships which can contribute to re-shaping the work climate. The dilemma for women is how to adapt to the present situation as well as to change it. At this point men and women have a great deal to offer to each other in the molding of new work climates.

Let us now turn to the second type of power, personal power. French and Raven (1959) have described five bases of power which people use to influence others. In addition to *legitimate* power, already discussed, there is *reward* and *coercive* power. This is the sort of influence a person wields who is able to supply resources or to apply sanctions or punishments. *Expert* power comes from an influential person's special skills or competencies, while *referent* power comes from the identification of the influence with the powerful person. As we consider these bases for power, it seems clear that all can be used in conjunction with role power to strengthen it. At the same time a most important power base, personal power, seems entirely missing. Perhaps this is because personal power, though acknowledged by organizational theorists as important, has not been studied systematically or thoroughly. We suggest that this is the kind of power that women use best.

Personal power is acquired from capacities which the person embodies. Without trying to be exhaustive we will suggest a few of the sources of personal power. Influence based on a collaborative relationship where trust and mutual respect are present is one aspect of personal power. In most organizational settings women have not had the formal role but they have had the ear of men in those roles, hence, "the power being the throne," "leading from behind" and other expressions characterize this unofficial but real kind of influence. Executive secretaries to influential persons in an organization often maintain an informal communication network which has great influence on their bosses and their decisions. The basis of this influence is partly informational and partly relational, that is, the person is experienced as insightful, trustworthy, of good judgment and permitted to have influence. Collaboration and trust, both relational qualities, are two aspects of personal power.

A second source of personal power is the capacity to generate good solutions to difficult problems. It may involve the creative capacity to think outside the givens of a situation. It may mean being able to think into the future before others have made those projections. It can be experienced either in work settings or in personal relationships. A model for the latter is Mary Poppins, that magical lady who always has just what you need in her carpetbag and whose medicine bottle dispenses your prescription in a flavor you adore. Mary Poppins stands for the intuitive quality of seeing what someone else wants or needs and working to make it happen. In reality as in fantasy, a finely tuned perceptiveness of others' needs can be the basis of great personal influence.

Charisma is the word currently in vogue to describe personal power. Since power is more often associated with men, it is easier to identify and describe charismatic men, such as, the Kennedy men, Leonard Bernstein, than charismatic women. Charisma is a combination of personal attractiveness which compels attention and liking, and a style of self-presentation in which affect and intellect combine to make the person difficult to ignore. Charisma in men is often associated with highly controlling assertive behavior (Lieberman Yalom, & Miles, 1973), as well as strength, humor, energy, warmth, and articulateness. But what of female charisma? We suspect that for a woman to be responded to as charismatic, she must combine personal attractiveness, strength and energy; sensitivity, warmth and humor; being "together" and self-aware in a way which is perceived as feminine—in other words, she does not defy the female sex-role stereotype. Perhaps as women enlarge their roles, new models of charisma in women will emerge.

A final source of personal power is that of a good idea presented at the right time. This is not the same thing as the problem-solving capacity previously described. Here, the idea itself is so compelling and inherently cogent that it is powerful and independent of its source. As a result, the one who is its source is experienced as powerful. Our view is that men and women are equal candidates for this type of power but that in settings where women are not listened to, they may have difficulty exercising this type of personal power.

Many well-known powerful women today have gained their power by associating with men who have real role power. Eleanor Roosevelt is an example of a woman who enlarged her role as first lady, which was without official power, and used it to extend her own influence into all kinds of important affairs. Her relationship to real power plus her capacity to use her own influence made her a formidable woman.

Ken Kesey has presented a model of negative personal power in Nurse Ratchett in his novel *One Flew Over the Cookoo's Nest*. Miss Ratchett is a tyrant with low role power who works her tyranny on others through the passive acquiescence of the ward doctor whom she influences to sanction her decisions officially. Miss Ratchett, who appears, on first impression, pleasant and helpful, is, on further inspection, manipulative and castrating, everyman's nightmare of the negative use of personal power. What we need in both literature and public life are women who can be positive models of role and personal power.

collusion

Another issue which confronts men and women who are trying to re-examine the sex-role stereotypes into which they have been socialized is collusion. Collusion, as we define it, means that an individual acts in order to fulfill others expectations rather than from his or her own needs. We will limit our discussion to situations where collusion occurs around sex roles. One of the authors, for example, lived for years in the firm belief that all things mechanical, including changing light bulbs, were not within her capacity. Since her husband traveled a lot, her view caused her no little inconvenience. As she came to recognize the collusion (women can't do mechanical tasks), she found herself able to do a number of mechanical jobs much to her own and her husband's satisfaction.

Since much of our early training teaches us how males and females behave, there is bound to be confusion when these patterns are questioned. Who opens doors? Who goes in and out of elevators first? Who swears in front of whom? Because of role-expected behaviors, the world is a place where men and women can interact predictably. We are not suggesting that all behavior which meets sex-role expectations is collusive. However, our experience is that many women, and probably men, too, act *before* they ask themself the question, "Do I really want to do this?", "Is this really the way I feel I want to continue to behave?", and only later realize that they did something not because it was appropriate but because they should, "because I am a woman." For example, a husband says to his wife, "Hey, why didn't you call me and let me carry in those grocery packages?" This man is indicating he is willing and able to carry in the packages; but his wife may be asking herself "Is he telling me that a man *should* carry in the packages? I'd better go get him to carry them in so he won't feel less manly." Suppose the wife is having these thoughts. If the relationship is collusive, she won't question her husband's need to carry the packages, she'll go get him. If the wife is conscious of herself, she may think, "Well, how do I feel about carrying packages? Sure it's nice to have help with a big load. But it isn't, so I'll do it myself."

Most men and women have been socialized to sex-role response without thinking through whether their real feelings match social expectations. The first step in beginning to examine collusive patterns is awareness. Growth in awareness of collusions proceeds by a series of steps. First, you see others acting in ways which are not collusive and you question your own behavior. For example, you may notice that a friend does not stop and wait for a man to open a door but opens it herself. You wonder, "Why do I wait? Do I want to wait?" Or, in another case, the only woman manager in a four-person management team is included with the women assistants in her office on the schedule of daily coffee making assignments while the three male managers are not. She does not protest. You wonder, "How would I handle that situation?"

The second step is often the discovery after the fact that you have been engaged in a collusion you did not like. For example, the owner of a shop you frequent makes a sexist comment to you and you laugh with him. As you leave the shop, you become conscious of what you did and become angry at him and at yourself. Our experience is that this "after-the-fact consciousness" is a common stepping-stone to awareness in the collusive situation itself. Gradually, as you become increasingly conscious of your feelings, you are able to experience them more and more within the situation that creates them. This process is a hanging on or a slowing down of the immediate sex-role response to others in order to give yourself time to figure out what you want to do. Talking about situations with others of the same sex who have had similar experiences is another means of bringing yourself into better touch with your feelings.

You may be aware that your behavior is collusive and want to change it, but you may not have the resources to do so. For example, you may have to let someone else change the porch light until you can learn how it is done. You might maintain collusion in order to keep a relationship going. For example, early in dating relationships the woman may be hesitant to put forth their own ideas or wishes before hearing from the man. "If he doesn't like my ideas he may not want to continue to see me." Here is another example. Recently we have been experimenting with paying for the lunch of male colleagues who often pay for ours. We say as we reach for the check, "It's my turn this time." If this is a first attempt to pick up the check, the lunch partner, registering, sheer horror, says, "No, I asked you." We may respond with anything from "Well then, let the drinks be on me this time," to "Well, I would really like to treat you. So if not this time, then let's agree that next time it's my check." All of these are ways of letting the other person know that the relationship is not entirely satisfactory and that you are committed to figuring out a way to change it. You are saying, in effect, "I will agree to colluding this time only if we agree jointly to begin to change."

Some anxiety will undoubtedly be experienced in the breaking of old collusions. Men, particularly, may experience a woman's new capacity to be "for herself" as somehow "against him." Suppose, for example, the old pattern has been that in matters of recreation the woman usually went along with what the man suggested. One day she asserts herself and chooses a different recreation from the one he has suggested. He may feel not only that she is asserting herself, but that this assertion is a challenge to him. It is urgently important when changing old patterns to discuss and thus clarify the intentions that are the unspoken part of the behavior. They need to be brought out into the open and shared so that in the face of new behavior, the other person will not assign wrong motives.

We can identify two types of collusive behavior. The first type, collusion with others' expectations, we have just been discussing. A secretary dusts her boss's office and brings coffee, not because it is part of her job, but because she thinks he expects it of her. The female graduate student laughs at a male faculty member's sly references to her body, not because she enjoys his appreciation, but because he would be offended if she expressed annoyance. This type of collusion is often conceptualized as a demand a woman feels that others are making on her. But she has not checked to see what the feelings of the others really are. Women whose self-esteem is primarily dependent on being useful to men may resist a close examination of collusive behavior because it would deprive them of the reinforcement that behavior brings.

The second type of collusion is equally interesting but more subtle; it is collusion with one's own internalized sex-role stereotypes. A prime example occurs when one of the authors finds herself dashing home to get dinner for her family with little attention to her own work or recreation. Her need to fulfill her own image of good mother and wife (Supermom) supercedes her need to have time for herself and the development of strategies for meeting both sets of needs.

Giving up collusion and really acting for oneself is a sweet freedom, but it is not won easily. Many women who put themselves first ask themselves (or others ask them) "Aren't you being selfish?" This fear is understandable and stems from their early training. Women are taught to put others' needs first and to get self-esteem from being rewarded by others. If women stop putting others first, there is the anxious question "Will anyone love me for myself? They love me now for being so sensitive to their needs."

It is easy to confuse knowing what you feel and what you want, with having to get what you want. The two are separable. It is quite possible to want very much to take a vacation alone with your husband, but to decide that particular needs of the children are urgent and that you will not take that vacation. Knowing you own needs means that even if you choose to suspend them, you do not pretend they do not exist and thus prevent yourself from seeking alternate ways of dealing with them. The capacity to feel strong needs and also to know that you can honor them or put them aside if necessary is very reassuring. It increases feelings of identity.

Seduction, the use of ritualized sexual behaviors to get what you want, can be a special case of collusion. Seductive messages are usually verbal or nonverbal cues inserted into another message that stands by itself. The person being addressed has to interpret the double message. The woman, for example, who asks her boss for a day off, eyelids aflutter, standing closer to him than usual, is trying to persuade at several levels. If he says "yes" because of her attractiveness when he really feels he should say "no," he has been part of a seductive collusion. The "sandwich" technique is another form of seduction. A man may open a conversation with a compliment to his female colleague about her appearance, make an unwelcome request for extra work, and then, squeezing her arm warmly, congratulate her on her excellent performance rating. If she accepts the extra work because of the compliments and his warmth, she has colluded. When one understands how seduction is used, it is possible to "play the game" that is, enjoy the seductive repartee, without letting it affect the decisions to be made.

intimacy-
sexuality

Two linked issues which raise anxieties as more and more women join the work force are intimacy and sexuality, the characteristics of personal relationships between men and women. Friendship does not mean the same thing to men as to women. Women are raised to cultivate close personal relationships with others, particularly men and often women. Men have no such training, so that the characteristics of what men and women refer to as "close friendships" are often quite different. For many men, friendships mean sports or recreational activities, having a good time with cronies, but no necessary self-disclosure or personal mutual exploration. Women, on the other hand seldom refer to anyone as "close" if they do not know a considerable amount about their thoughts and feelings at a quite personal level. Some if not many men make such self-revelations only to their wife or girlfriend.

Thus, personal closeness is linked in male experience with sexuality, physical intimacy. For women, there is no necessary link between personal closeness and sexuality; in some relationships it is present, in many it is not. Some women can move into a relationship and permit it to become close without feeling that sex is a necessary consequence. For men whose relationships do not usually separate intimacy and sexuality, the entrance of many women into the work world increases the potential for relationships which may involve closeness and thus lead to a sexual exchange. This is a source of anxiety for some, a threat and perhaps a promise. The anxiety about intimacy-sexuality is present in working men as well as their wives. Because of it, many resist the idea of women entering work settings where they are not currently employed.

When there are only a few women in an organization and they are in lower status positions, it is not uncommon to find that sex is the wampum being exchanged for advancement. Sex in this domain is power; the message is "If you sleep with me, I'll see that you are considered for the special opening . . ." Since women have been lower in status, it is women who have traditionally been exploited by the aggressive use of sex. What they have not been able to do until recently is get together and discuss their situation so that they could take action. In one company we worked with, women who had been divided by jealousy and competition with each other (and divided up by the men in the company), finally got together and as a group began to challenge the system. They were able to do it successfully through the support they gave each other and by sharing information. Men have traditionally discussed their female conquests, but when women began to discuss the

behavior of male coworkers, there were surprising revelations. The
women discovered that what they had thought were "private relationships" were widely shared by coworkers. They decided that if they all
refused to buy into the system, it could not survive.

Not all men are seeking sexual conquest, of course. There are
usually a group of men in organizations who are actively testing the
women's sexual availability and a group who ar not. If there is a small
number of women and a large male work force, the number of men who
test their availability may become an irritating problem to the women.
Men who are not seeking sexual relationships may be prone to deny
that the issue exists because they are not receiving continual interaction as are the women. These men, who might be supportive, may be
totally unaware of the situation in which the women find themselves.

Another issue for women is how to interact with the man who first
evaluates her attractiveness. If he does not find her physically appeal-
ing, he discounts her and she may have difficulty being heard or
accepted for her competence in role. If he finds her attractive, he may
either interact with her seductively, testing to see if she will respond or
he may withdraw because his sexual feelings get in the way of being
able to work easily with her. Either reaction creates stress in the working relationship. An additional anxiety some men experience is to wonder whether, as women become more assertive, they will also become
sexually aggressive and become the seducers.

In some sense the most acceptable relationship between men and
women is a sexual one because it is easy to understand. In a sexual
relationship, the traditional role of the male is the seducer and the role
of the woman is to be seducible. The great fear of many women is that
if they are not seducible, if they say no to a sexual request, then the
relationship will end. For women who are not very self-confident, it
may be easier to accede to a sexual request even if it does not make her
happy, than risk the loss of the relationship. We are not speaking only
about sexual intercourse. A great many behaviors are part of the ritual
of sex and fit this pattern. At a dance, for example, the woman who
regretfully refused a request to dance until she finished an interesting
conversation with a woman friend would be a raving nonconformist! A
request to dance has sexual overtones and insofar as the woman is
oriented toward being chosen by men it supercedes other involvements. The collusion around sexuality has been challenged in the physical sphere (Masters and Johnson, 1966) but less articulately in the
area of the rituals of seduction which lead to that final activity. It is
these rituals which are most apt to be a problem in the work setting.

As the numbers of women in organizations increase there is great
potential for moving beyond present anxieties into satisfying professional and personal relationships. The resistance of many men has dis-
solved after one good working relationship with a woman peer which

was personal but not sexual. Men who have never had to relate to women except as wife, lover, or family member may attempt to re-create the traditional role relationship with women colleagues unless he has experienced a peer relationship. Men often focus on fears of what they will lose! They won't feel comfortable, be able to swear or tell off-color stories, and so on. When women are part of the work setting, these fears can be tested in reality. Until that happens, they only breed resistance.

Lest we be misunderstood, let us make clear that we are not trying to reduce relationships between men and women in work settings to totally neutral ones. Our differences can be the source of much energy and enjoyment. Sexual attraction and the deeply internalized rituals surrounding it make personal relationships on the job or in the community sufficiently complicated that being able to face and discuss these issues openly is critical.

support

In order to do what they want to do, most people need to be in an environment of supportive relationships. This is particularly true for women moving into a position of responsibility in an institution where they have not traditionally carried these roles. When companies begin to promote women, they need more than a token woman. They need to promote enough women so that these women can form support groups for each other. Why do women need support? Not because they are extra fragile, but because they are outside of the male apprentice and support network. In most organizations, the more established officers of the company keep a sharp eye on, and encourage younger men of promise. Frequently, they advise with them, take them in as proteges and use influence to make possible their advancement. This is infrequently true of women. Therefore, if they are to realize their potential, women need other women to make the climate one in which they too feel supported.

As women try out new sensations and behaviors, they feel powerful and excited, but they also may experience some deprivation—a feeling that a familiar part of them has been lost and that their newly acquired behavior has made them very vulnerable. As a result of this feeling of deprivation, women often return to old sex-role stereotypes to escape for a while from the unfamiliarity and vulnerability of the new roles.

There are a number of ways in which women can be supportive of each other as they experiment with new roles. They can seek ways to share common dilemmas; they can support each other's experimental behaviors and learn from each other's experiences.

In organizations, two special groupings of women must learn the rewards of mutual support—those in peer groups and those in superior/subordinate relationships. For a while, women in key managerial positions will have few female peers. So women throughout an organization will have to seek each other out and build their own referent-group support system. Partially because of their greater numbers, men can more easily provide each other with a continuing support system.

All women who move up in an organization will undoubtedly share similar experiences, for example, how to feel comfortable in previously all-male staff meetings. Most women were taught early to orient to men; these patterns are carried into adulthood. An analysis of group interaction (see Aries' article in this volume) demonstrates what even a casual observation of groups will quickly reveal. In mixed-sex groups, most conversation is oriented toward the men. Women's comments are most often interrupted, overlooked, or unheard because men are not used to paying attention too what women are saying. Women have colluded with this pattern, and they ignore other women too. One way to break this collusion is for women to support other women by paying special attention to what they are saying (regardless of whether or not it is agreeable to them) and reinforcing them so that they will be heard and dealt with. This can be a very simple and powerful process once you begin to work with it. One example: after a woman begins to speak, another woman can watch the group carefully. If the speaker has been interrupted the other woman can remark, "I think we only heard half of your thought, what was the rest of it?" and help her to finish. Or if a woman who spoke was ignored, another woman can reinforce her statement with: "Barbara really had an interesting comment on what we were discussing" or "I would like to hear what Edie had to say again; I'm not sure it was clearly understood." In any group, women must not permit other women's ideas to be dropped.

During crises, support will also be greatly needed. Crises may range from the difficulty of entering into "Man's World," to encountering major problems on the job, to integrating home priorities with job priorities. Women can understand and support with much more empathy than men; they must be available to each other when critical situations arise.

In the superior/subordinate relationship, there are many opportunities for mutual support, and often these are totally missed or misused. Women in key positions can become important models for those who are striving, and for whom there are so few women models. They can become model androgynous women who have moved upward and retained their female attributes while at the same time incorporating more "masculine" characteristics (Bem, 1974). Women superiors can become respected colleagues, friends, "bosses."

Women subordinates are often jealous of the success of their superiors; they are not used to being responsible to, working for, and being rewarded by a woman. Often, they continue to respond to women in sex-role stereotypes, such as: women can type their own material, handle their own travel arrangements; their work has lower priority than a man's because it is not as important. These problems in the relationship must be confronted and the relationship redirected into ways in which superiors and superordinates can begin to support each other. Men often rely on sexuality in male/female superior/subordinate relationships to maintain human connectedness. Women must rely on mutual respect and competence for this kind of human connection with other women. If these ingredients are present in the relationship it becomes one of enormous support.

Women who try new ways of mutual support find it very satisfying. It is essential that organizations recognize this satisfaction, understand its potency, and encourage women to continue to build support systems for their survival and their productivity.

conclusion

The issues we have discussed: power, collusion, intimacy-sexuality, and support are crucial in this period when old sex-role stereotypes are giving way to more androgynous roles for men and for women. As women move into these new roles they feel anxious, angry, confused, curious, delighted, and liberated. As men experiment with enlarging the boundaries of the traditional male role, they will experience these same feelings. Our intent has been to help women understand the internal and the external sources for these feelings.

What is happening to women has implications for both personal relationships and for the organizations in which they work. Men need to be ready to engage in a re-education process around their relationships if they are to navigate this period of transition successfully. Organizations must be willing to re-examine the assumptions on which much organizational behavior is based. Most important, however, is the continued articulation of issues such as the ones raised in the paper and their discussion between the sexes in both personal and institutional conflicts. We can expect changes both in the climate of institutions and in the relationships of men and women as they head in the direction of increased authenticity and mutuality.

references

Bem, S. L. Sex-role adaptability: One consequence of psychological androgyny. *Journal of Personal and Social Psychology,* 1975, 31 (4), 634-643.

Bem, S. L. The measurement of psychological androgyny. *Journal of Consulting and Clinical Psychology,* 1974, 42 (2), 155-162.

Broverman, I. K., Vogel, S. R., Broverman, D. M., Clarkson, F. E., & Rosenkrantz, P. S. Sex-role stereotypes: A current appraisal. *Journal of Social Issues,* 1972, *28,* 59-78.

Deutsch, M. *The resolution of conflict: Constructive and destructive processes.* New Haven: Yale University Press, 1973.

French, J. R. P., & Raven, B. The bases of social power. In D. Cartwright (Ed.), *Studies in social power.* Ann Arbor, Mich.: Institute for Social Research, 1959.

Horner, M. S. Fail: Bright women. *Psychology Today,* November 1969, 3.

Kantor, R. M. *Commitment and community: Communes and utopias in sociological perspective.* Cambridge, Mass.: Harvard University Press, 1972.

Lieberman, M. A., Yalom, I. D., & Miles, M. B. *Encounter groups: First facts.* New York: Basic Books, 1973.

Masters, W. H., & Johnson, V. E. *Human sexual response.* Boston: Little, Brown, 1966.

Rapoport, R. & Rapoport, R. N. *Dual-career families.* Middlesex, England: Penguin, 1971.

women in organizations: sex roles, group dynamics, and change strategies

Rosabeth Moss Kanter

There are plenty of women in organizations. Except for football teams, monasteries, Wall Street law firms, coal mines, and the Harvard faculty, there are few organizations that do not somehow include a number of women. But where are they? Generally they are not in positions of power. To understand the behavior of women in organizations, we have to start with the structural facts, easily documented by a look at the Census, that practically all of the managers, administrators, and leaders in America are men (over 96 percent of those earning $15,000 a year); and practically all of the stenographers, typists, receptionists, secretaries, and telephone operators are women (93 to 96 percent of the holders of these jobs). Even female work units like offices and social work agencies often have men at the top (Kanter, 1975).

Thus, when men and women interact in organizations, they tend to do it across status lines in which power, leadership, decision making, and control are considered male functions; and support, nurturance, hostessing, and organizational housework are considered female functions. These expectations, caricatured to be sure, affect the behavior of even those women who play other roles, as professionals, production workers, or leaders. As a young professional and the only woman faculty member in my department years ago, I remember wanting to please my colleagues by bringing cookies and buying the Christmas gifts for staff, and I remember how carefully we decided I would not take the notes at faculty meetings, as though somebody might assume I should.

Sex is such an important variable in determining who does what in organizations, in fact, that many occupations are "sex-typed"—that is, they are held almost exclusively by members of one sex and come to be defined in ways considered appropriate for that sex. This sex-typing may vary from organization to organization; in one, the people to put the bottoms on shoes may be all men, while in another this might be

considered "woman's work." One of the first things that should be discovered about an organization in order to change it, then, is how its
functions are sex-typed and linked to opportunities for promotion and
self-expression. An organization's pattern of sex-typing (for example,
that the English department is 75 percent female but the math department is all-male) also affects the sex ratio of those with whom
members interact (all-male, all-female, mixed or a few of one sex and a
majority of the other), and this, in turn affects the norms that are set
and the ease with which members of either sex can demonstrate their
full competence.

I argue that structural factors like these play a major role in determining how women behave in organizations. What we know about
women's leadership, for example, we know from a context in which
very few women have power. What we know about women as professionals we often know from settings where a woman is the only
female in a group of men. What we know about the majority of women
workers we have learned from studying occupations carrying female
sex stereotypes, like nursing, teaching, or typing. The relative proportions of women and men in groups and organizations have many behavioral consequences; the lone woman among men faces very different issues from the woman in a more evenly balanced or all-female
group.

**mixed-sex
groups**

There is evidence that the presence of both men and women in the
same group heightens tension and may put women at a disadvantage. If
conformity to group judgment (measured by degree of agreement with
erroneous judgments) can be taken as a sign of self-consciousness and
unwillingness to take risks, then there is some evidence that women, at
least, and men in one study, may conform more in mixed than same-sex
groups (Tuddenham, MacBride, & Zahn, 1958; Reitan & Shaw, 1964).

In Aries' laboratory study described elsewhere in this book, the two
cross-sex groups were more self-conscious about the group itself, more
often engaging in analysis of the group's functioning, than were the
single-sex groups. Men were more tense, serious, and self-conscious,
speaking less of aggression and engaging in less practical joking. In the
cross-sex groups there were more references to self and more talk of
feelings than in the comparison groups, but there was also evidence of
sexual tension: heterosexual contact was valued, and concerns expressed about being attractive to the opposite sex. The sexual questions and "cross-cultural" issues that can arise in mixed-sex groups
are useful explanations for their tensions.

William Foote Whyte has also hypothesized, extrapolating from
studies of the ethnic composition of groups, that "other things being
equal, a one-sex work group is likely to be more cohesive" than a
mixed-sex group (1961, p. 511). A Parisian study found many male-
female as well as cross-generational conflicts when men and women

worked in the same office (Crozier, 1965, p. 110).

In addition to sexual and cultural issues, there are also status issues when men and women are both members of the same group. Males have generally higher status and power in American society than females, so that when men and women are ostensible peers, the male's external status may give him an advantage inside the group. A number of studies have indicated the importance of power and status in determining behavior in groups: for example, those low in power tend to engage in more approval seeking, while those high in power engage in more influence attempts; those in low-status positions favor communication upward in a hierarchy, a form of "substitute locomotion" or "vicarious achievement" (Lippitt, Polansky, Redl, & Rosen, 1952; Back et al., 1950; Kelley, 1951; Thibaut, 1950).

The differential behavior of the more and less powerful coincides with the observed group behavior of men and women. A field experiment tested more specifically the effects of high and low power on group relations, using 32 six-person groups at a one-day professional conference. Participants were labelled high and low-power on the basis of the prestige of their occupations, which were assumed to correlate with ability to influence. While the authors do not report the sex distribution of participants, it is likely from occupational sex-typing that men were found more often in the high power category (psychiatrists, psychologists) and women in the low power category (nurses, social workers, teachers). The researchers found that "highs" were liked more than "lows"; "highs" liked "lows" less than they liked other "highs"; "highs" talked more often than "lows"; "lows" communicated more frequently to "highs" than to other "lows"; and the amount of participation by "lows" was consistently overrated, as though people felt the "lows" talked too much (Hurwitz, Zander & Hymovitch, 1968).

The interpretation is straight-forward. In mixed groups of "peers," men and women may not, in fact, be equal, especially if their external statuses are discrepant. The resulting behavior, including frequency of participation, leadership, conformity, and acceptance, may reflect status and power differences more than sex-linked personality traits. The issues are familiar to me as a woman, too. Upon leaving a group in which men did most of the talking and were considered to be the "important" ones to direct comments to, I wondered whether I had talked too much. Are men in mixed-sex groups liked more than women, do they get the most attention, and do they feel women talk too much? Do women "hold back" in the presence of men? These are questions to test against our own experiences.

women and leadership

With the special handicaps women may operate under in mixed groups, it is not surprising that women are not generally found in positions of leadership. While sex does not affect leadership *style* (see

Crozier, 1965, p. 126), with men and women capable of the same wide range, it does affect the chances of being accepted as a leader. There is evidence that the general attitude toward working for a woman or taking orders from a woman have been very negative in the United States until the recent past, thus shaping one dimension of the interactional context for women leaders. Several surveys have indicated that most businessmen and some businesswomen prefer not to be subordinate to a woman. In a 1965 *Harvard Business Review* survey of 1,000 male and 900 female executives, over two-thirds of the men and nearly 20 percent of the women reported that they themselves would not feel comfortable working for a woman. Very few of either sex (95 of the men and 15 percent of the women) felt that men feel comfortable working for a woman; and a proportion of the male respondents said that women did not belong in executive positions. Fifty-one percent of the men responded that women were "temperamentally unfit" for management, writing in comments such as, "They scare male executives half to death . . . As for an efficient woman manager, this is cultural blasphemy . . ." (Bowman, Worthy, & Greyser, 1965).

Male resentment of taking orders from a woman influenced the work flow and the interaction between waitresses and countermen in the restaurants studied by William Foote Whyte during World War II. There were several devices in one restaurant by which countermen could avoid direct contact with waitresses (and hence direct orders) or could make their own decisions about the order in which to prepare food and drinks, thus taking initiative and forcing the waitresses to wait. Orders were written on slips and placed on a spindle, and a warming compartment imposed a high barrier between the waitresses and the countermen, thus eliminating face-to-face interaction. In a restaurant without these equalizing devices, satisfaction was low, and there was constant wrangling. Whyte's explanation is simple: people of higher status (men) like to do the directing for people of lower status (women) and resent reversals (1961, p. 128).

Therefore, even if women have formal authority, they may not necessarily be able to exercise it over reluctant subordinates. Margaret Cussler's (1958) study of female executives provides several examples of this. In one case a woman had formal leadership of a group of men, but the men did not accept this, reporting informally to her male superior. The subordinates further met together at lunch to share information, excluding her. More formal meetings then developed, "conceived of by the woman as meetings of her staff, by the men as a mutual protection society for the interchange of ideas" (p. 76-77).

At the same time, women tend to assume visible leadership reluctantly. A creative laboratory study discovered that, for women, the situational context rather than a dominant personality tended to predict a woman's exercise of visible leadership. Same-sex and cross-sex dyads were paired by scores on a "dominance" measure and given a task in which one member had to lead and one to follow. Assumption of leadership by high-dominance women paired with a low-dominance man was significantly lower than in any other pairing. The greatest assumption of leadership by high-dominance subjects occurred when a high-dominance man was paired with a low-dominance woman; the high-low-dominance single-sex pairings showed about the same intermediate distribution of leadership. However, in the situation which a high-dominance woman was paired with a low-dominance man, the woman made the final decision of who was to be the leader more often than in any other group, 91 percent of the time appointing the man. The study suggests that men are not necessarily more "dominant" in character than women, but women are more reluctant to assume leadership, particularly when the subordinate is male (Megaree, 1969). The leadership strategies chosen by successful women executives in Margaret Hennig's research (1970) tends to confirm this kind of laboratory finding. The women tended to minimize the authoritative exercise of power and maximize subordinate autonomy and learning through delegation.

But a leader's style may be ultimately less important for the impact on his or her subordinates than another resource unequally distributed between the sexes: power outside of the immediate work group. Early theory in organizational behavior assumed that there was a direct relationship between leader behavior and group satisfaction and morale. But Donald Pelz discovered in the early 1950s that perceived external power was an intervening variable. He compared high- and low-morale work groups to test the hypothesis that the supervisor in high-morale groups would be better at communicating, more supportive, and more likely to recommend promotion. Yet, when he analyzed the data, the association seemed to be nonexistent or even opposite. In some cases supervisors who frequently recommended people for promotion and offered sincere praise for a job well done had lower morale scores. The differentiating variable was whether or not the leader had power influence on his or her own superiors and how decisions were made in the department. The combination of good human relations and power was associated with high morale. Human relations skills and low power (a likely combination for women leaders) sometimes had negative consequences (Pelz, 1952).

The implications for female leadership in organizations are significant. A woman's generally more limited power in the surrounding society and often more limited power in an organization (partly a function of her rarity and isolation) may interfere with her effective exercise of leadership and morale in her subordinates regardless of her own style and competence. This hypothesis also helps explain the greater resistance to working for a woman. It also may account for the evidence of the importance of a male sponsor in the success of women executives and professionals (Cussler, 1958; Hennig, 1970; Epstein, 1970). A high-status man bringing the woman up behind him may provide the visible sign that the woman does have influence upward. While sponsors serve multiple functions (e.g., coaching and socialization in the informal routines) and are found in the careers of men, the reflected power they provide may be even more pivotal for women.

the case of the lone woman in a male group

A skewed-sex distribution affects the dynamics of the group in addition to whatever issues of leadership women face in the presence of men. Two quick generalizations can be made. When a man is the rarity in a female-dominated group, he is likely to be central, to be deferred to and respected. When a woman is the rarity in a male-dominated group, she is likely to be isolated, to be treated as trivial. (Effective intervention in such situations may depend upon understanding these dynamics as a function of the group and not necessarily of the individuals involved.)

Isolation and invisibility, sometimes self-imposed, are often consequences of status as a lone woman in an otherwise all-male collectivity. In one study, six small training groups with only one woman each in a group of eight to twelve men were observed: three sensitivity training groups for business school students and three work groups of psychiatric residents. In each case, the woman was eventually isolated, failed to become a leader or ally herself with the emergent leaders, and was defined by the researchers as a "casualty" of the group. They concluded, in addition, though without presenting comparison groups, that the six groups' productivity tended to be low, in part because of the problematic interactions around the solo woman (Wolman & Frank, 1973). The female executives studied by Margaret Hennig (1970) support the isolation hypothesis. They reported that their most difficult relationships were with male peers when they (the women) were in the early-to-middle stages of their careers. They had little contact or relationship with the men, tried to be unobtrusive or invisible, and practiced strategies of conflict avoidance. Epstein (1970) also suggests that team membership may be harder for the lone woman among male professional peers than for a man, pointing to institutionalized isolation (such as barriers to membership in male clubs or associations) as well as interactional isolation. As a consequence, she proposes that women have been less likely to be successful in fields that require participation on a team of peers as opposed to individual activity (1970, p. 175).

Lone women may reinforce their own isolation by a series of accommodative strategies. The limiting of visibility ("taking a low profile") is one such accommodation to and reinforcement of isolation. Hennig's respondents reported trying to minimize their sexual attributes so as to blend unnoticeably into the predominant male culture (before they reached top positions). One recalled in an interview:

You dressed carefully and quietly to avoid attracting attention; you had to remember to swear once in a while, to know a few dirty jokes, and never to cry if you got attacked. You fended off all attempts of men to treat you like a woman; you opened doors before they could hold them, sat down before a chair could be held, and threw on a coat before it could be held for you (Hennig, 1970, pp. VI-21).

At the same time, Epstein indicates that lone professional women may impose their own limits on interaction with male peers, avoiding social contact: such as not going to lunch, writing, or calling (1970, p. 76).

In other reports, lone women managers have also participated in the limiting of the visibility of their competence by not taking credit for accomplishments or letting someone else take the credit (Cussler, 1958). Some women, in interviews, even expressed pride that they could influence a group of men without the men recognizing the origin of the idea, or that they rejoiced in the secret knowledge that they were responsible for their boss' success. These reports match the Megaree finding reported above that high-dominance women may let a man assume official leadership while strongly influencing the decisions. Epstein points out that, in general, on elite levels, women have less visible jobs than men, promote themselves less often, feel the need to make fewer mistakes, and try to be unobtrusive (1970, pp. 180-182, 191-192).

stereotypical roles

When a woman is alone or virtually alone in a group of men, there is pressure on her to adopt one of four stereotypical roles: mother, sex object, pet, or "iron maiden." These are all ways of resolving the issues of sexuality, competence, and control that arise when a woman enters a group of men. Such roles help the men confine the woman to a limited place where she is not a competitive threat and her sexuality is comfortably defined in traditional ways. Some women may themselves choose to adopt these roles for the security they provide, while others may struggle against their limitations. Some women may find themselves simultaneously playing all of these roles with different men at different times. And men may adopt the male counterparts of the female roles, similarly behaving in stereotypical ways: father, stud, joker. In any case, whether accepted or fought, the four female stereotypes serve to limit the effective and flexible exercise of a woman's competence, for whether or not they confine her behavior to a narrow range, they at least give men a set of standards for interpreting her behavior and deciding if she is an "adequate" female. This pressure to be a "good woman" is difficult to resist.

1. mother

A solitary woman sometimes finds that she has become a "mother" to a group of men. They bring her their troubles, and she comforts them: The assumption that women are sympathetic, good listeners, and can be talked to about one's problems is a common one in male-dominated organizations (even though the majority of paid therapists are men). In a variety of groups solitary women have been observed acting out other parts of the traditional nurturant-maternal role: getting coffee, cooking for men, making doctors' appointments, doing their laundry, sewing on buttons. The mother role is comparatively safe; the mother is not necessarily vulnerable to sexual pursuit (for Freud it was the very idealization of the Madonna that was in part responsible for men's ambivalence toward women) nor to competition for her favors.

The typecasting of women as nurturers has three consequences: 1) The mother is rewarded by her male colleagues primarily for service to them and not for independent action. 2) The dominant, powerful aspects of the maternal image may be feared by men, and thus the mother is expected to keep her place as a noncritical, accepting, "good mother," or lose her rewards. Since the ability to differentiate and be critical is often an indicator of competence in work groups, the mother is prohibited from exhibiting this skill. 3) The mother becomes an emotional specialist. This provides her with a place in the life of the group and its members. Yet, at the same time, one of the traditionally feminine characteristics men in authority often criticize in women, as people trying to change the status of women in industry can attest, is excess "emotionality." Though the mother herself might not every cry or engage in emotional outbursts in the group, she remains identified with emotional matters. As long as she is in the minority, however, it is unlikely that nurturance, support, and expressivity will be valued, or that a mother can demonstrate and be rewarded for critical, independent, task-oriented behaviors.

2. sex object

The role of sex object or seductress (a perception on the part of others—the woman herself may not be behaving seductively) is fraught with more tension than the maternal role, for it introduces an element of sexual competition and jealousy. The mother can have many sons; it is more difficult for the sex object to have many lovers. Should the woman cast as sex object (that is, seen as sexually desirable and potentially available) share her attention widely, she risks the debasement of the whore. Yet, should she form a close alliance with any man in particular, she arouses resentment—particularly so because she represents a scarce resource; there are just not enough women to go around. In several situations observed, a high-status male allies himself with the seductress and acts as her "protector," partly, I think, because of his promise to rescue from sexually charged overtures of the rest of the men as well as because of his high status *per se*. The powerful male (staff member, manager, professor, etc.) can easily become the "protector" of the still-virgin seductress, gaining through masking his own sexual interest what the other men could not gain by declaring theirs. But this removal of the seductress from the sexual marketplace contains its own problems. The other men may resent the high-status male for winning the prize and resent the woman for her ability to get an "in" with the high-status male that they as men could not obtain. While the seductress is rewarded for her femaleness and insured attention from the group, she is also the source of considerable tension. And needless to say, her perceived sexuality blots out all other characteristics.

Men may themselves adopt the role of protector toward an attractive woman, regardless of her collusion, and by implication cast her as sex object, reminding her and the rest of the group of her sexual status. In the guise of "helping" her, self-designated protectors may actually put up further barriers to the solitary woman's full acceptance by inserting themselves, figuratively speaking, between the woman and the rest of the group. For example, at a weekend symposium attended by thirty men and four women, a woman with a doctorate was addressed as "Miss" by a male participant, while all the men were called "Doctor." The woman decided to wait until the end of the session to say something privately to the offender. Another man, the self-chosen protector, rushed over to her, in the presence of an audience, to assure her that he had heard the "insult" and would speak to the offender right away. Despite her declaration that she was about to say something herself, the protector called the offender over. The woman was then in the midst of a group of men who watched while two other men symbolically discussed her fate. The protectors' claim of "ownership" of the woman opened the door for other men in the group to pursue her, and for the rest of the evening, she was the object of sexual attention.

3.   pet

The "pet" is adopted by the male group as a cute, amusing little thing and symbolically taken along on group events as mascot, a cheerleader for the shows of male prowess that follow. Humor is often a characteristic of the pet. She is expected to admire the male displays but not enter into them; she cheers from the sidelines. Shows of competence on her part are treated as special and complimented just because they are unexpected (and the compliments themselves can be seen as reminders of the expected rarity of such behavior). One woman reported that when she is alone in a group of men and speaks at length on an issue, comments to her by men after the meeting often refer to her speech-making ability rather than the content of what she said ("You talk so fluently."), whereas comments the men make to one another are almost invariably content- or issue-oriented. Competent acts that are taken for granted when performed by males are often unduly "fussed over" when performed by women, considered "precocious or precious"—a kind of look-what-she-did-and-she's-only-a-woman attitude. Such attitudes on the part of men in a group encourage self-effacing girlish responses on the part of solitary women (who, after all, may be genuinely relieved to be included and petted), and prevent them from realizing or demonstrating their own power and competence.

4. iron maiden   The "iron maiden" is a contemporary variation of the stereotypical roles into which strong women are placed. Women who fail to fall into any of the first three roles and, in fact, resist overtures that will trap them in a role (such as flirtation), may consequently be responded to as "tough" or dangerous. If she insists on full rights in the group, if she displays competence in a forthright manner, or if she cuts off sexual innuendos, she may be asked "You're not one of those women's libbers, are you?" Regardless of the answer, she may henceforth be regarded with suspicion, undue and exaggerated shows of politeness (by inserting references to women into conversations, by elaborate rituals of *not* opening doors), and with distance, for she is demanding treatment as an equal in a setting which no person of her kind has previously been as equal. Women who become trapped in the "iron maiden" role are often behaving in healthy, self-actualizing ways, but the male response may stereotype them as tougher than they are (hence the name I've provided) and may trap them into a more militant stance than they would otherwise choose.

I am speaking, of course, of stereotypes and deliberately caricaturing the patterns and their response. I see the notion of the four roles as "sensitizing concepts" that make sense out of much subtler real-life behavior. What all four ideal conceptions of the roles and their real-life manifestations have in common is that they serve to isolate the solitary woman—one of one, two, or three in a much larger group of men—from the mainstream of group interaction. They prevent her from experiencing or being straightforwardly rewarded for what might be very real competences that contrast or conflict with the stereotypical role. Some of the roles, further, arouse resentment in the same male colleagues who, at the same time, might be promoting the roles, And, finally, each of the roles engenders conflicts in the woman that can easily interfere with effective performance.

It is the very loneliness of the token woman in such situations that contributes to the stereotyping and role traps. She lacks female role models that clearly demonstrate how it is possible to be both competent and female. She lacks a critical mass of other women, a sizable enough number to counteract stereotyping by evidencing a range of behaviors and characteristics—and a range of ways of being female. (Stereotyping becomes harder when face-to-face with evidence for its overgenerality and inaccuracy.) The token woman lacks other women with whom to generate a "counterculture" to the male-dominated culture which can provide support and its own indicators of status. If status and power positions in that situation are the monopoly of men, then the woman remains dependent on men for inclusion and for reward.

Further, if men alone control status, then it is to no man's advantage to curry favor with solitary women, for an alliance with a lower-status figure only lowers the man's own status—unless he is "taking" from the other in the form of nurturance (the Madonna) or sexual conquest (the whore). To the extent that the presence of only a handful of women indicates that few places in the group are open to women, the the solitary woman herself may have very ambivalent responses to other women—on the one hand, they represent a threat of replacement. Thus, even in the presence of one or two other women in a group, a token woman may still feel that her fate and future rests with "making it" with the men. Her possible antagonistic response to the few other women present heightens the conflicts both in her and in them. Finally, to the extent that each woman is seen as All Women because of her lone-ness—to the extent that her performance in the group will help determine whether women can, in fact, be effective in the new positions opening to them—she carries an extra burden of responsibility that cannot help but engender additional anxiety, not to mention the tendency to be excessively critical of her female colleagues.

change strategies

How do we change the situation of women in organizations, providing more opportunities for them to become leaders, to demonstrate competence, to gain their fair share of rewards? One way is simply to change the sex ratio in the power structure of organizations, to put more women in positions of visible leadership. But this "simple" solution has proven to be not an easy matter of just recruiting and promoting more women; both male and female expectations may get in the way. So may all the issues I have reviewed that occur when women try to exercise leadership or join a male peer group.

Human relations training (for example, running sensitivity workshops) is not an effective strategy by itself. The norms of human relations workshops are particularly suited for helping men develop new behavioral repertoires and self-insights counterbalancing the stereotypical tendencies of the male role. Where the male role stresses instrumental leadership, a task and power orientation, a humanistic approach emphasizes learning the expression of feelings; where the male role stresses analytic and intellectual reasoning, human relations emphasize learning to pay attention to emotions; where the male role stresses an identity based on achievement with respect to tasks, human relations norms emphasize learning to receive and be influenced by feedback from others; where the male role stresses aggression and competition, human relations norms emphasize learning to behave cooperatively. And so on. But the very norms that offer new learning for men are already a stereotypical part of the female role: expressive leadership, nurturance, and support; emotional reasoning; talking immediately and directly to one another; intuition; cooperation. Table 1 indicates this contrast.

Table 1. *human relations norms in the light of male and female stereotypical role tendencies*

Male role tendency	Human relations norm	Female role tendency
Instrumental leadership; task and power orientation	Learn to express feelings	Expressive leadership; nurturance and support
Analytic reasoning intellectualizing	Learn to pay attention to feelings	Emotional reasoning; intuition
Generalizing	Learn to speak for yourself	Personalizing
Identity based on achievement; how others see self less important	Learn to receive and be influenced by feedback	Identity dependent on feelings of others toward self; status traditionally based on relationships
Attention to issues of large systems; in a group, remarks impersonal and indirect	Learn to talk personally, directly to others	Attention to small number of others; in a group, remarks addressed personally to another
Anger and blame externalized; vengeance sought	Learn to take personal responsibility for own behavior	Blame internalized; difficulty expressing anger
Physical distance; hostility-violence in crowded conditions	Learn comfort with physical contact	Greater comfort with being touched; cooperation under conditions of crowding
Fear of failure in the organizational world; get ahead at all costs	Learn to value human concerns	Ambivalence about success in the organizational world;
Aggression; competition	Learn to behave cooperatively	Cooperation; support
Exhibit strength; hide weakness	Learn to show vulnerability	Exhibit weakness; hide or repress strength

Thus, while men may need help learning about relationships and emotional expression, *women need help learning just the opposite: the experience of power, task orientation, intellectualizing, behaving "impersonally" and addressing large groups, invulnerability to feedback,* and other new experiences in interpersonal behavior for many women.

There are two very different training agendas for men and women. Training and workshop designs would consequently differ if primarily men or primarily women were involved. Male managers and executives, foremen and administers, need to support and encourage the experience of power in women at the same time that they encourage expressiveness in men. They could consider helping men learn about relating and women learn about large groups, impersonality, and boundaries. In addition, men and women could be encouraged to see each other in the light of these new behavior possibilities and consequently redefine their usual modes of interacting with one another. Since most managers are male, they are probably not sensitive to the special needs and issues of women, and they need to learn to modify their style and assumptions. They need to understand the special issues of people who have been assumed to be powerless and have been confined to roles of support rather than independence. Men interacting with women should be aware of their own reinforcement of female stereotypes and when helping is *not* helping—for example, when a man adopts the "protector" role toward a lone woman.

The relative proportions of men and women in work groups and training groups should similarly be taken into account in designing programs. Whenever possible, a "critical mass" of females should be included in every working group—more than two or three, and a large enough percentage that they can reduce stereotyping, change the culture of the group, and offer support without being a competitive threat to one another. If there are only a few women in the sales force, for example, this analysis suggests that they should be clustered rather than spread widely. If men outnumber women in a training program and the participants are being divided into groups, perhaps it would be better to have a few equally balanced mixed-sex groups and the rest of the men together rather than putting one or two women in each group.

One of the primary barriers to increasing the participation of women in organizational areas usually excluded to them is the existence and persistence of cultural stereotypes. These stereotypes influence the decisions of managers and male colleagues concerning women and affect their behavior toward women as a social category, regardless of their relationships with individual women. Women as well as men sometimes hold these stereotypes and perceive themselves and other women in terms of them. Some common stereotypes reflect lack of knowledge and can be influenced simply by the transfer of information. Facts and examples, theory and research findings, can be potent tools in change efforts. Stereotypes are supported by more than interaction patterns and can persist despite a person's continued experience with women who are "different." Evidence from a wide variety of sources can sometimes be covincing where personal experience can be denied as an "exception."

A second barrier to women's full participation can also be challenged by information transfer: the uncertainty on the part of many men about how to treat a female subordinate, colleague, or superior. In this case uncertainty creates discomfort and a consequent desire to avoid an uncomfortable situation. Knowledge about how women prefer to be treated, where the general tendencies of female psychology converge or diverge from that of males, what kinds of women seek careers and for what reasons, as well as an opportunity to learn from professional or career women about women, can ease some of the discomfort, just as prior information about the norms and expectations of people from another culture can ease entry into that culture. Thus, giving a group of men and women an opportunity to "check out" their assumptions about the other sex with those people can be an effective change strategy. In one program I ran, we learned that men often assume that women have or will have family responsibilities that interfere with travel or with promotion to jobs involving greater responsibility. In many cases they do not test this with the woman involved and give her an opportunity to correct the assumption if it is wrong, nor do they let her make her own decision. (The notion that men's families help them with work but women's families held them back needs to be modified in the light of the large numbers of employed married women.) Both men and women can learn not to make *a priori* assumptions about the other sex but to test these with the people involved.

Finally, since the situation of women in organizations has been determined by complex structural factors, attention should be paid to the system as a system, with its own particular arrangements, structure, traditions, and sex-typing of jobs. We might ask about:

the patterns of job segregation with respect to sex

salary differentials by sex and their relationship to length of service and organizational level

the existence of a male support network and the opportunities for women to build their own support network

the difference between a dead-end job in the organization and one from which people are promoted; how to change dead-end into promotable jobs

whether formal training or informal on-the-job training makes the difference in effective performance; if the informal system is more effective than the formal, how do informal arrangements include/exclude women? (Similar questions can be asked about other aspects of the incongruency between the formal and informal systems.)

the nature of career development for men and whether this can easily include women

traditional barriers to change in general in the organization; organizational politics and who must be included to make effective change

conclusion

There was a time when social scientists seemed to assume that sex played no role in the functioning of modern organizations. Indeed, the "passionless organization," the neuter bureaucracy, was the very ideal model theorists and planners tried to promote, often excluding women in the process (Kanter, 1975). But we now know differently—that sex and its behavioral consequences may play an important role in determining who does what and who gets ahead in organizations. Our recent knowledge can serve as an impetus for change, for extending equal opportunities to both women and men, and for changing the structural factors that tend to give women a limited place in organizations. In the process we can work to reintegrate the socially imposed polarizations that give power and rationality to men and nurturance and human caring to women, but can, instead, allow all people to learn both leadership and support. If organizations of the future help make this possible, then neither women nor men will need to waste half of their human capacities.

references

Back, K. The methodology of studying rumor transmission. *Human Relations.* 1950, *3*, 307-12.

Bowman, G. W., Worthy, N. B., & Greyser, S. A. Are women executives people? *Harvard Business Review*, 1965, *43*, 14-30.

Crozier, M. *The world of the office worker.* trans. by David Landau. Chicago: University of Chicago Press, 1971.

Cussler, M. *The woman executive.* New York: Harcourt, Brace, 1958.

Epstein, C. F. *Woman's place: Options and limits on professional careers.* Berkeley, Calif.: University of California Press, 1970.

Hennig, M. Career development for women executives. Doctoral Dissertation, Harvard University Graduate School of Business Administration, 1970.

Hurwitz, J. I., Zander, A. F., & Hymovich, B. Some effects of power on the relations between group members. In D. Cartwright & A. Zander (Eds.), *Group dynamics.* New York: Harper & Row, 1968.

Kanter, R. M. *Commitment and community.* Cambridge: Harvard University Press, 1972.

Kanter, R. M. The impact of hierarchical structures on the work behavior of women and men. *Social Problems*, 1976, *23*, in press.

Kanter, R. M. *Men and women of the corporation.* New York: Basic Books, in press.

Kanter, R. M. Women and the structure of organizations: Explorations in theory and behavior. *Sociological Inquiry*, 1975, *45*, 34-75.

Kelly, H. Communication in experimentally created hierarchies. *Human Relations*, 1951, *4*, 39-56.

Lippitt, R., Polansky, N., Redl, F., & Rosen, S. The dynamics of power. *Human Relations,* 1952, *5,* 37-64.

Megaree, E. I. Influence of sex roles on the manifestation of leadership. *Journal of Applied Psychology,* 1969, *53,* 377-382.

Pelz, D. C. Influence: A key to effective leadership in the firstline supervisor. *Personnel,* 1952, *29,* 3-11.

Reitan, H. T., & Shaw, M. E. Group membership, sex-composition of the group, and conforming behavior. *The Journal of Social Psychology,* 1964, *64,* 49-51.

Thibaut, J. An experimental study of the cohesiveness of underprivileged groups. *Human Relations,* 1950, *3,* 251-278.

Tiger, L. *Men in groups.* New York: Random House, 1969.

Tuddenham, R. D., MacBride, P., & Zahn, V. The influence of the sex composition of the group upon yielding to a distorted norm. *Journal of Psychology,* 1958, *46,* 243-251.

Whyte, W. *Men at work.* Homewood, Ill.: Irwin-Dorsey, 1961.

Wolman, C., & Frank, H. The solo woman in a professional peer group. *American Journal of Orthopsychiatry,* 1975, *45*(1), 164-171.

men in organizations: some reflections

Herbert A. Shepard

The second piece of advice is: Observe the cormorant in the fishing fleet. You know how cormorants are used for fishing. The technique involves a man in a rowboat with about half a dozen or so cormorants, each with a ring around the neck. As the bird spots a fish, it would dive into the water and unerringly come up with it. Because of the ring, the larger fish are not swallowed but held in the throat. The fisherman picks up the bird and squeezes out the fish through the mouth. The bird then dives for another and the cycle repeats itself.

To come back to the second piece of advice from the neo-Taoist to the American worker. Observe the cormorant, he would say. Why is it that of all the different animals, the cormorant has been chosen to slave away day and night for the fisherman? Were the bird not greedy for fish, or not efficient in catching it, or not readily trained, would society have created an industry to exploit the bird? Would the ingenious device of a ring around its neck, and the simple procedure of squeezing the bird's neck to force it to regurgitate the fish have been devised? Or course not.

Greed, talent, and capacity for learning then are the basis of exploitation. The more you are able to moderate and/or hide them from society, the greater will be your chances of escaping the fate of the cormorant.

... It is necessary to remember that the institutions of society are geared to make society prosper, not necessarily to minimizing suffering on your part. It is for this reason, among others, that the schools tend to drum it into your mind the high desirability of those characteristics that tend to make society prosper—namely, ambition, progress and success. These in turn are to be valued in terms of society's objectives. All of them gradually but surely increase your greed and make a cormorant out of you.*

some history about men in organizations

Among the other spectacular, violent, and possibly catastrophic developments in America in the twentieth century was the emergence of a new breed of men: the managers. Managers are the focus of this

---

*Ralph G. H. Siu. Work and Serenity. *Journal of Occupational Mental Health*, 1971, 1 (1), 5.

387

chapter, because they are the men who have been successful in organizations. Our society has learned how to produce managers by the millions. The childrearing and schooling practices needed for the production of farmers were modified to produce managers. The school became a socializing model of the adult bureaucracy. Fathers increased their emphasis on filial obedience and conformity to formal rules within the home and community, prolonged their sons' dependency on the parent's ability to provide, demanded that the son engage in win-lose competitiveness with peers outside the home, that he earn straight A's across the board in school, and that he deny any confused feelings stirred by these anomalous requirements. Of the schooling provided to the boys as the country moved to the city and the one-room multi-age schoolhouse became the depersonalizing cell-block of concrete, vinyl and glass hallways, washrooms and peer-group classrooms, it could be said that any lad who could survive it through high school without dropping out would survive adult organizations as well. The school provided an adequate experience in pleasing authorities, competing with one's peers, working on intrinsically meaningless tasks, and associating feelings of success and failure—self-worth and self-worthlessness—with status symbols in the form of grades. Cormorants notwithstanding, the proudest thing a father could say was that his son was ambitious, talented, and had a high capacity for learning.

During most of the period of urbanization, industrialization, professionalization and bureaucratization, the church, as well as home and school, played an important role in preparing men for organizations. By rewarding conformity and obedience, by inducing guilt and a sense of sin for deviance, and by stressing the necessity for loyalty to a supreme authority, the church helped lay a foundation for organizational discipline. Loyalty was readily transferable to other authorities—the boss, the mission, the nation, the corporation or the chief. Even the church's geographical heritage in the positioning of heaven and hell supported the notion of up and down in social life, identifying hierarchy with pyramid—a metaphor that is perhaps our most pervasive myth.

Some of the religions also provided a simple model of traditional bureaucratic organization. But in this respect, the military tradition had much greater impact. For as technology and organization grew symbiotically, we experienced a series of wars, some very large and involving many of our young men. In numerous ways military experience facilitated mastery of the art of being a superior and a subordinate, served to teach and reinforce the mentality and skills needed in large organizations, and provided a language suitable for use in an expanding, competitive organization: mission, strategy and tactics, mobilization and deployment. Much military slang became the slang of civilian organization: the top brass or the big guns on the one hand, the troops on the other. Managers learned to be hard-nosed and to bite the bullet.

Standards of managerial appearance were also reinforced by military experience. Beards and long hair are dysfunctional when dealing with wounds, mud, lice, and dangerous equipment. A heritage of the wars seems to have been a norm that having a face as hairless as a woman's and hair almost as short as a convict's was an important symbol of masculinity and managerial respectability. In matters of dress, the limits of what constitutes proper managerial clothing became narrow, clear, and somber—in some organizations, almost uniform.

The experience of managers in organizations coupled with the work of social scientists and engineers heightened our awareness of and created concepts for organizational structure and process. Early in the period, concepts like authority, delegation, responsibility, span of control, line and staff, supervision and efficiency became fundamental principles. Some of the principles could be summed up in phrases like one man—one boss; no responsibility without commensurate authority. On such fundamentals more complex and refined policies, procedures and practices were erected. Organization charting and the writing of job descriptions became identifiable arts. Compensation and industrial engineering became professional fields. Management information and control systems became more sophisticated. The growth of technology and the image of the organization as a command system encouraged the use of mechanistic concepts. An organization was like an automatic factory in which some functions could not yet be economically mechanized, and were therefore performed by human parts operating to specification.

The impact of all these intertwined forces and processes was to produce an adult male who was dedicated to the disciplined performance of his organizational role, and who was capable of subordinating himself for the purpose of moving upward, that is, of subordinating himself at a higher level. In doing so, he also subordinated any personal needs that were irrelevant to the organization. As one manager put it, "Your work day is to earn your salary; your overtime is to gain your promotion." This depersonalization with respect to work extended to interpersonal communication. Articulate, rational, fact-based, cause-effect discourse was a critical success skill. Interaction with the boss should be businesslike. Subordinates were to be directed and evaluated. Issues among peers should be resolved by the boss.

Relationships with subordinates were to be impersonal—firm but fair. Should a subordinate have to be "terminated," an impersonal relationship would make the action less awkward or painful. The psychological power of the organization over the man is suggested in the last statement. Success could never be securely and permanently acquired. There were always higher levels to aspire to: but the people at higher levels had the power to offer not only a little more success, but also complete failure—a traumatic blow to self-esteem.

If men experienced the anxiety generated by this threat, they were not to show it. The emphasis on rational communication and decision making meant that all emotion was considered dysfunctional; and careers could be damaged by a show of feelings, especially the warmer emotions. In spite of what was known about "positive reinforcement," it was rarely used as a managerial method: more attention was paid to the punishment of unwanted behaviors than to the reinforcement of wanted behaviors. Supportive behavior of any kind was rare; admitting a need for help from others was a sign of weakness; offering help was a putdown.

Organizational disciplines and symbols came to pervade the life of the manager. Automobiles, homes, and tastes conformed to the requirements of organizational role and status almost as much as office size and furnishings. The manner and content of greeting other men, engaging in small talk, and joking became ritualized and differentiated at and between different levels of organization, in the same way that communication around tasks or the making of formal presentations conformed to certain standards.

The above historical sketch highlights some aspects of male socialization and organization development to the neglect of others, and perhaps to the point of caricature. Though no precise dates can be ascribed to the oversimplified description given above, it is intended to suggest the early 1950s. In succeeding years the demands of organization on men and of men on organization have begun to shift dramatically, and this shift is affecting male roles and relationships, and also changing the characteristics of female roles in organizations.[1]

The impact of these historical developments on domestic life over a period of a few generations was dramatic. As the roles of men became more status-oriented, more performance-oriented, more oriented toward organizational success, less personally expressive, and more disciplined—with all the attendant qualities of orderliness, rationality, articulateness, neatness, efficiency, punctuality, conformity, and structure—the demands on household organization became more stringent. (It was during these years that the pressure-cooker became popular.) When money and status became important measures of male suc-

---

[1]Historically, the roles of women in organizations are relevant to the focus of this chapter largely because women came to replace men as adjuncts to managers. Girls were not brought up to aspire to compete in organizations. In fact, girls who excelled in school or were active competitive tomboys after school, like girls who appeared to have the female equivalent of wild oats to sow, were a source of concern to parents and teachers. Learning to provide the support system that a man needed—to be decorative, emotionally supportive, and competent in support tasks like housekeeping and childrearing—these were the important things. During this period the male confidential clerk disappeared from organizations. In military organizations male aides began to be replaced by members of the women's services. These support jobs came to be seen as somewhat demeaning for men, and it seemed appropriate to have women in roles analogous in their supportive characteristics to the wifely role.

cess there was increased emphasis on the husband—father's role as provider of these commodities to his family, and de-emphasis on emotional support and interpersonal relations. As his discipline and dedication to work increased, his wife seemed to develop excellence in housekeeping, the management of children, the art of being a hostess and decorative companion, and in maintaining the family image. At the same time, the nuclear family became more isolated from external sources of emotional support. Moving up in the organization meant moving around the country. Bonds of kinship, friendship, and familiarity became superficial and transitory. The family became an impoverished social system, a prison in which the children had only two significant adults to turn to, and the adults had only each other. Families broke up at an increasing rate, leaving bewildered men, bitter women, and children in conflict.

During the fifties conditions were ripening for radical change in family life, sex roles, human values, and organizations. The theme of human relations had been of concern to management for some time, but primarily with respect to the work force. The spread of unionism was in part a response to the dehumanization of work and workers, but the human relations movement was intended more as a counterforce to unionism than as an effort to make the job worthwhile.

During the forties and fifties there was increasing awareness of the inadequate bureaucratic principles governing organizational structure and process. As organizations grew larger and more complex, internal interdependencies could no longer be managed by the clumsy hierarchy of authority-responsibility delegations; for example, teamwork and collaboration among specialists and managers was needed for the solution of complicated problems. And as organizational environments became more dynamic, the awkward communication and decision-making processes of traditional firms prevented them from making a rapid, adaptive response to external changes. Not only were organizations becoming unfit to work in, they were becoming unfit to work.

During this period, various organizational experiments were undertaken. The "Scanlon Plan" in which participants in interpersonal and intergroup collaboration were rewarded was one such experiment. National Training Laboratories began to offer interpersonal relations training for executives. A naval laboratory began to hold periodic "retreats" for its management to resolve interpersonal conflicts and develop teamwork among the members. The first major organization development experiments were conducted at Esso Standard Oil in the late fifties.

All these experiments emphasized the need for collaboration, teamwork, openness, trust, and the expression and use of emotion. People began to recognize that organizations had to become less mechanistic and more organic if they were to be effective: the parts of any thriving organism are fully alive and in good communication with one another and actively in touch with internal and external environments. There were radical implications for how men would perform their organizational roles. In the sixties, TRW Systems, a leader in the aerospace industry, was also a leader in developing new concepts of organization (matrix organization) and in developing resocializing methods (organization development) for its members. Matrix organization dispensed with the one man-one boss rule, required that responsibility and authority be shared by people rather than divided among them, and relied on teamwork within and between many groups of specialists for organizational effectiveness. Organization Development provided members with opportunities to learn how to build relationships with one another that would permit the organization to function. These were "rehumanizing" experiences that emphasized personal growth, interpersonal openness, reaching out to others to confront conflict, or to seek or offer help. Such learnings were out of keeping with traditional concepts of organizational role or masculine role—forerunners of the learnings that were to become more widespread in the seventies.

some current history about men in organizations

It is not possible to have a perspective on the multifaceted crunch we are now entering, but some observations can be offered on recent developments related to the topic of this chapter—men in organizations.

The day of the simple hierarchy, chain of command, or bureaucracy has passed, and with it the relevance and utility of many of the disciplines, concepts, and skills that men in organizations learned. Some of the "fundamentals" are applicable in specific contexts, but they have moved from a position of absolute value to one of relative value. The increasing complexity of internal and external interdependencies and the increasingly turbulent environment make unprecedented demands on managers. The socializing institutions of family, school, and church have not kept pace with the requirements of organization in the adult world. Organizations are becoming resocializing institutions, providing intensive continuing education to their members.

A transformation of values accompanies the acquisition of new organizational skills. Competition among individuals has become dysfunctional where problem-solving and the achievement of organizational objectives require intense collaboration and commitment to each other's success. Intense collaboration requires more than the learning of some new skills. It requires learning how to earn trust and how to extend it to others; it requires personalization rather than depersonalization of relationships; it means giving emotional as well as technical support to others; it involves learning to confront conflict with others and to resolve conflicts on a win-win basis; it requires the ability to learn from and with others; it requires a willingness to transcend the boundaries of one's own and others' job descriptions; it requires learning how to use each other's resources strategically in the accomplishment of shared objectives. All these learnings imply a change in life values from those implicit in the older concepts of organization.

Control is still the central concern of the manager. In the past, control was associated with aggressiveness and domination as an aspect of male sexism. Under the emerging organizational conditions, these attributes are likely to be dysfunctional. Controlling has become a dynamic, adaptive, learning process, an aspect of organizational communication depending on openness, responsiveness and trust, on the one hand, and on the capacity to process large amounts of complex information, on the other. Controlling means continuously seeking a strategic comprehension of complicated processes.

Similarly, authority and obedience are no longer the cement of organization, just as money and status are no longer adequate as motivators. There is no unitary authority over the multiple resources involved in the accomplishment of organizational goals, nor can there be. Men in organizations must learn a broad range of influence skills besides those of command, persuasion, manipulation, and negotiation. They must learn a whole range of collaborative influence strategies for which there is little historical precedent: how to create common interests, how to resolve conflict on a win-win or superordinate goal basis, how to build on one another's strengths.

In the area of motivation, psychic income is becoming as important as money and more important than status. As organizations begin to demand the full range of human potential, the educational processes involved cause a continuous raising of levels of awareness. A new kind of selfishness is emerging from the resocialization experiences that organizations are providing for their members; for example, Gestalt Therapy, Transactional Awareness, Transcendental Meditation, Life Planning, Conflict Management, Personal Growth, Team Development, Intercultural Skills, Achievement and Power Motivation, Creativity, Awareness Training, Consciousness Expansion. Many of these experiences have certain themes and implications in common: learning to care for and nurture oneself; learning to recognize and accept responsibility for one's choices rather than projecting them onto others; learning to appreciate the right side of the brain and develop latent capacities that were regarded as irrational and dysfunctional (and effeminate!) in organizations— like intuition, nonverbal imagery, empathic apprehension of others, the existence of auras, extrasensory perception, and energy exchange among people; re-examining one's fundamental preconceptions about oneself, about the meaning of life, about religious, social and moral values and behavior, about war, progress, government and nationalism, about the roles of women and men, about sex and race, childhood, youth, adulthood and old age, and about organizational life.

It would be folly to claim that these developments have as yet brought about a revolution in men's values or organizational life or family relationships or relationships with women. Most managers still feel guilty if they leave the office early; most managers continue to play variations of the games they learned in college to impress the professor at the expense of their fellow students; most managers are still seeking money and status in the shadow of the fear of failure rather than seeking beauty in life and work; most managers still want their children to be good status symbols; most managers still want to think of themselves as good providers for their wives and other dependents. And as all the above implies, most managers are men.

But men are changing, and by no means solely in response to changing women. Many women are adjusted to the man-manager of the past and are alarmed as he becomes more human; many women have rebelled against the man-manager of the past and are striving to become like him. But current and future organizational requirements demand a higher level of human functioning. Organizations need both men and women who are developing and using all their multifaceted potentials.

teachers as mediators
of sex-role standards

Marcia Guttentag

Helen Bray

Educational institutions are becoming more and more responsible for socialization of children which previously had been reserved for parents. This socialization occurs at earlier and earlier ages. Schools reflect the values of the society at large, and transfer these standards of behavior to children. Thus, girls are trained to be passive and boys to be single-minded achievers. Recent concerns about such sexist socialization practices in school systems, voiced by concerned layman and educators, have already resulted in some changes.

No research program has yet systematically studied all of the dynamics of differential boy/girl treatment, expectations, and age differences in classrooms to make it possible to predict what changes are necessary, what changes are ineffectual, and what changes will have effects of the longest duration. One practical measure of current effects of sexism in the educational process is that boys come out of it believing that they are competent for full-time careers, while girls emerge able to handle only full-time homemaking opportunities. Of course, given wider cultural currents, these beliefs are changing. Yet we know little about why and how stereotyping is perpetuated in our educational system. To be effective, interventions and changes in current educational processes must be informed. Schools and teachers have long believed they treat boys and girls equally and fairly and yet have had little idea about how children were actually influenced in sexist directions. For this reason, research done in the classroom which documents behaviors, attitudes, and expectancies of the teacher is critical in pinpointing those actions that subtly distinguish between boys and girls. This chapter reviews relevant research on those classroom practices which have encouraged differential achievement and aspiration patterns for boys and girls, and focuses on the teacher's role in the mediation of sex-role standards.

achievement patterns of boys and girls

Differences between boys and girls are accentuated over time in the school setting. As measured by tests of ability, boys and girls enter kindergarten with similar levels of intelligence, motor skills, perceptual performance, and patterns of reasoning (Korner, 1973). Activity level at birth are quite similar, but by age five the previously more fragile boy shows greater muscular vigor, with more aggression and a more disorganized reaction to frustration. Observational studies show that girls are not more timid and fearful than boys in kindergarten (Maccoby, 1974).

Early in the school years, boys are underachievers, especially in reading tasks, and girls, supposedly stimulated by the external social reinforcement of the teacher, excel in most academic areas. Boys, suspicious of demands for conformity in the classroom, display more disruptive behaviors which call for more disciplinary actions by the teacher. By the middle elementary school years, girls believe their occupational choices are limited to the stereotyped roles of teacher, nurse, artist, stewardess, and so on. Girls generally define their roles around marriage and the family, while boys picture themselves in work and careers (Hartley, 1964; Iglitzin, 1972). Children sex-type all kinds of activities and show definite preferences for same-sex stereo-typical hobbies, activities, and interests (Guttentag, Bray; Amster, Jane; Donovan, Virginia; Legge, Gordon; Wilson-Legge, Wendy; Littenberg, Ronnie; Stotsky, Sandra, 1975). Performance on tasks can, to some extent, be predicted by their sex-typing, (Stein, Pholy, & Mueller, 1969). Thus, in the junior high school years, the pattern is for boys to be mathematicians and for girls to excel in all the verbal skills of writing, verbal comprehension, and languages.

Girls, who were generally excellent students in elementary school drop off in their high school achievement and a core of female underachievers develops. There is a trend for girls' IQ scores to decline in late adolescence and early adulthood. Boys in high school become more studious, and as they orient themselves toward careers, try to gain definite skills for vocational or college opportunities. Until quite recently, boys had more objective opportunities to continue training or college, while girls gradually dropped out of the job market and into family life.

Despite the fact that girls receive better grades until high school, their declared expectations of success are lower than their actual achievements. Girls consistently underestimate their ability, while boys are more realistic and accurate in their self-concepts, with a slight trend to overestimate their talents (Stein & Smithells, 1969; Grandall & Rabson, 1960). Both sexes judge that boys do better on achievement tasks (Torrance, 1963).

how do schools emphasize sex differences

Why do these sex stereotypical patterns appear so clearly? Before turning to the interactions between teachers and students in the classroom, sex-role stereotyping on the organizational level of the educational system must be examined. First, men run the system; women work in it. Men hold the administrative jobs of superintendents, principals, and coordinators and also dominate the policy-making school boards. Women are concentrated in positions at the early childhood level. Some research indicates that by the age of five, children attribute more power and prestige to the male role (Kohlberg, 1966). This is hardly more than an accurate appraisal of the current society's imbalance of power, reinforced for the child by observation within the educational system itself.

Second, the teaching materials used in schools have been evaluated as discriminatory (D'Uren, 1971; Federbush, 1973). For instance, Saario, Tittle & Jacklin (1973) analyzed four elementary reading textbook series in detail. They discovered that characters and plots centered around females less frequently than around males. Boys in these materials showed greater amounts of aggression, physical assertion, and problem solving, while girls were displayed as characters enveloped in fantasy, carrying out directive behaviors, and being self-concerned. Adult males demonstrated constructive-productive behavior while adult females were conforming and talked rather than accomplished anything. The roles of males and females became increasingly differentiated from first-grade primers to third-grade readers, indicating a tightening of sex-role stereotype with age within the school curriculum.

From these books children learn not only basic skills but become acquainted with images of men and women that were reduced to a set of prescribed, limited roles and personality characteristics, hardly a realistic presentation of most people with individualistic and complex perferences and values which cross sex lines.

Third, activities are segregated by sex. Young girls and boys are organized to play different games; they form separate lines, carry out different classroom tasks, and learn different things. Later in school, adolescents are directed either to sewing or woodworking, with little concern for the desires and talents of the individual child. Recently, considerable attention has been paid to the inequalities in funding for girls' sports on both the high school and college level. Teachers have reported that recent changes in dress codes which allow girls to wear slacks are the most important factors in erasing distinctions in activities, since the elementary school girls can now climb and jump and run as fast as the boys without the hinderance of a skirt.

teachers' attitudes toward sex differences

The fourth major way in which children are differentially socialized is through attitudes and behaviors of teachers. Since the avowed goal and personal commitment of teachers is to introduce the children to skills and stimulate their thirst for knowledge, teachers probably do not purposely guide girls into limited future options and boys into more open and fulfilling aspirations.

In a survey of teachers from a variety of school systems, across grades and sex of teacher (Donovan, 1973, unpublished), no teacher reported feeling differently toward boys and girls or treating them differently. Yet classroom observations of the same teachers revealed clear differences in teacher-girl-boy interaction patterns. Unspoken beliefs about sex differences in boys and girls, their occupational roles, and differential parental expectations for the children seem to influence the dynamic interactions between teachers and students, although teachers are not aware of it.

Teachers apparently believe that boys and girls have different needs that must be met by differential treatment by the teacher. A fairly recent study re-examined the issue of sex differences from an attitudinal perspective by focusing on how the teacher perceives the preferences of the class and other teachers. Ricks and Pyke (1973) carried on interviews with 30 male and 30 female teachers (age range 25-57 years). As expected, a majority (73 percent) of the teachers in the sample reported that boys and girls perform or behave differently. This percentage was the same for male and female teachers. In another item which asked whether students expected to be treated differently, 55 percent of the females and 50 percent of the males thought that boys and girls expected differential treatment. A similar percentage indicated that teachers had neither the responsibility nor the right to influence childrens' attitudes toward sex roles.

The picture these findings present is one in which teachers perceive that boys and girls are different and want to be treated differently. The teachers' role is one of meeting rather than shaping these "needs." For the teacher to be a nonstereotyped model is important, but it is not enough. Children in schools are accustomed to receiving information about new concepts and skills. Issues of competency, self-confidence, sensitivity towards people, and equality of opportunity are suitable for any classroom and are directly relevant to the discussion of sex roles.

Some studies of teachers' general attitudes toward boys and girls, have set up hypothetical instances and asked the teachers to rate them and describe their feelings. For instance, one study (Levitin & Chananie, 1972) paired hypothetical boys and girls with the characteristics of dependency, aggression, or achievement. The teachers were asked how much they approved of the student, how much they liked the student, and how typical the student was. Trends indicated that the dependent male received less approval than the dependent female, and the aggressive male and dependent female were acknowledged to be fairly typical. Teachers liked the achieving girl and the dependent girl more than the dependent male. Perhaps in the school situation, where there is a press for obedience and consistent performance, the dependent girl is the one who listens to the teacher, follows directions, and produces correct papers, thus becoming a submissive kind of achiever. This study distinguished between attitudes appropriate to the teacher's job and more personal evaluations of boys and girls as likeable. Both direct and indirect expectations and approval are communicated to the dependent girl who is liked and the dependent boy who is not. Yet it is independence, not dependence, which later correlates with creative intellectual ability.

teachers' be-
haviors which
reinforce sex
differences

The attitudes and beliefs that a person holds are uncertainly connected to consistent daily behaviors. Few studies about teacher-student interaction have tried to pinpoint how teacher attitudes affect teacher behaviors with students. Felsenthal (1970) attempted to connect teacher's perceptions of sex differences as measured by an attitudinal scale to actual variations in student reading achievement. She attempted to relate teacher attitudes to classroom activities and related both to pupil performance in reading. In the first-grade groups, Felsenthal found some significant sex differences in teacher treatment. Results showed boys received more interaction of both a positive and negative kind than girls. Boys were questioned more, criticized more, and had more ideas accepted and rejected. Girls volunteered significantly more often but were not called on. They had higher reading achievement scores. Felsenthal also measured teacher attitudes to educational issues. No classroom behavioral differences were observed between the attitude groups.

Although the direct effects of teachers' attitudes on their behaviors is difficult to evaluate, there have been many studies on the discrete behaviors of teachers and students in the classroom. These use systematic observational methods in which trained observers code and count specific actions, for instance: "child asks questions," "teacher scolds," or "student ignores teacher." Diverse but significant sex differences have appeared in many of these studies. One of the earliest (Meyer & Thompson, 1956) tested the hypothesis that boys receive more disapproval contacts with teachers than girls. In the sixth-grade classes that were examined, this hypothesis was supported. A trend indicated that boys also received more praise than girls did. Jackson and Lahaderne (1967) found sixth-grade boys had more prohibitory, managerial, and instructional contacts with the teachers than girls. There was a positive correlation between the three kinds of contacts for boys, though not for girls. In fourth- and sixth-grade classrooms, Spaulding (1963) found teachers interacted more with boys in each of four categories: approval, disapproval, instruction, and listening. Research focusing on verbal interaction at the preschool level, (Cherry, 1974) demonstrated that teachers talked with boys more than with girls and were more likely to initiate the talking.

the teacher and dicipli- nary action

Disruptive and dependent behaviors by students and the teacher's reactions to them were chosen as the focus of a recent study of sex differences in preschool classrooms (Serbin, O'Leary, Kent, & Tonick, 1973). Close observational sessions of interaction indicated that teachers reacted in a louder and stronger fashion to the aggressive behavior of boys than they did to the aggressive behavior of girls. This may have occurred because of the teacher's belief that boys cause more disruption and need to be dealt with immediately and forcefully, or a belief that boys are less responsive to reprimands so that the discipline must be more noticeable. The researchers used a proximity measure of interaction from which they learned that boys and girls receive equal amounts of attention only when they are very close to the teacher. Boys receive more attention than girls when they are out of the immediate vicinity of the teacher. This teacher behavior encourages girls to stay near the teacher and emphasizes all the supportive elements of physical contact, including nodding praise, slight helping, and eye contact. Boys who are appropriately at work in the classroom out of the teacher's reach still receive encouragement and attention from the teacher, thus supporting their adventurous and independent activities. Obviously, this is a subtle, yet powerful form of differential treatment by teachers. It clearly supports a policy of training boys for individualistic behaviors and girls for socially approved behaviors.

A study by Martin (1972) qualified the generalization that boys receive more disapproval contacts. He suggested that teachers respond negatively not so much to boys in general as to a certain kind of boy. The bulk of negative reaction to boys is directed toward a minority of boys with low status in the classroom, or those termed as behavior problems. As Good and Brophy have pointed out (1973), teacher's reinforcements are made first on the basis of achievement level, then by sex. Achieving boys receive substantially more praise and support than normal boys, while underachievers receive substantially more punishment from the teacher. Girls fall in between the extreme ranges of praise and punishment given the boys. Female underachievers tend to be passive rather than disruptive. Because of this they may be overlooked in a classroom and receive little stimulation or guidance from teachers. Male underachievers are constantly directed toward achievement possibilities.

On the whole, it is clear that boys receive more behavioral criticism in the elementary classrooms. They also seem to be generally more active and to have more interactions of all kinds with teachers. When differences are found on student-initiated contacts, it is in favor of boys. When a pupil is not called on, the pupil is more likely to be a girl. In teacher-initiated interactions, boys are called on more often and given more evaluative and elaborated feedback than girls.

If teachers initiate more contact with boys and give them more evaluative feedback on their performance, this will help boys to evaluate their own efforts realistically and will help to lay the groundwork for independent intellectual activity. In contrast, if girls are ignored or given more global feedback, they will neither be able to evaluate their own performance realistically nor feel the confidence to do things on their own. Research has shown that by early elementary school, girls tend to underestimate their abilities (Crandall, et al. 1962), prefer easy tasks, show less task persistence when they have failed, and they may try to avoid difficult tasks altogether (Moriarity, 1961). They also have a lower expectancy of success at tasks than boys (Montanelli & Hill, 1969).

teacher preference and evaluation of boys and girls

Other studies have provided evidence that teachers perceive boys more differentially and evaluatively than girls. Jackson and Getzels (1959) and Jackson (1968) found teachers able to more accurately distinguish boys who were dissatisfied with school from those who were satisfied, though this was not the case for girls. Jackson and Lahaderne (1967) found teachers made more negatively evaluative statements about boys, but their statements also indicated more overall personal involvement with boys. Sears and Feldman (1966) had elementary school teachers rate their pupils: They had different preferences for bright boys and those of average ability, emphasizing self-sufficiency for the former and good work habits for the latter. Teachers did not distinguish bright from average ability girls: for both groups the emphasis was on friendly, agreeable, behavior—not on work habits or performance. McIntyre et al. (1966) found a similar lack of differentiation in teachers' evaluations of girls, while boys were differentiated both on social class and ability-performance variables.

These studies seem to indicate that boys appear to mean more to their teachers: they are perceived more analytically and accurately, and teachers interacted with them more differentially and frequently. To some extent, this may reflect actual differences in the children's behavior. Boys are more active and variable in behavior from birth. They show more learning and behavior disorders in the early grades, and there some research suggests that this may have a constitutional basis. However, the differential perception and treatment of the sexes is undoubtedly largely a function of the teacher's different expectations and stereotypes.

The survey by Ricks and Pyke (1973) reports two interesting and consistent preferences. First, More teachers, especially female teachers prefer male students to female students. Teachers reported that males were more outspoken, active, willing to exchange ideas, open, honest, and easier to talk with. The sole reason they gave for preferring female students was a lack of discipline problems. Second, 41 percent of the teachers believe that students prefer male teachers. Not one teacher felt that students preferred female teachers, although few teachers evaluated the female teacher as less effective. They reported that male teachers speak with more knowledge, authority, directness, and clarity than female teachers. There can be little doubt that prevalent beliefs such as these strongly influence the dynamic interaction between teacher and student.

In many studies, children's perceptions of the expectations and pre-ferences of the teacher have been used as measures for the evaluation of the teacher. Some studies (Meyer & Thompson, 1956; Davis & Slobodian, 1967) suggest that elementary school children generally perceive their teachers as favoring girls over boys in amount of approval versus disapproval and in giving them opportunities to read. An adjective check list was distributed to boys and girls by Davidson and Lang (1960) to evaluate their perception of the teacher's attitude towards them. The list contained favorable and unfavorable traits and the children were instructed to complete the statements: "My teacher thinks I am . . ." and "I think I am . . .". More girls than boys thought the teacher would attribute favorable qualities to them (although we know this is not so). This seems, in part, due to the way the girls pay particular heed to the approval contacts from teachers. Girls more often do what the teacher wants; for example, they show docility, relia-bility, neatness, and attentiveness, and believe they will therefore be liked more. There was also a strong relation between how favorably girls believed the teacher saw them and how favorably they saw them-selves. This effect seems to be stronger for the girls who rely more on social approval than on objective measures, a fair self-estimate of abil-ities. Self-deluded, the girls believe that conformity will bring approval.

are female teachers at fault?

Periodically, suspicions and complaints arise about the feminine atmosphere in the elementary school and the female teacher's possible bias against boys. Do female teachers feminize boys, and in so doing hinder achievement for boys? What effects would male teachers have on boys and girls?

The much-cited work of Fagot and Patterson (1969) indicates that nursery school teachers reward both boys and girls for traditionally feminine activities. These investigators defined feminine behaviors as listening to stories, painting, art work, playing in the doll corner and in the kitchen; masculine behaviors included playing in the block and truck corners, and generally climbing, running, and riding tricycles. The researchers found that teachers rewarded the girls 353 times for "feminine" behavior and only 10 times for "masculine" behavior. The boys were rewarded only 232 times for any sex-typed behavior, but 199 of those were for feminine behaviors. Over the year, however, boys did not become more apt to prefer the feminine behaviors than when they started. Peer groups were noticeably powerful in reinforcing same-sex valued by reminding each other that boys liked the boys' toys, and boys did boy things together. Girls also kept to their stereotypically proper play groups during free play.

Girls in the primary grades learn to read faster than boys. Boys demonstrate more learning and behavior disorders, repeat grades more often, and are referred for clinical help more often. Researching sex differences in reading, Felsenthal (1970) suggests that identity shifts of boys from femaleness (mother) to maleness are complicated by the dominantly feminine environment of the elementary school. At early ages, boys neglect classroom achievement and performance, because in their struggle to form masculine values, they are receiving strong cues against aggressive or independent behavior rather than encouragement toward achievement. Girls, on the other hand, flourish under the tutelage of a female teacher who expects docility and performance from them. They are not in the same conflict as the boys.

Whether or not pupils approve or respond, the school environment of the young child as represented by the female teacher pressures all students into conformity with the standards of behavior and ideals of the educational system. But, this general process differentially influences boys and girls. As mentioned before, some theorists hold that boys benefit from the external control as they learn to gauge limits and direct energies. The same process reemphasizes already existing conformity and dependency on the part of girls. Thus, girls are more solidly entrenched into sex-typed behaviors, stereotypically female. Even the close-at-hand role model of a strong, dependable, authoritative woman such as the teacher herself may do little to encourage independence in the girl at that age. It is the prescribed role of the teacher, rather than the female sex of the teacher which predicts the teacher's type of interaction with boys and girls in the classroom. It is likely that male teachers, conscious of the delineated teacher role, also maintain these patterns of interaction with students.

female versus male teachers

What happens in a classroom taught by a man? Can there be a "masculine" atmosphere in the classroom? Very few studies have controlled for sex of teacher because of the obvious scarcity of male teachers in elementary classrooms. The exact influence of male teachers on boys and their achievements is unclear. Nevertheless, the idea of male role models has been popularized as a reason for putting men into nursery and elementary school positions. There is some indication (Mueller & Cooper, 1972 unpublished) that, in a preschool setting, teacher teams of a man and a woman had the effect of increasing area use and social play for children of the opposite sex. Male teachers attracted the girls to the blocks and truck, while female teachers increased the boys' use of dressing up and art areas. The findings suggest that male-female team-teaching might maximize both boys and girls' play with cross-sex type toys, and may increase cross-sex cooperative and assertive play.

On the issue of teacher effectiveness, one study rather weakly asserts that a small number of young boys taught by a male teacher improved their reading achievement while a control group under a female teacher did not (Shinedling & Pederson, 1970). However, a variety of other projects (reported in Brophy & Good, 1973) indicate strongly that the sex of the teacher has little to do with increasing boys' reading ability. In a comparison of a husband-wife kindergarten teaching team (Brophy & Laosa, 1971) which consciously tried to associate reading skills with the man, and mathematical and spatial skills with the woman, there were no significant effects at all on sex-role differentiation, interests, motivational measures, or achievement.

Good, Sikes, & Brophy (1973) set out to compare the behavior of male and female teachers with boys and girls in 16 classes at the junior high school level. Interaction analyses showed the expected student sex difference: boys were much more active and interacted more frequently with the teachers. Teachers were more apt to ask boys process questions and to ask girls product and choice questions. Proportionately, boys' interactions with teachers were more likely to be negative than were girls' interactions. Results showed that although males and females have different teaching styles, they do not treat boys and girls differently. Only one of the 62 measures of interaction between teacher sex and student sex reached significance, and even then it showed female teachers more likely to seek out boys on work-related topics. The same kind of sex differences recorded as repeatedly occurring in classes taught by females also appear in classes taught by males.

a teacher alleviation of sex-role stereotyping

What innovations in the educational system will ensure that both sexes are treated equally while encouraging the greatest possible individual achievement? How can teachers socialize boys to control impulsive behavior and motivate girls to independent actions? How can boys be directed to verbal skills and school achievement and girls be encouraged toward creative thinking and problem solving?

Torrance, as part of his study on creativity, observed significant sex differences and attempted to manipulate these informally through the expectations of teachers (Torrance, 1965). First he asked teachers to describe incidents in which they had rewarded creative behavior in the classroom, either by listening, helping, or allowing continuation. Teachers reported 224 incidents. In 172 incidents, the sex of the children was mentioned. The ratio of 26 percent girls to 74 percent boys suggests that teachers recognize the creative behavior of the boys more often and may possibly reward the boys for creativity, while they communicate conformity to the girls. Other sections of Torrance's work show that children do much better at creativity tasks which are sex-typed. This suggests that girls may be choosing their level of creativity, based on the sex-role appropriateness of the task. In two studies where children played with scientific toys, the boys produced many more creative ideas. Torrance discussed these findings with teachers and parents and enlisted their aid in encouraging girls toward creative thinking with nonfeminine toys. The next year, when the children were retested, girls had significantly increased in creative behavior. However, during both years the student participants reported that the boys contributed better ideas than the girls. Small-scale interventions such as this provide invaluable information about the potential for change and the methodology through which teacher can encourage change. This study identified sex-typed toys and playing as a source which limits children's creativity.

Studies on the "female motive to avoid success" (Horner, 1970) indicates that group competition causes more conflict for girls and increases the likelihood that they will reject achievement opportunities in favor of social-femininity opportunities. Teachers should know that the direct mixed-sex competition (like spelling bees) is not an effective teaching tool at the high-school level. They need to be aware of the strength of same-sex peer groups and use them to make the best of interactions. Care should be taken not to jeopardize a girl's desire to be competent and a boy's neccessity to look competent by prematurely overplaying direct competition. Yet students should learn to evaluate their intellectual potential in reference to their peers. Perhaps more attention could be paid to curriculum and teaching methods designed to promote individual abilities and dispel sex typing.

A research project headed by Guttentag (1975) used a six-week curriculum intervention with 24 teachers at 3 different grade levels participating. This work examined the role of curriculum and classroom procedure in encouraging or inhibiting sex-role stereotyping. The climax of the study focused on an intervention program in which teachers consciously monitored the classroom, encouraging students to discuss sex roles and to consider nonsexist alternatives in daily classroom life.

The aim of the project was to develop and test measures, materials, and methods which could be used in schools for the purpose of expanding children's cognitive category width for the occupational, familial and socio-emotional roles of men and women. The age groups of 5 years, 9 years, and 14 years were selected since these represented strikingly different social, cognitive, and sexual periods in a child's development. The five-year-old probably experiences his first separation from the home. He has well-formed preferences that can be verified as sex-typed. In other words, he knows that boys play with bulldozers and girls play with dolls. Sex differences, he believes, are irreversible and are linked to physical or concrete facts, such as men are bigger and stronger and drive trucks. The curriculum in the Guttentag study thus was geared to change the sex-role attitudes of kindergarteners by its ties to the everyday world of the child. The category most easily changed was related to occupations. Children were informed that women can be aviators and men can be typists, that boys can be good at jumping rope and girls adept at hammering nails.

Fifth graders are at the stage of believing that social roles reflect social duties and desires. They believe that people do sex appropriate things because they want to. Fifth graders say children can do anything they want, and yet they clearly prefer sex-typed activities and hobbies. Girls and boys often are equally active, though the tomboy is beginning to feel the pressure of girls' social expectations, while the boy is trying to gain prowess in sports and games. The curriculum used with fifth graders was concerned with concepts of discrimination and prejudice against both men and women as depicted in the media and throughout history.

Ninth graders are well into the dating concerns brought on by puberty. Peer groups are an important source of values and the groups provide support for status hierarchies. Boys devote an increasing amount of energy to the instrumental concerns of achievement and independence. In return, they receive the approval of their group which supports their sense of competence and self-determination. Girls are increasingly directed toward the expressive area, especially the development of the interpersonal skills, which gained opposite-sex approval for them. Since, at this age, they have largely achieved the level of formal operational thought, the curriculum dealt with the relativistic ideas of individual rights and social roles. Issues of occupation and homemaking become increasingly powerful throughout high school. Therefore, the curriculum gave students the opportunity to discuss vocational and family expectations in the present and future.

The teachers, who voluntarily involved themselves in the intervention program, were from three school systems which represented diverse socioeconomic situations and differences in educational policies. Teachers received training in the use of the curriculum and were invited to weekly consultations to discuss the quality of work and any problems with the material. Teachers were also introduced to the research in which boys and girls were treated differently in the classroom. Teachers were shown how to treat boys and girls equally. Strategies which promote cross-sex play and cooperation were shared and discussed. Throughout the intervention program, it became clear that the teachers were the vital links in promoting nonsexist attitudes in the children in this short-term intervention, although the curriculum, activities, administration, peer groups, and parents provided the necessary tools and support for the teachers.

descriptions and results from the intervention effort

The intervention effort had diverse effects on the three different age groups. Initially, the kindergartners categorized people in a stereotypical way. They emphasized that men and women had different jobs and spent their time doing different things. A woman could not be a mother and an aviator and a father always went to work, except on weekends, when he would play with the children. Following the intervention, kindergartners significantly increased their ability to understand that the same job could be held by either a man or a woman. After the intervention, the girls especially were more likely to place men in interpersonal jobs like social worker, teacher, and salesclerk. However, the children did not change their attitudes toward the socio-emotional roles which men and women could play.

The fifth graders presented a mixed picture on the issue of sexism. They believed that women could have jobs, but that sometimes, women were not good at their work and sometimes had to desert helpless children to have jobs. Fifth graders always put men and women in sex-stereotyped private routines and hobbies. Boys and men were ascribed particularly restrictive socio-emotional roles: they lacked problems, they were active in sports, and they were seen as economically successful. Girls readily accepted a socio-emotional emphasis as an important part of their roles. They also showed a tendency toward negative self-esteem (for instance, being socially desirable) reflected in their feeling that they were not as beautiful as they should be. At the fifth-grade level, the intervention primarily affected the girls. Their belief that women could have varied and successful careers was strengthened. Their perceptions of the qualities of ideal boys and ideal girls converged, denoting a new sensitivity toward non-sexist qualities of personhood. They were only scattered changes in attitudes about men's roles. The boys showed virtually no change on any item.

Ninth graders had fairly well-developed attitudes about sex roles. They believed that socio-emotional qualities were essential for women, but also important for men. Girls were forceful in supporting women in occupations, while boys were suspicious of employed women. Girls more often presented the women in a dual career and marriage situation. Interestingly, ninth-grade girls were privately sure that they were ugly, although they wanted to be beautiful, that is, socially desirable. Ninth graders in general reacted negatively to the non-sexist message of the intervention. Boys' views became more stereotyped after the intervention. Peer-group support for boys was particularly strong in discounting the import of the non-sexist issues.

Yet ninth-grade girls, following the intervention, improved their sense of personal attractiveness and self-esteem. Apparently the intervention succeeded in showing them a variety of alternative ways in which women could achieve status, other than through social attractiveness. Although both sexes were more stereotyped in their attitudes toward the opposite-sex role, than their own, nevertheless, boys were stronger in upholding the stereotypes for girls' roles and vise versa. From these results, it appears that a little intervention of a nonsexist type may be worse than none at all for ninth-grade boys. Yet, a strong, thorough, and intense classroom exploration of nonsexist role possibilities can have a liberating effect even on the sex-role stereotypes of ninth-grade boys.

Perhaps the most meaningful and relevant finding from the intervention program came from the examination of changes in individual classrooms. The amount of children's attitude change in the direction of non-stereotyping closely correlated with an independent measure of the individual teacher's effectiveness in implementing the curriculum. In other words, the teacher who cared about the issue of sexism in roles and society and who used the provided curriculum regularly and creatively, could change the attitudes of their students even in a six-week intervention effort. Even in a ninth-grade classroom, where the teacher used the nonsexist curriculum regularly and enthusiastically, not only were there significant attitudinal changes in girls, but boys changed to nonstereotyped views in many areas. It is the teacher's use of nonsexist curricula and classroom intervention patterns which can dramatically open up children's sex role stereotypes.

summary

In conclusion, it is clear that teachers play a major role in inculcating and supporting children's sex-role values and standards. The educational system, through its curriculum, activities, administration, budgeting, and explicit policies, either passively or actively supported differential treatment for boys and girls. In schools, where the primary emphasis is on achievement, girls have relied on the social approval of teachers in elementary school for their classroom reinforcements. During adolescence, girls receive more group pressure to emphasize social skills and tend to drop off in their intellectual endeavors. Boys receive constant and consistent feedback in classrooms which helps them to establish and realistically evaluate their abilities, while controlling their impulses. In adolescence, they receive strong encouragement in the schools to achieve. Teachers often unknowingly support these patterns by their classroom policies of discipline and approval.

Having a male or female teacher makes little difference. The problem lies with the teacher's own role conception. The teacher attempts to meet students' needs, which are stereotypically viewed as calming down the boys and giving emotional support to the girls. Teachers who are aware of the circular sex differences/sex-differential reinforcement pattern can intervene and can stimulate each individual student to his/her fullest intellectual, social, and physical potential.

The impact of nonsexist curricular interventions and nonsexist education policies lies in the hand of the teachers. Even the influences of peer groups can be mediated by the teacher's classroom interactions. Teachers control the bases for reinforcement in the classroom. Both men and women can effectively use nonsexist curricula in the classroom to undo the sex-role stereotyping of boys and girls.

references

Brophy, J., & Good, T. Feminization of American elementary schools. *Phi Delta Kappan*, 1973, *54*, 564-566.

Brophy, J., & Good, T. Teacher communication of differential expectations for children's classroom performance: Some behavioral data. *Journal of Educational Psychology*, 1970, *61*, 365-374.

Brophy J., & Laosa, L. *Effect of a male teacher on the sex typing of kindergarten children*. Proceedings, APA 79th Annual Convention, 1971, *6*, 169-170.

Cherry, L. Pre-school teacher-child dyad: Sex differences in verbal interaction. *Child Development*, 1975, *46*, 532-537.

Crandall, V. J., Katkowsky, W., & Preston, A. Motivational and ability determinants of young children's intellectual achievement behaviors. *Child Development*, 1962, *33*, 643-661.

Crandall, V. J., & Rabson, A. Children's repetitive choices in an intellectual achievement situation following success and failure. *Journal of Genetic Psychology*, 1960, *97*, 161-168.

Davidson, H. H., & Lang, G. Children's perceptions of their teacher's feeling toward them related to self-perception, school achievement and behavior. *Journal of Experimental Education*, 1960, *29*, 107-118.

Davis, O. L., & Slobodian, J. J. Teacher behavior toward boys and girls during first grade instruction. *American Educational Research Journal*, 1967, *4*, 261-269.

Donovan, V. *Elementary school teachers' sex role attitudes and classroom behavior towards girls and boys*. Unpublished paper, June 1973.

D'Uren, M. The image of women in textbooks. In Gornick & Moran (Eds.), *Women in sexist society*. New York: Basic Books, 1971.

Fagot, B., & Patterson, G. R. Analysis of reinforcing contingencies in sex-role behaviors in the pre-school child. *Developmental Psychology*, 1969, *1*, 563-568.

Federbush, M. *Let them aspire: A report on the Ann Arbor schools*. Pittsburgh, Pa.: KNOW, Inc., 1975.

Felsenthal, H. *Sex differences in teacher-pupil interaction in first grade reading instruction*. Paper presented at American Educational Research Associates, Minneapolis, 1970.

Felsenthal, H. *Pupil sex as a variable in teacher perception of classroom behavior*. Paper presented at AERA, New York, 1971.

Good, T., & Brophy, J. Behavioral expression of teacher attitudes. *Journal of Educational Psychology*, 1973, *63*, 617.

Good, T., Sikes, J. N., & Brophy, J. Effect of teacher sex and student sex on classroom interaction. *Journal of Educational Psychology*, 1973, *65*, 74-87.

Guttentag, M., & Bray, H. *Undoing sex stereotypes*. New York: McGraw Hill, in press.

Hartley, R. A developmental view of female sex role definition and identification. *Merril-Palmer Quarterly*, 1964, *10*, 3-16.

Horner, M. S. Feminity and successful achievement: Basic incongruity. In J. Bardwick, E. Douvan, M. S. Horner & D. Gutman, *Femine personality and conflict.* Belmont, Calif.: Brooks Cole Publishing Co., 1970.

Iglitzin, L. B. A child's eye view of sex roles. *Today's Education,* 1972, *61*(9), 23-25.

Jackson, P. W. *Life in classrooms.* New York: Holt, Rinehart & Winston, 1968.

Jackson, P. W., & Getzels, J. W. Psychological health and classroom functioning: A study of dissatisfaction among adolescents. *Journal of Educational Psychology,* 1959, *50,* 295-300.

Jackson, P. W. & Lahaderne, H. M. Inequalities of teacher-pupil contacts. *Psychology in the Schools,* 1967, *4,* 204-211.

Kohlberg, L. A cognitive-developmental analysis of children's sex-role concepts and attitudes. In E. Maccoby, *The development of sex differences.* Palo Alto, Calif.: Stanford University Press, 1966.

Korner, A. F. Sex differences in newborns with special reference to differences in the organization of oral behavior. *Journal of Child Psychology and Psychiatry,* 1973, *14,* 19-29.

Lee, P., & Gropper, N. Sex-role culture and educational practice. *Harvard Educational Review,* 1974, *44,* 369-410.

Levitan, T. E., & Chananine, J. D. Responses of female primary teachers to sex-typed behavior in male and female children. *Child Development,* 1972, *43,* 1309-1316.

Levy, B. The school's role in the sex-role stereotyping of girls: A feminist review of the literature. *Feminist Studies,* 1972. *1*(1), 5-23.

Maccoby, E. E. *The development of sex differences.* Stanford: Stanford University Press, 1966.

Maccoby, E., & Jacklin, C. N. *The psychology of sex differences.* Stanford: Stanford University Press, 1974.

Martin, R. Student sex and behavior as determinants of the type and frequency of teacher-student contacts. *Journal of School Psychology,* 1972, *10,* 339-344.

McIntyre, D., Morrison, A., & Sutherland, J. Social and educational variables relating to teachers' assessments of primary school pupils. *British Journal of Educational Psychology.* 1966, *36,* 272-279.

Meyer, W., & Thompson, G. Sex differences in the distribution of teacher approval and disapproval among sixth grade children. *Journal of Educational Psychology,* 1956, *47,* 385-396.

Meyers, R. E., & Torrance, E. P. *Invitations to speaking and writing creatively.* Eugene, Oregon: Perceptive Publishing, 1962.

Montanelli, P. S., & Hill, K. T. Children's achievement expectations and performance as a function of two consecutive reinforcement experiences, sex of self, and sex of experimentor. *Journal of Personality and Social Psychology,* 1969, *13,* 115-128.

Moriarity, A. E. Coping patterns of preschool children in response to intelligence test demands. *Genetic Psychology Monographs.* 1961. *64,* 3-127.

Mueller, E., & Cooper, B. The effect of preschool teacher's sex on children's cognitive growth and sexual identity. Final Report to H.E.W. Office of Education, August, 1972.

Polansky, L. Group social climate and the teacher's supportiveness of group status systems. *Journal of Education Sociology,* 1954, *28*; 115-123.

Ricks, F., & Pyke, S. Teacher perceptions and attitudes that foster or maintain sex role differences. *Interchange,* 1973, *4,* 26-33.

Saario, T., Jacklin, C., & Tittle, C. Sex role stereotyping in the public schools. *Harvard Educational Review*, 1973, *43*, 386-416.

Sears, P., & Feldman, D. H. Teacher interventions with boys and girls. *National Elementary Principal*, 1966, *46*, 30-35.

Sears, R. R. Relation of early socialization experiences to self concepts and gender role in middle childhood. *Child Development*. 1970, *41*(2), 267-289.

Serbin, L., O'Leary, K. D., Kent, R., & Tonick, I. A comparison of teacher response to the preacademic and problem behavior of boys and girls. *Child Development*, 1973, *44*, 796-804.

Shinedling, M., & Pederson, D. Effects of sex of teacher and student on children's gain in quantitative and verbal performance. *Journal of Psychology*, 1970, *76*, 79-85.

Spaulding, R. L. *Achievement, creativity, and self-concept correlates of teacher-pupil transactions in elementary schools*. Cooperative Research Project No. 1352, D.H.E.W. Office of Education, Washington, D.C., 1963.

Stein, A. H., Pholy, S. R., & Mueller, E. *Sex typing of achievement areas as a determinant of children's efforts and achievement*. Paper presented at Sex-Research in Child Development, Santa Monica, Calif., March 1969.

Stein, A. H., Smithells, J. Age and sex difference in children's sex-role standards about achievement. *Journal of Developmental Psychology*, 1969, *1*, 252.

Torrance, E. P. Changing reactions of preadolescent girls to tasks requiring creative scientific thinking. *Journal of Genetic Psychology*, 1963, *102*, 217-223.

Torrance, E. P. *Rewarding creative behavior: Experiment in classroom creativity*. Englewood Cliffs, New Jersey: Prentice-Hall, 1965.

women and work around the world: a cross-cultural examination of sex division of labor and sex status

It has been suggested that there are three main roads to power: economic, political, and military (for example, Lenski, 1966). For women, the empirical evidence shows no society where their political or military power even equals that of men. However, there are a number of groups where women enjoy more economic power than men—and fairly equal status in other areas as well (Blumberg, 1974a).

So for women, the only feasible route to equal status has proved to be the economic one. But the evidence also suggests that there is a toll that must be paid to enter the economic route to power and equal status. This toll is labor in the main productive activities of the society. On the one hand, work is not enough, and there are a number of societies where women do most of the labor yet are treated little better than slaves (for instance, the Azande; see Sanday, 1973). But, on the other hand, in groups where women do not contribute much to "bringing home the bacon," their status has been found to be invariably low (Sanday, 1973).

In short, productive labor is for women an apparently necessary (although insufficient) precondition for equality. To what extent are women involved in productive labor? And under what conditions do women work? These are the two main topics of the present paper.[1]

[1]As I shall discuss in the Summary and Conclusions, I am engaged in a larger research project on factors affecting the position of women. I have formulated a preliminary theory, which begins by predicting under what conditions women work in productive activities. The theory hypothesizes conditions under which women's labor may be translated into economic power. Finally, it predicts the kinds of equal opportunities that women's economic power will pay for (Blumberg, 1974a). Presently, I am attempting a partial and preliminary test of the theory. Toward this end, I have coded most of the main variables of my theory in a pilot sample of 61 preindustrial societies, using the Human Relations Area Files. Some preliminary results are indicated at various points in this paper (to be reported in Blumberg, forthcoming). Finally, to get additional data for this paper, I have done some special computer runs on Murdock's 1170-society Ethnographic Atlas. Results from these runs are referred to at several places in the paper.

As we shall see, societies where women do not contribute much to family support are in a great minority from an evolutionary or worldwide perspective. The fact that today's industrial societies all have recently emerged from an agrarian past of low female economic productivity and subjugated female status helps explain the ethnocentrism of the predominant view of women's work and worth. But we should not let this ethnocentric heritage cloud our theories of woman's past position and—more important in an era of rapid social change—her future potential.

At one extreme of the prevailing view of women and work, Charlotte Perkins Gilman wrote in 1894: "The female of genus *homo* is economically dependent on the male. He is her food supply" (Babcox & Belkin, 1971, p. 139). In the 1940s and 1950s, Talcott Parsons, perhaps the most influential American sociologist of those decades, was writing a somewhat more technically phrased version of the same view: The husband is the main provider, "whereas the wife is primarily the giver of love . . ." (Parsons & Bales, 1955, p. 151).

How much more than love do women contribute? George Peter Murdock has compiled data on hundreds of contemporary groups in his life work, *Ethnographic Atlas* (1967). Using it, Aronoff and Crano (1975) calculate that women contribute 44 percent of the food supply as a world average. Women are not parasites.

Nevertheless, the range of variation of women's work is quite great. In my own calculations from the Ethnographic Atlas (using the 1170-society computer tape version), I found that in about 2 percent of the societies, the women contributed virtually nothing to the food supply; at the other extreme, in roughly 2 percent of societies women contributed two-thirds or more. Since women's economically productive work is the first precondition to power and equality, and the empirical evidence shows such high variation, how can we predict how much productive labor women in a given society are likely to do?

Specifically, I suggest that two major factors influence female's economic productivity: first, the extent to which the activity is compatible with childrearing, especially nursing babies (Brown, 1970). Second, labor demand versus supply—whether an excess of available men means that some take women's jobs away, or whether a shortage of men means that women are brought in to do even those tasks which are incompatible with simultaneous childraising obligations.

The evidence for both pre-industrial and industrial societies is given in the next part of this paper. Part 1 is an evolutionary overview of women and work in societies at four levels of societal complexity. For the three pre-industrial levels (hunting and gathering, hoe horticulture, and plow agriculture), the broad outlines of female contribution to the food supply can be ascertained largely from the first factor, that is, mainly by examining the compatibility of the main subsistence activities with baby-tending. Thus, in gathering and hoe horticulture groups, women tend to be the major economic providers. Their status in such societies tends to be considerably better than in the plow agrarian—and some industrial—societies where their productivity is also much less. Part 2 of the paper consists of brief sketches of selected modern societies, industrial or industrializing ones. Here, the main activities are done away from home and children and thus are relatively incompatible with simultaneous child care, yet women work in varying proportions in all these groups. So in Part 2 the focus is more strongly on the second factor, demand for labor vs. supply, in accounting for the position of women in their group's labor force.

1.   an evolutionary overview

In this section, we shall examine four types of societies, representing increasing levels of societal complexity: 1) hunting and gathering, the least complex; 2) horticultural, based on shifting hoe cultivation; 3) agrarian, which necessitates plow cultivation on permanent fields (hoe and plow cultures are quite different as we shall see); and finally, 4) industrial and industrializing societies, the most complex.[2]

hunting and gathering societies

In the two million or more years that humans have walked the earth, for all but about the last ten thousand we were hunters and gatherers. The mystique surrounding hunting and gathering societies is that of "Man the Hunter" (Lee & DeVore, 1968), and indeed, evidence from hundreds of societies shows that hunting is almost exclusively a male activity (Murdock & Provost, 1973). But although men hunt, these same sources show that it is women who do most of the gathering. Moreover, in virtually all but arctic hunting-gathering groups, the major part of the food supply, typically 60 to 80 percent, according to Lee and DeVore, is not hunted—it is gathered. In my calculations with the *Ethnographic Atlas* computer tape, I found information on the sexual division of labor for 85 groups whose main economic activity was gathering, and in 86 percent of these women proved to be the predominant labor force. In sum, women tend to bring home the main part of the diet. Nonetheless, most hunting-gathering groups prefer the food hunted by the men (Woodburn, 1968), and some even have a word in their language for "meatlessness." As Margaret Mead (1949) has observed, whatever men do is considered more important by the culture.

But what, then, of the position of women? In general, anthropological evidence from Hobhouse, Wheeler and Ginsberg (1915) onwards agrees that it is fairly good. Hunting-gathering societies generally are the world's most egalitarian (Lenski, 1970). Despite the strong sexual

[2]I am characterizing societies in terms of their main economic activity, or "subsistence base." This is a common technique in social science articles written from an evolutionary slant (see Goldschmidt, 1959; Lenski, 1970; Lomax et al., 1968, for related typologies).

division of labor, women tend to be full economic partners (Leacock, 1972). They also tend not to be repressed sexually: In my own work based on a pilot sample of 61 preindustrial societies, including ten hunting-gathering groups, I have found that the hunters and gatherers rank highest in warm, cooperative relations between the sexes. Moreover, brides rarely are required to be virgins (a rule corelated with female oppression).

horticultural
societies

Originally, it was thought that cultivation was some sort of discovery, as though one day in the Middle East about ten thousand years ago, Thor informed an incredulous Og: "Seeds sprout into plants!" Whereupon the entire society proceeded to take advantage of Thor's magnificent finding (Macneish, 1964 p. 533). But recent archeological and anthropological evidence has drawn a very different picture. First, no known hunt-gathering group is ignorant of the connection between plants and the seeds from which they sprout (Flannery, 1971 p. 81). Second, cultivation developed gradually over millennia; and it appears that since intensification of cultivation is usually more and harder work (Boserup, 1965), people adopted it only when driven to increase their food supply, most likely because of local population pressure (Binford, 1971; Meyers, 1971). Third, given the sexual division of labor in hunting-gathering societies, early cultivation and its development almost surely seems to have been the work of women (Childe, 1964, pp. 65-66). Given the many archeologists who agree with V. Gordon Childe in viewing the emergence of horticultural societies as the first great social revolution in human history (Lenski, 1970 p. 194), the continuing invisibility of women in most books about this era seems unjustified, although not surprising.

Yet, probably "the earliest Neolithic (prehistoric horticultural) societies through their range in time and space gave woman the highest status she has ever known" (Hawkes & Woolley, 1963, p. 264). These same authors consider that the widespread remains of mother goddess clay figurines and shrines indicate that woman was religiously as well as economically important in nearly all Neolithic groups from Southwest Asia to Britain (cited in Leavitt, 1971, p. 394).

What about the horticultural societies surviving into the present era? Most of these are located in sub-Saharan Africa or in the islands of the Pacific. In computer runs using the *Ethnographic Atlas*, I have found that only about one-fifth of the societies in which shifting hoe cultivation is the main economic activity have predominantly male labor forces. This formation is based on the 376 such societies for which sex division of labor data are available. For Africa as a whole, it recently has been estimated that 70 percent of the cultivation is in the hands of women (Economic Commission for Africa, 1974). In general, hoe horticulture is an activity which easily can be coordinated with child care—and the contemporary data show that it is.

The majority of women in contemporary horticultural societies live in Africa in groups where they must reside with their husband's kin, and are brought in as an outside labor force to farm lands they do not own.[3] Moreover, they are still quite likely to live in groups practicing polygyny. To the extent that women do not control property and the products they produce, female status seems to suffer. Nevertheless, women in horticultural societies more often than not can dispose of part of their production, often in market trading. In fact, there are few horticultural groups that seem to give women a really low status or treat them little better than slave labor. Finally, in my own 61-society pilot sample, which includes 13 horticultural groups, I found considerable equality between the sexes on certain "life options." This proved especially true of divorces where horticulturist women usually enjoy equal or greater rights than their husbands to end a union. Also, I found considerable premarital sexual freedom for young women. The horticultural societies in my sample rank first in having egalitarian (vs. male supremacist) sexual ideology.

agrarian societies

Of the four types of societies discussed in this section, agrarian ones as a group represent the low point of women's status. The evidence in the Ethnographic Atlas shows us that most agrarian societies have a male-dominated division of labor; moreover, Michaelson and Goldschmidt's comparative study of 46 peasant societies reveals the near-universal prevalence of female subjugation (1971). Among the upper classes of traditional agrarian societies, who typically have lived in the cities (Sjoberg, 1960), such institutions of female seclusion as purdah (in India), foot-binding (in China), veiling, and the harem have reached their greatest intensity (Boserup, 1970). In other words, among the poor peasants of agrarian societies, women could not be totally shackled to the house because for certain tasks their labor was needed, especially during the peak agricultural season. Thus, while subservient to their husbands, they were less restricted in their activities than their less poverty-stricken counterparts. Upper-class women, while outranking lower-class people of both sexes, nevertheless typically spent their lives as caged birds. Compared to the peasant women, they were virtually without economic value for their men.

[3]It should be noted that in those horticultural societies in which male-dominated hunting and herding are least important (accounting for less than 15 percent of subsistence), Lenski and Lenski (1974:192) show the maximum incidence of maternal kin institutions. Fully 39 percent of such societies are "matrilineal" (have organized descent groups traced through the mother only), and in addition, 22 percent of them are "matrilocal" (require the newly wed couple to live with the bride's kin). Matrilineal or matrilocal groups do not automatically mean high status for women, although their status seems generally better in such societies than in those dominated by patriarchal institutions (Leavitt, 1971).

Agrarian societies, which replaced the hoe with the plow, arose in the Middle East around 5,000 years ago and spread through Asia and Europe. Specifically, agrarian societies are based on plow cultivation of cereal crops in permanent fields. There are two main kinds of agrarian groups, those practicing dry cultivation of these crops versus those who irrigate. In general, the labor contribution and status of women is higher among the irrigationists, particularly if the crop is paddy rice and especially if the women do market trading as well. Labor demands in wet rice agriculture are so great that societies rarely have the option or the luxury of freezing their women out of production. Boserup (1970) has shown that in the agrarian societies of Southeast Asia and Indonesia, which are based on irrigated rice agriculture (and where females are active in trade), the position of women is better than in agrarian societies practicing dry farming (such as Northern India and much of the Middle East). In these dry agrarian regions there usually is a surplus, not a shortage, of male labor (Lenski, 1966) and, conversely, the tasks of tending the distant fields often are difficult to combine with baby care. So the women's economic importance is not great.

In these societies, even religion is patriarchal, and reinforces women's lowly status (Boserup, 1970). But religion per se does not seem responsible for this. For example, in those areas of Indonesia where women have long been active in rice cultivation and market trading, hundreds of years of Islam, following centuries of Hinduism, have not undermined most aspects of their relatively high status (Vreede-de Stuers, 1967). Despite such bright spots, however, agrarian societies tend to oppress women sexually, economically, legally, politically, and religiously.

industrial societies

Except for horticultural Africa, where the process of modernization seems to be partially undermining women's traditional economic importance (Boserup, 1970), industrialization seems to have provided women with new opportunities. For example, the emergence of widespread wage labor has constituted a new option for women, even if the work is ill-paid.

Industrialization flowered first in nineteenth century England. Employers learned early in the industrialization process that women (and children) were cheaper to hire than men. In England, for example, Smelser cites figures showing that the introduction of the power loom meant that "women and boys in factories replaced men who had worked (as weavers) at home" (Smelser, 1959, p. 200, quoting Hammond, 1920). However, sex segregation of occupations also emerged quite early (Oppenheimer, 1973), so that males were able to limit competition from lower-paid females. Notwithstanding, industrialization greatly increased the size of a nation's economy and its demand for labor. As a result, female employment has gradually increased to the point where it is now important in all industrial nations, capitalist and socialist alike. In these countries, women comprise about a quarter to a half of the entire labor force (see, for example, Sullerot, 1971). Nevertheless, numerous studies show that females still earn much less than their male counterparts.

Industrialization also marks the first time that women have participated on a large scale in production away from home, family property, and children. Furthermore, we should note that the status of women, sexually, economically, legally, politically, and religiously, slowly tended toward general improvement as industrialization advanced in previously agrarian societies. And, of course, all of Europe, as well as the United States and Japan, were characterized by agrarian economies at the start of industrialization.

To speculate, perhaps this agrarian heritage of low female productivity and status has played a part in the persistent view of both social scientists and mass media that economically, women are excess baggage. In contrast to this erroneous ethnocentrism, we have seen that in the two types of society where the main subsistence activity is easily compatible with care of unweaned children (gathering and hoe horticulture), women tend to bring home the major share of the food. On the whole, their status in such societies tends to be considerably better than that of their less productive sisters in agrarian (and some industrial) societies.

Let us continue our exploration of the economic role of women by turning now to sketches of women's work and position in a small number of industrial or industrializing groups. In all of the cases, the main subsistence activities are not easily compatible with child-care responsibilities (even though bottle feeding now makes this a cultural, not a biological, constraint), so we must look to the economy's needs for specific types of labor to interpret women's changing economic participation.

2. women's work and women's status in the contemporary world: selected cases

United States

The first case to be considered is that of the United States, a country where many authors assumed that the revolution for sexual equality had been fought and won, until a rising women's movement raised their consciousness. (In 1940, for example, a book actually entitled *Victory, How Women Won It* was published.) In the United States, most sociology, both popular and professional, is built up around a mythical and model white middle-class way of life. Among this group we long have been told that the husband is the principal breadwinner, while the wife stays home reading *McCall's*, tending the children, and buying the consumer goods on which the economy flourishes (see, for example, Parsons, 1942). Furthermore, it was long held that even though their roles are so disparate, husband and wife are relatively equal in the United States.

The actual facts are quite different. In the first place, United States women are increasingly likely to work. In 1900, only 20 percent of American females ages 18 to 64 were in the labor force, but by 1970, this figure had risen to 50 percent (U.S. Bureau of Labor Statistics, 1971, p. A-10). Also, by that year, 60 percent of female workers were married women living with their husbands (Sokoloff, 1974). But even though labor force participation has been increasing in recent years, rewards have been declining relative to those of American males. Knudsen (1969) shows from United States Census data that there was a gradual but persistent decline in women's occupational, economic, and educational achievements, compared to those of men, in the period 1940 to 1964. And Ehrlich (1974, p. 2) also uses United States Census Bureau figures to document the increasing gap in the ratio of women's to men's earnings. Comparing only full-time, year-round workers, Ehrlich shows that in 1955, American women made 64 percent as much as men. By 1970, the figure had declined to 59 percent (women's median—$5,403 vs. male median—$9,104, so that for every dollar a man earned, a woman earned only fifty-nine cents).

If the relative reward has been declining, why has the female labor force increased so sharply, especially in the period beginning with the 1940s? Sokoloff (1974) has shown empirically that most women in the United States work out of sheer economic necessity, for the standard of living of even middle-class households often can be maintained only by more than one wage earner. And the reason these women have been able to work has been shown by Oppenheimer (1973) to be economic demand.

Oppenheimer notes that in 1900, the few women who participated in the labor force tended to do so before marriage and children. As it happened, women by that year were increasingly monopolizing precisely those sectors of the labor force destined to undergo the greatest expansion in subsequent decades: clerical and service jobs. Slowly, between 1900 and 1940, labor demand pulled in married women, but mainly those without school-age children. By World War II, not only was Rosie the Riveter fully employed, but the economy had expanded to the point where married women with school-age children had joined their sisters in the labor force. After World War II, the likes of Rosie—highly paid women in "male preserve" manufacturing jobs—were forcibly laid off (Tobias & Anderson, 1973), and, as Betty Friedan (1963) has it, the feminine mystique settled upon the land.

But Oppenheimer shows that more women continued to join the labor force, especially after 1960. By then, the economy had grown to a state where it could fulfill its labor needs only by bringing in the last major untapped female group, mothers of preschool children. In the decade 1960-1969, for example, the proportion of working married women, aged 20-24 (husbands present) with preschool children rose by 82 percent from 18 percent in 1960 to 33 percent in 1969 (Oppenheimer, 1973, p. 947). More generally, during the years of the "feminine mystique," the 1950s, as few as six out of 100 women with preschool children worked, but by 1970, the overall figure was about 30 percent (Blakkan, 1972).

Given prevailing attitudes toward working mothers of young children, the mothers of preschoolers who worked during the 1950s included mostly lower-income women, plus a few career women who did not leave their jobs when their children were born. Recently, however, the range of mothers of preschool children entering the labor force has broadened considerably to include many middle-class mothers. Some of these may be working for reasons of personal fulfillment; more of them are probably working in order to provide the standard of living to which they aspire but for which their husbands' income alone is insufficient (Sokoloff, 1974). In support of this view, Oppenheimer (1974) shows that within each professional category, it is the wives of the relatively lower-paid men in the category who are most likely to be in the labor force.

The lesson of the United States might be that economic demand was powerful enough in every instance to draw workers into the production force, even female workers constrained by the then-prevailing ideology from working outside the home. If this is the case, we should be able to test whether this lesson can be generalized across other industrializing and industrial societies.

Soviet Union

In the case of the Soviet Union, women are a much more important part of the labor force, both in status and in numbers. Many more Russian than American women have high-status jobs as scientists and professionals. Partly as a result of the tremendous number of men killed during World War II, about one-half of the Soviet labor force is female. According to Goldberg (1972), 80 percent of urban women in the prime child-rearing years, 20 to 39, are in the labor force. In Russia, women not only do urban industrial jobs, but since World War II it is women—and often middle-aged ones at that—who also do the traditionally male farming jobs. In fact, it is estimated that up to 73 percent of unmechanized and very strenuous farming activities are being done by females (Goldberg, 1972). Moreover, this percentage represents millions of women because as Goldberg notes, agricultural workers accounted for close to half of the labor force until recently.

Yet, in the Soviet Union, for all their economic importance, women do not share very greatly in the political power centralized in the Communist Party. Only about 3 percent of the current Central Committee consists of women; and, as in the United States, they are found as rarely in top government jobs (Goldberg, 1972).

Japan

The women's labor situation is much more oppressive in another industrial country, Japan. Because of the great World War II casualties and close to thirty years of economic expansion, Japanese women are necessary to the labor market, but they are less than equal to men in the market. Ginzberg (1971) paints the following picture: about 40 percent of the work force is female, a high proportion for a nonsocialist industrial nation. More than 50 percent of females work; the highest rate is 71 percent of women 20 to 24, dropping to about 50 percent of women 25 to 29, and fluctuating between 50 and 60 percent until the rate starts declining for women aged 55 to 64 (Ginzberg, p. 94).

But these rates are deceptive. Ginzberg shows that the large numbers of older working women are mainly agricultural workers, and these are mainly unpaid. Fully 36 percent of the 19 million Japanese women in the labor force work on farms, and there are a million more women farmers than men. But about 80 percent of female farmers are unpaid family workers, and more than half of all farm families' incomes are earned away from the farm. This has meant that "the high rate of savings that has been of critical importance to the country's rapid growth was stimulated by the fact that many women ran the family farm while their husbands found industrial jobs" (Ginzberg, p. 95).

What about females not employed on farms? Ginzberg documents that these are typically low-paid young women who work until marriage and then are forced to leave by employer and tradition. Ginzberg discusses Japan as a land where male wages are geared to seniority. Thus:

The importance of a supply of female employees who will work at low wages is underscored by the fact that for women production workers, taking the wages of the age group from 20-24 as 100, the wages of the next group, 25-29, is 101. For men, meanwhile, for whom the seniority principle operates, those aged 40-49 earn 170! When the wage differentials of nonproduction workers are compared, for men the wages rise to 256 in the 40-49 group, while the comparable figure for women is 150 (p. 95).

In short, the sharply rising costs of keeping men on the payroll are avoided by the employment of women, especially young ones whose rapid turnover results in their earning little more than the entry wage. And that wage is low.

The other major gain that accrues to employers in hiring women evolves from the fact that even today a woman production worker earns only about half the salary of the average male with the same tenure. The discrepancy with respect to new production workers is even wider (pp. 95-96).

As for the future, Ginzberg notes that the supply of young women workers "is being radically reduced by a combination of demographic and educational developments." The solution would seem to be the incorporation of large numbers of mature married females into the non-agricultural work force. But it remains to be seen whether this will be accompapanied by an improvement in the relative position of women workers in male-dominated Japan.

Venezuela

So far we have looked briefly at economically expanding *industrial* nations—The United States, the Soviet Union, and Japan. Venezuela is a good example of that much rarer breed—the economically expanding *industrializing* nation. For the last generation, Venezuela's oil-based economy has been having a fairly consistent boom. During the early years of the boom, the nation was under the Perez-Jimenez dictatorship (1948-1958). His immigration policies brought hundreds of thousands of Southern Europeans to the small country (see, for example, Kritz, 1973). When he was overthrown, the immigration laws were revised and employment laws changed to force the oil companies and other modern industrial enterprises to employ more native Venezuelans. This was of immediate benefit to Venezuelan men, especially educated ones. The oil boom continued (except during the years 1958 through 1961) and the government's share of oil revenues grew larger and larger during the course of the 1960s and early 1970s. At the same time the government also expanded and the need for professionals of many kinds became more pressing.

The only way to fill the ever-growing demands for bureaucrats and professionals from many different fields was to tap the last legal market for such jobs, namely Venezuelan women (Blumberg, 1973). Employers were of course, highly selective, hiring only the women with most education and skills. At this time Venezuelan women are only about 20 percent of the labor force (*Encuesta del Hogar*, 1970), half the rate of Japan. But at upper levels, 18.8 percent of Venezuelan working women versus only 6.3 percent of their male counterparts held professional or technical jobs in 1970 (*Encuesta del Hogar*, 1970). (In the United States for that year, the percentages were roughly 14 percent for each sex). And Venezuelan women are being well educated; large numbers of them are obtaining degrees in fields where American women receive only a tiny fraction of the diplomas.

Let us examine the figures for Venezuelan women graduated in a selection of "nontraditional" fields. The most recent figures (1969) unfortunately do not include the graduates of Central University, the country's largest institution for higher education. The numbers are small, in proportion to the relatively small population of Venezuela, but they do present an interesting picture.

Table 1. *proportion of Venezuelan university degrees earned by women in selected "non-traditional" fields, 1969**

Fields	*Percent*	*(N)*
Pharmacy	81.4	(35)
Dentistry	67.4	(43)
Architecture	51.5	(33)
Economics	41.4	(70)
Law	36.7	(188)
Business Administration-Accounting	35.7	(70)

*Excludes Central University, the nation's largest; data shown are for Universidad Central Occidental, Universidad del Zulia, Universidad de los Andes, Universidad Catolica Andres Bello. Source: Urbaneja and Millar (1971:43), based on *Memoria y Cuenta 1969-70*, Ministry of Education, pp. 494, 501, 513, 519.

Not all nontraditional fields have been "invaded" to the same extent by Venezuelan university women. The same source shows, for example, that 23.2 percent of the 297 medicine degrees went to females in 1969. But, interestingly enough, only 66.7 percent of the 12 nursing degrees were won by women in this traditionally all-female field. How does this table compare with United States data? There's almost no comparison! In the United States, to give two examples, women received only 0.8 percent of the dentistry degrees and 3.4 percent of the law degrees in 1964-1965 (Epstein, 1970:60).

Israel — the kibbutz

We have been discussing the labor forces of three nations, in which an expanding economy or a sudden hole in the demographic pyramid caused by war or by migration has increased the demand for women in the market, regardless of previously prevailing ideology. In contrast to these situations, there is the case of the Israeli kibbutz, where the opposite condition prevails.

In Israel, a group of idealistic East European Jewish founders (who were largely male) established an agrarian socialist experiment which has thrived for half a century. In fact, the kibbutz has remained true to its founding principles in almost every respect save that of sexual equality. One of the principles which the kibbutz was founded upon was the emancipation and equal status of women and their participation in production. As it happened, kibbutz women, in a process of attrition, were eased out of agrarian production and into the domestic and child-care services from which they were supposed to have been liberated.

The main reason for this attrition was the techno-economic base of the kibbutz, namely agriculture. Everywhere it exists, an agrarian economy has proven unfavorable to women (see Blumberg, 1974b; 1976a). In fairness, the kibbutz founders undoubtedly were unaware of the cross-cultural evidence that the agrarian labor force tends to be predominantly male. (This is so, I suggest, largely because the demands of agrarian production cannot conveniently be combined with child rearing. And, except for planting and harvesting, agrarian production does not need sufficient labor to require female participation when the demographic pyramid is normal.)

Another problem was that although the kibbutz attempted to free women from child rearing and domestic chores by collectivizing such services, they never specified in advance who would be doing those collectivized services. As it turned out, the kibbutz never sent men to the nurseries (Rabin, 1970; Gerson, 1972) and even though both sexes were supposed to work in the domestic drudgery services, women soon came to predominate. Ultimately, about 90 percent of kibbutz women became engaged in services, but many of them, especially those in the low-regarded kitchen and laundry branches, were so dissatisfied with their lot as to constitute a serious problem (see, for example, Spiro, 1963; Rosner, 1967).

The process can be traced as follows: when the early socialist kibbutzim were founded in the 1920s[4] both sexes labored side by side in agricultural production. In those days survival was difficult; children were rare. Then, as the kibbutzim turned the corner on survival, the women (who numbered only 20 to 35 percent of the founders, according to Talmon, 1972 p. 9) began to have babies. On these points, all the major authorities on the kibbutz (including Talmon, Spiro, and Rabin)

[4]The first kibbutz, Degania, actually was founded in 1909, but not until 1921, with the formation of Ein Harod, was the deliberately large (over 100 members), full-collective socialist kibbutz born. The 1920s and early 1930s then, constitute the pioneering period. In recent years, kibbutz growth has leveled off (most of it now coming from natural increase, not immigration), and as of late 1972 there were just over 100,000 kibbutzniks, living in 233 kibbutzim. The kibbutzim, representing around 3½ percent of Israeli population, are largely organized into three major federations, varying mainly in the purity of their socialist ideology.

are in agreement.

These authors, however, do no mention what I believe to have been a crucial factor—the continuing arrival of *immigrants*—which the kibbutz was ideologically and economically bound to absorb. Like the kibbutz' founding generation, these immigrants were young, childless, and predominantly male. These characteristics of the immigrants were to prove important, I suggest.

The earlier kibbutzim had chosen agrarian production as their economic base, and any examination of an aerial photo of a kibbutz will reveal that the field crops are located farthest from the center of the settlement. Therefore, the women farmers, once they became mothers, were really hindered by another aspect of kibbutz ideology. This was the kibbutz emphasis on breast feeding and frequent contact of the mother with the child, even though child care was collectivized in unique "children's houses." Women forced to walk in the blazing midday sun from the distant fields, might be expected to dislike agrarian activities. In fact, they often did (Padan-Eisenstark, 1973). If however, the historical evidence of the kibbutz shows that the women did not want to be taken out of *production*, a removal which they saw, rightly, as the road to second-class status. What they argued for was a change in the kibbutz production mix. Specifically, at a 1936 conference (held by the largest of the three kibbutz federations), the women strongly urged more emphasis on the kinds of horticultural activities which, as we have seen in our previous overview, have been done by women throughout history, namely cultivating garden crops and tree crops, and the care of such small animals as poultry (Viteles, 1967 pp. 323-324). These activities take place close to the children's nurseries at the center of the kibbutz.

Unfortunately for the women though, in the kibbutz accounting system these horticultural activities appear less profitable than agrarian production. This is because horticulture uses proportionally more labor (that is for a given level of output) than agriculture, and the kibbutz' socialistic accounting method is based exclusively on the amount of labor devoted to production. Specifically, the kibbutzim, despite the fact that they exist as islands in a larger capitalist sea, almost from the start based their bookkeeping on the socialist "labor theory of value." (In this view, of the three factors of production—land, capital, and labor—only labor results in value added.) The kibbutzim measure labor by the criterion "income per labor day," so that which uses much more land (excluded from the bookkeeping) but less labor per unit of output than horticultural crops, win hands down.

In spite of all this, had there been no immigration, the women might have gotten their request for the production mix to be changed to emphasize their preferred horticultural activities (Blumberg, 1974b, 1976a). But the immigrants *did* arrive and I propose that increasing numbers reduced the pressure on the kibbutz to emphasize horticultural activities, which were accounted as less profitable.[5]

The result was attrition. The immigrants gradually replaced, first, the pioneer mothers; ultimately male arrivals replaced almost all women in agricultural production. In recent years, kibbutz women have been less than 10 percent of the productive agricultural labor force (see, for example, Spiro 1963, p. 225; Viteles, 1967, pp. 333, 336). The service sector, meanwhile, grew in size but not in mechanization so that they needed increasing numbers of workers. Ultimately these services absorbed more than half of all kibbutz workers, and 90 percent of the women, in the average kibbutz (see, for example, Talmon, 1972).

Thus, in the case of the kibbutz, ideology was insufficient to counteract structural tendencies caused first by the agrarian techno-economic base they chose; and second by demographic pressures in the form of the arrival of an immigrant labor force viewed as preferable to the kibbutz pioneer mothers.

Happily, especially since the 1960s, industrialization has reached the kibbutz (Barkai, 1971; Leviatan, 1972), and it appears that the deck is being reshuffled again. Specifically, the techno-economic base is changing to give greater weight to industrial activities. However, since immigration to the kibbutz has slowed to a trickle in recent years (Stern, 1973) and outside hired labor is still regarded with great ideological disapproval, women have been brought into kibbutz industry in increasing numbers. Already they are over 30 percent of the industrial labor force (Leviatan, 1972), although for a generation they were only 10 percent of the agricultural work team.

To reiterate, it appears that structure more than ideology caused the initial erosion of kibbutz women's role in production and then, after a generation of second-class status, the recent upswing of kibbutz women's participation in production followed the introduction of industrialization. This latter change in the productive mix occurred at a time when immigration to the kibbutz had largely dried up, so that if the kibbutzim were to avoid what was for them the ideologically repellent use of large numbers of outside hired workers, they had to turn to their own members for labor. Since few additional men could be freed from the kibbutz' highly mechanized agriculture (see Leviatan, 1972), this meant mechanizing services to reduce their labor needs and sending the women thus freed to work in kibbutz industry. Apparently this is

[5]I do not yet have data as to whether, during the period in question, kibbutz agrarian field crops proved consistently more profitable in the world market than their horticultural output. According to Barkai (1973), the picture seems mixed. (It should be noted that much of my discussions concerning the kibbutz involve hypotheses that are supported by a data base varying greatly in quality. For example, most of the materials on the early days of the kibbutzim are anecdotal, not statistical or empirical. Much of the literature on the kibbutz is based on these same anecdotal sorts of sources.)

happening today (Barkai, 1971).

In short, in various settings—the United States, the Soviet Union, Japan, Venezuela, and the Israeli kibbutz—structural considerations concerning the nature of economic activities, and the nature of the balance between labor-force demand and supply, have been more important than ideological considerations in determining female participation in the economy.

summary and conclusions

At the beginning of this paper, I argued that for women, economic power was the only one of the three main types of power (the others are power of political position and power of force) in which they have been known to equal or dominate the men of their group. Economic power means control over the means and fruits of production, and it is not all that uncommon that women achieve substantial economic control. In fact, in my own research based on a pilot sample of 61 preindustrial societies, women's economic control equals or exceeds that of their menfolk in one-fourth to one-third of the cases for which I have data. Furthermore, there are well-known cases where women controlled virtually the entire economic pie (for instance, the Iroquois; see Martin & Voorhies, 1975).

How do women achieve economic power? The first step on the road seems to be participation in productive labor, in that women's position (economic and otherwise) has been low in groups where females do not contribute to the family's support.

Hence, women's productive labor has been the principal focus of this paper. First, we have seen that from a worldwide or evolutionary perspective, women are much more economically productive than ethnocentric stereotypes in our society give them credit for. Second, I have asserted—and provided varied cross-societal data—that the extent and nature of women's productive labor is influenced by two main factors: the degree of compatibility of the task with tending small children; and the state of the labor supply versus the need for workers. But women's productive labor is not an automatic road to economic power or other manifestations of equality. After all, slaves work too, and in some societies women may do most of the work and still be treated as virtual slaves.

If this paper has analyzed female productive labor as the first precondition for female economic power and equality, it has neglected two crucial subsequent questions concerning the position of women. First, under what circumstances can women's productive labor be translated into economic power over production and property? Second, for what other aspects of equality can women's economic power be cashed in?

My own recent research has been aimed at these questions (Blumberg 1974a; 1976b; forthcoming). Space limitations preclude their full treatment in this paper, but let me indicate the proposed answers suggested by my paradigm and the direction of the research.

Two main conditions permit women's work to be translated into women's economic control: the power women have via their group's kinship system; and how indispensable and strategic the women producers and their activities are to their society's survival. I view women's "strategic indispensibility," as more important.[6]

Finally, what are the practical advantages of women's economic power? As I see it, women's power (largely economically derived) is a kind of "poker chips" which may be "cashed in" for the various assets of equal status. I am interested not in which sex is held up on a pedestal, but in the extent to which women can determine their fate in major (noneconomic) life decisions or "life options."[7] After all, Victorian ladies were given the pedestal treatment but rarely allowed out of the house.

In summary, my findings indicate that productive labor does not lead women directly to freedom and equality. Rather, under certain circumstances, it can lead them to economic power. And economic power, in

---

[6]Broadly speaking, there are three main sorts of kinship arrangements in the world: those emphasizing paternal relatives, those emphasizing maternal kin, and those in which both paternal and maternal kin ties are reckoned (what anthropologists call bilateral systems). In general, women fare better in societies emphasizing links through female kin than in those with patriarchal institutions (see, for example, Leavitt, 1971). Especially important in my theory of sexual equality is whether residence is with the husband's kin, the wife's kin, both, or neither (Blumberg, 1974a). Where women can live near their own families after they marry, I have found them significantly more likely to exert economic power (Blumberg, forthcoming). Concerning the "strategicness" of women's productive labor, I suggest that there are a number of aspects above and beyond the kinship system, that affect the degree to which women's labor may bring them control over the means and fruits of production. Women seem more likely to gain economic power from their labor if their activities produce a large fraction of the group's output or diet, and, more importantly, are difficult to replace. Similarly, if the women themselves are virtually irreplaceable (because of their unique skills and/or the lack of replacement personnel), their probable power is enhanced. This would seem especially true if the women can manage to organize on their own behalf. Finally, if the women workers or their output are needed by competing segments of the society, their power position should also be enhanced.

Thus far, I have been unable to measure these proposed "indispensability" factors to see if they do, in fact, add to women's economic power. However, I have been able to collect data relevant to the last unexplored question of this paper—what other aspects of equality are affected by womens economic power.

[7]Specifically, there seem to be a series of "life options" which exist in every known human society. As the operational measurement of women's status I propose the freedom of women relative to the men of their group to decide these life options. These life options include relative freedom to: decide whether and whom to marry; terminate a marriage; engage in pre- and extramarital sex; regulate fertility (i.e., as far as possible to decide number, spacing, and sex ratio of children and the means of fertility control, such as contraception, abortion, and infanticide); control freedom of movement; have access to adult educational opportunity; and exercise de facto household authority. Thus far, in my analysis of a 61-society pilot study, my predictions have been supported by the data. "Life options" are proving much more strongly affected by women's economic power than by any other variable.

turn, seems to be the strongest influence on women's relative freedom and equality versus that of their menfolk in controlling their personal destiny—marriage, divorce, sex, children, free movement, education, and household power.

Actually, the connection between female work and economic power may be somewhat more direct and assured in Western industrial societies than in the preindustrial societies of my pilot sample, even though a handful of people, overwhelmingly male, control productive resources in industrial countries.[8] The reason for this slightly more direct link between work and power is that women in our kind of society work almost exclusively for wages, which are paid to the individual. The women worker may put all money in the family account but she brings home her own paycheck. And her paycheck usually permits her some say as to its disposition, as well as in other household decisions (see, for example, Blood & Wolfe, 1960). Even though she typically earns considerably less than a similarly qualified male, a woman with earnings does have more autonomy not just in the house, but also with respect to marriage and divorce. She may be less likely to marry just anyone and less afraid of terminating a bad marriage if she can earn a living on her own.

What does all this imply for the future of the American female? To the extent that American women's "paycheck power" continues and is supplemented by their organizing on their own behalf, as in the current Women's Liberation Movement, it seems logical to expect some degree of increasing equality between men and women in their basic life options. But it should be stressed that "paycheck power" is only a small part of what I have conceptualized as economic power. And it is an even smaller part of the larger political economy (which influences, among other things, who gets to work for what size paycheck) in which women currently play a negligible role in both capitalist and socialist countries. Accordingly, it would seem that organized attempts to change the system will weigh more heavily than even a hypothetical situation of 100 percent female employment if American women's life chances really were to be made equal to those of men.

[8]In the United States, for example, a growing number of studies have found that income distribution has been substantially unchanged since World War II (or earlier), with the richest fifth receiving over 40 percent of total income, and the poorest fifth receiving only around 5 percent (see, for example, Ackerman, et al., 1972). Income, however, is only part of the story. Projector and Weiss' study for the Federal Reserve (1966) shows that in 1962, the wealthiest 20 percent of American households owned 76 percent of total national wealth and 96 percent of corporate stock. Considering only the wealthiest 1 percent, the survey found that these households controlled 31 percent of total wealth and 61 percent of corporate stock. For the corporate owners and managers overwhelmingly male who make up the major controllers of American productive capital, see Navarro, 1975. Of course, in socialist industrial countries such as the Soviet Union, income is more equally distributed, but control over the economy is retained by the central apparatus of the Communist Party, with a membership of less than 1 percent of the population.

references

Ackerman, F., Birnbaum, H., Zimbalist, J. A. The extent of income inequality in the United States. In R. C. Edwards, M. Reich & Thomas E. Weisskopf (Eds.) *The capitalist system.* Englewood Cliffs, N.J.: Prentice-Hall, 1973.

Anonymous. *Victory: How women won it.* New York: Wilson, 1940.

Aronoff, J., & Crano, W. D. A re-examination of the cross-cultural principles of task segregation and sex-role differentiation in the family. *American Sociological Review,* 1975, 40, 12-20.

Babcox, D., & Belkin, M. (Eds.) *Liberation now!* New York: Dell, 1971.

Barkai, H. *The kibbutz: An experiment in microsocialism.* Research report No. 34. Jerusalem: Hebrew University of Jerusalem, 1971.

Barkai, H. Interviews and communications with author, January-September, 1973.

Binford, L. R. Post-pleistocene adaptations. In S. Streuver (Ed.) *Prehistoric agriculture.* Garden City, New York: Natural History Press, 1971.

Blakkan, R. Women workers in America. *The Guardian.* London, England: March 29, April 5, April 12, and April 19, 1972.

Blood, R. O., Jr., & Wolfe, D. M. *Husbands and wives.* New York: Free Press, 1960.

Blumberg, R. L. Technological change and the role of women: Multi-national oil companies and women in Venezuela. Presented at the World Affairs Institute, Iowa State University, Ames, Iowa, December, 1973.

Blumberg, R. L. Structural factors affecting women's status: A cross-societal paradigm. Paper read at the meeting of the International Sociological Association, Toronto, 1974a.

Blumberg, R. L. From liberation to laundry: A structural interpretation of the retreat from sexual equality in the Israeli kibbutz. Revised version of paper read at the meeting of the American Political Science Association, Chicago, 1974b.

Blumberg, R. L. Kibbutz women: From the fields of revolution to the laundries of discontent. In L. Iglitzin and R. Ross (Eds.) *Women in the world: A comparative study.* Santa Barbara, Calif.: ABC Clio, 1976a, in press.

Blumberg, R. L. *Stratification: Socioeconomic and sexual inequality.* Dubuque, Ia.: Wm. C. Brown, 1976c, in press.

Blumberg, R. L. Woman's fate: A cross-societal paradigm and study of sexual stratification. Unpublished manuscript. 1976.

Boserup, E. *The conditions of agricultural growth: the economics of agrarian change under population pressure.* Chicago: Aldine, 1965.

Boserup, E. *The role of women in economic development.* New York: St. Martin's, 1970.

Brown, J. K. A note on the division of labor by sex. *American Anthropologist,* 1970, 72, 1074-1079.

Childe, V. G. *What happened in history?,* rev. ed. Baltimore: Penguin, 1964.

Economic Commission for Africa. *The data base for discussion on the interrelations between the integration of women in development, their situation and population factors in Africa.* Addis Ababa, Ethiopia: Economic Commission for Africa, United Nations Economic and Social Council. Document E/CN.14/SW/37 June, 1974.

Ehrlich, H. J. *Selected differences in the life chances of men and women in the United States.* Research Group One, Report No. 13, 1974.

Encuesta del Hogar, Venezuela: Ministerio de Fomento, April, 1970.

Epstein, C. F., *Woman's place: Options and limits in professional careers.* Berkeley, Calif.: University of California Press, 1970.

Flannery, K. V. Archeological systems theory and early meso-America, In Stuart Struever (Ed.) *Prehistoric Agriculture,* Garden City, New York: Natural History Press, 1971.

Friedan, B. *The feminine mystique.* New York: Norton, 1963.

Gerson, M. Lesson from the kibbutz: A cautionary tale. In L. K. Howe (Ed.) *The future of the family.* New York: Simon & Schuster, 1972.

Gilman, C. P. Women and economics. (Originally published in 1894.) In D. Babcox & M. Belkin (Eds.) *Liberation now!* New York: Dell, 1971.

Ginzberg, E. *Manpower for development: Perspectives in five continents.* New York: Praeger, 1971.

Goldberg, M. P. Women in the Soviet economy. *The Review of Radical Political Economics,* 1972, *4* (3).

Goldschmidt., W. *Man's way: A preface to the understanding of human society.* New York: Holt, Rinehart and Winston, 1959.

Hawkes, J., & Woolley, L. *Prehistory and the beginning of civilization.* New York: Harper & Row, 1963.

Hobhouse, L. T., Wheeler, G. C., & Ginsberg, M. *The material culture and social institutions of the simpler peoples.* London: Chapman & Hall, 1915.

Hammond, J. L., & Hammond, B., *The skilled labourer, 1760-1832.* London: Longmans, Green, & Co., 1920.

Knudsen, D. D., The declining status of women: Popular myths and the failure of functionalist thought. *Social Forces,* 1969, *48* (2).

Kritz, M. M., *Immigration and social structure: The Venezuelan case.* Unpublished Ph.D dissertation, University of Wisconsin, 1973.

Leacock, E. Introduction. In F. Engels, *The origin of the family, private property and the state.* New York: International Publishers, 1972.

Leavitt, R. R. Women in other cultures. In V. Gornick & B. K. Moran, *Woman in sexist society.* New York: Basic Books, 1971.

Lee, R. B., & DeVore, I. *Man the hunter.* Chicago: Aldine, 1968.

Lenski, G. E. *Power and privilege: A theory of social stratification.* New York: McGraw-Hill, 1966.

Lenski, G. E. *Human societies: A macrolevel introduction to sociology.* New York: McGraw-Hill, 1970.

Lenski, G. E., & Lenski, J. *Human societies,* 2nd ed. New York: McGraw-Hill, 1974.

Leviatan, U. The industrial process in the Israeli kibbutzim: Problems and their solution. Paper presented at the International Conference on Trends in Industrial and Labor Relations, Tel Aviv, 1972.

Lomax, A. *Folk song style and culture.* Washington, D.C.: American Association for the Advancement of Science, No. 88, 1968.

Macneish, R. S. Ancient meso-American civilization. *Science,* 1964, *143,* 531-537.

Mandel, W. *Soviet women.* Garden City, New York: Anchor, 1975.

Martin, M. K., & Voohies, B. *Female of the species.* New York: Columbia University Press, 1975.

Mead, M. *Male and female.* New York: Morrow, 1949.

Meyers, J. T. The origin of agriculture: An evaluation of three hypotheses. In Stuart Struever (Ed.), *Prehistoric agriculture.* Garden City, New York:

Natural History Press, 1971.

Memoria y Cuenta, 1969-1970. Caracas, Venezuela: Ministerio de Educacion, 1970.

Michaelson, E. J. & Goldschmidt, W. Female roles and male dominance among peasants, *Southwestern Journal of Anthropology*, 1971, *27*, 330-352.

Murdock, G. P. Ethnographic atlas: A summary. *Ethnology*, 1967, *6*, 109-236.

Murdock, G. P., & C. Provost, Factors in the division of labor by sex: A cross-cultural analysis. *Ethnology*, 1973, *12*, 203-225.

Navarro, V. Women in health care. *New England Journal of Medicine*, 1975, *292*, 398-402.

Oppenheimer, V. K. Demographic influence on female employment and the status of women. *American Journal of Sociology*, 1973, *78*, 946-961.

Oppenheimer, V. K. The sociology of women's economic role in the family: Parsons revisited and revised. Paper read at the meeting of the American Sociological Association, Montreal, 1974.

Padan-Eisenstark, D. Personal communication, October, 1973.

Parsons, T. Age and sex in the social structure of the United States. *American Sociological Review*, 1942, *7*, 604-616.

Parsons, T., & Bales, R. *Family, socialization and interaction process.* Glencoe, Ill.: Free Press, 1955.

Projector, D. S., & Weiss, G. *Survey of financial characteristics of consumers.* Washington, D.C.: Federal Reserve System, 1966.

Rabin, A. I. The sexes: Ideology and reality in the Israeli kibbutz. In G. H. Seward & R. C. Williamson (Eds.) *Sex roles in changing society.* New York: Random House, 1970.

Rosner, M. Women in the kibbutz: Changing status and concepts. *Asian and African Studies, 3,* 35-68, reprinted in Rosner, no date. *The Kibbutz as a Way of Life in modern society: A collection of articles.* Givat Haviva, Israel: Center for Research on the Kibbutz, 1967.

Sanday, P. R. Toward a theory of the status of women. *American Anthropologist*, 1973, *75*, 1682-1700.

Sjoberg, G. *The pre-industrial city.* New York: Free Press, 1960.

Smelser, N. J. *Social change in the industrial revolution.* Chicago: University of Chicago Press, 1959.

Spiro, M. E. *Kibbutz: Venture in utopia.* New York: Schocken Books, 1963.

Sokoloff, N. J. A description and analysis of the economic position of women in American society. Paper presented at the meeting of the American Sociological Association, Montreal, 1974.

Stern, S. The kibbutz: Not by ideology alone. *The New York Times Magazine,* May 6, 1973.

Sullerot, E. *Woman, society and change,* trans. Margaret Sicher, New York: McGraw-Hill, 1971.

Talmon, Y. *Family and community in the kibbutz.* Cambridge, Mass.: Harvard University Press, 1972.

Tobias, S., & Anderson, L. *What really happened to Rosie the Riveter: Demobilization and the female labor force 1944-47.* Mss. Module 9, 1973.

U.S. Bureau of Labor Statistics. *Marital and family characteristics of workers,* Special Labor Force Reports, No. 120, Washington, D.C.: Government Printing Office, 1971.

Urbaneja, R. de I., & Millar, B. L. *La participacion de la mujer in el desarrollo.*

Caracas, Venezuela. Promocion Popular, 1971.

Viteles, H. *Book two: The evolution of the kibbutz movement.* In *A history of the cooperative movement in Israel: A source book in seven volumes.* London: Vallentine-Mitchell, 1967.

Vreede-de Stuers, C. Indonesia. In Raphael Patai (Ed.) *Women in the modern world.* New York: Free Press, 1967.

Woodburn, J. An introduction to Hadza ecology. In R. B. Lee & I. DeVore, *Man the hunter.* Chicago: Aldine, 1968.

women's equality:
implications of the law*

Carol Agate
Colquitt Meacham

Not long ago a Connecticut judge upheld the exclusion of girls from a high school track team with these words:

The present generation of our younger male population has not become so decadent that boys will experience a thrill in defeating girls in running contests, whether the girls be members of their own team or of an adversary team. It could well be that many boys would feel compelled to forego entering track events if they were required to compete with girls on their own team or adversary teams. With boys vying with girls . . . the challenge to win, and the glory of achievement, at least for many boys, would lose incentive and become nullified.[1]

The symbol of the law is the statue representing Justice, her blindfold and her scales signifying an impartial weighing of the facts. But laws are made and interpreted by people—legislators and judges—who are products of their socialization. As one sees in the above quotation, the values, attitudes, and beliefs that develop from each judge's exposure to our culture determine how he or she will interpret the law.

The law is, by and large, a duality. The statutory law consists of the codes as written by legislators, and the common law consists of judicial decisions in areas not covered by statute. Justice can be applied to women and men impartially only when the legislators and judges who constitute the legal system are able to transcend the socialization that led them to believe men and women are meant to have distinct roles in life.

*Our appreciation to Bernice Sandler, of the Project on the Status and Education of Women, Association of American Colleges for her helpful comments on this paper.
[1]Hollander v. Connecticut Interscholastic Athletic Conference, Case No. 12-49-27 (Super. Ct., New Haven City, Conn., Mar. 29, 1971).

This chapter explains our legal system with respect to the ways in which it reinforces or eradicates differential treatment of men and women. The authors will examine the equal protection clause—the often technical, but also flexible, constitutional promise of freedom from arbitrary discrimination, and how it operates in specific areas of the law; federal statutes aimed at eliminating sex discrimination, and how it operates in specific areas of the law; federal statues aimed at eliminating sex discrimination; and finally the implications of the Equal Rights Amendment.

equal protec-
tion clause

Prior to 1963, the only legal tool used to challenge sex discrimination was the Equal Protection Clause of the Fourteenth Amendment to the United States Constitution, which provides that "no State shall . . . deny to any person within its jurisdiction the equal protection of the laws."

Despite the unequivocal wording of this clause, courts have recognized that total equality is not feasible nor desirable and certain differences between people do warrant legal distinctions if there is a rational basis for such distinction. For example, separate public schools may be provided for children who are mentally retarded but not for those who are black.[2]

Until recently, sex was always held to be a difference that warranted different legal treatment. The judicial system operated on the premise that the legal rights of women were defined by their societal roles, and that such treatment did not violate the Equal Protection Clause. A classic statement of the limitations imposed upon women by their socially defined role was made in 1873 by United States Supreme Court Justice Bradley in explaining why a state was constitutionally permitted to ban women from practicing law:

The civil law, as well as nature herself, has always recognized a wide difference in the respective spheres and destinies of man and woman. Man is, or should be, a woman's protector and defender. The natural and proper timidity and delicacy which belongs to the female sex evidently unfits it for many of the occupations of civil life. The constitution of the family organization, which is founded in the divine ordinance, as well as in the nature of things, indicates the domestic sphere as that which properly belongs to the domain and functions of womanhood.[3]

Nearly one hundred years later, the Supreme Court first ruled that sex was an impermissible basis for differential legal treatment.[4] The case involved an Idaho law under which preference in administering an estate between persons of equal relationship to a deceased had to

[2]Brown v. Board of Educ., 347 U.S. 483 (1954).
[3]Bradwell v. Illinois, 83 U.S. (16 Wall.) 130, 141.
[4]Reed v. Reed, 404 U.S. 71 (1971).

be given to males. The Court held the law in violation of the Equal Protection Clause because the state had failed to show that the sex of the applicant for letters of administration had any rational relationship to a valid state objective. Therefore the choice of an administrator could not be mandated solely on the basis of sex. This 1973 ruling opened the way to other recent decisions which have expanded women's rights as full persons under the law.

state action
The first requirement in bringing suit under the Equal Protection Clause is that the act of discrimination must involve action by the state. Action by a city or town also qualifies as "state action" because municipal governments are agents of the state. If the discrimination in question involves only private wrongs with no element of state involvement, the courts must dismiss the suit as not coming within the protection of the Constitution.

Examples of sex-biased state action are:

a law that allows women to marry at sixteen but requires men to wait until they are eighteen;
a municipal swimming pool that requires women to wear caps regardless of their hair length while men must wear caps only if their hair is long; and
a lease of state-owned property to a private club that excludes women from membership.

On the other hand, there is no state action if:

a private school does not accept boys as students;
a private country club establishes hours when only men can play; or
a private organization does not accept women as voting members.

In a case involving a privately owned restaurant that leased space from a municipal parking garage, the Supreme Court showed how far the concept of state action can be carried.[5] There was sufficient state action in the public ownership of the space to make it unconstitutional for the restaurant to refuse to serve blacks. On the other side of the state-action/private-action borderline was a case in which the Court held that the granting of a liquor license did not constitute sufficient state action to require a men's club to serve blacks.[6] The Court reasoned that to hold otherwise would involve virtually everything as state action since even a connection to municipal water lines involves the state as much as does the granting of a liquor license.

If state action is not involved, the discrimination in question is not

[5]Burton v. Wilmington Parking Authority, 365 U.S. 715 (1961).
[6]Moose Lodge No. 107 v. Irvis, 407 U.S. 163 (1972).

invalid under the Fourteenth Amendment. If state action is established, the next step is to determine whether the discrimination is unconstitutional.

tests for constitu- tionality

The methods used in analyzing sex-discrimination cases have precedent in cases involving racial discrimination. The Supreme Court originally used what is called the "rational basis" test to evaluate state action which creates classifications resulting in differential treatment of people. It then evolved the more stringent "strict scrutiny" standard which was applied to certain types of suspect classifications such as those based on race.

1.   rational basis test

The traditional method of analysis, the rational basis test, is derived from a 1920 Supreme Court case.

[T]he classification must be reasonable, not arbitrary, and must rest upon some ground of difference having a fair and substantial relation to the object of the legislation, so that all persons similarly circumstanced shall be treated alike.[7]

The rational basis test was used when the United States Supreme Court sustained a Michigan statute which provided that a woman could not obtain a bartender's license unless she was "the wife or daughter of the male owner" of the bar.[8] (The challenge was directed to the classification between the two types of women—those who were wives or daughters of owners and those who were not. The constitutionality of the unequal treatment between men and women was assumed.) The state's reason for its restriction was that a husband or father would protect a woman from the "hazards that may confront a barmaid." The Court concluded that since the line the state had drawn "is not without a basis in reason, we cannot give ear to the suggestion that the real impulse behind this legislation was an unchivalrous desire of male bartenders to try to monopolize the calling."

It has not been difficult for courts to justify sex discrimination where the articulated object of the legislation is to protect women. In a few state and federal court cases, sex discrimination has been held unconstitutional even under this test. For example, the Court of Appeals for the Eighth Circuit found it was not rational to exclude girls from competing for places on a boys' tennis team when the school did not provide girls' teams.[9] However, the more usual result is that sex discrimination is upheld under the rational basis test. An example is a

[7] F. S. Royster Guano Co. v. Virginia, 253 U.S. 412, 415.
[8] Goessart v. Cleary, 335 U.S. 464 (1948).
[9] Brenden v. Independent School Dist. 742, 477 F. 2d 1292 (1973).

case in which the Supreme Judicial Court of Maine upheld a law which provided longer sentences for men than for women who attempted to escape from prison. The court found the discrimination rational because:

the Legislature could reasonably conclude that the greater physical strength, aggressiveness and disposition toward violent action so frequently displayed by a male prisoner bent on escape from a maximum security institution presents a far greater risk of harm to prison guards and personnel and to the public than is the case when escape is undertaken by a woman. . .[10]

2. strict strutiny standard

In recent years, the United States Supreme Court has developed what is referred to as the strict scrutiny standard when examining certain types of legislative classifications. There are two prongs to judicial review under the strict scrutiny test. If the type of classification made in the statute is in a "suspect" category *or* the statute infringes upon a fundamental right of the party, the discrimination in question may be unconstitutional.

a. suspect classification

First, it must be decided whether a suspect classification is involved. Among classifications that have been labelled as suspect are race, national origin, and alienage.

The first court to label sex as a suspect classification was the Supreme Court of California in 1971. The case involved a Fourteenth Amendment challenge to a state law which excluded women from the occupation of bartender. In the opinion, which stated that the law violated the Equal Protection Clause, Justice Peters wrote,

What differentiates sex from nonsuspect statuses, such as intelligence or physical disability, and aligns it with the recognized suspect classifications is that the characteristic frequently bears no relation to ability to perform or contribute to society. (Citations omitted.) The result is that the whole class is relegated to an inferior legal status without regard to the capabilities or characteristics of its individual members.[11]

Members of the United States Supreme Court are divided on the question of whether sex is a suspect classification which evokes the application of the strict scrutiny test. The Court, in *Reed* v. *Reed*,[12] for the first time in its history, held a state statute to be unconstitutional because it discriminated against women. It refrained, however, from

[10]Wark v. State, 266 A. 2d 62, 65 (1970), *cert. denied,* 400 U.S. 952 (1970).
[11]Sail'er Inn, Inc. v. Kirby, 5 Cal. 3d 1, 18, 485 P. 2d 529, 540.
[12]404 U.S. 71 (1971).

labelling sex a suspect classification, basing its holding on the less stringent rational basis test.

The more recent case of *Frontiero v. Richardson*[13] involved an armed-services regulation which provided housing and medical benefits to its members' dependents. Men needed merely to claim their wives as dependents while women had to prove their husbands were actually dependent on them for over one-half of their support. The Court found that the regulation violated the Equal Protection Clause and was unconstitutional. Four justices based their decision on the fact that classifications based on sex are inherently suspect and must be subjected to strict judicial scrutiny, which the regulation in question could not pass.

In a concurring opinion, three other justices agreed the statute was unconstitutionally discriminatory. Their decision was based on the holding in *Reed* v. *Reed* which, they said, "did not add sex to the narrowly limited group of classifications which were inherently suspect." The remaining concurring opinion, by Justice Stewart, avoided taking a stand on the issue of sex as a suspect classification by saying merely that the statutes "work an invidious discrimination in violation of the Constitution." Justice Rehnquist, in the sole dissenting opinion, stated that there was a rational basis for the statutory distinction between men and women and therefore the legislation was not unconstitutional.

In a case following the decision in *Frontiero, Kahn* v. *Shevin,*[14] six members of the Court upheld a Florida law which granted widows a property tax exemption but did not extend the benefit to widowers. The Court used the reasonable basis test and found that Florida was within constitutional bounds in "cushioning the financial impact of spousal loss upon the sex for whom that loss imposes a disproportionately heavy burden."

It seems clear, after *Kahn*, that only a minority of the Supreme Court justices are ready to label sex as a suspect classification and that challenges to sex based distinctions must still overcome the rational basis analysis.

b.   *fundamental right*

Assuming that sex is not a suspect classification, the next step in using the strict scrutiny standard is to ask whether a fundamental right is involved. Among the rights which have been held to be fundamental are voting, interstate travel, and procreation. For example, strict scrutiny is not applied to a classification based on poverty, but a poll tax which

[13]411 U.S. 677 (1973).
[14]Kahn v. Shevin 42 U.S.L.W. 4591 (1974).

inhibits the fundamental right to vote does get a more rigorous judicial review.[15]

If a suspect classification or a fundamental right is involved, the strict scrutiny standard of review is used rather than the rational basis test. Under strict scrutiny the state may continue to discriminate only if it can show it has a compelling interest in doing so. It is extremely difficult for a state to show it has a compelling interest in discriminating against a suspect class, or denying a fundamental right. As Chief Justice Burger commented:

> So far as I am aware, no state law has ever satisfied this seemingly insurmountable standard, and I doubt one ever will, for it demands nothing less than perfection.[16]

Actually, the Court had earlier[17] found a state interest sufficiently compelling to warrant an infringement upon a fundamental right, but it was indeed rare.

specific areas of discrimination

Although most law suits challenging discrimination include equal protection arguments as outlined above, many are also based on laws that prohibit specific types of discrimination. For example, the California law that discriminated against female bartenders was challenged under both the Civil Rights Act of 1964, and the Equal Protection Clause.[18]

In each of the specific areas examined below, the Equal Protection Clause is relevant where there is state action involved. However, where there is no state action, there may be state and/or federal laws that can be used to fight sex discrimination.

employment

Women's search for job equality was long hampered by the law's paternalism. In 1908, the Supreme Court first decided that there could be different employment regulations for men and women. Around the turn of the century, the Court had held that a state could not enact legislation limiting working hours and conditions because to do so was to interfere with a man's constitutional freedom to contract for his labor.[19] But when later presented with the same question in regard to women, the Court held that a state could step in to protect them.

> Differentiated by these matters (lesser physical strength and business experience, greater dependency) from the other sex, she is properly placed in a class by herself, and legislation designed for her protection may be sustained,

---

[15]Harper v. Virginia Bd. of Elections, 383 U.S. 663 (1966).
[16]Dunn v. Blumstein, 405 U.S. 330, 363-64 (1972) (Burger, C.J., dissenting).
[17]Jeness v. Fortson, 403 U.S. 431 (1971).
[18]*See* Sail'er Inn, *above.*
[19]Lochner v. New York, 198 U.S. 45 (1905).

even when like legislation is not necessary for men and could not be sustained. It is impossible to close one's eyes to the fact that she still looks to her brother and depends upon him.[20]

The outcome of this decision was the enactment of a rash of laws "protecting" women from certain jobs and working conditions. Even after the Supreme Court accepted the constitutionality of laws restricting men's working conditions, those relating to women tended to be more restrictive. Predictably, employers preferred to hire men who could legally work more than nine hours, or for whom they did not have to provide a seat on the job, or who were not forbidden to lift heavy weights. When women were hired it was because they could be paid less.

title VII of the
civil rights act of 1964

To alleviate discrimination in employment, Congress passed the Civil Rights Act of 1964, Title VII of which provides:

It shall be unlawful employment practice for any employer to fail or to refuse to hire or to discharge any individual, or otherwise to discriminate against any individual with respect to his compensation, terms, conditions, or privileges of employment, because of such individual's race, color, religion, sex, or national origin. . .[21]

The word "sex" was added by a southern representative for the purpose, as commonly believed, of defeating the entire act, but even with this amendment, the act passed. It included the establishment of the Equal Employment Opportunity Commission (EEOC) to enforce the provisions of the Act.

The courts were slow to implement the sex discrimination provisions of Title VII. It was not until the late 1960s that courts recognized that the laws designed to "protect" women were, in fact, robbing them of equal employment opportunities. Weight and hour restrictions, whether imposed by the state or by the employer, have been struck down as inconsistent with Title VII. Job applicants must be treated as individuals and judged according to their own capacities rather than by assumptions about the characteristics of their sex.[22]

Under the most recent amendment to Title VII, no one employing fifteen or more persons may refuse to hire or promote any person because of her or his sex. (Smaller firms may be covered under a similar state law.) No assumptions may be made by the employer based on sex

[20]Muller v. Oregon, 208 U.S. 412, 422 (1908).
[21]42 U.S.C.A. §2000e (1970).
[22]*See, e.g.*, Rosenfeld v. Southern Pacific Co., 444 F. 2d 1219 (9th Cir. 1971); Weeks v. Southern Bell Tel. & Tel. Co., 408 F. 2d 228 (5th Cir. 1969).

or any characteristic related to sex. Thus, a company cannot refuse to hire mothers of small children based on the unproven assumption that they are less reliable than fathers of small children.[23] A company cannot advertise its positions as being for one sex or another, nor can it establish different retirement ages or benefits for men and women.

Title VII includes a provision allowing the employer to discriminate on the basis of sex when hiring an employee for a job for which sex is a bona fide occupational qualification (BFOQ).[24] In many cases challenging sex discrimination, employers have attempted to defend their actions on the basis of the BFOQ exception. Courts however, have construed the BFOQ exemption so narrowly that very few cases will warrant its application.[25]

The Equal Employment Opportunity Commission has also interpreted the BFOQ exemption narrowly. Its Guidelines provide that the Commission will consider sex a BFOQ where it is necessary for the purpose of authenticity or genuineness, for example an actor or actress.[26]

A complaint under Title VII is made to the nearest office of the EEOC, located in most major cities. If there is a comparable state law—usually called a Fair Employment Practice (FEP) Law—the charge will first be sent to the state agency. If the state does not act within 60 days, the EEOC has a duty to investigate the complaint. If it does not act within another 180 days, the complaint may institute a private suit by requesting permission from the EEOC in the form of a "notice of right to sue" letter. Since the Commission has a backlog of complaints which often results in a long delay of investigations, many people prefer to institute their own suits. They are aided in this by Title VII's provision for the awarding of attorneys' fees, which encourages lawyers to take cases for a contingent fee.

The most noteworthy EEOC accomplishment to date is its settlement with American Telephone and Telegraph Company. When AT&T applied in 1970 to the Federal Communications Commission for a rate increase, its application was opposed by the EEOC which charged employment discrimination. In 1973, AT&T agreed to settle the case, awarding back pay and salary increases to women and minorities totalling an estimated $38 million. The company also agreed to set goals and timetables under which the number of women and minorities in managerial and technical positions and men in clerical and operator jobs would be increased.

[23]Phillips v. Martin Marietta Corp., 400 U.S. 542 (1971).
[24]42 U.S.C. Sec. 2000e-2(e).
[25]Weeks v. Southern Bell Tel. and Tel. Co., 408 F. 2d 228 (5th Cir. 1969); Rosenfeld v. Southern Pacific Co., 444 F.2d 1219 (9th Cir. 1971); Diaz v. Pan American World Airways, Inc., 311 F. Supp. 559 (S.D. Fla. 1970), 442 F.2d 385(5th Cir. 1971), cert. denied, 404 U.S. 950 (1971).
[26]29 C.F.R. Sec. 1604.1.

equal pay act of 1963

Title VII is the most important and useful federal legislation for protection against sex discrimination. However, the Equal Pay Act [27] which mandates "equal pay for equal work" may be helpful in some types of cases. Under the Act the complainant must show that the jobs in question are roughly equal, although not necessarily identical, in skill, effort, and responsibility, and that the working conditions are similar. The Act is enforced by the Wage and Hour Division of the Department of Labor, as part of the Fair Labor Standards Act. The Department usually files suit on behalf of the complainant, and has won back pay awards for thousands of employees despite the narrow scope and application of the Act.

executive order

Additional prohibitions against sex discrimination are found in Executive Order 11246 as amended by Executive Order 11375. Under the Executive Order, any entity that has a contract with the federal government must agree that neither they, their subcontractors nor their agents will discriminate on the basis of race, color, national origin, religion, or sex and that they will establish an affirmative action policy to increase opportunities for women and minorities and to remedy the effects of past discrimination where appropriate. If the contractor has a Federal contract for $50,000 or more, it must write a formal Affirmative Action Plan and have it available for inspection by the appropriate enforcement agency. The Affirmative Action Plan must detail what the employer will do to ensure the hiring and promotion of women and minorities, including timetables and numerical goals where problems or deficiencies are identified.

The direct work of enforcement is performed by 15 compliance agencies, each regulating a category of contractors which include various industries, construction companies, school districts, public and private colleges and universities, hospitals, and museums. A list of the agencies and the industries they regulate may be obtained from Director, OFCC, U.S. Department of Labor, Washington, D.C. 20210. If someone who wants to file a complaint pursuant to the Executive Order should send a letter, including the complainant's name, address, and phone number, the name and address of the contractor, and a description of the discrimination to the above address or to the proper compliance agency.

education

Sex discrimination institutions are exempt from the provisions of Title VII, the Civil Rights Act of 1964. This deficiency was compensated for

---

[27] 29 U.S.C. Sec. 206(d).

by Title IX of the Education Amendments of 1972,[28] which prohibits schools and colleges from discriminating on the basis of sex in any education program or activity receiving Federal funds. This Act applies to the admission and treatment of students as well as the hiring and promotion of employees.

The law provides significant exemptions in the area of admissions. Private undergraduate colleges may set their own policies as to whether they will admit members of both sexes, and to what extent they will become coeducational. However, they may not discriminate against students on the basis of sex once they are admitted. Public undergraduate institutions that have traditionally and continually had a policy of admitting only students of one sex may continue to do so. Once they admit members of the opposite sex, however, they lose their exemption and must admit students in a nondiscriminatory manner.

The Act allows military schools to discriminate in admissions. It also grants an exemption to educational institutions controlled by a religious organization if the application of the Act would not be consistent with the religious tenets of the organization.

The Act specifically allows educational institutions to maintain separate living facilities for women and men. However, the Regulation implementing the Act[29] requires comparability as to the facilities themselves and nondiscrimination as to their availability and to the rules by which they are operated.

An additional exemption enacted into law in 1974 allows discriminatory membership practices by social fraternities and sororities at the postsecondary level, the Boy Scouts, Girl Scouts, Campfire Girls, Y.W.C.A., Y.M.C.A., and certain voluntary youth services organizations.[30]

As mentioned above, the Department of Health, Education and Welfare wrote a Regulation implementing the Act which became effective July 21, 1975. The Regulation sets forth in detail what will be required of recipient institutions in order to comply with Title IX.

The Regulation addresses a broad range of issues involving the treatment of students—housing and facilities, courses, counseling, student financial aid, student health and insurance benefits, marital or parental status of students, and athletics.

The Regulation exempts discriminatory scholarships for study abroad provided the institution makes available to the opposite sex reasonable opportunities for similar study. Additionally, scholarships administered pursuant to a will, trust, or bequest may be sex-restricted as long as the overall effect of the institution's financial aid policy is not discriminatory.[31]

---

[28]Public Law 92-318 (1972).
[29]45 C.F.R. Part 86.
[30]Public Law 93-568 (1974).
[31]45C.F.R.86.37. This was evidently designed to accommodate the Rhodes scholarship.

Sections of the Regulation dealing with athletics have been highly controversial and the issue has received a great deal of publicity. As finally approved, the Regulation provides that separate teams for men and women are permissible in contact spots or where selection for teams is based on competitive skill. The definition of contact sport is one where the purpose or major activity involves bodily contact. In the case of noncontact sports, where one single sex team is maintained, members of the opposite sex must be allowed to try out for membership.

The Regulation does not require an institution to make equal expenditures on sports for men and women, but the athletics opportunities must be equal. In making a determination as to compliance with the Act the Department of Health, Education, and Welfare will consider a number of factors such as facilities, equipment, coaching, when measuring equality of opportunity.[32]

In dealing with employment practices of recipient institutions, the Regulation provides that an employer may not discriminate against an employee on the basis of pregnancy or related conditions. A temporary disability resulting from these conditions must be treated as any other temporary disability for all job-related purposes. If the employer has no temporary disability policy, pregnancy must be considered justification for leave without pay and the employee reinstated to her original or comparable status when she returns to work.[33]

The authors have not attempted to give an exhaustive discussion of Title IX and its implementing Regulation, but rather have highlighted some of its more notable provisions. Persons who think they have been discriminated against on the basis of sex by a school district, college, or university should consult the Regulation and contact the appropriate regional office of the Department of Health, Education, and Welfare, which has responsibility for enforcing Title IX.

sports

In the area of sports, role expectations play the greatest part both in determining behavior and in interpreting the law. Women are not supposed to be competitive or physically strong, the two essentials for athletic success. Since laws reflect societal expectations, sports has been a difficult area in which to achieve equality.

Problems of discrimination in sports involve consideration of laws covering employment and education. The added factor of physical contact complicates the issues and distinguishes them from other cases in those areas. Thus, wherever courts have held that women must be allowed to join athletic teams, the decisions have been limited to non-contact sports such as tennis, golf, track, and cross-country running.[34]

[32]45 C.F.R. 86. 41.
[33]45 C.F.R. 86.51-86.55.
[34]*See, e.g.,* Morris v. Michigan State Bd. of Educ., 472 F.2d 1207 (6th Cir. 1973); Haas v. South Bend Community School Corp., 289 N.E. 2d 495 (1972).

The Title IX Regulation accepts this contact-noncontact dichotomy. The State Supreme Court of Washington held that the prohibition of women high school students from playing on the football team violated The Washington State Constitution.[35]

The Title IX Regulation is weak in the provisions covering sports. Equal funding for men's and women's teams is not required. Schools are not required to allow women to compete in men's contact sports, nor are they required to establish women's teams in these sports. There are no affirmative action requirements for upgrading women's athletic programs.

Another basis for legal challenges to sports discrimination may be in the various state public accommodations acts. Examples of possible violations of such acts are: golf courses that do not allow women to play on weekend mornings; bowling alleys that sponsor segregated teams, YMCA's that set aside daytime hours for women and evening hours for men, or ski areas that give women reduced rates on ladies' day.

Sports discrimination is probably more difficult to challenge than any other form of sex discrimination because, as a rule, women do not perform as well as men, even given two persons of the same height and weight. Their lower level of performance can be attributed to a number of handicaps, including lack of encouragement, unavailability of facilities, absence of role models, parental and societal suppression of competition, and lack of incentive in the form of scholarships and prize money.

Whatever the reasons, the fact of unequal ability exists. A policy, therefore, of single teams with equal access would result in few girls or women getting onto teams. Therefore, it is necessary for schools and recreational facilities to sponsor teams requiring different levels of strength and ability so both sexes will have access to a team on which they can compete.

family planning

The issues in family planning revolve around the fight, especially among women, for control of one's own body. This fight originally focused on the issue of birth control. In the early days of the efforts to change abortion laws, the emphasis was on their liberalization. The American Law Institute, a scholarly group of theoreticians, recommended that in given situations—rape, incest, possibility of fetal deformity, or danger to the woman's physical or psychological health—abortions should be permitted. Several states enacted laws embodying these recommendations.

As the feminist movement grew and adopted the abortion issue, the focus changed. The concept of establishing grounds for an abortion was rejected in favor of the argument that women had the right to con-

---

[35]Darrin v. Gould, 85 Washington 2d 859, 540 Pacific 2d 882 (1975).

trol their own bodies. In 1973, the Supreme Court struck down state laws that prohibited or restricted abortion.[36] The Court ruled that the state could not interfere with a woman's right to an abortion during the first three months of her pregnancy. During the second three months the state can regulate abortion for the purpose of making it safer, but cannot ban abortion entirely. Only during the last three months can abortion be prohibited, but only if the woman's life or health is not at stake.

As soon as the decision was announced, a number of congressmen started introducing bills for constitutional amendments to prohibit abortion. These bills vary in their scope, going so far as to define "person" as including the embryo from the moment of conception.

The other major fight for control of one's own body, the right to use birth control, may largely be considered won. The Supreme Court has held that a state may not ban contraceptives[37] nor may it limit their use to married persons.[38] Along with the legality of contraceptives and public concern about their safety, has gone the increased acceptance of sterilization. After a stormy history of prohibitions and lawsuits the operation is now legal in every state.[39] A few states have enacted restrictions, such as mandatory waiting periods or a spouse's consent. Many hospitals have their own regulations, also requiring a spouse's consent or limiting sterilization to those women who have reached a given age and/or borne a given number of children. Courts have generally overturned such regulations[40] and it is doubtful many of the others would stand if challenged. Such a challenge has not yet gone to the United States Supreme Court.

The acceptance of voluntary sterilization has increased the problem of involuntary sterilization. Welfare mothers have charged that statutes allowing eugenic sterilizations on persons who are feeble-minded have been used to operate on them without any finding of mental incompetence.[41]

community property

Although community property exists in only eight states,[42] it is an important concept in equalizing the value of the roles of each partner

---

[36]Roe v. Wade, 410 U.S. 113; Doe v. Bolton, 410 U.S. 179.

[37]Griswold v. Connecticut, 381 U.S. 479 (1965).

[38]Eisenstadt v. Baird, 405 U.S. 438 (1972).

[39]The last two states to ban voluntary sterilization were Connecticut and Utah. The Connecticut law, CONN. GEN. STAT. § 53-33 (9158), was repealed by the legislature, P.A. 69-828, § 214, eff. Oct. 1, 1971. The Utah law, UTAH CODE ANN. § 64-10-12 (1968), which prohibited "destroying the power to procreate the human species" was interpreted by the Supreme Court of Utah as applying to eugenic sterilization only. Parker v. Rampton, 38 Utah 2d 36, 497 P.2d 848 (1972).

[40]*See, e.g.,* Coe v. District of Columbia Gen. Hosp., D.C. Dist. Ct., June 5, 1972, as reported in REPORTER IN HUMAN REPRODUCTION AND THE LAW; McCabe v. Nassau County Medical Center, 453 F.2d 698 (2d Cir. 1971).

[41]Relf v. Weinberger, 372 F. Supp. 1190 (D.D.C. 1974).

[42]Arizona, California, Idaho, Louisiana, Nevada, New Mexico, Texas, and Washington.

in a marriage. The theory is that each spouse owns one-half of the earnings of the "community"—a term analogous to "partnership" in business—regardless of who earned it. Thus, housework is recognized as a contribution to the marriage equal in value to work outside the home.

In practice, the status of the woman who stays home to keep house has been no better in community-property states than in common-law states. But that status has been improving. Although the actual laws vary, the trend is evident in each community-property state. California will be used as an example of the gradual increase in the wife's rights.

As originally enacted, California law provided that even though the wife owned one-half the property, she could not exercise the rights of ownership until she was divorced or widowed. She could challenge her husband's use of the property only if he was guilty of gross mismanagement. Through statutory revisions and court decisions, the husband's obligation to act as fiduciary became better defined. Ultimately, he lost the right to sell real property or give away any community assets without his wife's consent. With the exception of those restrictions, he could manage and control the property of the community.

The first major change came in 1951, when the woman was given management and control over her own earnings and personal injury damages awarded to her in lawsuits. However, if she mingled her money with that of her husband, she lost her right to manage it.

The spouses did not become equal in their rights over the community property until January 1, 1975. Now the rule in California is that either spouse can manage the property of the community. Major exceptions are that both must join in sales or long leases of real property and a spouse who operates a business has sole management and control of the business property. How these provisions will work in practice remains to be seen.

credit

A much needed Federal law giving protection to women who seek to establish credit went into effect October 28, 1975. The Equal Credit Opportunity Act[43] states that it shall be unlawful for any creditor to discriminate against any applicant on the basis of sex or marital status with respect to any aspect of a credit transaction.

Pursuant to the Act, the Board of Governors of the Federal Reserve System developed Regulation B,[44] which sets forth in detail the rights and obligations of creditors and applicants for credit.

The Regulation provides that a creditor shall not ask the applicant's marital status if the applicant applies for an unsecured separate account, except in a community property state or as required to comply

[43]15 U.S.C. sec. 1691 *et seq.*
[44]12 C.F.R. 202.

with state law governing permissible finance charges or loan ceilings.[45]

A creditor may request and consider information concerning an applicant's spouse if the spouse will be permitted to use the account, or will be contractually liable on the account, or the applicant is relying on community property, the spouse's income, alimony, child support or maintenance payments from a spouse or former spouse as a basis for repayment of the credit requested.[46]

Women should note that a creditor may not request information about birth-control practices or child-bearing intentions or capability, nor make generalized assumptions concerning childbearing when evaluating the applicant.[47]

Of particular importance to married women is the requirement that accounts reflect participation by both spouses if they each use the account or are contractually liable for it. This provision will allow a married woman to develop a credit history in her own name.[48]

A creditor who fails to comply with the Act risks civil liability for actual and punitive damages. Additionally, an aggrieved applicant who brings a successful action under the Act may be awarded costs and reasonable attorney fees.[49]

equal rights amendment

Legal rights are often derived from social expectations. Countless times judges have ignored the plain words of the Equal Protection Clause, secure in the knowledge that it was not meant to apply to women. The authors of the Fourteenth Amendment, when using the word "persons," were thinking of the newly freed male slaves and did not have women, either black or white, in mind.

But the genius of our system is the continual reinterpretation of the Constitution in light of changing cultural and economic conditions. The *Reed* case, rejecting a legislative classification based on sex, was a large step forward. But it did not go far enough. Unless the Supreme Court gives sex the status of a suspect classification, it is too easy for legislators to enact discriminatory laws and devise a "rational basis" for doing so.

The Equal Rights Amendment should settle the question of whether sex discrimination can be justified on a mere showing of rational basis or whether the state must prove it has a compelling interest in discriminating. In fact, the three justices in *Frontiero* who refused to call sex a suspect classification did so because the amendment was pending, and they did not want their judgment to render the decision of the people meaningless.

[45] 12 C.F.R. 202.4.
[46] 12 C.F.R. 202.5(b)(1).
[47] 12 C.F.R. 202.5(h).
[48] 12 C.F.R. 202.6.
[49] 12 C.F.R. 202.13.

The Equal Rights Amendment provides: Equality of rights under the law shall not be denied or abridged by the United States or by any state on account of sex. This Amendment, which has been introduced in its present or similar form in every Congress since 1923, finally passed the House and Senate in 1972. By the end of 1974, thirty-three states had ratified it, with five more needed before the deadline in 1979.

The probable effect of the Equal Rights Amendment was summarized in a leading textbook on sex discrimination.

In sum, the amendment would eliminate the historical impediment to unqualified judicial recognition of equal rights and responsibilities for men and women as constitutional principle; it would end legislative inertia that keeps discriminatory laws on the books despite the counsel of amendment opponents that removal or revision of these laws is "the way"; [footnote omitted] and it would serve as a clear statement of the nation's moral and legal commitment to a system in which women and men stand as full and equal individuals before the law.[50]

references

Boslooper, T., & Hayes, M., *The femininity game.* New York: Stein & Dat, 1973.

Davidson, K., Ginsburg, R., & Kay, H. *Sex-based discrimination.* St. Paul, Minn.: West, 1974.

DeCrow, K., *Sexist justice,* New York: Random House, 1974.

Kanowitz, L., *Sex roles in law and society.* Albequerque: University of New Mexico Press, 1973.

Summary of the Regulation for Title IX Education Amendments of 1972 by the Project on the Status and Education of Women, Association of American Colleges, Washington, D.C.

Ross, S. *The rights of women.* New York. Discus/Avon, 1973.

Valparaiso University Law Review, Symposium—Women and the law, 1971.

[50]Davidson, Ginsburg, & Kay, *Sex-Based Discrimination and the Law,* 116.

racism, sexism, and class elitism: change-agents' dilemmas in combatting oppression

Orian Worden

Gloria Levin

Mark Chesler

Racism, sexism, and class elitism are deeply rooted expressions of the structural relations upon which this nation was founded.[1] The realization that social oppression is a function of our social structure has crucial implications for change-agents[2] who wish to bring about social justice. We begin with an historical and contemporary analysis of some of the structures of racism, sexism, and class elitism. We argue that structurally rooted problems require structurally based analyses and strategies if solutions are to be effective. The change-agent's own position within that social structure invariably generates a series of significant personal dilemmas in the move toward social justice. A major focus of this paper is on a variety of dilemmas facing change agents. These dilemmas have their roots in questions of personal identity, institutional security, relationships with clients and constituencies, to name a few. Finally, we review a range of tactics that may be used to alter social oppression.

introduction

Our social structure includes people's basic assumptions about the social order and their social values. Some socially affirmed values are formally legitimized through the Constitution (e.g., the supremacy of private property); others are informal, although still intrusive and powerful in impact (e.g., individual achievement through competition). Some of our many formally stated values are belied by the realities of

[1] Although we focus this discussion on the systematic exclusion and oppression of persons along race, sex, and class lines, our conceptual framework is no less applicable to all socially oppressed classes including certain religious and ethnic groups, children, students, the physically and mentally handicapped, and the aged.

[2] For purpose of our paper, change-agents refers to a category of people who are committed to bringing about social change.

life in the United States of America (e.g., equal justice under law). Indeed, the reality of American life is often contrary to democratic rhetoric, and our values then are cultural rationalizations of elite political and economic interests.[3]

The dominant assumptions or ideologies of our society, legitimize the behaviors of those people in power, and justify the exclusion or subjugation of others. They also allow elites to maintain their grip on power and thus perpetuate serving their self-interests at the expense of non-elites.

Racial minorities were explicitly excluded from full participation in American society from the earliest days of our nation's history. Despite the doctrine that "all men are created equal," blacks were treated as three-fifths of a white male for the purpose of apportioning Congressional seats. Native Americans were not counted at all. Although racial minorities have won some legal rights, informal exclusionary practices continue to operate in support of white material interests and cultural affirmation. For instance, the definition of "white-Anglo intelligence" as a superior commodity assigns inferior status to the cultural and linguistic styles of racial minorities. Since white elites determine the standards by which intelligence is judged, and those standards, in turn, determine one's access to social mobility and econommic rewards, white elites can exclude racial minorities while assuring that their own children will be favored. And, they can do that on the ideological basis of presumed "merit," not prejudice.

Women were excluded from the right to vote until 1920 and today they are still virtually excluded from positions of political and economic power. One biologically determined function of women, the ability to reproduce, was used to justify their exclusion from power when the nation was primarily agrarian. (For a thorough discussion see Rae Blumberg's chapter in this book.) The widespread industrialization of our society and the movement of women into the work force in large numbers have only shifted the main site of sexual oppression from the home to the workplace. The restriction of women to low-paying jobs is justified by elites on the ideological basis of their supposed physical weakness (even when physical strength is not salient to the job function) and their temperamental "makeup."

Monopoly capitalism is the central organizing reality in our society for which a wide variety of functional mythologies or ideologies are constructed. For instance, one myth given wide currency is that an individual is wholly responsible for his or her own success in life, rather than being the potential victim of those structural arrangements

---

[3]Myrdal (1944) and others have suggested that simplistic notions of rhetoric and real values may not be the most useful concepts, and that on most basic issues Americans hold conflicting values or have "value dilemmas."

which systematically include or exclude him or her. The principle of individual responsibility (and its correlates of individual achievement and competition) is central to the capacity of our economic system to reward or penalize its workers differentially. Inequality in the allocation of rewards serves to spur members to higher productivity levels and higher profits for upper-class elites. Until recently, the rapid growth of the economy and a rising standard of living masked the fundamental and continuing inequality between social classes. But poor people and many middle-class people, are functionally oppressed by our politico-economic system.

The dominant ideology is being increasingly challenged by social activists with diverse racial, sexual, and class identities and interests. But disclosure of our underlying myths and structural realities is not sufficient for change; a coordinated and strategically effective challenge must also be mounted. Historical awareness of the roots of institutionalized racism, sexism, and class elitism sensitizes the change-agent to his or her own personal identity and membership in elite or nonelite groups. Self-awareness can then provide a foundation for the development of antiracist, antisexist, and anticlass elitist attitudes and behaviors. It also establishes for each of us a set of dilemmas and choice points; our resolution of these problems provides the direction of our work. Then we can discuss some specific tactics, guided by the need to be tuned to our own identities and capacities, and by our own analysis of the larger society. Those who attempt to correct structurally determined injustices must find ways to confront and alter the root inequities of our politico-economic system.

an historical perspective

Even at the time of the American Revolution, the political and social structure of the colonial society was profoundly and systematically limited by the colonists' conscious and unconscious notions of who was a citizen. Access to power in the New World was only accorded to representatives of Western European civilization, that is, to the white, Anglo-Saxon, affluent, male, adult, and Protestant (WAAMAP). The great social struggles of the ensuing two-hundred year history of the Republic have been between and among: a) those who wanted to broaden participation and include more people in the governance and reward structures of the society (led primarily by people who considered themselves outsiders); and b) those who wanted to maintain the initial exclusionary categories of participation—WAAMAP (led primarily by people who considered themselves insiders).

exclusion based on race

At the beginning of the twentieth century, W. E. B. DuBois made one of the most startlingly accurate observations and predictions about Western society generally, and American society particularly. He stated that, "the problem of the twentieth century is the problem of the color line, the relation of the darker to the lighter races of men in Asia and Africa, and America and the islands of the sea" (DuBois, 1969, p. 54). DuBois based his observation on three hundred years of European attempts at military, economic, political, social, and cultural domination of people of color. William Lowndes Yancey, a southern legislator speaking in 1860 before a northern audience stated: "Your fathers and my fathers built this government on two ideas: the first is that the white race is the citizen and the master race and the white *man* is the equal of every other white *man* (italics added). The second idea is that the negro is the inferior race." (Frederikson, 1971, p. 61) Seventy-five years into the twentieth century both men have been proven correct about America.

The leaders of capitalist America's economic, political, and social institutions have successfully used racism among other things to maintain their dominance. Racism has been, and continues to be, a readily available tool for the systematic political and economic exclusion of "inferior" groups.

exclusion based on sex

The dominant ideology promulgated by white male elites defined women's "natural" roles in terms of their reproductive ability rather than their wider range of human talents and contributions. In a production-conscious society women have been defined primarily in terms of their relationship to their men and their men's roles in the means of production. The exclusion of women from positions of power was also reflected in their virtual absence, until very recently, from the recorded political, economic, and social history of the nation (Brown & Seitz, 1970).

Yet, women played essential roles in the building of our society. In the primarily agricultural economy of colonial America, women had a diversity of roles at the side of the men. Women selected for their physical strength and skills settled the frontier lands. But industrialization brought about a separation of home and productive labor; work performed by homebound women was undervalued in the commodity-oriented economy. Even those laws passed to protect women's supposed physical weaknesses were used to exclude them from access to higher pay and status.

The myth of women's physical and intellectual inferiority was accompanied by a myth of their moral superiority, and both were used to oppress them. As agents for socialization, women were expected to be the custodians of the culture's morality even when that culture was based on deep-rooted inequalities and injustices. Upper-class women were encouraged to volunteer for progressive welfare activities partly to deflect attention from their husband's exploitative business practices (Domhoff, 1970).

exclusion
based on class

One genius of the American capitalist elite is its ability to obscure society's historical and contemporary economic and social-class distinctions. Capitalists have successfully obscured the reality of oppression with ideological homilies such as "people are rewarded for merit, not situations of their birth," and "the society is open and classless, with plenty of opportunity for mobility." As a result, white workers have identified the "enemy" as blacks, other racial minorities, or women.

Historically, white elites took advantage of the great majority of whites, male and female, and co-opted the nonlanded, largely uneducated, but security-seeking laboring classes.[4] Poor whites have been free from slavery, but that freedom has been a floundering and drifting search for a clear identity and a secure life. In fact, the reality of our class situation is that a few white males dominate and exploit great masses of other white males: as a group white males are more powerful and privileged than white females and males or females of color.

**summary for a
contemporary
analytic
framework**

Racism, sexism, and class elitism interlock and overlap. These relationships support a white male-dominated politico-economic-socio-cultural system. The system holds out small, motivating incentives while it continues to exclude racial minorities, the poor, and females. However, there is evidence that increasing numbers of people in these excluded groups know that failure to achieve in the system is related to the structure of the system, not to their "personal defects." The winds of present and future change flow from that growing awareness.

The core issues in fundamental or institutional change rest on the reallocation of these structures and resources. Power is the master variable; whoever controls or changes it determines the distribution of other social rewards and resources. Those now in control of societal power administer it in ways that speak to their continuing advantage and privilege.

To be in control in our society means to possess various forms of power privileges and benefits.

concentration
of economic
power

One form of control is the concentration of economic power among the elite and is reflected in the following benefits: their receipt of the greater portion of economic resources, salaries, and investment returns; their control of offices and positions of economic leadership in the public and private sectors; their use of women as supporters of working men in economic policies from which they will be the prime beneficiaries; their use of black and other racial minorities as cheap labor pools exploited by corporations; and their positions at the top of

---

[4]A thorough analysis of this reality is far beyond the scope of this effort; however, for a series of excellent treatments see: Aronowitz, 1973; Baltzell, 1964; Campbell, 1974; Domhoff, 1967; Lundberg, 1968; Mills, 1956.

monetary and security hierarchies that create permanent classes of unemployed and underemployed minorities and women.

**political
power**

Another form that benefits the elite is the concentration of political power; their access to and control of membership positions in representative organizations; their leadership in voluntary political agencies and social movements; and their designing of legislative and executive policies and programs from which they benefit.

**cultural
power**

The control of the elites is further reflected in the concentration of cultural power: their manufacturing and maintenance of ideologies which support democratic centralism and the concentration of political power; their support of the notion that the rich have worked harder and have better genes, are more intelligent or at least somehow merit their superior economic and political positions; and their continuing beliefs that women are less rational, less decisive, weaker, more emotional, less able to cope, or are different in crucial economic and political aspects of life, and that blacks, browns, reds, and members of other racial minorities are the creators of their own oppression in America.

**professional
change-agentry
and the fight
against social
oppression**

Programs to alter racism, sexism, and class elitism must focus upon the structure of American society. Various social movements use different forms of economic, political, and cultural power—power now vested primarily in the hands of white, male, and affluent elites.

All movements for social change need workers especially wise in the ways of change-making. That wisdom includes skill in understanding social systems and organizations, in helping people to clarify their values, in improving group processes, and in providing leadership in negotiating, organizing demonstrations, and so on. People with such skills always have played vital roles in the history of change. As in all sectors of our highly technocratic society, however, the field of change-agentry has become highly specialized and technologically sophisticated. We have developed special training programs and peer associations for people identified with the social change profession.

The professional change-agent is presumed to have unique expertise in change-making, primarily as a result of special training in a university or other advanced educational system, and usually buttressed by state and peer association. She/he is also assumed to be able to work for others' goals, and to be able to subordinate personal priorities to the needs of a client group.[5] Most professional change-agents are recognizable by their identification with the applied behavioral

[5]In general, these are the essential characteristics of any profession, as outlined in: Friedson (1971); Haug and Sussman (1969); Wolfe (1970).

sciences—a broad categorization including educational managers and consultants, social workers, community organizers and planners, group process consultants, human relations trainers, and applied social scientists.

It should be clear that one need not be a professional to be a competent change-agent.[6] Yet, professional change-agents are also the most visible kind in our society, the subjects or objects of an overwhelming portion of the scholarly literature on change.

choice points for dealing with social justice and power

Professional change-agents can proceed with their efforts to alter aspects of social systems in many ways. *Some change-agents are not explicitly concerned with goals of social justice and with the eradication of racism, sexism, and class elitism.* Rather, they see the maintenance of the societal status quo, or at least their role in it, as tied to the welfare of ruling elites. They are committed, overtly or covertly, to maintaining the privileged position of white, male, and affluent power holders. Others see this as the natural order, perhaps even as a reflection of the "survival of the fittest." Direct service to elites often is justified by presenting them as the caretakers of a chaotic society, our "best hope" for a better future for all.

Some justify working with elites or with any one else as a way of making everyone happier, irrespective of racial, sexual, and class barriers and issues. Such views assume that elites and oppressed racial, sexual, and economic groups share the same interests and values. The essential underlying political principle is that we all have a lot in common; if we work together, especially under the leadership of the "best qualified" among us, we can all do well. Little attention is paid to the historic evidence that what is justified by society's leaders as being in the best interests of "all the people" turns out to be best mostly for the political, economic, and cultural elites.

Some change-agents are explicitly concerned with issues of justice, but fail to consider the power of institutions to maintain or alter injustice. Rather, they see it as possible to alter societal patterns of racism, sexism, and class without altering centers of societal power. For instance, some specialists in changing organizational systems attribute economic injustice to an inefficient economic system; hence they commit themselves to the expansion of industrial productivity, the improvement of industrial morale, or the greater rationalization of industrial

[6]Crowfoot and Chesler (1974) have provided a useful categorization of professionals and other change-agents operating from different assumptions and meeting different criteria for performance—as well as the differences that makes. In their view, professional change-agents are typified in the writings of Bennis, Benne, & Chin (1969), Likert (1961), Rogers & Shoemaker (1971), and Schein (1969). Change-agents writing from a frankly political perspective include Alinsky (1969), Carmichael & Hamilton (1967), and Machiavelli (1957). And a countercultural perspective on change-agentry is evident in the writings of Fairfield (1972), Fromm (1955), and Schutz (1971).

management methods. Of course, such an analysis and prescription proceeds from one of the central myths of monopoly capitalism—that economic growth will lead to economic/social equality.

Another approach is taken by those who try to handle racism or sexism on an individual basis; they attempt to change individuals' attitudes rather than institutional structures and norms. Unless the activities of change-agents alter the underlying norms of our culture rather than solely individuals, these agents are unlikely to counter the power of racist and sexist institutions and cultural patterns. Moreover, until their activities effectively plan to resist institutional racism and sexism, the minor changes in attitude or life styles they are able to effect will be obliterated by the weight of traditions, daily rules and roles, and the general cultural press.

Some change-agents are explicitly concerned with issues of social justice and try to bring it about by manipulating social power. They attempt to design programs to resist the prevailing power elites; they try to activate the potential power of oppressed groups; they coordinate their activities with on-going social movements for reform. The choices made by these agents contrast sharply with the choices of those not explicitly committed to social justice, and those apparently committed to social justice but who do not know how to make changes or are unwilling or unable to alter patterns of ruling power.

major dilemmas facing change-agents fighting injustice

Change-agents who employ power to fight social injustice are inevitably confronted by a series of major dilemmas and existential choice points. Each requires clear thinking and action in the face of substantial cultural ambiguity and personal risk. We feel personally qualified to discuss these complex dilemmas, alternative role definitions, and strategic options because we are faced with them daily. We also experience the doubts and anxieties which accompany these dilemmas, and any particular resolution of them.

dilemma #1

With whom do I identify and on what basis? In the most extreme instance, one may choose to identify with owners and managers of the corporate establishment or with those who are excluded from institutional centers of power and privilege. Each person begins to solve this dilemma according to race, sex, and class membership. Affluent white males are most likely to identify with the ruling elites; at least, this is an expected outcome of normal socialization and professionalization. The sense of privilege accruing to these hereditary roles and statuses usually precludes effective identification with "out groups." However, although race and sex clearly are immutable, some class mobility does exist in the society. Change-agents committed to social justice goals can renounce their affluence by taking "vows of poverty" and working for subsistence wages. Others have found it possible or necessary to develop new forms of white or male or affluent consciousness that are less exploitative than previous commitments and styles.[7] It is probably impossible for whites to be fully antiracist (or for males to be completely antisexist, etc.), but one can be resocialized to relatively non-exploitative modes of involvement in social justice movements with and on behalf of third-world groups, poor people, and women.

Still other change-agents have determined that being socialized as affluent white males has inevitably prevented them from effectively serving nonprivileged groups. Consequently, they elect to work with their own kind, to try to alter group consciousness, oppressive behaviors, and the nature of their relationships with each other and oppressed peoples. This is accomplished through rap groups, workshops in value clarification, and so on.[8]

The change-agent who is third-world, female, and/or nonaffluent confronts this dilemma differently. She or he is not "of" the society, even if "in" it, and this exclusion creates different alternatives for identification and work with varied groups. The struggle to deal with a society that oppresses because of one's birthright is easily shared with people who have had the same experience.

In working with elites, however, there is a greater potentiality for doubt, uncertainty, lack of clarity, and confusion. As a representative of an oppressed group, or as an oppressed person working with the oppressor, a primary danger, of course, is isolation, especially immediate isolation from one's own membership cadre. When this occurs the identity issues can become blurred, and with them clarity of analysis and strategy. The seduction of apparent acceptance on the basis of perceived merit or untested friendship, or other material and symbolic rewards, increases with increased contact with the elites. The elites will not grant *full* membership in the majority society to the nonelites, and recognition of this reality allows the change-agent to have a clearer analysis of situational dynamics and of effective change strategies. Thus, it may be possible to appear to support elite power arrangements while actually working to increase the contradictions in ideology and in practice, and also to help mobilize oppressed groups to action.

dilemma #2   Can I overcome being centered on the interests of my own group in order to analyze effectively concentrations of power and privilege, patterns of exclusion and oppression, and strategies for their eradication?

[7]This redefinition of self-interest in less exploitative form requires one to learn to be "in" but not "of" the majority system . . . to be aware of the privileges of one's group of origin, but to resist identifying, depending, or capitalizing on those privileges.
[8]Some materials extending this argument and providing examples of organizing or retraining activities of this sort are described for males in Bradley, et al., 1971; Pleck & Sawyer, 1974; Farrell, n.d. Similar descriptions for whites can be found in Terry, 1970; Heyer & Monte, 1969; Karenga, 1969. Some class parallels are explored in Grosser, 1967.

Since each of our locations in the social system predisposes the kinds of analyses we make as well as the blinders we wear, how can I learn to see clearly beyond these limitations?

The American tradition of social science research often neglects the operations of power in our institutions. This omission strongly effects our ability to design effective change efforts through valid institutional and macro-societal diagnoses. That diagnostic failure helps maintain the invisibility and hence invulnerability of corporate centers of power. For if power is not effectively diagnosed, or is systematically overlooked, it cannot be altered.[9]

An effective diagnosis raises anew the difficulties encountered in dilemma #1. For instance, when a female change-agent is able to diagnose clearly the operations of male power, she is free to develop strategies that combat that monopolistic control. On the other hand, a male who tried to make that diagnosis is encumbered by his own collusive self-interest in the maintenance of male privilege and control. How can he do this himself, partly blinded by the myopia that sexism engenders?

Similarly, third-world groups probably see more clearly than whites the racist operations of our corporate production and welfare systems. Their own self-interest does not require them to see America as the land of equal opportunity; rather they are healthier if they understand the way their life opportunities are limited by racism.* In a culture that teaches us that merit is rewarded and achievements result from individual effort, the privileges of class are seen as the just rewards of a perservering Horatio Alger even against substantial odds. For affluent white men to see it otherwise might suggest that they attained their privileges on other than meritorious bases. The affluent view might also suggest changing those mechanisms that guarantee advantages to successive generations of the affluent young, and that protect them from failure, downward mobility, and other outcomes common to oppressed groups.

dilemma #3   From what base can a person work most appropriately for social change? Every change-agent has to organize his or her efforts in some way, and these modes generally are influenced by one's institutional "home base."

Change-agents operating from the base of a contemporary university carry with them the professional norms and sanctions of one of the primary bastions of affluent white male ideology. The university may be a center of action for social reform or social amelioration. But since it is

[9]Chesler and Worden (1974) indicate how important and neglected this issue is in the conduct of social-change programs.

*There can, of course, be myopia on the part of oppressed groups that clouds their analysis of objective conditions and confuses their subjective consciousness. A change-agent must be prepared to deal with this self-interest problem as well.

controlled by and accountable to dominant interests of monopoly capitalism, it cannot be a meaningful base of operations for fundamental social change (Smith, 1974). A change-agent who uses the university for these purposes, nevertheless, will encounter the following:

The commitment to credentialization (through the norm systems of white males and the affluent) screens out otherwise qualified or competent people who differ from the majority.

The emphasis on theory and analysis discourages actual application, involvement, commitment, and work in social system change.

Screening and admission procedures for students and faculty favor the white and the affluent.

Anxiety about disturbing trustees, legislators, contributors and alumni who form the base of support for the university prevents the making of significant social justice reforms.

The protection of university investments in portfolios is tied to the success of monopoly capitalism.

Norms of "academic freedom" and "individual merit" are invoked to support racist, sexist, and class elitist practices (in hiring, promoting, teaching, counseling, etc.).

The appearance of neutrality and detachment from overt action masks actual consultation with and covert support for the ruling elites.

Those change-agents who do operate on social justice objectives from within the universities do so with full attention to the duality of their position. They usually operate on the "soft money" margin, or in a subversive way, wherein they deliberately violate the letter and/or spirit of traditional academic norms.

Some change-agents interested in moving towards social justice have elected to resolve this dilemma by working with organizations directly committed to anti-elitist goals. Here they may be relatively free of some identity confusions, but still vulnerable to anxieties about status, security, and professional credibility. For example, the female change-agent who works with a women's organization is potentially vulnerable to charges that she is a narrow specialist or too partisan to be objective. The third-world professional who acts on his or her commitments to social justice often is narrowly slotted into jobs that call only for specialists on black or Chicano affairs, or native American affairs. Consequently, minority change-agents are isolated from other issues and from centers of mainstream power, so their opportunity and impact are further limited.[10] White and male change-agents who elect to work for social justice from the anti-elitist base are subject to many

---

[10]Covert discussions often are held among members of the white male elite about the "personal needs," "identity hang-ups," or "acting out mechanisms" being employed by such highly committed female and third-world change-agents.

of the same exclusions and sanctions. As past members of the privileged club, they may be seen as unpredictable defectors and perhaps as even more dangerous and threatening to their former colleagues.

A third major institutional base for effecting change is through self-employment. Some change-agents operate in a free-lance style, hiring themselves out to a variety of institutional clients who seek and can afford their services (or to whom they volunteer). For those willing to make less money, this can be a very effective mode. Yet, this freedom of action must be accompanied by occasional monitoring by friends; otherwise it slips too easily into self-serving interests potentially divorced from social justice objectives. The concern for survival may turn many heads.

dilemma #4   How will I relate to the people I wish to serve or work with—my client, consumer group, or constituency group? This broad question contains at least three issues: 1) What will be my reward for services? 2) What controls will groups exert on me and on my work? and 3) What are the resources or services I will provide, discover, create, and so on? Clearly defined and reciprocal contracts on those issues can help overcome change-agents' exploitation of clients.

Different change-agents have different definitions and priorities for rewards. Some are concerned primarily with financial remuneration for their services or consider this vital to any helping transaction. For others, doing research or gaining knowledge and experience in something new and interesting is most important. In yet other cases, prestige, being appreciated by people in need, or acting out one's general social commitments may be most salient. Of course, these rewards are not necessarily mutually exclusive, but for any change-agent at any specific time, some rewards have priority over others.

If financial rewards are paramount, the change-agent is probably limited to working with the economic elites. This is especially likely when the change-agent has no other financial base of operations. If she/he has met survival needs otherwise, or can work for financial rewards part time, she/he can contribute volunteer time to economically oppressed groups as well.

Many applied behavioral scientists greatly value their intellectual and operational autonomy, and do not wish to share real control of their activities with client or constituency groups. Thus, they operate without a contract, or with a very vague contract, or without clear client understandings ("informed consent") of their intended methods and/or goals. Even when a contract is made, its basic ideology and format are usually controlled by the professional. Mindful of the many ways the social system operates to deny self-determination to oppressed peoples, other change-agents explicitly make contracts that provide oppressed groups with clear monitoring devices and control over change-agent activities. It is essential to agree on specific resources and services that are needed and can be delivered. Rather than relying on mystical expertise, the change-agent is obligated to disclose and account for the precise elements of his or her professional know-how and the ways in which it can or cannot be useful to client groups. In such circumstances, the change-agents' role is more that of a technical aide than as an independent professional with unchecked influence over clients.

dilemma #5   Is it possible and desirable for me to retain my status and privileges as a professional and still work effectively for social justice objectives? This is a central dilemma running through the entire section and can help us summarize earlier portions of the discussion.

Assumed hallmarks of professional status include: access to specialized expertise through a selective academic training process; commitment to broad goals of public welfare and an altruistic willingness to serve others; legitimation by the state or professional peers; and substantial autonomy in the conduct and evaluation of work. Chesler and Lohman (1971) question whether it is possible for persons with such training and commitments to serve the interests of oppressed groups. They argue that such service runs counter to the self-interest of the professional class and requires contradictions almost impossible to resolve.

Reiff (1974) raises other questions about the inherently antidemocratic and oppressive tendencies of professionalism.[11] For instance, the state certifies legal, medical, educational and welfare professionals and then delegates control over these jobs to the same professionals. When the right to decide upon the nature of service, control the delivery system, judge staffing competencies, and evaluate performance reside within the profession, it has a virtual monopoly on practice. Moreover, the professional has a monopoly on the knowledge that underlies legal, medical, educational, or welfare programs. Thus, it is hard for oppressed groups (or any served group for that matter) to advocate their own service needs in light of their alleged "ignorance" and alleged inability to evalute "objectively" the quality of professional services.

The democratization of the professions and the demystification of professional knowledge may provide people with greater control over their own lives. Any professionalism that totally controls services and knowledge stands in the way of such self-determination. Examples of such efforts include: the promulgation of preventive or self-help measures and the wider diffusion of expertise, as well as information

[11]Most current "paraprofessional" programs neither democratize nor demystify the professions. Because professionals still control both knowledge and practice, the potential reform thrust of paraprofessionalism is vitiated.

about professional error (demystification); and client formulation of needs; client monitoring and control of services; and client definition of professional membership as well as practice (democratization).

tactics

We are aware of a variety of appropriate tactics for countering racism, sexism, and class elitism. Although the potential tactical range is broad, the following depend upon the reallocation of power or the alteration of centers of power that support systems of oppression. We continue to believe that the resolution of the aforementioned five dilemmas of social change-agentry underlie any tactical choice. These tactics vary according to the target, the change-agent's skills, his or her own group membership; and personal orientation to and awareness of that membership.

helping organize oppressed groups

One can provide support to oppressed people in their own struggles to gain and assert power for change. Generally we can distinguish three stages of the organizing process, in each of which the change-agent can serve a useful function:

1. Consciousness-raising or the development of oppressed people's awareness of their common situation and of the need for collective action. The professional change-agent may be useful at this stage in helping develop or diffuse diagnostic information that reflects the realities of common oppression and which counters societal myths of individual achievement, merit and minority "satisfaction."
2. Mobilization or activation of groups on the basis of their common values, interests, and goals for change. The professional change-agent may be helpful at this stage in sharing the experiences of other movements in this regard.
3. Confrontation, bargaining or some other means of implementing goals and programs in ways that capture or influence power centers and improve the rewards of oppressed peoples. The professional change-agent who has information and skill of a tactical sort can be very useful at this stage.

We have indicated that one of the central dilemmas facing the professional change-agent and the oppressed group is whether the one can be really helpful to the other and if so, how? Doesn't "helping" reflect the continuing dominance of the powerful over the powerless and thus retard oppressed peoples' abilities for self-determination? Oppressed groups must develop and actualize their own skills and resources, using external change-agents as technical assistants in order to insure that the professional is not in charge of the control pattern, but is controlled by it.

2. threatening elites

If we assume that it is in the self-interest of ruling classes to retain their power, and thus their privileged share of societal resources and rewards, we can also assume that threats or challenges to the maintenance of such power and privilege might alter their practices. Thus, it would seem possible and appropriate to promote social justice goals by influencing the material self-interests of elite classes.

Oppressed groups may be able to mobilize strategic threats to the well-being and continued domination of ruling classes in several ways:

1. By threatening to withhold key resources which they control and which are essential to elite status or reward. Examples of such resources may include cheap labor, consumership (through product boycotts), and sexual activity.
2. By disrupting the orderly fabric of society in ways that prevent monopoly capitalism from maintaining its economic and political control. Examples of such actions might include urban violence and insurrections, wildcat strikes, cattle spoilage, industrial sabotage, mass resignation, and building takeovers.
3. By identifying and threatening individual members of oppressor groups with their personal safety, comfort, and security. Examples of such actions might include harassment, kidnapping, personal liability litigation, and exposure.

Several of these tactical possibilities appear to violate the canons of professional change-agentry; as such they may threaten the rewards one might expect from continued alliance with professional status and institutional bases. This not only represents a personal dilemma, but raises anew the question of how one can serve a group whose tactics may threaten one's own self-interest.

3. promoting and encouraging values of social justice and democracy

Many social theorists have assumed that persons operate at least in part on the basis of their preferred social values. For many Americans the constitutional concerns with social justice and social equality are not mere rhetoric, but are deeply internalized arbiters of feeling and action. Thus, an outright appeal to values of social justice and equality may help change unjust attitudes and practices, promote humanism in social structures and otherwise have a positive impact upon the policy positions and programs governed by the elites.

On the other hand, many theorists of human behavior argue that we do not act primarily on the basis of our values, but on the basis of psychic, economic, or political forces. They argue that our apparent free choices of values really are outgrowths of our roles and status in the cultural and politico-economic system. Certainly we have indicated such a bias in our own thinking, since we have noted the natural barriers to social justice commitments and actions in persons of white, male, and affluent backgrounds. In this context it is appropriate to consider once again the dilemma of the professional role itself. Are the ideologies and institutions of professionalism themselves inconsistent with democratic practice in public service systems?

4. exploiting contradictions in the elite

It is clear that ruling groups of white, male, and affluent persons do not always see eye-to-eye or collaborate with each other. At certain times and places they contradict and compete with each other, and then change-agents working with or for oppressed groups can heighten the instability of these ruling classes. "Divide and conquer" tactics can be used to decrease elite control just as the elites have used those tactics to fragment the potential unity of oppressed groups.

One example of work of this sort can be found in recent white ethnic movements which redefine these identities. The differences between our Germanic and English heritages are substantial, and every attempt to focus attention on those differences helps to crack the monolith of white Protestant power. The power of affluent classes also is challenged by the splits between the older and younger generation of privileged white Americans. The factions within the leadership of the Democratic Party during the elections of 1972, and the developing factions within the top echelons of the Republican Party post-Watergate, also indicate how the old coalition politics among elites are changing—at least temporarily or potentially over the long haul.

The change-agents' role amidst these developments are to lend support to them. That requires a sophisticated analysis that does not take past alliances as givens, but tests their future potentials. Diagnostic data and training experiences that highlight the inconsistencies among ideology, role behavior, and future promises are among the most helpful devices.

5. create alternative societal forms

One way to restructure the society along radically different lines is to create alternative forms for cooperative material production, distribution, and consumption. These forms, together with compatible new modes for family, schooling, religion, and so on, can be the start of a new culture that stands as a model for the old. In order to lessen the functional dominance of the ruling elite it is necessary to lessen our dependence on them, especially our material dependence. Therefore, the first steps usually require adoption of a simpler life style, one less materially oriented, or at least less materially dependent on the majority culture and its artifacts.

Change-agents' roles in this tactical approach are to learn and practice values and life styles that are humane and nonexploitative, life styles detached from the prior emphasis of monopoly capitalism. Personal resocialization is an important component of the ability to join with other groups and persons in the creation of communes, cooperatives, free schools, new family networks, and so on. For the professional change-agent, this tactic also implies giving up professional prerogatives and credentials. Rewards in alternative cultural systems are generally provided for survival skills in land management and food or craft production, areas far from the training of the professional change-agent. Skills in human resource development and in the creation of human living and working groups may be quite relevant, but as practiced by a member, not as an outside consultant.

This tactic represents a form of withdrawal from direct confrontation or relationships with elites and elite structures. But it is not a retreat as such from the effort to bring about social change. The goal here is social change; the tactics are to pull back and create alternatives that can serve as full or partial models for the dominant society or for certain of its institutions. It argues that change cannot be created from within, and that we must step outside of the mainstream society in order to change it.

One of the problems of this tactic is that is has been hard for oppressed people wrestling with the problems of material survival to elect further deprivation for the sake of social change. As a result, the primary emphasis upon developing alternative cultural forms has come from relatively privileged portions of the population, especially the young, white, and affluent. But many from this class have been successful, at least in the short run. They have been able to overcome the myriad problems engendered by prior socialization and cultural resistance, and have created new life styles and important new images of social life. Some have even successfully projected alternative models back onto segments of the mainstream society. For instance, the development of new ecological styles, the increasing use of marijuana by middle-class persons, the creation of new family structures and child-centered day-care centers and schools. The changes in consciousness and commitment of children of the elite sooner or later also has other effects—on their families, on the recruitment of others into slots they vacate, and on their later use of inherited wealth.

6. let the system rot

A final group of tactics starts from the position that there is little hope of this society holding together in its present form much longer, and little hope of peaceful reform. The general assumptions behind this view seem to be threefold:

1. Basic contradictions among the elites and between the elite and oppressed groups are so great that the system can not hope to hold together much longer.
2. Society is so shot through with the self-destructive seeds of racism, sexism, and classism that there is little hope of turning this situation around.

3. No elite group will or has given up its privileges and control of the social system without a fight. And, given the state of our technology, and the machinery of state violence at their beckon, elite resistance mandates disaster.

Professional change-agents, therefore, might as well not bother making serious investments of time and energy in trying to alter historic patterns of social injustice. Rather, they might better plan for their own survival and for the survival of the ones they love.

If the system will rot of its own accord and has the potential to explode in cataclysmic ways, it will also mean the end of the privileged rewards the change-agent gathers from his or her professional status and operations.

conclusion

Indeed, why not sit back and wait for the system to consume itself? That certainly would justify affluence and leisure, as well as a more relaxed approach to change. But if we recognize the many ways in which elites can maintain their control despite blundering inefficiencies, we cannot be content to sit back, placing total faith in "historic inevitability." Nor can we afford to be patient when confronted daily with widespread suffering.

One essential characteristic of all change-agents has to be a shared conviction or hope that social change is possible. But this conviction cannot rest on naive faith; it must begin with an accurate analysis which reflects the cultural, political, and economic realities of American society. And, it must be an analysis tied to effective tactics which provide impetus to change efforts in the direction of social justice and equality.

Those who would commit their efforts to combating the institutional determinants of racism, sexism, and class elitism participate in the daily struggles of oppressed peoples. Their energies, in concert with the actions of many others, may help bring this society closer to a vision of true justice and equality—for all. We either move in that direction or we do not; there is no middle ground, no neutrality, and no escape.

references

Alinsky, S. *Reveille for radicals.* New York: Random House, 1969.
Aronowitz, S. *False promises: The development of American working class consciousness.* New York: McGraw-Hill, 1973.
Baltzell, D. *The Protestant establishment.* New York: Random House, 1964.
Bennis, W., Benne, K. and Chin, R. (Ed.) *The planning of change.* New York: Holt, Rinehart and Winston, 1969.
Bradley, M., Danchik, L., Fager, M., & Wodetzki, T. *Unbecoming men: A men's consciousness-raising group writes on oppression and themselves.* N.J.: Times Change Press, 1971.

Brown, C., & Seitz, J. You've come a long way, Baby. In R. Morgan (Ed.) *Sisterhood is powerful*. New York: Vintage, 1970.

Campbell, W. The world of the redneck. *Katallagete*, 1974, *5* (1), 34-40.

Carmichael, S., & Hamilton, C. *Black power: The politics of liberation in America*. New York: Random House, 1967.

Chesler, M., & Lohman, J. Changing schools through student advocacy. In R. Schmuck and M. Miles (Eds.), *Organizational development in schools*. Palo Alto, Calif.: National Press Books, 1971.

Chesler, M. & Worden, O. Persistent problems in 'Power and Social Change.' *Journal of Applied Behavioral Sciences*, 1974, *10*, 462-472.

Crowfoot, J., & Chesler, M. Contemporary perspectives on planned social change: A comparison. *Journal of Applied Behavioral Sciences*, 1974, *10* 278-303.

Domhoff, W. *Who rules America?* Englewood Cliffs, N.J.: Prentice-Hall, 1967.

Domhoff, W. *The higher circles*, New York: Random House, 1970.

DuBois, W. E. B. *Souls of black folk*. New York: New American Library, 1969.

Fairfield, R. *Communes, U.S.A.* Baltimore: Penguin, 1972.

Farrell, W. *NOW masculine mystique Kit*. Chicago: Publication of NOW.

Fredrickson, G. *The black image in the white mind*. New York: Harper & Row, 1971.

Freidson, E. Professionalism: The doctor's dilemma, *Social Policy*, January February 1971, 35-40.

Fromm, E. *The Sane Society*. New York: Holt, Rinehart and Winston, 1955.

Grosser, C., Class orientations of the indigenous staff. In G. Brager and F. Purcell (Eds.) *Community action against poverty*, New Haven Conn.: College and University Press, 1967.

Haug, M. & Sussman, M. Professional autonomy and the revolt of the client. *Social Problems*, 1969, *17*, 153-161.

Heyer, R., & Monte, F. *Am I a racist?* New York: Association Press, 1969.

Karenga, R. The black community and the university: A community organizer's perspective. In A. Robinson, (Eds.), *Black studies in the university*. New Haven, Conn.: Yale University Press, 1969.

Likert, R. *New perspectives of management*. New York: McGraw-Hill, 1961.

Lundberg, F. *The rich and the super-rich*. New York: Lyle Stuart, 1968.

Machiavelli, N. *The prince*. New York: Mentor, 1957.

Mills, C. W. *The power elite*. New York: Oxford University Press, 1956.

Mydral, G. *An American dilemma*. New York: Harper & Row, 1944.

Pleck, J., & Sawyer, J. *Men and masculinity*. Englewood Cliffs, N.J.: Prentice-Hall, 1974.

Reiff, R. The control of knowledge: The power of the helping professions. *Journal of Applied Behavioral Sciences*, 1974, *10*, 451-462.

Rogers, E., & Shoemaker, F. *Communication of innovations*. New York: Free Press, 1971.

Schein, E. *Process consultation: Its role in organizational development*. Reading, Mass.: Addison-Wesley, 1969.

Shutz, W. *Here comes everybody*. New York: Harper & Row, 1971.

Smith, D. *Who rules the universities: A class analysis*. New York: Monthly Review Press, 1974.

Terry, R. *For whites only*. Grand Rapids, Mich.: Eerdmans, 1970.

Wolfe, A. The perils of professionalism. *Change*, September-October 1970, 51-54.

about the contributors

Dee G. Appley

Dee G. Appley is presently a member of the clinical faculty, Department of Psychology, University of Massachusetts, Amherst. She is also a therapist and a human relations consultant. She taught previously at York University (Toronto), Southern Illinois University, and Connecticut College for Women. For more than a decade, she has been associated with change projects both inside and outside the university, and presently defines desirable change as a function of consciousness, choice, commitment, caring, and collaboration. The keystone of her theory and practice is collaboration which she sees as a process as "natural" as competition. Some recent publications include: *Work and the Human Condition; Making a Living, Making a Life* (in press); *Collaboration in Higher Education: Development of a Behavioral Science Alliance* with William Kraus and Donald Carew (Development, CREDR Corp., Calif., 1974); and *T-Groups and Therapy Groups in a Changing Society* with Alvin Winder (Jossey-Bass, 1973). She is presently working on two major projects: She is researching changing attitudes of men and women towards work and marriage; and with several colleagues, she is working on a theory of collaboration as an alternative model for human relations. At present, art is an avocation. She looks forward to the time when art will be her "work."

Carol Agate

Carol Agate received her B.A. from Brown University in 1955 and her J.D., with honors, from the University of Connecticut School of Law in 1974. She was an associate editor of the *Connecticut Law Review* and recipient of the American Jurisprudence Award for research and writing. While in law school she lived in Westport, Connecticut, where she served as Justice of the Peace, alter-

nate member of the Zoning Board of Appeals, director of Fairfield County Legal Services, and trustee of the Westport Public Library. She has been active in the feminist movement as a member of NOW, WEAL, NWPC, and the Women's Right Project of the ACLU. She is also a Deputy City Attorney in Los Angeles.

Elizabeth Aries

Elizabeth (Buffy) Aries holds a Ph.D. from Harvard University in social relations and in social psychology and is presently an assistant professor of psychology in the Department of Psychology at Amherst College. Her major area of research is interaction styles of men and women in groups.

Judith Bardwick

Judith Bardwick is an associate professor of psychology at the University of Michigan. Her research has become increasingly philosophic and existential, focusing on issues of values, feelings of worth and of morality, crises of aging, and the psychodynamics of work and of success. In addition to papers, speeches and book chapters, she has written *Psychology of Women* (New York: Harper & Row, 1971), co-authored *Feminine Personality and Conflict* (Monterey, Calif.: Brooks-Cole, 1970), and edited *Readings on the Psychology of Women* (New York: Harper & Row, 1972).

Sandra Lipsitz Bem

Sandra Lipsitz Bem received her B.A. in psychology at Carnegie Mellon University in Pittsburgh and her Ph.D. in developmental psychology at the University of Michigan. After earning her Ph.D., she returned to Carnegie

470

Mellon to teach for several years and then joined the faculty of Stanford University in 1970. Dr. Bem is a feminist and her research on the psychology of sex roles represents a coming together of both her intellectual and her political concerns. In addition to her research on psychological androgyny, Dr. Bem has also researched the effects of sex biased job advertising and she has testified as an expert witness in two court cases involving discrimination against women. She has also served as a member of a Citizen's Advisory Committee to the Women's Traffic Officer Project of California Highway Patrol. Together with her husband, Daryl, she has given literally hundreds of speeches across the country on the topics of sex-role stereotyping and equalitarian marriage.

Rae Lesser Blumberg

Rae Lesser Blumberg is a member of the Department of Sociology at the University of California—San Diego. Her primary research interests have been comparing and relating the areas of economic development, the position of women, and childbearing. She held a Ford Foundation Faculty Fellowship on the Role of Women in Society in 1973-1974, and served as resident advisor in sociological research in the Venezuelan Ministry of Education. She lived for five and one-half years in Latin America, mostly Venezuela, where she began as a Peace Corps Volunteer teaching sociology in a Caracas university. She received her Ph.D. in sociology from Northwestern University in August, 1970. Her publications include an article in *American Journal of Sociology*, another in *American Sociological Review*, and a forthcoming book on socioeconomic and sexual stratification. Her son, David, who has just turned six, has logged over 100,000 air miles accompanying her on some of her research and job travels.

Helen Bray

Helen Bray participated in the Sex-role Stereotypy Project as a major research assistant while a student at Radcliffe College. She works in development of sex-role attitude measures, conducting field interviews with children, coding procedures, and conducting teaching seminars and training sessions for teachers about sexism in the educational process. She anticipates continuing in research and clinical work with women.

Barbara Benedict Bunker

Barbara Benedict Bunker is an associate professor of social psychology at the State University of New York at Buffalo where she also does research on self-disclosure and on teaching psychology in high schools. She is active in the training of graduate students at Buffalo for careers in applied behavioral science. She is an accredited charter member of IAASS (International Association of Applied Behavioral Science) and is on the Board of Directors of National Training Laboratories Institute. Her consulting is primarily with educational systems, voluntary agencies, and corporations. She has a "dual-career" family: Her husband, Douglas, teaches in the Policy Sciences Program in the School of Management at SUNYAB and is an organizational consultant. The Bunkers' four children in their teens and early twenties have experienced several reorganizations of household tasks as part of Barbara's own experimentation with sex-role behavior at home and seem to have survived admirably.

Cecilia Preciada de Burciago

Cecilia Preciada de Burciago received her M.A. in sociology of education from University of California, Riverside. She is currently assistant to the president of Chicano Affairs at Stanford University. She is a board member at the Center for Research On Women at Stanford, and also serves on the board of Mid-Peninsula Urban Coalition. From 1968-1972, when Ms. Burciago was with the United States Commission on Civil Rights, she was on the research staff of The Mexican American Study. Her current research interest is the role of women in higher education, specifically that of chicano women in education.

Mark Chelser

Mark Chelser is an associate professor of sociology at the University of Michigan, and Project Director Community Resources Limited, Ann Arbor. He is currently doing research and consultation for social-change programs in schools and communities. He is especially concerned with new definitions and strategies for using powerful social science tools, ideologies, and institutions in the pursuit of social justice.

Charlotte Darrow

Charlotte Darrow is a sociologist and a member of the Department of Psychiatry at Yale University. She also works in the Research Unit for Social Psychology and Psychiatry, Connecticut Mental Health Center. Originally trained at Michigan, Ms. Darrow is now completing her doctorate at New York University.

Ellen Levine Ebert

Ellen Levine Ebert is a painter and free lance photographer. She was born in Cincinnati, Ohio, in 1943. She received her education at Wellesley College (1965), Boston University School of Fine Arts, the Art Academy of Cincinnati, and the Skowhegan School of Painting and Sculpture. She has had one-person and group exhibitions, and her work is in numerous private collections. She now lives in Bethesda, Maryland, with her husband, Mike, a psychiatrist, and two young children.

Robert Fein

Robert Fein is a psychologist who is working to understand and facilitate examinations of male roles in the United States. He has lectured and written about men's experiences with childbirth, fathering, and men who work with children. Work on "Examining the Nature of Masculinity" was supported in part by an independent grant from the Ford Foundation. Dr. Fein lives in Cambridge, Massachusetts.

Viola Gonzalez

Viola Gonzalez is a native of Corpus Christi, Texas—an economically depressed city which severely limits the political participation of Chicanos. This motivated her to graduate with honors from high school and college; leave Texas; and complete a MBA from Harvard Business School. She went on to pursue a career in corporate management which has enabled her to contribute administrative skills to nonprofit Chicano organizations.

Leonard D. Goodstein

Leonard D. Goodstein is professor of psychology and chairman of the Psychology Department at Arizona State University in Tempe. He is the co-author (with Richard I. Lanyon) of *Adjustment, Behavior, and Personality* (Addison-Wesley, 1975) and *Personality Assessment* and *Readings in Personality Assessment* (John Wiley, 1971). Since January, 1974, he has served as editor of the *Journal of Applied Behavioral Science*. Dr. Goodstein is married and has two sons from a former marriage, Richard and Steven.

Marcia Guttentag

Marcia Guttentag, a developmental social psychologist, at the Harvard Graduate School of Education, is president-elect of the Division of Personality and Social Psychology of the American Psychological Association. She has served as evaluation consultant to many agencies and written many chapters and articles on evaluation. She was director of the Sex-role Stereotypy Project dealing with measuring and intervening in children's attitudes about sex roles.

Nancy Henley

Nancy Henley received her doctorate in experimental psychology from Johns Hopkins University, specializing in social psychology and psycholinguistics, and did postdoctoral research in nonverbal communication at Harvard. She has taught at the University of Maryland (Baltimore County campus), worked on the critical mental health journal *Rough Times (Radical Therapist)*, and is now assistant professor of psychology at the University of Lowell in Massachusetts. She is currently writing a book on the politics of nonverbal communication.

Ruth A. Hepburn

Ruth A. Hepburn has been researching and teaching the history of American Women, specializing in the history of feminism for the past six years. Her Ph.D. dissertation, "Revolutionary Feminists in the United States 1900-1930" is presently being expanded to include the entire political spectrum of feminism during the period in her book, *The Politics of American Feminists 1900-1930*. She has been politically active throughout her life and has taught at community colleges: California Polytechnic State University (San Louis Obispo, Ca.) and the University of California at Santa Barbara.

Rosabeth Kanter

Rosabeth Kanter brings her own "lone woman" experience to her teaching, writing, and consulting in the field of organizational behavior. Dr. Kanter has taught at the Harvard University Graduate School of Education and is now an associate professor of sociology at Brandeis University. Her publications include *Commitment and Community* (Harvard University Press, 1972), *Men and Women in the Corporation* (New York: Basic Books, In Press). She received her Ph.D. from the University of Michigan. She likes early music and tending gardens, as well as learning about and participating in efforts to build humane working and living environments.

Edward Klein

Edward Klein is currently in the Department of Psychiatry at Yale and the Research Unit for Social Psychology and Psychiatry, Connecticut Mental Health Center. He is a clinical—social psychologist with strong social science interests.

Diane F. Kravetz

Diane F. Kravetz is an associate professor in the School of Social Work, University of Wisconsin, Madison. She teaches social work methods courses and a course entitled Sexism and Social Work Practice. She is also a member of the Women's Studies Program faculty at the university. She received her Ph.D. from the University of Michigan in social work and social psychology in 1970 and an M.S.W. from the University of Michigan School of Social Work in 1967. Dr. Kravetz has focused her research and writings on sex-roles.

Gloria B. Levin

Gloria B. Levin is a Ph.D. candidate in community psychology at the University of Michigan, Ann Arbor. Over the past ten years she has worked as a community organizer in the United States and a Peace Corps Volunteer in Peru. Her consultant and research interests and activities are in the areas of social change, public policy, social movement, and community organization.

Daniel Levinson

Daniel Levinson's study of adult development, the result of several years' research with support from the National Institute of Mental Health, links both sociology and psychiatry. Originally a psychologist (University of California, Berkeley, 1947), he is now a member of the Department of Psychiatry at Yale University and the Research Unit for Social Psychology and Psychiatry, Connecticut Mental Health Center.

Maria Levinson

Maria Levinson is currently in the Department of Psychiatry at Yale and the Research Unit for Social Psychology and Psychiatry, Connecticut Mental Health Center. She and Dan Levinson are a wife-husband team whose collaboration goes back to graduate school and their work on the *Authoritarian Personality* (Adorno, T.W., et. al., New York: Harpers, 1950), and *Seasons of a Man's Life* (New York: Knopf, in press).

Jerry Lynch

Jerry Lynch graduated from San Fernando Valley State University with a B.S. in education. He received his M.S. in counseling from San Diego State University under a NDEA grant.

He was a group leader at the 1970 White House Conference on Children, was a writer and group leader on a research project for Chicano Housing, and a trainer of teachers in the Magic Circle since 1969 throughout the United States and more recently in Mexico.

At the present time, Jerry and Luanne Lynch are developing consciousness-raising workshops for children and parents, which are based at the Children's School in San Diego and are also co-authors of *The Loving Family* (unpublished manuscript) and workshop.

Luanne Lynch

Luanne Lynch was trained as an elementary teacher at San Fernando Valley State University and taught middle grades in Los Angeles and at a United States radar site dependent school in Spain.

She has worked as a Magic Circle consultant for two years in the United States training educational leaders in humanistic skills. Luanne and Jerry have developed a family workshop where they worked in depth with families in Mexico. She is working as illustrator and co-author, along with Jerry Lynch and Harold Bessel on a book called *The Loving Family* (unpublished manuscript), which is for single parents as well as larger families.

Luanne has worked as a leader and organizer of women's awareness groups in Mexico, and is currently teaching an open classroom at The Children's School in San Diego.

Colquitt L. Meacham

Colquitt L. Meacham received her LL.B. from Emory University and her LL.M. from Harvard University. Ms. Meacham has taught courses on sex-based discrimination at several law schools, and has published articles concerning the legal status of women. She has served as assistant dean of the law school at the University of California at Berkeley, and as a teaching fellow at the Harvard Law School. Presently, she is chief of the Higher Education Branch, Office for Civil Rights, at HEW, where she has responsibility for enforcement of Title IX of the Education Amendments of 1972.

Norma McCoy

Norma McCoy received her B.A. (1956) in psychology from Stanford University, and her M.A. (1960) and Ph.D. (1963) in child psychology from the Institute of Child Development at the University of Minnesota. She is currently an associate professor of psychology at San Francisco State University. Except for three semesters as a visiting professor at Amherst College, she has been at SFSU ever since. She has a son, (1968), and a daughter (1970). Her work on the biological basis of sex differences arose out of her experiences creating and teaching a course in the development of sex differences.

Braxton McKee

Braxton McKee is currently on the clinical faculty of the Department of Psychiatry at Yale and in the Research Unit for Social Psychology and Psychiatry, Connecticut Mental Health Center. He is a psychiatrist in private practice and is completing his psychoanalytic training.

Carol Pierce

Carol Pierce is a partner in New Dynamics Associates and a trainer for Women's Awareness and Man/Woman Interaction groups. She has served as chairwoman of the New Hampshire Commission on the Status of Women and is a member of the New Hampshire State Legislature. She is a community organizer with particular experience in the mental health, aging, and grant-managing fields. Ms. Pierce is a graduate of the University of Wisconsin, 1954.

Nancy Richardson

Nancy Richardson teaches assertiveness training in a First School in Cambridge, Massachusetts, which is an implementation of Lawrence Kohlberg's theory of moral education. She is a doctoral student in psychology at Harvard. She was a member of the social ecology program at the University of California at Irvine and interned at the counseling center there.

Michele Russell

Michele Russell has been active in the broad movement for social change since 1958 through vehicles such as Students for Democratic Society, Student Non-violent Coordinating Committee, New University Conference, RESIST, and the Labor Defense Coalition. Now living in Detroit, she has worked as a college teacher, writer, industrial consultant, foundation program officer, and political publicist. She received her B.A. in comparative literature from the University of Southern California and was a Woodrow Wilson Fellow at Brown University in the American Civilization Department. Ms. Russell is currently on the staff of Wayne County Community College developing a Workers Education Center.

Janice Sanfacon

Janice Sanfacon has been interested in developing new techniques to teach problem solving to women, helping skills to men, and collaborative skills to both. She is executive director and a partner of New Dynamics Associates, a consulting firm which specializes in developmental programs for individuals and organizations. She is active in both industry and education in the areas of affirmative action, awareness training, and assertiveness training programs. She is a graduate of Ohio Wesleyan University, 1957.

Alice G. Sargent

Alice G. Sargent is an organizational consultant with specific interest in developing proactive affirmative action programs. She is currently coordinator of the National Conference on Women in Education under a joint contract from the Assistant Secretary for Education, Department of Health, Education, and Welfare and the Institute for Educational Leadership in Washington, D.C. She received her Ed.D. from the University of Massachusetts, her M.A. in English literature from Brandeis University and her B.A. from Oberlin College. She has taught management at San Diego State University and English literature at Temple University. She is a core faculty member for Union Graduate School of Antioch College.

Edith Whitfield Seashore

Edith Whitfield Seashore is an organization and training consultant in human relations and leadership training. She develops programs for industry, colleges, voluntary organizations, and school systems. She has worked with many organizations helping them implement their affirmative action programs. She is president of the National Training Laboratories Institute, an accredited Charter Member of the International Association of Applied Social Scientists, and a member of the Board of Trustees of the Center for a Voluntary Society. Ms. Seashore lives in Washington, D.C. with her husband, Charles, a social psychologist, and two daughters who are 9 and 7 years old.

Herbert A. Shepard

Herbert A. Shepard conducted the first large-scale experiments in organization development at Esso in the late fifties, and founded the first doctoral program in that field at Case Western Reserve University. He holds a Ph.D. in industrial economics from Massachusetts Institute of Technology and has worked as a consultant for industrial, governmental, educational, health, and military organizations.

Carol Tavris

Carol Tavris received a B.A. in sociology and comparative literature from Brandeis University, and then went to the University of Michigan for social psychology. In 1971, she did her thesis on a survey of attitudes toward women and the newly emerging women's movement, which caught both her personal and professional interest. She is assistant managing editor of *Psychology Today*. In addition, she was editor of *The Female Experience*, a *Psychology Today* special publication (1973). She has written educational filmstrips for Schloat Productions, "A Woman's Place," and is currently writing a psychology series. She compiled a survey similar to the

Psychology Today questionnaire for *Redbook*, is currently preparing another survey for *Redbook* on women's experiences with marriage and recently prepared a survey on masculinity for *Psychology Today*.

Barrie Thorne

Barrie Thorne is an assistant professor of sociology at Michigan State University, where she teaches courses in sex roles, social movements, social psychology, and field research methods, and is helping organize an interdisciplinary women's studies program. She received a B.A. from Stanford University, and an M.A. and Ph.D. in sociology from Brandeis University. In addition to research on language and sex, she did a participant-observer study of the draft resistance movement, and coauthored a book on professional education.

R. C. Townsend

R. C. Townsend is a professor of American literature.

Richard Vittitow

Richard Vittitow is cofounder of the Center for Designed Change in Mill Valley, California. His major interests are in developing support systems for men, increasing his own sense of self-management and social responsibility, understanding the processes of transitions, and developing humanistic organizations.

Elizabeth Wales

Elizabeth Wales received her B.A. in Theatre Arts from the University of Kansas, and her M.A. and Ph.D. from the University of Cincinnati in Clinical Psychology. She is currently an associate professor of psychology and psychiatry at Wright State University School of Medicine in Dayton, Ohio.

For the past five years, her private therapy case load has been primarily focused on areas of sexual dysfunctions. Her primary teaching responsibilities include the teaching of human sexuality and sexual therapy to advanced doctoral students in clinical psychology. Her major research interests in the past few years have been in the area of sex-role attitudes and stereotypes for both men and women.

Orian Worden

Orian Worden is a group and organization development consultant in private practice in Detroit. He provides direct services in program planning and OD, psychological evaluation and treatment; conducts professional in-service training programs and human relations laboratories. Clients include universities and school systems, business and industry, religious and volunteer organizations, public officials on the international, national, and local levels, and minority and community groups.

name index

subject index